FILM 73/74

FILM 73/74

An Anthology by the
National Society of Film Critics

*Edited by Jay Cocks
and David Denby*

THE BOBBS-MERRILL COMPANY, INC.
Indianapolis / New York

ISBN 0-672-51988-7   Hardcover
ISBN 0-672-51989-5   Paperback

Library of Congress catalog card number 74-248
Designed by Sheila Lynch
Manufactured in the United States of America

First printing

The reviews and articles in this book originally appeared, for the most part, in the publications for which the contributors regularly write. Thanks are hereby given by the contributors as follows:

HOLLIS ALPERT, reviews of *Last Tango in Paris* and *Jesus Christ Superstar* and articles, "The American Film Theatre" and "The Making of *The Exorcist*," reprinted by permission of *Saturday Review/World*, copyright © 1973 by Saturday Review/World, Inc.

GARY ARNOLD, reviews of *The New Land, Paper Moon, Last Tango in Paris, Walking Tall, Day for Night,* and *The Adversary,* reprinted by permission of the *Washington Post,* copyright © 1973 by the Washington Post Company, Inc.

VINCENT CANBY, reviews of *Love, Deep Throat, Tout Va Bien, I. F. Stone's Weekly, Day for Night,* and *David Holzman's Diary,* and article, "Abel Green (1900–1973)," reprinted by permission of *The New York Times,* copyright © 1973 by the New York Times Co.

CHARLES CHAMPLIN, reviews of *The Long Goodbye, Save the Tiger,* and *The Exorcist,* reprinted by permission of *The Los Angeles Times,* copyright © 1973 by the Los Angeles Times Company, Inc.

JAY COCKS, reviews of *Pat Garrett and Billy the Kid, Don't Look Now, The Spider's Stratagem, Kid Blue,* and *American Graffiti,* reprinted by permission of *Time,* copyright © 1973 by Time, Inc.

JUDITH CRIST, reviews of *Summer Wishes, Winter Dreams, Serpico, Paper Moon,* and *The Sting,* appeared in *New York* and are reprinted by permission of Judith Crist, copyright © 1973 by Judith Crist.

DAVID DENBY, articles "Men Without Women, Women Without Men" and "Law and Disorder," reprinted by permission of *Harper's,* copyright ©

1973, 1974 by Harper's Magazine Company; review of *Bang the Drum Slowly*, copyright © 1973 by the Regents of the University of California; reprinted from *Film Quarterly*, Vol. 27, No. 2, Winter 1973–1974, pp. 49–52, by permission of The Regents; and reviews of *Days and Nights in the Forest* and *Fists of Fury*, reprinted by permission of *The Fun City Observer*, copyright © 1973 by The Fun City Observer, Inc.

BERNARD DREW, reviews of *The Sting* and *A Touch of Class*, reprinted by permission of the Gannett News Service, copyright © 1973 by the Gannett News Service, Inc.

ROGER EBERT, reviews of *The Day of the Jackal, Blume in Love*, and *Wedding in White*, reprinted by permission of the *Chicago Sun-Times*, copyright © 1973 by the Chicago Sun-Times Company, Inc.

JOSEPH GELMIS, reviews of *Mean Streets, The Way We Were, Live and Let Die*, and article, "Making America Dance to *Last Tango*," reprinted by permission of *Newsday*, copyright © 1973 by Newsday, Inc.

PENELOPE GILLIATT, reviews of *State of Siege, Memories of Underdevelopment, Playtime, Love, O Lucky Man!, Such a Gorgeous Kid Like Me*, and *Heavy Traffic*, reprinted by permission of *The New Yorker*, copyright © 1973 by The New Yorker Magazine, Inc.

ROGER GREENSPUN, review of *The Last American Hero*, and article, "John Ford (1895–1973)," reprinted by permission of *The New York Times*, copyright © 1973 by The New York Times Co.; reviews of *American Graffiti* and *A King in New York*, reprinted by permission of *Penthouse*, copyright © 1973, 1974 by Penthouse, Inc.; review of *Day for Night* reprinted by permission of *Viva*, copyright © 1973 by Viva International Ltd.

MOLLY HASKELL, reviews of *Blume in Love* and *A Touch of Class, The Iceman Cometh, Sleeper, La Grande Bouffe*, and *A Doll's House*, and article, "Sisterhoodwinked," reprinted by permission of *The Village Voice*, copyright © 1973, 1974 by The Village Voice, Inc.; review of *Marilyn*, reprinted by permission of *The Real Paper*, copyright © 1973 by The Real Paper.

ROBERT HATCH, reviews of *Slither, La Grande Bouffe, O Lucky Man!*, and *An Autumn Afternoon*, reprinted by permission of *The Nation*, copyright © 1973 by The Nation, Inc.

PAULINE KAEL, reviews of *Mean Streets, Don't Look Now, The Long Goodbye, Sleeper,* and *If I Had a Gun,* reprinted by permission of *The New Yorker,* copyright © 1973 by The New Yorker Magazine, Inc.; review of *Last Tango in Paris,* copyright © 1972 by The New Yorker Magazine, Inc.; review of *The Exorcist,* copyright © 1974 by The New Yorker Magazine, Inc.

MICHAEL KORDA, reviews of *Pat Garrett and Billy the Kid* and *Jonathan Livingston Seagull,* reprinted by permission of *Glamour,* copyright © 1973 by Condé Nast Publications, Inc.

WILLIAM S. PECHTER, reviews of *The Long Goodbye, Blume in Love, Save the Tiger, American Graffiti, Mean Streets,* and *Pulp,* reprinted by permission of *Commentary,* copyright © 1973, 1974 by the American Jewish Committee.

ANDREW SARRIS, reviews of *Charley Varrick, The Mattei Affair, State of Siege, Heavy Traffic, The Merchant of Four Seasons,* and article on *The Grapes of Wrath,* reprinted by permission of *The Village Voice,* copyright © 1973 by The Village Voice, Inc.; review of *Marilyn,* reprinted by permission of *Book World,* copyright © 1973 by the Washington Post Company, Inc.; review of *Ten from "Your Show of Shows,"* reprinted by permission of *Television Quarterly,* copyright © 1973 by Television Quarterly.

RICHARD SCHICKEL, reviews of *The Friends of Eddie Coyle, Sisters, Playtime,* and *Bang the Drum Slowly,* reprinted by permission of *Time,* copyright © 1973 by Time, Inc.

BRUCE WILLIAMSON, reviews of *La Grande Bouffe, Payday, Scarecrow,* and *Godspell,* reprinted by permission of *Playboy,* copyright © 1973 by Playboy, Inc.

PAUL D. ZIMMERMAN, reviews of *The Way We Were, The Day of the Dolphin, The Homecoming* and *A Delicate Balance, Papillon, Jesus Christ Superstar, Summer Wishes, Winter Dreams,* and article, "Imaginary Movies," reprinted by permission of *Newsweek,* copyright © 1973, 1974 by Newsweek, Inc.

DAVID BINDER's article on the award to Tomás Gutiérrez Alea reprinted by permission of *The New York Times,* copyright © 1974 by The New York Times Co.

CONTENTS

ix

INTRODUCTION

One: The Anthology

Once more, dear friends, into the breach—this time literally (see the second part of this introduction). The National Society of Film Critics here presents its seventh annual selection of film reviews plus commentary on trends and other happenings of the film year. And we make the usual disclaimers: *Film 73/74* has been designed as an informal reference volume and a sampler of American film criticism in its many forms and styles, but the volume does not pretend to be comprehensive; we cover only about one-fifth of the movies—the most important and interesting—that actually opened in the country during 1973. We say "important and interesting," but any anthology that was absolutely consistent in its criteria would be a dull book indeed. Thus you will find some lively writing here on movies that were not very important but were nevertheless part of the year's excitement. You will also find a section called "Favorites," which is made up of articles on movies that never caught fire commercially but which appealed to one critic or another as an original or demanding piece of work. We hope this feature of the anthology will be retained in future volumes.

We have tried whenever possible, as in the past, to include longer, essayistic pieces, on the grounds that anyone interested enough in movies to buy this volume would welcome the depth of the detailed analysis offered in these articles. Also as in the past, this policy means that several contributors who write under severe space and deadline limitations are relatively underrepresented in this volume; to them we offer apologies.

We should like to thank Diane Giddis of Bobbs-Merrill for numerous editorial suggestions and emendations. Finally, we should like to welcome the five new members of the National Society of Film Critics—elected to the group in January, 1974—whose work will appear in next year's volume. They are Joy Gould Boyum of *The Wall Street Journal*, Stuart Byron of *The Real Paper* (Boston), Jon Landau of *Rolling Stone*, Nora Sayre of *The New York Times*, and Colin Westerbeck, Jr. of *Commonweal*.

JAY COCKS
DAVID DENBY

xiii

Two: The Alea Affair

For the past two years, as part of its annual awards, the Society has been administering two cash prizes provided by the Richard and Hinda Rosenthal Foundation. After our voting meeting (January 2, 1974) the Society announced its awards for the year 1973, including the information that one of the Rosenthal Awards would go to Tomás Gutiérrez Alea, the Cuban director of *Memories of Underdevelopment,* a fine Cuban film of 1968, which was finally distributed in the United States in 1973. To its considerable surprise, the Society immediately found itself embroiled in a political and legal struggle with the United States government. The editors have decided not to add anything at this writing (late February, 1974) to a set of circumstances that may be much altered by litigation or changes in American foreign policy by the time this volume appears. But we should like to reprint, for the record, an article from *The New York Times* describing the reaction of the United States State and Treasury Departments to our award, and then two statements that were read at the Society's annual awards party at the Algonquin Hotel on January 20, 1974—one from Tomás Gutiérrez Alea (a cable from Cuba), and the other from Andrew Sarris, chairman of the Society. All three are self-explanatory and require no further introduction.

U.S. Refuses Visa to Cuban Director to Get Film Award

By David Binder
Special to the New York Times

Washington, Jan. 16—The State Department announced today that it had denied a request by the Cuban film director Tomás Gutiérrez Alea for an entry visa to accept the award of the National Society of Film Critics in New York Sunday.

A visa application was also turned down for Saul Yelin, director of Cuba's National Film Institute, who had asked to accompany Mr. Gutiérrez as an interpreter.

The award of $2,000 and a plaque was to honor the 45-year-old director's 1968 film, *Memories of Underdevelopment*.

Hollis Alpert, chairman of the critics group, said he was warned today by a United States Treasury official that it would be a violation of the Trading With the Enemy Act for anyone to accept the award on behalf of Mr. Gutiérrez.

The filmmakers applied for visas through the Swiss Embassy, which represents American interests in Cuba. A United States official said the request was turned down after a routine review.

The official said the United States had granted visas to "well under 100 Cubans" in the last year to attend international conferences, to go to the United Nations, and to participate in certain amateur and professional athletic events, and "for humanitarian purposes."

"The denial represents a continuation of U.S. policy toward Cuba," he added.

Memories of Underdevelopment, first shown in the United States in 1972, recounts the experiences of an alienated writer. Vincent Canby, film critic of *The New York Times*, called it superb and listed it among the ten best films of 1973.

Mr. Andrew Sarris, Chairman
National Society of Film Critics
Algonquin Hotel, Oak Room
New York, New York

It is with deep regret that we are unable to attend the ceremonies at which we were to accept the award conferred by you upon the Cuban film *Memories of Underdevelopment*.

We write these lines first of all to express our satisfaction with the interest with which the film has been received and with the esteem that you have displayed for it. But, above all, these lines will inform you of the unavoidable explanation for our absence at the ceremonies as well as certain other things.

The reason for our failure to attend is very simple: the State Department has denied us a visa to enter your country and has not given any explanation in this regard.

But that is not all. The Treasury Department has threatened your Society with judicial proceedings that could put some of your officers in prison if you grant us the award (U.S. $2,000) or even if you merely give us a plaque.

None of this is new. It should not come as a surprise to us. This superpower has subjected us to acts of aggression, to a blockade decreed against our country, and to misinformation ever since our revolutionary process began. These acts of aggression—which are to a certain extent reflected in our film—and all acts which are intended to impede any kind of contact between our people and the people of the United States have the immediate result of keeping the American people in ignorance and preventing them from getting to know the truth about what is happening in our country. Last year, using the same absurd pretexts and the crudest of repressive measures, the U.S. Treasury Department prohibited the New York showing of a group of Cuban films brought together for what was to be a festival of Cuban Cinema. On that occasion as well, the State Department denied visas to a group of our film directors, thus preventing them from entering into direct contact with the North American public. All of this is obviously contrary to the principles of freedom supported by the people of the United States and proclaimed—with an insistence that is quite suspect—by the U.S. Government. We believe that the threats which the Treasury Department has aimed at the officers of the National Society of Film Critics are ridiculous and that nothing they do can take away the recognition that Cuban cinematography has received from your Society.

We would also point out, in closing, that all of these manifestations of pompousness and arrogance on the part of the Empire toward a country that stopped being its servile colony fifteen years ago also affect—in some important ways—the interests of the North American people. Among other things, they are thus forbidden to receive information which a very nearby people are offering to communicate about their process of finding their own identity, becoming masters of their own destiny, and liberating all of their own creative energy.

Tomás Gutiérrez Alea

As Chairman of the National Society of Film Critics, I speak for the members of our group in condemning the action of the U.S. State Department in denying a visa to Tomás Gutiérrez Alea, director of *Memories of Underdevelopment*. We meet here today at what Lionel Trilling has called the bloody crossroads of art and politics. Ironically, our award was dictated more by artistic than by political considerations. Unfortunately, the politics has been thrust upon us, not only by the woefully short-sighted decision of the State Department, but also by some of the questionable political rhetoric of the film's American distributor, Tricontinental Films. I cite in particular the following sentence in a recent press release: "Mr. Gutiérrez Alea and his work are products of socialist Cuba." I would submit that *Memories of Underdevelopment* has no more been honored by us as a product of socialist Cuba than *Day for Night* has been honored as a product of capitalist France or *American Graffiti* and *Payday* as products of capitalist America. We vote for the works of individuals, and not of systems. Indeed, what has struck most of us most favorably about *Memories of Underdevelopment* is its very personal and very courageous confrontation of the artist's doubts and ambivalences regarding the Cuban Revolution. Some of us had even expressed the hope that our award might assist Mr. Gutiérrez Alea's career since, to the best of our knowledge, he does not seem to have made a film in five years, *Memories of Underdevelopment* having been originally released in 1968.

If Mr. Gutiérrez Alea had been here today, he might have shed some light on conditions in Cuba for a creative artist of his caliber. He might have disabused us of any misplaced concern for his future as a filmmaker. Indeed, he could have provided a high level of educational experience for film students in the New York area. In his absence, he joins such previous victims of bureaucratic bigotries and blacklists as Charles Chaplin and Luis Buñuel, John Garfield and Arletty, the Hollywood Ten and Leni Riefenstahl, Alexsandr Solzhenitsyn, Pablo Neruda, Ezra Pound, and many many other creative people of various political persuasions.

As an association of film critics and scholars dedicated to artistic excellence in the cinema, we must stand with Gutiérrez Alea against the functionaries of our own government in the name of the professed principles of our own country. At the very least, we must protest this State Department discrimination against a film director of a country from which athletes and artists from other fields have been previously admitted to our shores. We trust that Mr. Gutiérrez Alea will not have to take up ping-pong in order to secure a visa to the United States. In the hope of better official relations in the future between the United States and Cuba, the National Society of Film Critics has empowered me to announce that the $2000 monetary prize from the Society and the Richard and Hinda Rosenthal Foundation will be placed in a blocked account of a New York City bank, and his plaque will be held in escrow, until such time as he is able to pick up the money and the plaque personally. In addition, several members of the group have volunteered to constitute a litigation committee in order to cooperate with the New York Civil Liberties Union in securing a judicial reversal of the State Department's decision. Meanwhile, we hope that more people will have an opportunity to see the film, and judge for themselves whether the award was artistically justified. I should hope that some people in Washington might benefit from a special screening. Thank you all for coming.

ANDREW SARRIS

THE AWARDS

The National Society of Film Critics, in its eighth annual awards, voted *Day for Night* the best picture of the year. The Society named François Truffaut, director of *Day for Night,* as the best director of the year. Liv Ullmann won the best actress award for her performance in *The New Land,* and Marlon Brando was chosen best actor for his performance in *Last Tango in Paris.*

The Society also picked Valentina Cortese as best supporting actress for her performance in *Day for Night,* and Robert De Niro as best supporting actor for his role in *Mean Streets.*

The best screenplay award was shared by George Lucas, Gloria Katz, and Willard Huyck for their work on *American Graffiti.* Vilmos Zsigmond won best cinematography award for *The Long Goodbye.*

In this year's second voting for the Richard and Hinda Rosenthal Foundation Awards, the prize for a film released in the past twelve months which, although not sufficiently recognized by public attendance has nevertheless been an outstanding cinematic achievement, went to Tomás Gutiérrez Alea for *Memories of Underdevelopment.* The second prize, to a person working in cinema whose contribution to film art has not yet received due public recognition, was awarded to Daryl Duke, director of *Payday.* The awards were accompanied by cash prizes of $2,000 to each recipient.

A posthumous special award was voted to Robert Ryan for his performance in *The Iceman Cometh,* "a consummate demonstration of acting skill at the end of a long, distinguished career."

Participants in the voting included Hollis Alpert of *Saturday Review/World*; Gary Arnold of *The Washington Post*; Vincent Canby of *The New York Times*; Charles Champlin of *The Los Angeles Times*; Jay Cocks of *Time*; Judith Crist of *New York*; David Denby of *Harper's*; Bernard Drew of the Gannett News Service; Roger Ebert of *The Chicago Sun-Times*; Joseph Gelmis of *Newsday*; Penelope Gilliatt of *The New Yorker*; Roger Greenspun of *Penthouse*; Molly Haskell of *The Village Voice*; Pauline Kael of *The New Yorker*; Michael Korda of *Glamour*; Andrew Sarris of *The Village Voice*; Richard Schickel of *Time*; Bruce Williamson of *Playboy*; and Paul D. Zimmerman of *Newsweek.*

Voting for 1973 Awards
The National Society of Film Critics

Each critic was asked to vote for three candidates in each category. The first choice was worth three points; the second, two; the third, one; and a simple plurality established the winner.

Best Picture

HOLLIS ALPERT:
  Mean Streets; American Graffiti; Bang the Drum Slowly
GARY ARNOLD:
  The New Land; Mean Streets; The Adversary
VINCENT CANBY:
  Day for Night; Memories of Underdevelopment; Mean Streets
CHARLES CHAMPLIN:
  Day for Night; Last Tango in Paris; American Graffiti
JAY COCKS:
  Don't Look Now; Pat Garrett and Billy the Kid; Love
JUDITH CRIST:
  Serpico; O Lucky Man!; Sleeper
DAVID DENBY:
  Mean Streets; Memories of Underdevelopment; American Graffiti
BERNARD DREW:
  Day for Night; Last Tango in Paris; Don't Look Now
ROGER EBERT:
  Last Tango in Paris; Mean Streets; American Graffiti
JOSEPH GELMIS:
  American Graffiti; Mean Streets; Sleeper
PENELOPE GILLIATT:
  Memories of Underdevelopment; Day for Night; Playtime
ROGER GREENSPUN:
  Day for Night; American Graffiti; The Merchant of Four Seasons

MOLLY HASKELL:

> *Day for Night; The Merchant of Four Seasons; The Spider's Stratagem*

PAULINE KAEL:

> *Last Tango in Paris; Mean Streets; Memories of Underdevelopment*

MICHAEL KORDA:

> *Day for Night;* no second or third choice

ANDREW SARRIS:

> *Day for Night; The Merchant of Four Seasons; A King in New York*

RICHARD SCHICKEL:

> *Day for Night; American Graffiti; Bang the Drum Slowly*

BRUCE WILLIAMSON:

> *Last Tango in Paris; The New Land; American Graffiti*

PAUL D. ZIMMERMAN:

> *Last Tango in Paris; American Graffiti; Mean Streets*

Best Director

HOLLIS ALPERT:

> Martin Scorsese (*Mean Streets*); George Lucas (*American Graffiti*); John Hancock (*Bang the Drum Slowly*)

GARY ARNOLD:

> Jan Troell (*The New Land*); Martin Scorsese (*Mean Streets*); Satyajit Ray (*Days and Nights in the Forest*)

VINCENT CANBY:

> François Truffaut (*Day for Night*); Tomás Gutiérrez Alea (*Memories of Underdevelopment*); Martin Scorsese (*Mean Streets*)

CHARLES CHAMPLIN:

> François Truffaut (*Day for Night*); Bernardo Bertolucci (*Last Tango in Paris*); George Lucas (*American Graffiti*)

JAY COCKS:

> Nicolas Roeg (*Don't Look Now*); Sam Peckinpah (*Pat Garrett and Billy the Kid*); Károly Makk (*Love*)

JUDITH CRIST:

> Lindsay Anderson (*O Lucky Man!*); George Roy Hill (*The Sting*); Sidney Lumet (*Serpico*)

DAVID DENBY:

> George Lucas (*American Graffiti*); Martin Scorsese (*Mean Streets*); Tomás Gutiérrez Alea (*Memories of Underdevelopment*)

BERNARD DREW:

> François Truffaut (*Day for Night*) ; Bernardo Bertolucci (*Last Tango in Paris*) ; Martin Scorsese (*Mean Streets*)

ROGER EBERT:

> Werner Fassbinder (*The Merchant of Four Seasons*); Martin Scorsese (*Mean Streets*) ; George Lucas (*American Graffiti*)

JOSEPH GELMIS:

> George Lucas (*American Graffiti*) ; Martin Scorsese (*Mean Streets*) ; Woody Allen (*Sleeper*)

PENELOPE GILLIATT:

> François Truffaut (*Day for Night*) ; Satyajit Ray (*Days and Nights in the Forest*) ; Jacques Tati (*Playtime*)

ROGER GREENSPUN:

> François Truffaut (*Day for Night*) ; George Lucas (*American Graffiti*) ; Werner Fassbinder (*The Merchant of Four Seasons*)

MOLLY HASKELL:

> François Truffaut (*Day for Night*) ; Werner Fassbinder (*The Merchant of Four Seasons*) ; Bernardo Bertolucci (*Last Tango in Paris*)

PAULINE KAEL:

> Bernardo Bertolucci (*Last Tango in Paris*) ; Robert Altman (*The Long Goodbye*) ; Martin Scorsese (*Mean Streets*)

MICHAEL KORDA:

> François Truffaut (*Day for Night*) ; no second or third choice

ANDREW SARRIS:

> François Truffaut (*Day for Night*) ; Werner Fassbinder (*The Merchant of Four Seasons*) ; Don Siegel (*Charley Varrick*)

RICHARD SCHICKEL:

> François Truffaut (*Day for Night*) ; George Lucas (*American Graffiti*) ; John Hancock (*Bang the Drum Slowly*)

BRUCE WILLIAMSON:

> Bernardo Bertolucci (*Last Tango in Paris*) ; George Lucas (*American Graffiti*) ; Jan Troell (*The New Land*)

PAUL D. ZIMMERMAN:

> Bernardo Bertolucci (*Last Tango in Paris*) ; George Lucas (*American Graffiti*) ; Martin Scorsese (*Mean Streets*)

Best Actress

HOLLIS ALPERT:

> Glenda Jackson (*A Touch of Class*) ; Liv Ullmann (*The New Land*) ; Vivien Merchant (*The Homecoming*)

GARY ARNOLD:
    Liv Ullmann (*The New Land*); Sharmila Tagore (*Days and Nights in the Forest*); no third choice
VINCENT CANBY:
    Lili Darvas (*Love*); Mari Töröcsik (*Love*); Vivien Merchant (*The Homecoming*)
CHARLES CHAMPLIN:
    Marsha Mason (*Cinderella Liberty*); Liv Ullmann (*The New Land*); Maria Schneider (*Last Tango in Paris*)
JAY COCKS:
    Mari Töröcsik (*Love*); Vivien Merchant (*The Homecoming*); Susan Anspach (*Blume in Love*)
JUDITH CRIST:
    Marsha Mason (*Cinderella Liberty*); Joanne Woodward (*Summer Wishes, Winter Dreams*); Rachel Roberts (*O Lucky Man!*)
DAVID DENBY:
    Mari Töröcsik (*Love*); Barbra Streisand (*The Way We Were*); Julie Christie (*Don't Look Now*)
BERNARD DREW:
    Maria Schneider (*Last Tango in Paris*); Lili Darvas (*Love*); Liv Ullmann (*The New Land*)
ROGER EBERT:
    Liv Ullmann (*The New Land*); Julie Christie (*Don't Look Now*); Susan Anspach (*Blume in Love*)
JOSEPH GELMIS:
    Barbra Streisand (*The Way We Were*); no second or third choice
PENELOPE GILLIATT:
    Lili Darvas (*Love*); Vivien Merchant (*The Homecoming*); Liv Ullmann (*The New Land*)
ROGER GREENSPUN:
    Mari Töröcsik (*Love*); Sarah Miles (*The Hireling*); Lili Darvas (*Love*)
MOLLY HASKELL:
    Mari Töröcsik (*Love*); Sarah Miles (*The Hireling*); Joanne Woodward (*Summer Wishes, Winter Dreams*)
PAULINE KAEL:
    Liv Ullmann (*The New Land*); Maria Schneider (*Last Tango in Paris*); Julie Christie (*Don't Look Now*)
MICHAEL KORDA:
    Barbra Streisand (*The Way We Were*); no second or third choice

ANDREW SARRIS:

    Joanne Woodward (*Summer Wishes, Winter Dreams*); Sarah Miles (*The Hireling*); Hanna Schygulla (*The Merchant of Four Seasons*)

RICHARD SCHICKEL:

    Joanne Woodward (*Summer Wishes, Winter Dreams*); Liv Ullmann (*The New Land*); Julie Christie (*Don't Look Now*)

BRUCE WILLIAMSON:

    Liv Ullmann (*The New Land*); Maria Schneider (*Last Tango in Paris*); Glenda Jackson (*A Touch of Class*)

PAUL D. ZIMMERMAN:

    No first choice; Susan Anspach (*Blume in Love*); Marsha Mason (*Cinderella Liberty*)

Best Actor

HOLLIS ALPERT:

    Al Pacino (*Serpico*); Robert De Niro (*Mean Streets*); George Segal (*A Touch of Class*)

GARY ARNOLD:

    Yves Montand (*César and Rosalie*); Jeff Bridges (*The Last American Hero*); Gian Maria Volonte (*The Mattei Affair*)

VINCENT CANBY:

    Marlon Brando (*Last Tango in Paris*); Sergio Corrieri (*Memories of Underdevelopment*); Al Pacino (*Serpico*)

CHARLES CHAMPLIN:

    Marlon Brando (*Last Tango in Paris*); Robert Ryan (*The Iceman Cometh*); Al Pacino (*Serpico*)

JAY COCKS:

    Robert Ryan (*The Iceman Cometh*); second choices: Robert De Niro and Harvey Keitel (*Mean Streets*); Marlon Brando (*Last Tango in Paris*)

JUDITH CRIST:

    Al Pacino (*Serpico*); Jack Lemmon (*Save the Tiger*); Robert De Niro (*Mean Streets*)

DAVID DENBY:

    Marlon Brando (*Last Tango in Paris*); Robert Ryan (*The Iceman Cometh*); Sergio Corrieri (*Memories of Underdevelopment*)

BERNARD DREW:

    Robert De Niro (*Mean Streets*); Marlon Brando (*Last Tango in Paris*); Al Pacino (*Serpico*)

Roger Ebert:

Marlon Brando (*Last Tango in Paris*); Robert Ryan (*The Iceman Cometh*); Harvey Keitel (*Mean Streets*)

Joseph Gelmis:

Robert De Niro (*Mean Streets*); Marlon Brando (*Last Tango in Paris*); James Caan (*Cinderella Liberty*)

Penelope Gilliatt:

Sergio Corrieri (*Memories of Underdevelopment*); Marlon Brando (*Last Tango in Paris*); Donald Pleasence (*Wedding in White*)

Roger Greenspun:

Elliott Gould (*The Long Goodbye*); Harvey Keitel (*Mean Streets*); Charles Chaplin (*A King in New York*)

Molly Haskell:

Hans Hirschmuller (*The Merchant of Four Seasons*); Jeff Bridges (*The Last American Hero*); Jack Lemmon (*Save the Tiger*)

Pauline Kael:

Marlon Brando (*Last Tango in Paris*); Robert Ryan (*The Iceman Cometh*); Harvey Keitel (*Mean Streets*)

Michael Korda:

George Segal (*A Touch of Class*); no second or third choice

Andrew Sarris:

Charles Chaplin (*A King in New York*); Rip Torn (*Payday*); Robert Blake (*Electra Glide in Blue*)

Richard Schickel:

Marlon Brando (*Last Tango in Paris*); Robert Ryan (*The Iceman Cometh*); Rip Torn (*Payday*)

Bruce Williamson:

Marlon Brando (*Last Tango in Paris*); Al Pacino (*Serpico*); Paul Rogers (*The Homecoming*)

Paul D. Zimmerman:

Marlon Brando (*Last Tango in Paris*); Robert Ryan (*The Iceman Cometh*); Al Pacino (*Serpico*)

Best Supporting Actress

Hollis Alpert:

Valentina Cortese (*Day for Night*); P. J. Johnson (*Paper Moon*); Candy Clark (*American Graffiti*)

GARY ARNOLD:
Valentina Cortese (*Day for Night*) ; Daisy Granados (*Memories of Underdevelopment*) ; no third choice

VINCENT CANBY:
Mari Töröcsik (*Love*) ; Valentina Cortese (*Day for Night*) ; Diane Keaton (*Sleeper*)

CHARLES CHAMPLIN:
Sylvia Sidney (*Summer Wishes, Winter Dreams*) ; Marsha Mason (*Blume in Love*) ; Valentina Cortese (*Day for Night*)

JAY COCKS:
Valentina Cortese (*Day for Night*) ; Janice Rule (*Kid Blue*) ; E. J. Peaker (*The All-American Boy*)

JUDITH CRIST:
Valentina Cortese (*Day for Night*) ; Eileen Brennan (*The Sting*) ; Diane Keaton (*Sleeper*)

DAVID DENBY:
Mari Töröcsik (*Love*) ; P. J. Johnson (*Paper Moon*) ; Valentina Cortese (*Day for Night*)

BERNARD DREW:
Valentina Cortese (*Day for Night*) ; Sylvia Sidney (*Summer Wishes, Winter Dreams*) ; Geraldine Fitzgerald (*The Last American Hero*)

ROGER EBERT:
Irm Herman (*The Merchant of Four Seasons*) ; Amy Robinson (*Mean Streets*) ; Cindy Williams (*American Graffiti*)

JOSEPH GELMIS:
Nina Van Pallandt (*The Long Goodbye*) ; Mackenzie Phillips (*American Graffiti*) ; Dorothy Tristan (*Scarecrow*)

PENELOPE GILLIATT:
Mari Töröcsik (*Love*) ; Diane Keaton (*Sleeper*) ; Anne Kreis (*Such a Gorgeous Kid Like Me*)

ROGER GREENSPUN:
Mari Töröcsik (*Love*) ; Valentina Cortese (*Day for Night*) ; Marsha Mason (*Blume in Love*)

MOLLY HASKELL:
Mari Töröcsik (*Love*) ; Valentina Cortese (*Day for Night*) ; Andrea Ferreol (*La Grand Bouffe*)

PAULINE KAEL:
P. J. Johnson (*Paper Moon*) ; Cindy Williams (*American Graffiti*) ; Madeline Kahn (*Paper Moon*)

MICHAEL KORDA:
Rachel Roberts (*O Lucky Man!*) ; no second or third choice

ANDREW SARRIS:
> Sylvia Sidney (*Summer Wishes, Winter Dreams*); Valentina Cortese (*Day for Night*); Mari Töröcsik (*Love*)

RICHARD SCHICKEL:
> Sylvia Sidney (*Summer Wishes, Winter Dreams*); Valentina Cortese (*Day for Night*); Amy Robinson (*Mean Streets*)

BRUCE WILLIAMSON:
> Valentina Cortese (*Day for Night*); Andrea Ferreol (*La Grand Bouffe*); Clarice Taylor (*Five on the Black Hand Side*)

PAUL D. ZIMMERMAN:
> Valentina Cortese (*Day for Night*); Cindy Williams (*American Graffiti*); Andrea Ferreol (*La Grand Bouffe*)

Best Supporting Actor

HOLLIS ALPERT:
> Robert De Niro (*Mean Streets*); Michael Hordern (*England Made Me*); Denholm Elliott (*A Doll's House*)

GARY ARNOLD:
> Michael Hordern (*England Made Me*); Robert De Niro (*Mean Streets*); John Houseman (*The Paper Chase*)

VINCENT CANBY:
> Fredric March (*The Iceman Cometh*); Ian Holm (*The Homecoming*); Robert De Niro (*Mean Streets*)

CHARLES CHAMPLIN:
> John Houseman (*The Paper Chase*); Kris Kristofferson (*Blume in Love*); Michael Hordern (*England Made Me*)

JAY COCKS:
> Ian Holm (*The Homecoming*); second choices Ralph Richardson (*O Lucky Man!*) and Fredric March (*The Iceman Cometh*); Mickey Rooney (*Pulp*)

JUDITH CRIST:
> John Houseman (*The Paper Chase*); Mark Rydell (*The Long Goodbye*); Martin Balsam (*Summer Wishes, Winter Dreams*)

DAVID DENBY:
> Robert De Niro (*Mean Streets*); John Houseman (*The Paper Chase*); Kris Kristofferson (*Blume in Love*)

BERNARD DREW:
> Robert Ryan (*The Iceman Cometh*); Robert De Niro (*Mean Streets*); Cyril Cusack (*The Homecoming*)

ROGER EBERT:
> Kris Kristofferson (*Blume in Love*); Fredric March (*The Iceman Cometh*); John Houseman (*The Paper Chase*)

JOSEPH GELMIS:
> Alan Price (*O Lucky Man!*); Peter Boyle (*Steelyard Blues*); François Truffaut (*Day for Night*)

PENELOPE GILLIATT:
> Denholm Elliott (*A Doll's House*); Ian Holm (*The Homecoming*); Arthur Lowe (*O Lucky Man!*)

ROGER GREENSPUN:
> John Houseman (*The Paper Chase*); Vincent Gardenia (*Bang the Drum Slowly*); Fredric March (*The Iceman Cometh*)

MOLLY HASKELL:
> Art Lund (*The Last American Hero*); John Houseman (*The Paper Chase*); Fredric March (*The Iceman Cometh*)

PAULINE KAEL:
> Robert De Niro (*Mean Streets*); Robert Ryan (*The Iceman Cometh*); Fredric March (*The Iceman Cometh*)

MICHAEL KORDA:
> John Houseman (*The Paper Chase*); no second or third choice

ANDREW SARRIS:
> Ian Bannen (*The Mackintosh Man*); Jack Gilford (*Save the Tiger*); Massimo Girotti (*Last Tango in Paris*)

RICHARD SCHICKEL:
> Vincent Gardenia (*Bang the Drum Slowly*); Kris Kristofferson (*Blume in Love*); Robert De Niro (*Mean Streets*)

BRUCE WILLIAMSON:
> Robert De Niro (*Mean Streets*); Fredric March (*The Iceman Cometh*); John Houseman (*The Paper Chase*)

PAUL D. ZIMMERMAN:
> Robert De Niro (*Mean Streets*); Mark Rydell (*The Long Goodbye*); John Houseman (*The Paper Chase*)

Best Screenplay

HOLLIS ALPERT:
> George Lucas, Gloria Katz and Willard Huyck (*American Graffiti*); Woody Allen and Marshall Brickman (*Sleeper*); Paul Mazursky (*Blume in Love*)

GARY ARNOLD:
   Paul Mazursky (*Blume in Love*) ; Satyajit Ray (*Days and Nights in the Forest*) ; Claude Sautet (*César and Rosalie*)
VINCENT CANBY:
   Tomás Gutiérrez Alea (*Memories of Underdevelopment*) ; François Truffaut, Suzanne Schiffman and Jean-Louis Richard (*Day for Night*) ; Woody Allen and Marshall Brickman (*Sleeper*)
CHARLES CHAMPLIN:
   George Lucas, Gloria Katz and Willard Huyck (*American Graffiti*) ; François Truffaut, Suzanne Schiffman and Jean-Louis Richard (*Day for Night*) ; Bernardo Bertolucci and Franco Arcalli (*Last Tango in Paris*)
JAY COCKS:
   François Truffaut, Suzanne Schiffman and Jean-Louis Richard (*Day for Night*) ; Bernardo Bertolucci, Edoardo De Gregori and Marilu Pavolini (*The Spider's Stratagem*) ; George Lucas, Gloria Katz and Willard Huyck (*American Graffiti*)
JUDITH CRIST:
   Stewart Stern (*Summer Wishes, Winter Dreams*) ; Woody Allen and Marshall Brickman (*Sleeper*) ; David Sherwin (*O Lucky Man!*)
DAVID DENBY:
   Bernardo Bertolucci and Franco Arcalli (*Last Tango in Paris*) ; Tomás Gutiérrez Alea (*Memories of Underdevelopment*) ; George Lucas, Gloria Katz and Willard Huyck (*American Graffiti*)
BERNARD DREW:
   François Truffaut, Suzanne Schiffman and Jean-Louis Richard (*Day for Night*) ; Bernardo Bertolucci and Franco Arcalli (*Last Tango in Paris*) ; Martin Scorsese and Mardik Martin (*Mean Streets*)
ROGER EBERT:
   George Lucas, Gloria Katz and Willard Huyck (*American Graffiti*) ; Satyajit Ray (*Days and Nights in the Forest*) ; Paul Mazursky (*Blume in Love*)
JOSEPH GELMIS:
   George Lucas, Gloria Katz and Willard Huyck (*American Graffiti*) ; Arthur Laurents (*The Way We Were*) ; Martin Scorsese and Mardik Martin (*Mean Streets*)
PENELOPE GILLIATT:
   Alain Tanner (*Return to Africa*) ; Harold Pinter (*The Homecoming*) ; Satyajit Ray (*Days and Nights in the Forest*)
ROGER GREENSPUN:
   François Truffaut, Suzanne Schiffman and Jean-Louis Richard (*Day

for Night); George Lucas, Gloria Katz and Willard Huyck (*American Graffiti*); William Roberts (*The Last American Hero*)

MOLLY HASKELL:

Howard Rodman and Dean Riesner (*Charley Varrick*); Edwin Shrake (*Kid Blue*); Stewart Stern (*Summer Wishes, Winter Dreams*)

PAULINE KAEL:

Tomás Gutiérrez Alea (*Memories of Underdevelopment*); Paul Mazursky (*Blume in Love*); Martin Scorsese and Mardik Martin (*Mean Streets*)

MICHAEL KORDA:

François Truffaut, Suzanne Schiffman and Jean-Louis Richard (*Day for Night*); no second or third choice

ANDREW SARRIS:

Edwin Shrake (*Kid Blue*); François Truffaut, Suzanne Schiffman and Jean-Louis Richard (*Day for Night*); L. M. Kit Carson (*David Holzman's Diary*)

RICHARD SCHICKEL:

François Truffaut, Suzanne Schiffman and Jean-Louis Richard (*Day for Night*); George Lucas, Gloria Katz and Willard Huyck (*American Graffiti*); Woody Allen and Marshall Brickman (*Sleeper*)

BRUCE WILLIAMSON:

George Lucas, Gloria Katz and Willard Huyck (*American Graffiti*); François Truffaut, Suzanne Schiffman and Jean-Louis Richard (*Day for Night*); Bernardo Bertolucci and Franco Arcalli (*Last Tango in Paris*)

PAUL D. ZIMMERMAN:

George Lucas, Gloria Katz and Willard Huyck (*American Graffiti*); Paul Mazursky (*Blume in Love*); Woody Allen and Marshall Brickman (*Sleeper*)

Best Cinematographer

HOLLIS ALPERT:

Kent Wakeford (*Mean Streets*); Haskell Wexler (*American Graffiti*); Vilmos Zsigmond (*The Long Goodbye*)

GARY ARNOLD:

Jan Troell (*The New Land*); Kent Wakeford (*Mean Streets*); no third choice

VINCENT CANBY:
Kent Wakeford (*Mean Streets*); Vilmos Zsigmond (*The Long Good-bye*); Pierre-William Glenn (*Day for Night*)

CHARLES CHAMPLIN:
Jan Troell (*The New Land*); Haskell Wexler (*American Graffiti*); Vittorio Storaro (*Last Tango in Paris*)

JAY COCKS:
Vittorio Storaro (*Last Tango in Paris*); Nicolas Roeg (*Don't Look Now*); Miroslav Ondricek (*O Lucky Man!*)

JUDITH CRIST:
Vilmos Zsigmond (*The Long Goodbye*); Laszlo Kovacs (*Paper Moon*); Miroslav Ondricek (*O Lucky Man!*)

DAVID DENBY:
Kent Wakeford (*Mean Streets*); Haskell Wexler (*American Graffiti*); Nicolas Roeg (*Don't Look Now*)

BERNARD DREW:
Vittorio Storaro (*Last Tango in Paris*); Vilmos Zsigmond (*The Long Goodbye*); Kent Wakeford (*Mean Streets*)

ROGER EBERT:
Vilmos Zsigmond (*The Long Goodbye*); Kent Wakeford (*Mean Streets*); Ralph Woolsey (*The Iceman Cometh*)

JOSEPH GELMIS:
Haskell Wexler (*American Graffiti*); Owen Roizman (*The Exorcist*); Kent Wakeford (*Mean Streets*)

PENELOPE GILLIATT:
Jan Troell (*The New Land*); Vittorio Storaro (*Last Tango in Paris*); Miroslav Ondricek (*O Lucky Man!*)

ROGER GREENSPUN:
Haskell Wexler (*American Graffiti*); Pierre-William Glenn (*Day for Night*); Kent Wakeford (*Mean Streets*)

MOLLY HASKELL:
Fred Konenkamp (*Papillon*); Pierre-William Glenn (*Day for Night*); Haskell Wexler (*American Graffiti*)

PAULINE KAEL:
Vittorio Storaro (*Last Tango in Paris*); Jan Troell (*The New Land*); Vilmos Zsigmond (*The Long Goodbye*)

MICHAEL KORDA:
Jack Couffer (*Jonathan Livingston Seagull*); no second or third choice

ANDREW SARRIS:
Pierre-William Glenn (*Day for Night*); Fred Konenkamp (*Papillon*); Michael Butler (*Charley Varrick*)

RICHARD SCHICKEL:
  Vilmos Zsigmond (*The Long Goodbye*) ; Vittorio Storaro (*Last Tango in Paris*) ; Jan Troell (*The New Land*)
BRUCE WILLIAMSON:
  Miroslav Ondricek (*O Lucky Man!*) ; Vittorio Storaro (*Last Tango in Paris*) ; Owen Roizman (*The Exorcist*)
PAUL D. ZIMMERMAN:
  Vilmos Zsigmond (*The Long Goodbye*) ; second choices: Kent Wakeford (*Mean Streets*) and Vittorio Storaro (*Last Tango in Paris*) ; Mario Vulpiani and Pascuali Rachini (*La Grand Bouffe*)

Voting Tabulation

(First choice = three points, second choice = two points, third choice = one point)

Best Picture 1973 : *Day for Night*

24 points	*Day for Night*
16 points	*Last Tango in Paris*
16 points	*Mean Streets*
15 points	*American Graffiti*
8 points	*Memories of Underdevelopment*
5 points	*The Merchant of Four Seasons*
5 points	*The New Land*
4 points	*Don't Look Now*
3 points	*Serpico*
2 points	*Pat Garrett and Billy the Kid*
2 points	*Sleeper*
2 points	*O Lucky Man!*
2 points	*Bang the Drum Slowly*
1 point	*Love*
1 point	*The Spider's Stratagem*
1 point	*A King in New York*
1 point	*Playtime*
1 point	*The Adversary*

Best Director 1973 : François Truffaut
Day for Night

25 points François Truffaut—*Day for Night*
18 points George Lucas—*American Graffiti*
15 points Martin Scorsese—*Mean Streets*
14 points Bernardo Bertolucci—*Last Tango in Paris*
 8 points Werner Fassbinder—*The Merchant of Four Seasons*
 4 points Jan Troell—*The New Land*
 3 points Lindsay Anderson—*O Lucky Man!*
 3 points Nicolas Roeg—*Don't Look Now*
 3 points Tomás Gutiérrez Alea—*Memories of Underdevelopment*
 3 points Satyajit Ray—*Days and Nights in the Forest*
 2 points Robert Altman—*The Long Goodbye*
 2 points John Hancock—*Bang the Drum Slowly*
 2 points George Roy Hill—*The Sting*
 2 points Sam Peckinpah—*Pat Garrett and Billy the Kid*
 1 point Don Siegel—*Charley Varrick*
 1 point Sidney Lumet—*Serpico*
 1 point Jacques Tati—*Playtime*
 1 point Károly Makk—*Love*
 1 point Woody Allen—*Sleeper*

Best Actress 1973 : Liv Ullmann
The New Land

19 points Liv Ullmann—*The New Land*
14 points Mari Töröcsik—*Love*
 9 points Lili Darvas—*Love*
 9 points Joanne Woodward—*Summer Wishes, Winter Dreams*
 8 points Maria Schneider—*Last Tango in Paris*
 7 points Marsha Mason—*Cinderella Liberty*
 6 points Vivien Merchant—*The Homecoming*
 6 points Sarah Miles—*The Hireling*
 5 points Julie Christie—*Don't Look Now*
 4 points Barbra Streisand—*The Way We Were*
 4 points Glenda Jackson—*A Touch of Class*
 4 points Susan Anspach—*Blume in Love*
 1 point Rachel Roberts—*O Lucky Man!*
 1 point Sharmila Tagore—*Days and Nights in the Forest*
 1 point Hanna Schygulla—*The Merchant of Four Seasons*

Best Actor 1973:   Marlon Brando
Last Tango in Paris

31 points   Marlon Brando—*Last Tango in Paris*
15 points   Robert Ryan—*The Iceman Cometh*
12 points   Al Pacino—*Serpico*
10 points   Robert De Niro—*Mean Streets*
6 points   Sergio Corrieri—*Memories of Underdevelopment*
5 points   Harvey Keitel—*Mean Streets*
4 points   Charles Chaplin—*A King in New York*
4 points   Jeff Bridges—*The Last American Hero*
3 points   Yves Montand—*César and Rosalie*
3 points   Elliott Gould—*The Long Goodbye*
3 points   Hans Hirschmuller—*The Merchant of Four Seasons*
3 points   Rip Torn—*Payday*
3 points   Jack Lemmon—*Save the Tiger*
2 points   George Segal—*A Touch of Class*
1 point   Gian Maria Volonte—*The Mattei Affair*
1 point   Robert Blake—*Electra Glide in Blue*
1 point   Donald Pleasence—*Wedding in White*
1 point   Paul Rogers—*The Homecoming*
1 point   James Caan—*Cinderella Liberty*

Best Supporting Actress 1973:   Valentina Cortese
Day for Night

32 points   Valentina Cortese—*Day for Night*
16 points   Mari Töröcsik—*Love*
11 points   Sylvia Sidney—*Summer Wishes, Winter Dreams*
7 points   P. J. Johnson—*Paper Moon*
5 points   Cindy Williams—*American Graffiti*
4 points   Diane Keaton—*Sleeper*
4 points   Andrea Ferreol—*La Grand Bouffe*
3 points   Irm Herman—*The Merchant of Four Seasons*
3 points   Marsha Mason—*Blume in Love*
3 points   Nina Van Pallandt—*The Long Goodbye*
3 points   Amy Robinson—*Mean Streets*
2 points   Eileen Brennan—*The Sting*
2 points   Mackenzie Phillips—*American Graffiti*
2 points   Janice Rule—*Kid Blue*
1 point   Candy Clark—*American Graffiti*

1 point   Dorothy Tristan—*Scarecrow*
1 point   E. J. Peaker—*The All-American Boy*
1 point   Clarice Taylor—*Five on the Black Hand Side*
1 point   Geraldine Fitzgerald—*The Last American Hero*
1 point   Madeline Kahn—*Paper Moon*
1 point   Anne Kreis—*Such a Gorgeous Kid Like Me*
1 point   Daisy Granados—*Memories of Underdevelopment*
1 point   Rachel Roberts—*O Lucky Man!*

Best Supporting Actor 1973:   Robert De Niro
Mean Streets

21 points   Robert De Niro—*Mean Streets*
18 points   John Houseman—*The Paper Chase*
11 points   Fredric March—*The Iceman Cometh*
 8 points   Kris Kristofferson—*Blume in Love*
 7 points   Ian Holm—*The Homecoming*
 6 points   Michael Hordern—*England Made Me*
 5 points   Vincent Gardenia—*Bang the Drum Slowly*
 5 points   Robert Ryan—*The Iceman Cometh*
 4 points   Denholm Elliott—*A Doll's House*
 4 points   Mark Rydell—*The Long Goodbye*
 3 points   Ian Bannen—*The Mackintosh Man*
 3 points   Art Lund—*The Last American Hero*
 3 points   Alan Price—*O Lucky Man!*
 2 points   Jack Gilford—*Save the Tiger*
 2 points   Peter Boyle—*Steelyard Blues*
 1 point   François Truffaut—*Day for Night*
 1 point   Martin Balsam—*Summer Wishes, Winter Dreams*
 1 point   Arthur Lowe—*O Lucky Man!*
 1 point   Cyril Cusack—*The Homecoming*
 1 point   Massimo Girotti—*Last Tango in Paris*
 1 point   Mickey Rooney—*Pulp*
 1 point   Ralph Richardson—*O Lucky Man!*

Best Screenplay 1973:   George Lucas, Gloria Katz
and Willard Huyck
American Graffiti

24 points   George Lucas, Gloria Katz and Willard Huyck—*American Graffiti*

21 points François Truffaut, Suzanne Schiffman and Jean-Louis Richard
           —*Day for Night*

9 points Paul Mazursky—*Blume in Love*

8 points Tomás Gutiérrez Alea—*Memories of Underdevelopment*

7 points Woody Allen and Marshall Brickman—*Sleeper*

7 points Bernardo Bertolucci and Franco Arcalli—*Last Tango in Paris*

5 points Edwin Shrake—*Kid Blue*

5 points Satyajit Ray—*Days and Nights in the Forest*

4 points Stewart Stern—*Summer Wishes, Winter Dreams*

3 points Martin Scorsese and Mardik Martin—*Mean Streets*

3 points Alain Tanner—*Return to Africa*

3 points Howard Rodman and Dean Riesner—*Charley Varrick*

2 points Arthur Laurents—*The Way We Were*

2 points Bernardo Bertolucci, Edoardo De Gregori and Marilu Pavolini
           —*The Spider's Stratagem*

2 points Harold Pinter—*The Homecoming*

1 point David Sherwin—*O Lucky Man!*

1 point L. M. Kit Carson—*David Holzman's Diary*

1 point William Roberts—*The Last American Hero*

1 point Claude Sautet—*César and Rosalie*

Best Cinematography 1973:   Vilmos Zsigmond
The Long Goodbye

18 points Vilmos Zsigmond—*The Long Goodbye*

17 points Vittorio Storaro—*Last Tango in Paris*

17 points Kent Wakeford—*Mean Streets*

13 points Haskell Wexler—*American Graffiti*

12 points Jan Troell—*The New Land*

8 points Pierre-William Glenn—*Day for Night*

6 points Miroslav Ondricek—*O Lucky Man!*

5 points Fred Konenkamp—*Papillon*

3 points Owen Roizman—*The Exorcist*

3 points Nicolas Roeg—*Don't Look Now*

2 points Laszlo Kovacs—*Paper Moon*

1 point Mario Vulpiani and Pascuali Rachini—*La Grand Bouffe*

1 point Michael Butler—*Charley Varrick*

1 point Ralph Woolsey—*The Iceman Cometh*

1 point Jack Couffer—*Jonathan Livingston Seagull*

AWARDS FROM PREVIOUS YEARS

1966 Awards

Best Picture: *Blow-Up*
Best Director: Michelangelo Antonioni
Best Actor: Michael Caine (*Alfie*)
Best Actress: Sylvie (*The Shameless Old Lady*)

1967 Awards

Best Picture: *Persona*
Best Director: Ingmar Bergman
Best Actor: Rod Steiger (*In the Heat of the Night*)
Best Actress: Bibi Andersson (*Persona*)
Best Supporting Actor: Gene Hackman (*Bonnie and Clyde*)
Best Supporting Actress: Marjorie Rhodes (*The Family Way*)
Best Screenplay: David Newman and Robert Benton (*Bonnie and Clyde*)
Best Cinematography: Haskell Wexler (*In the Heat of the Night*)

1968 Awards

Best Picture: *Shame*
Best Director: Ingmar Bergman (*Shame, Hour of the Wolf*)
Best Actor: Per Oscarsson (*Hunger*)
Best Actress: Liv Ullmann (*Shame*)
Best Supporting Actor: Seymour Cassel (*Faces*)
Best Supporting Actress: Billie Whitelaw (*Charlie Bubbles*)

Best Screenplay: John Cassavetes (*Faces*)
Best Cinematography: William A. Fraker (*Bullitt*)

Special Awards were presented to Allan King's *Warrendale* and Eugene S. Jones's *A Face of War* for feature-length documentary, and to *Yellow Submarine* for feature-length animation.

1969 Awards

Best Picture: *Z*
Best Director: François Truffaut (*Stolen Kisses*)
Best Actor: Jon Voight (*Midnight Cowboy*)
Best Actress: Vanessa Redgrave (*The Loves of Isadora*)
Best Supporting Actor: Jack Nicholson (*Easy Rider*)
Best Supporting Actress: Sian Phillips (*Goodbye, Mr. Chips*)
Best Screenplay: Paul Mazursky and Larry Tucker (*Bob & Carol & Ted & Alice*)
Best Cinematography: Lucien Ballard (*The Wild Bunch*)

Special Awards were presented to Ivan Passer for *Intimate Lighting*, "a first film of great originality," and to Dennis Hopper for his achievements in *Easy Rider* as director, co-writer, and co-star.

1970 Awards

Best Picture: *M*A*S*H*
Best Director: Ingmar Bergman (*The Passion of Anna*)
Best Actor: George C. Scott (*Patton*)
Best Actress: Glenda Jackson (*Women in Love*)
Best Supporting Actor: Chief Dan George (*Little Big Man*)
Best Supporting Actress: Lois Smith (*Five Easy Pieces*)
Best Screenplay: Eric Rohmer (*My Night at Maud's*)
Best Cinematography: Nestor Almendros (*The Wild Child* and *My Night at Maud's*)

Special Awards were presented to Donald Richie and the Film Department of the Museum of Modern Art for the three-month retrospective of Japanese films they held in 1970; and to Daniel Talbot of the New Yorker Theater for "the contribution he has made to the cinema by showing films that otherwise might not have been available to the public."

1971 Awards

Best Picture: *Claire's Knee*
Best Director: Bernardo Bertolucci (*The Conformist*)
Best Actor: Peter Finch (*Sunday, Bloody Sunday*)
Best Actress: Jane Fonda (*Klute*)
Best Supporting Actor: Bruce Dern (*Drive, He Said*)
Best Supporting Actress: Ellen Burstyn (*The Last Picture Show*)
Best Screenplay: Penelope Gilliatt (*Sunday, Bloody Sunday*)
Best Cinematography: Vittorio Storaro (*The Conformist*)

A special award was presented to *The Sorrow and the Pity*, directed by Marcel Ophuls, "a film of extraordinary public interest and distinction."

1972 Awards

Best Picture: *The Discreet Charm of the Bourgeoisie*
Best Director: Luis Buñuel
Best Actor: Al Pacino (*The Godfather*)
Best Actress: Cicely Tyson (*Sounder*)
Best Supporting Actor: Joel Grey (*Cabaret*) and Eddie Albert (*The Heartbreak Kid*)
Best Supporting Actress: Jeannie Berlin (*The Heartbreak Kid*)
Best Screenplay: Ingmar Bergman (*Cries and Whispers*)
Best Cinematography: Sven Nykvist (*Cries and Whispers*)

Richard and Hinda Rosenthal Foundation Awards: *My Uncle Antoine* (director: Claude Jutra), "a film which, although not sufficiently recognized by public attendance, has nevertheless been an outstanding cinematic achievement"; and Ivan Passer, director of *Intimate Lighting* and *Born to Win*, and Robert Kaylor, director of *Derby* (splitting the award), "a person working in cinema whose contribution to film art has not yet received due public recognition." The Awards were accompanied by cash prizes: $2000 to Mr. Jutra and $1000 each to Mr. Passer and Mr. Kaylor.

One

PERSONAL
VISIONS

DAY FOR NIGHT

Vincent Canby

When we are children we build sandcastles and snowmen and marionette theaters. We have electric trains we can wreck at will without serious damage to any lives, limbs or trains. We play make-believe games that give us power over the uncertain universe, which otherwise rules our lives without knowing we exist. In these things we bring reality to its knees so it can see us. Some children grow up to paint, to sculpt, to make constructions of aluminum and barbed wire, to write stories and novels and plays, to create movies.

One of the propelling impulses still is the need to make ordered and comprehensible a world that is disordered and incomprehensible. It's not the only impulse but it is an important one, and it has always seemed to me that one of the most moving aspects of the work of any artist is this ability to continue to function when, deep down, he must suspect an ultimate futility.

This suspicion is apparent throughout the best work of François Truffaut, whose newest and most exhilarating comedy, *Day for Night* (original French title: *La Nuit Américaine*), was the opening attraction at the 11th New York Film Festival at Lincoln Center and will begin its commercial engagement at the Fine Arts Theater here today. It's not the final disposition of things that is important, Truffaut's films keep saying, but the adventures and the risks en route, the mad and often doomed challenges that are accepted in living.

In *Bed and Board*, the fourth and, according to Truffaut, the last of his semi-autobiographical films about Antoine Doinel, Antoine's wife Christine, the lovely, sweet representative of a middle class that Antoine envies without quite being able to become a part of, turns on Antoine with fury. "I'm not like you," Christine says. "I hate what is vague . . . illusory. I hate the ambiguous. I like what is clear-cut."

La Nuit Américaine, which is what French filmmakers call the technique by which, through the use of filters, a scene shot in daylight is made to look like night, is Truffaut's love letter to people who, for one reason or another, choose to live their lives halfway between reality and illusion. It's the highly comic and affecting chronicle of the members of a movie crew who gather at the Victorine Studios in Nice to make what looks to be (at least, from the bits we see of it) a sudsy romantic melodrama about a young wife who falls tragically in love with her father-in-law.

On its surface, *Day for Night* is a very inside movie, decorated with references to dozens of movies and moviemakers, packed with behind-the-scenes information about how movies are made, how technicians manufacture rain and snow, how stuntmen crash cars without suffering fatalities themselves, how bits and pieces of seemingly disconnected footage are finally put together to make an intelligible whole. It is full of marvelous anecdotes about moviemaking, some dramatized, some simply recounted, like the story of an actress who, after attending the preview of her first film, asked with surprise: "Did I do that? All I remember is the waiting."

In *Day for Night*, Truffaut is emulating two earlier artists he admires a great deal, Balzac and Hawks, each of whom in his own way was fascinated by the details of a profession which, in turn, could express the essence of a character. If *Day for Night* were simply about how movies are made, however, it would be no more than a pleasantly frivolous film, charming in its details, perhaps, but as easily forgotten as a successful soufflé. It is, I think, a great deal more than that, since this profession, which Truffaut happens to know best, also happens to be an almost perfect metaphor for life as Truffaut seems to see it in his films.

Beautifully expressing one of the essential thoughts of the film is a line spoken by Severine (Valentina Cortese), a once-popular Hollywood actress who has returned to Europe to live and to play roles like that of the middle-aged mother in *"Meet Pamela,"* which is the title of the film-within-the-film. After a party celebrating her last day of shooting, Severine says of movie-making: "As soon as we grasp things, they're gone." Which, I suspect, is also the way a lot of non-movie people may feel about their lives.

Day for Night is about seven weeks—the time allotted to the production of *"Meet Pamela"* by the American backers of the film—in the lives of the members of the crew, including Ferrand (Truffaut), the director of the film within, a man who wears a hearing aid and is obsessed with movies; Julie Baker (Jacqueline Bisset), the Hollywood actress imported to play the title role in *"Meet Pamela"*; Alexandre (Jean-Pierre Aumont) who, like Severine, is a refugee from an earlier Hollywood career; Alphonse (Jean-Pierre Léaud), who as the young leading man of *"Meet Pamela"* is a kind of grotesque extension of Antoine, so self-absorbed that he's the last one on the set to realize that the girl he thinks he loves, Lilianne, the script girl, played by Dani, is having quickie affairs with almost everyone who has five minutes free.

The film uproariously details the minutiae of temperament and disaster in the course of the production, which becomes a sort of lifetime. Everything is as temporary as the sets, as illusory as a prop candle that has an electric light hidden inside. Everything is obviously disguised, a substitute for reality, or a reflection of it. Real-life dialogue is transformed into the art of the film within. When Julie is discussing her role in *"Meet Pamela"* at a press conference on her arrival in Nice, she explains the plot of the film within by saying that the heroine falls in love with her father-in-law when she realizes that her husband is just a so-so reflection of the father.

For all of its inside details, *Day for Night* seems to me to be less about moviemaking than about a way of facing the conundrum of human existence. A candle may turn out to be fake, life-long friendships may simply be temporary alliances, and what seems to be love may only be infatuation or simply a cheering gift, a one-night stand. Art may be actual experience, ransacked and reformed. This awareness, however, need not diminish the quality of the experience or art. It can, in fact, enhance it. To deprecate it is to deprecate the grand possibilities of life itself.

I don't want to freight *Day for Night* with too much drug-store philosophy. It's such a buoyant, charming film, though, I fear that its wisdom, and the clear eye with which it regards some of life's more troubling aspects, will be overlooked.

October 7, 1973

Roger Greenspun

It is now 14 years and a dozen movies since *The 400 Blows*, and François Truffaut has proved himself in just about everybody's eyes the most durable, the most consistently successful of those directors who, at the turn of the 1960s, formed the brilliant first rank of the French New Wave. That he is also the most serious, the most dedicated, the most intelligent, may be less self-evident. With a few significant exceptions, all of Truffaut's films are entertainments—murder melodramas, domestic comedies, farces— which people go to see and enjoy but don't usually consider important. Like the great master he most admires, Jean Renoir, he is cursed with an attraction to conventional plots and trivial subjects. But for my money, a curse like that is a blessing. In movies, more than in life, the greatest beauties come dressed in unpretentious, sometimes careless, attire.

So *Day for Night*, the latest Truffaut, looks like fun, which it is. But it doesn't look so obviously like a kind of thinking, which it also is: a meditation on aspects of a life, and the meaning and also the meaningless-ness of a career.

Day for Night is a movie about making a movie. The movie is to be called *"Meet Pamela"* (*Je Vous Présente Pamela* in French; I can't imagine a dumber title), and Truffaut has cast himself as its director. He has also cast a substitute for himself, Jean-Pierre Léaud, as its leading man. Léaud has virtually grown to adulthood playing Truffaut's surrogate, as Antoine Doinel, the slightly dopey hero of *The 400 Blows, Stolen Kisses, Bed and Board*. Here his name is Alphonse, but he's still Truffaut's surrogate. And while the director Truffaut ponders his production, asks himself questions like "What is a movie director?" (which he also answers) and repeatedly dreams at night of a boy who pushes a cane through a locked gate to steal promotional stills of *Citizen Kane*, the actor, the substitute Truffaut, makes a fool of himself with women, gets deeply hurt by one, and almost ruins the life of another purely out of childish, self-centered dependency.

But the use of Léaud is only part of it. Anyone who has seen enough of his work could put together a whole history of Truffaut scenes and motifs from this movie: a costume and a mysterious car ride out of *Jules and Jim;* a parcel of books out of *Fahrenheit 451;* a balcony scene out of *Love at Twenty;* a motel room, a saucer of milk, and a fatal jealousy out of *Soft Skin*—perhaps the most important of the film's sources. The hero of *"Meet Pamela"* has found his young British wife in Yorkshire—through a pair of sisters, her cousins it so happens, two English girls.

That's just a beginning. No other Truffaut movie lives so fully in its references, and I'm not sure what it will be like for someone to whom those references are totally unknown. No more puzzling, I suspect. They don't really explain anything. More surprising and unsettling is the direct, dense lyricism that I first saw more than ten years ago in *Shoot the Piano Player* and *Jules and Jim*. Early in *Day for Night* there is a scene in which Léaud argues with the apprentice script girl, with whom he's fallen in love, whether they should go out that night to a good restaurant—as she wants—or once again just go to the movies of which he can never get enough. He finally gives in, "on one condition"—we wait with her for the proposition; but it isn't a proposition, it's a proposal, solemn, elegant, rather theatri-cal—"that you marry me." The scene fades out on that. It doesn't matter—yet—that the girl neither desires nor quite accepts the proposal. It does matter that we have been shocked into a mood of romantic seriousness that is typical of Truffaut, but for which you can never be prepared.

Something of the same mood lingers in the corridors and on the grand staircase of the Hotel Atlantic in Nice, where the cast and crew of *"Meet Pamela"* are staying—and in the studio-lot reconstruction of a Paris square where they do so much of their work. In the course of the film, *"Meet*

Pamela" does get made—the tragic story of an English girl who falls in love with her French husband's father. But *Day for Night* is not just the story of a show-biz success.

In the first place, Truffaut's film isn't altogether a success story. *"Meet Pamela"* culminates in a winter street murder (with detergent suds for snow, sprayed from fire trucks). There has been one major disaster, and several near escapes, and almost everyone in the company ends the film less happy than when he began it. In the second place, almost everybody has an outside interest that is far more important than anything that happens on the set. The father in *"Meet Pamela"* (Jean-Pierre Aumont), a famous international lover in his day, has a young man, perhaps also a lover, whom he now wants to adopt. The mother (Valentina Cortese, in a marvelous performance) has a drinking problem brought on not by a career crisis but by the existence of a son off somewhere dying of leukemia. The father's secretary (Alexandra Stewart) has an unexplained pregnancy that fouls up the shooting schedule. And the young wife (Jacqueline Bisset) has a nervous breakdown in her past and a new, much older, husband—her doctor—in her present. That is, in a sense, a parallel with her movie role. Not such an important parallel; there are other things about her that matter more.

From time to time Léaud runs up to people to ask the amazing question: "Are women magic?" He gets various answers—like "No," or "Yes, at least their legs are magic," or "Yes, but men are magic, too." Jacqueline Bisset is as close as this movie gets to magic in its people. In her physical beauty, and her combination of warmth and kindness and extreme vulnerability, it is as close as it gets to an ideal humanity as well. Such ideals are always charged against their opposites in Truffaut—in this case, the cruel and fickle apprentice script girl who jilts Léaud and runs off with an English stuntman come to stand in for Jacqueline Bisset in the fatal car crash that climaxes *"Meet Pamela."*

But you have to understand that the script girl is also magic. To leave the star and follow the stuntman is in its way an act of fine and reckless romanticism. Everybody has his reasons, and the longer you stay with *Day for Night*, the deeper, the more just, the more poignant those reasons become.

Of course, you can choose between reasons, but you can't simply dismiss the ones you haven't chosen. Truffaut's greatness—a very real greatness—rests in some measure on all the alternatives he is unwilling to get rid of.

The movie's French title is *La Nuit Américaine,* and it refers to a filmmaking process (which the French call "American") that uses special filters to shoot nighttime scenes during the day. I like the English title better. It connects with a series of dislocating substitutions that pervade the film and run all the way up from, say, "Nice for Paris," through "stuntman for leading lady," to "summer for winter," and ultimately to "life for death." Like "day for night," all the substitutions tend to soften or to lighten reality, which is often very dark. The business of filmmaking—not the films themselves—seems to have a quality of strenuous but ameliorating make-believe that only a few rather special people can live with for long. The passions, the true depths, the exaltations exist either in movies or in life; in *"Meet Pamela"* or in the real world, and not in between. Having placed himself squarely in between, Truffaut has made a movie about being outside—like the dream child with his cane—a funny movie, a comedy that is full of longing and lost chances, sadness and farewells, and the memories of those who are only passing through.

October, 1973

Gary Arnold

François Truffaut's *Day for Night* is a pleasant, enjoyable anecdotal movie about the making of a movie. Several reviewers have characterized the picture as a valentine to the business of filmmaking, and it's an apt description. For people whose steady moviegoing history doesn't date back much farther than the beginning of The New Wave, Truffaut's kind of valentine may prove definitive as well as beguiling—a favorite image of their favorite form of entertainment.

Day for Night has the sentimental appeal of a valentine, but it also has a valentine's expressive limitations. Truffaut's account of life behind the scenes is peculiarly charming but also peculiarly placid and undramatic. After 40 or 50 minutes you begin to realize that the material isn't going to deepen, that the characters won't become more than casual new acquaintances and that the scenes are no more than funny little anecdotes about the business.

Truffaut casts himself as an earnest, hard-of-hearing director named Ferrand who is shooting a romantic melodrama, *"Meet Pamela,"* at the Victorine Studios in Nice. Nothing very drastic or memorable happens in the course of the shooting, and the few potentially drastic incidents that do arise are quickly brushed aside or glossed over or reported by messenger after happening behind closed doors or off-screen. How strongly one responds to the film may depend upon how successfully one can overlook its dramatic limitations. If you harbor a fond desire to work with a movie company, *Day for Night* may seem like a vicarious delight: Truffaut appears to be a very nice, untemperamental boss, and you can imagine yourself as one of his devoted, capable crew members. If you'd prefer to see something of dramatic consequence happen within this filmmaking family, *Day for Night* leaves a lot to be desired.

The film is at its best when Truffaut is revealing little tricks or aggravations of the trade. For example, an Italian actress played by Valentina Cortese keeps blowing her lines and asking why Ferrand can't do it "the way Federico does," with the actors reciting numbers instead of dialogue. Later we watch the company wait through take after take for a cat to perform the cute bit he's supposed to perform. This is nice, authentic stuff, but it's also superficial stuff, and you may feel disappointed if you go to *Day for Night* anticipating a level of observation that's more than anecdotal.

If filmmakers and critics frequently find themselves at odds about the nature of a particular movie or the movies in general, it's because they work in different ways and approach the object of their mutual affection from different perspectives, which can become antagonistic perspectives in extreme cases. Directors, preoccupied with projects and the process of filmmaking itself, can often lose sight of the finished product, the cumulative effect of all those arduously assembled bits and pieces upon people who are not associated with the process. It's not unusual for directors to become so wrapped up in the filmmaking process that they romanticize it, imagine it to be an end in itself rather than a means of expression and communication.

On the other hand, critics are obliged to evaluate the finished product, which becomes their inescapable preoccupation. Even if they're aware of the problems a director or a film company were up against and even if they're sympathetic, critics can't honestly avoid the necessity of dealing with the finished product, the movie that ends up being projected on theater screens rather than the movie the director intended or the experiences he relished while shooting it.

Truffaut was, of course, a movie-loving kid who became a movie critic and then a movie director. For a while it appears that *Day for Night* might be a fresh, original movie about moviemaking, dealing with a younger generation at work in a somewhat changed business and using firsthand experience of the filmmaking process as the basis for a dramatic creation. However, Truffaut declines to supply the dramatic elaboration, to venture beyond brief introductions and amusing sidelights.

There was a lot of hambone and fraud in Hollywood's typical accounts of backstage or backlot life, but they were also vivid and involving in a way that *Day for Night* never is. One almost comes away with the impression that Truffaut wants to share his infatuation with a colorless business. *Day for Night* flows along smoothly on a very low current of inspiration:

It's a pleasantly fleeting account of an apparently insignificant film production. I think audiences respond willingly to Truffaut's affectionate temperament, but they may also miss the intensity and vigor that used to be characteristic of show business melodramas.

One would like to believe that Truffaut could avoid the excesses of the tradition while still involving us in the feelings and conflicts of show people. The opening reels of *Day for Night* are crisp and invigorating; there's a constant parade of characters and a constant bustle of activity. You're having a good time and you're eager to learn more about the milieu and the people. Two of the characters—Valentina Cortese and another actress played by Jacqueline Bisset—are even set up as potentially volatile, disruptive elements in the company.

You wait but nothing happens. Cortese comes on with a wonderfully flamboyant impression of the late Anna Magnani and then disappears from the film. The explosive possibilities in Bisset's character never advance beyond the rumor stage. Tragedy enters in a most soft-spoken way when we hear that a member of the cast who didn't make much of an impression to begin with has been killed in a car accident. It's all so transitory that the movie has begun to vanish before the house lights come up again.

It may be difficult to duplicate the pleasures of a Hollywood-on-Hollywood melodrama like *Sunset Boulevard* or a Hollywood-on-Hollywood farce like *Singin' in the Rain,* but those pictures left indelible impressions. They have an enduring glamor, definition, and vitality that one starts to long for when it becomes clear that Truffaut is only skimming the surface of his experience behind the cameras. It seems a little early in his career for Truffaut to be offering us a thin little memory album. Perhaps the movies are a less rewarding subject for his particular sensibility than, for example, the general subject of childhood and adolescence.

Truffaut has said that *Day for Night* will be his last movie for at least a year, while he makes yet another effort to master the English language. He has also said that he expects the filmmaking process to become a dominant theme of films made in the seventies. One accepts *Day for Night* as a token of his affection for both the art and the audience, and one wishes him a speedy, productive return. At the same time I hope *Day for Night* does not set a style for movies about the movies, because the approach Truffaut takes is unlikely to lead us to anything emotionally stimulating, revealing, or sustaining.

October 19, 1973

LAST TANGO IN PARIS

Tango

Pauline Kael

Bernardo Bertolucci's *Last Tango in Paris* was presented for the first time on the closing night of the New York Film Festival, October 14, 1972; that date should become a landmark in movie history comparable to May 29, 1913—the night *Le Sacre du Printemps* was first performed—in music history. There was no riot, and no one threw anything at the screen, but I think it's fair to say that the audience was in a state of shock, because *Last Tango in Paris* has the same kind of hypnotic excitement as the *Sacre*, the same primitive force, and the same thrusting, jabbing eroticism. The movie breakthrough has finally come. Exploitation films have been supplying mechanized sex—sex as physical stimulant but without any passion or emotional violence. The sex in *Last Tango in Paris* expresses the characters' drives. Marlon Brando, as Paul, is working out his aggression on Jeanne (Maria Schneider), and the physical menace of sexuality that is emotionally charged is such a departure from everything we've come to expect at the movies that there was something almost like fear in the atmosphere of the party in the lobby that followed the screening. Carried along by the sustained excitement of the movie, the audience had given Bertolucci an ovation, but afterward, as individuals, they were quiet. This must be the most powerfully erotic movie ever made, and it may turn out to be the most liberating movie ever made, and so it's probably only natural that an audience, anticipating a voluptuous feast from the man who made *The Conformist,* and confronted with this unexpected sexuality and the new realism it requires of the actors, should go into shock. Bertolucci and Brando have altered the face of an art form. Who was prepared for that?

Many of us had expected eroticism to come to the movies, and some of us had even guessed that it might come from Bertolucci, because he seemed to have the elegance and the richness and the sensuality to make lushly erotic movies. But I think those of us who had speculated about erotic movies had tended to think of them in terms of Terry Southern's deliriously comic novel on the subject, *Blue Movie;* we had expected *artistic* blue movies, talented directors taking over from the *Shlockmeisters* and making sophisticated voyeuristic fantasies that would be gorgeous fun—a real turn-on. What nobody had talked about was a sex film that would churn up everybody's emotions. Bertolucci shows his masterly elegance in *Last Tango in Paris*, but he also reveals a master's substance.

The script (which Bertolucci wrote with Franco Arcalli) is in French and English; it centers on a man's attempt to separate sex from everything else. When his wife commits suicide, Paul, an American living in Paris, tries to get away from his life. He goes to look at an empty flat and meets Jeanne, who is also looking at it. They have sex in an empty room, without knowing anything about each other—not even first names. He rents the flat, and for three days they meet there. She wants to know who he is, but he insists that sex is all that matters. We see both of them (as they don't see each other) in their normal lives—Paul back at the flophouse-hotel his wife owned, Jeanne with her mother, the widow of a colonel, and with her adoring fiancé (Jean-Pierre Léaud), a TV director who is relentlessly shooting a 16-millimeter film about her, a film that is to end in a week with their wedding. Mostly, we see Paul and Jeanne together in the flat as they act out his fantasy of ignorant armies clashing by night, and it *is* warfare—sexual aggression and retreat and battles joined.

The necessity for isolation from the world is, of course, his, not hers. But his life floods in. He brings into this isolation chamber his sexual anger, his glorying in his prowess, and his need to debase her and himself. He demands total subservience to his sexual wishes; this enslavement is for him the sexual truth, the real thing, sex without phoniness. And she is so erotically sensitized by the rounds of lovemaking that she believes him. He goads her and tests her until when he asks if she's ready to eat vomit as a proof of love, she is, and gratefully. He plays out the American male tough-guy sex role—insisting on his power in bed, because that is all the "truth" he knows.

What they go through together in their pressure cooker is an intensified, speeded-up history of the sex relationships of the dominating men and the adoring women who have provided the key sex model of the past few decades—the model that is collapsing. They don't know each other, but their sex isn't "primitive" or "pure"; Paul is the same old Paul, and Jeanne, we gradually see, is also Jeanne, the colonel's daughter. They bring their cultural hangups into sex, so it's the same poisoned sex Strindberg wrote about: a battle of unequally matched partners, asserting whatever dominance they can, seizing any advantage. Inside the flat, his male physical strength and the mythology he has built on it are the primary facts. He pushes his morose, romantic insanity to its limits; he burns through the sickness that his wife's suicide has brought on—the self-doubts, the need to prove himself and torment himself. After three days, his wife is laid out for burial, and he is ready to resume his identity. He gives up the flat: he wants to live normally again, and he wants to love Jeanne as a *person*. But Paul is forty-five, Jeanne is twenty. She lends herself to an orgiastic madness, shares it, and then tries to shake it off—as many another woman has, after a night or a twenty years' night. When they meet in the outside world, Jeanne sees Paul as a washed-up middle-aged man—a man who runs a flophouse.

Much of the movie is American in spirit. Brando's Paul (a former actor and journalist who has been living off his French wife) is like a drunk with a literary turn of mind. He bellows his contempt for hypocrisies and ortho-doxies; he keeps trying to shove them all back down other people's throats. His profane humor and self-loathing self-centeredness and street "wisdom" are in the style of the American hard-boiled fiction aimed at the masculine-fantasy market, sometimes by writers (often good ones, too) who believe in more than a little of it. Bertolucci has a remarkably unbiased intelli-gence. Part of the convulsive effect of *Last Tango in Paris* is that we are drawn to Paul's view of society and yet we can't help seeing him as a self-dramatizing, self-pitying clown. Paul believes that his animal noises are more honest than words, and that his obscene vision of things is the way things really are; he's often convincing. After Paul and Jeanne have left the flat, he chases her and persuades her to have a drink at a ballroom holding a tango contest. When we see him drunkenly sprawling on the floor among the bitch-chic mannequin-dancers and then baring his bottom to the woman official who asks him to leave, our mixed emotions may be like those some of us experienced when we watched Norman Mailer put himself in an in-defensible position against Gore Vidal on the Dick Cavett show, justifying all the people who were fed up with him. Brando's Paul carries a yoke of masculine pride and aggression across his broad back; he's weighed down by it and hung on it. When Paul is on all fours barking like a crazy man-dog to scare off a Bible salesman who has come to the flat,* he may—to the few who saw Mailer's *Wild 90*—be highly reminiscent of Mailer on his hands and knees barking at a German shepherd to provoke it. But Brando's barking extends the terms of his character and the movie, while we are disgusted with Mailer for needing to prove himself by teasing an unwilling accomplice, and his barking throws us outside the terms of his movie.

Realism with the terror of actual experience still alive on the screen—that's what Bertolucci and Brando achieve. It's what Mailer has been trying to get at in his disastrous, ruinously expensive films. He was right about what was needed but hopelessly wrong in how he went about getting it. He

---

* This scene was deleted by the director after the New York Film Festival showing.

tried to pull a new realism out of himself onto film, without a script, depending wholly on improvisation, and he sought to bypass the self-consciousness and fakery of a man acting himself by improvising within a fictional construct—as a gangster in *Wild 90*, as an Irish cop in *Beyond the Law* (the best of them), and as a famous director who is also a possible Presidential candidate in *Maidstone*. In movies, Mailer tried to will a work of art into existence without going through the steps of making it, and his theory of film, a rationale for this willing, sounds plausible until you see the movies, which are like Mailer's shambling bouts of public misbehavior, such as that Cavett show. His movies trusted to inspiration and were stranded when it didn't come. Bertolucci builds a structure that supports improvisation. Everything is prepared, but everything is subject to change, and the whole film is alive with a sense of discovery. Bertolucci builds the characters "on what the actors are in themselves. I never ask them to interpret something preexistent, except for dialogue—and even that changes a lot." For Bertolucci, the actors "make the characters." And Brando knows how to improvise: it isn't just Brando improvising, it's Brando improvising as Paul. This is certainly similar to what Mailer was trying to do as the gangster and the cop and the movie director, but when Mailer improvises, he expresses only a bit of himself. When Brando improvises within Bertolucci's structure, his full art is realized. His performance is not like Mailer's acting but like Mailer's best writing: intuitive, rapt, princely. On the screen, Brando is our genius as Mailer is our genius in literature. Paul is Rojack's expatriate-failure brother, and Brando goes all the way with him.

We all know that movie actors often merge with their roles in a way that stage actors don't, quite, but Brando did it even on the stage. I was in New York when he played his famous small role in *Truckline Café* in 1946; arriving late at a performance, and seated in the center of the second row, I looked up and saw what I thought was an actor having a seizure onstage. Embarrassed for him, I lowered my eyes, and it wasn't until the young man who'd brought me grabbed my arm and said "Watch this guy!" that I realized he was *acting*. I think a lot of people will make my old mistake when they see Brando's performance as Paul; I think some may prefer to make this mistake, so they won't have to recognize how deep down he goes and what he dredges up. Expressing a character's sexuality makes new demands on an actor, and Brando has no trick accent to play with this time, and no putty on his face. It's perfectly apparent that the role was conceived for Brando, using elements of his past as integral parts of the character. Bertolucci wasn't surprised by what Brando did; he was ready to use what Brando brought to the role. And when Brando is a full creative presence on the screen, the realism transcends the simulated actuality of any known style of *cinéma vérité,* because his surface accuracy expresses what's going on underneath. He's an actor: when he shows you something, he lets you know what it means. The torture of seeing Brando—at his worst—in *A Countess from Hong Kong* was that it was a *reductio ad absurdum* of the wastefulness and emasculation (for both sexes) of Hollywood acting; Chaplin, the director, obviously allowed no participation, and Brando was like a miserably obedient soldier going through drill. When you're nothing but an inductee, you have no choice. The excitement of Brando's perfor-mance here is in the revelation of how creative screen acting can be. At the simplest level, Brando, by his inflections and rhythms, the right American obscenities, and perhaps an improvised monologue, makes the dialogue his own and makes Paul an authentic American abroad, in a way that an Italian writer-director simply couldn't do without the actor's help. At a more complex level, he helps Bertolucci discover the movie in the process of shooting it, and that's what makes moviemaking an art. What Mailer never understood was that his *macho* thing prevented flexibility and that in terms of his own personality he *couldn't* improvise—he was consciously acting. And he couldn't allow others to improvise, because he was always challenging them to come up with something. Using the tactics he himself compared to "a commando raid on the nature of reality," he was putting a gun to their heads. Lacking the background of a director, he reduced the art of film to the one element of acting, and in his confusion of "existen-tial" acting with improvisation he expected "danger" to be a spur. But acting involves the joy of self-discovery, and to improvise, as actors mean it, is the most instinctive, creative part of acting—to bring out and give form to what you didn't know you had in you; it's the surprise, the "magic" in acting. A director has to be supportive for an actor to feel both secure enough and free enough to reach into himself. Brando here, always listening to an inner voice, must have a direct pipeline to the mystery of character.

Bertolucci has an extravagant gift for sequences that are like arias, and he has given Brando some scenes that really sing. In one, Paul visits his dead wife's lover (Massimo Girotti), who also lives in the run-down hotel, and the two men, in identical bathrobes (gifts from the dead woman), sit side by side and talk. The scene is miraculously basic—a primal scene that has just been discovered. In another, Brando rages at his dead wife, laid out in a bed of flowers, and then, in an access of tenderness, tries to wipe away the cosmetic mask that defaces her. He has become the least fussy actor. There is nothing extra, no flourishes in these scenes. He purifies the characterization beyond all that: he brings the character a unity of soul. Paul feels so "real" and the character is brought so close that a new dimension in screen acting has been reached. I think that if the actor were anyone but Brando many of us would lower our eyes in confusion.

His first sex act has a boldness that had the audience gasping, and the gasp was caused—in part—by our awareness that this was Marlon Brando doing it, not an unknown actor. In the flat, he wears the white T-shirt of Stanley Kowalski, and he still has the big shoulders and thick-muscled arms. Photographed looking down, he is still tender and poetic; photographed looking up, he is ravaged, like the man in the Francis Bacon painting under the film's opening titles. We are watching *Brando* throughout this movie, with all the feedback that that implies, and his willingness to run the full course with a study of the aggression in masculine sexuality and how the physical strength of men lends credence to the insanity that grows out of it gives the film a larger, tragic dignity. If Brando knows this hell, why should we pretend we don't?

The colors in this movie are late-afternoon orange-beige-browns and pink—the pink of flesh drained of blood, corpse pink. They are so delicately modulated (Vittorio Storaro was the cinematographer, as he was on *The Conformist*) that romance and rot are one; the lyric extravagance of the music (by Gato Barbieri) heightens this effect. Outside the flat, the gray buildings and the noise are certainly modern Paris, and yet the city seems muted. Bertolucci uses a feedback of his own—the feedback of old movies to enrich the imagery and associations. In substance, this is his most American film, yet the shadow of Michel Simon seems to hover over Brando, and the ambience is a tribute to the early crime-of-passion films of Jean Renoir, especially *La Chienne* and *La Bête Humaine*. Léaud, as Tom, the young director, is used as an affectionate take-off on Godard, and the movie that Tom is shooting about Jeanne, his runaway bride, echoes Jean Vigo's *L'Atalante*. Bertolucci's soft focus recalls the thirties films, with their lyrically kind eye for every variety of passion; Marcel Carné comes to mind, as well as the masters who influenced Bertolucci's technique—von Sternberg (the controlled lighting) and Max Ophuls (the tracking camera). The film is utterly beautiful to look at. The virtuosity of Bertolucci's gliding camera style is such that he can show you the hype of the tango-contest scene (with its own echo of *The Conformist*) by stylizing it (the automaton-dancers do wildly fake head turns) and still make it work. He uses the other actors for their associations, too—Girotti, of course, the star of so many Italian films, including *Senso* and *Ossessione*, Visconti's version of *The Postman Always Rings Twice*, and, as Paul's mother-in-law, Maria Michi, the young girl who betrays her lover in *Open City*. As a maid in the hotel (part of a weak, diversionary subplot that is soon dispensed with), Catherine Allegret, with her heart-shaped mouth in a full, childishly beautiful face, is an aching, sweet reminder of her mother, Simone Signoret, in her *Casque d'Or* days. Bertolucci draws upon the movie background of this movie because movies are as active in him as direct experience—perhaps more active, since they may color everything else. Movies are a past we share, and, whether we recognize them or not, the copious associations are at work in the film and we feel them. As Jeanne, Maria Schneider, who has never acted before, is like a bouquet of Renoir's screen heroines and his father's models. She carries the whole history of movie passion in her long legs and baby face.

Maria Schneider's freshness—Jeanne's ingenuous corrupt innocence—gives the film a special radiance. When she lifts her wedding dress to her waist, smiling coquettishly as she exposes her pubic hair, she's in a great film tradition of irresistibly naughty girls. She has a movie face—open to the camera, and yet no more concerned about it than a plant or a kitten. When she speaks in English, she sounds like Leslie Caron in *An American in Paris,* and she often looks like a plump-cheeked Jane Fonda in her *Barbarella* days. The role is said to have been conceived for Dominique Sanda, who couldn't play it, because she was pregnant, but surely it has been reconceived. With Sanda, a tigress, this sexual battle might have ended in a draw. But the pliable, softly unprincipled Jeanne of Maria Schneider must be the winner: it is the soft ones who defeat men and walk away, consciencelessly. A Strindberg heroine would still be in that flat, battling, or in another flat, battling. But Jeanne is like the adorably sensual bitch-heroines of French films of the twenties and thirties—both shallow and wise. These girls know how to take care of themselves; they know who No. 1 is. Brando's Paul, the essentially naïve outsider, the romantic, is no match for a French bourgeois girl.

Because of legal technicalities, the film must open in Italy before it opens in this country, and so *Last Tango in Paris* is not scheduled to play here until January. There are certain to be detractors, for this movie represents too much of a change for people to accept it easily or gracefully. They'll grab at aesthetic flaws—a florid speech or an oddball scene—in order to dismiss it. Though Americans seem to have lost the capacity for being scandalized, and the Festival audience has probably lost the cultural confidence to admit to being scandalized, it might have been easier on some if they could have thrown things. I've tried to describe the impact of a film that has made the strongest impression on me in almost twenty years of reviewing. This is a movie people will be arguing about, I think, for as long as there are movies. They'll argue about how it is intended, as they argue again now about *The Dance of Death.* It is a movie you can't get out of your system, and I think it will make some people very angry and disgust others. I don't believe that there's *anyone* whose feelings can be totally resolved about the sex scenes and the social attitudes in this film. For the very young, it could be as antipathetic as *L'Avventura* was at first—more so, because it's closer, more realistic, and more emotionally violent. It could embarrass them, and even frighten them. For adults, it's like seeing pieces of your life, and so, of course, you can't resolve your feelings about it—our feelings about life are never resolved. Besides, the biology that is the basis of the "tango" remains.

October 28, 1972

Gary Arnold

Although Washington is one of the first half-dozen or so American cities to get a commercial engagement of Bernardo Bertolucci's *Last Tango in Paris*, I find myself imagining that today's opening at the Avalon must be a revival. And, since I feel no enthusiasm for the movie itself, not exactly an eagerly awaited revival.

It's been a mere six months since the semi-legendary American premiere of *Last Tango* on the final night of the 1972 New York Film Festival, and the movie opened commercially in New York less than three months ago. But between those two dates *Last Tango* had already become the beneficiary of an overwhelming amount of publicity, much of it sensationalistic. Assuming one kept up with the reviews and the mushrooming interviews and cover stories, it was virtually impossible to suppress a growing sense of skepticism and apprehension. What movies could possibly live up to this buildup?

Whether friendly, hostile or just mercenary in nature, the publicity has proved essentially misleading. It conditions one to expect a movie that simply isn't there. To take the most banal misconception, many people have been led to believe that they will see parts of Marlon Brando's anatomy they never expected to see before. They will have to go away satisfied with a flash of bare buttocks in long shot. At a more sophisticated level of disillusionment, customers anticipating emotional conflicts and revelations more naked than any ever dramatized on the screen may need to adjust to something far more tentative and inconclusive. The vision of modern sexual antagonisms in *Last Tango* is brooding and intriguing, yet also confused and opaque. Bertolucci's vision is anything (or everything) but lucid.

The initial break for *Last Tango in Paris* was, of course, the advance rave review by Pauline Kael in the October 28, 1972 issue of *The New*

Yorker, in which she wrote, "The movie breakthrough has finally come. Exploitation films have been supplying mechanized sex—sex as a physical stimulant but without any passion or emotional violence. The sex in *Last Tango in Paris* expresses the characters' drives. . . . This must be the most powerfully erotic movie ever made, and it may turn out to be the most liberating movie ever made. . . ."

Coming from one of our most respected, demanding, and responsive movie critics, such a rave was bound to have a dramatic effect. Indeed, it set off the *Last Tango* publicity bandwagon, which then got shoves from every journalistic quarter that considered itself in the know, with *Time* grabbing dubious honors as the most opportunistic joyrider. Still, what serious moviegoer wouldn't sit up and take notice when Pauline Kael described "a film that has made the strongest impression on me in almost twenty years of reviewing"?

Her review had an ecstatic and even intimidating quality that seemed utterly extraordinary. For example, the one hint that she may have harbored a few reservations about the film was formulated in a way that would make one feel downright philistine to pursue the matter: "There are certain to be detractors, for this movie represents too much of a change for people to accept it easily or gracefully. They'll grab at aesthetic flaws—a florid speech or an oddball scene—in order to dismiss it."

Far from being a powerfully erotic movie, *Last Tango* impresses me as one of the most oppressively anti-erotic movies ever made. If this film expresses a comprehensive vision of sexual relationships at all, it's a despairing and rather self-pitying male vision of irreconcilable conflict and misunderstanding in which the man, aggressive as he may be, is inevitably victimized, in part by his own humiliating behavior but also by the inscrutable, perfidious behavior of women.

The premise of the film is interesting and promising, but the characters are thinly and sordidly imagined. I don't think they support as much generalization about contemporary sexual roles and attitudes as they're intended to support. The ill-fated lovers of *Last Tango* are Brando as Paul, a middle-aged American failure residing in Paris, and Maria Schneider as Jeanne, a ripe, compliant young hedonist from the bourgeoisie. They meet by chance in an empty flat, couple on impulse and then spend several days in renewed sexual encounters. The arrangement is initiated, controlled, and sustained by the man, who insists there be no personal, emotional involvement—no names, histories, or obligations; only sexual contact.

This sexual retreat is Paul's way of coping with a domestic tragedy: his wife, a Frenchwoman and the owner of a second-rate hotel, has just committed suicide for no apparent reason. Paul takes out his frustration, anger, and incomprehension on the girl, dominating her sexually, humiliating her

Last Tango in Paris   19

and himself, insisting that she share his embittered, contemptuous perception of the world. At the end of a few days he appears to have passed his emotional crisis, having exorcised whatever demons were tormenting him. Paul declares his love for Jeanne, but her initial fascination and submission have turned into fear. When Paul attempts to pursue her, the pursuit leads to homicide.

In Kael's opinion Brando and Schneider are enacting "an intensified, speeded-up history of the sex relationships of the dominating men and the adoring women who have provided the key sex model of the past few decades—the model that is collapsing." This may be the idea, but the enactment itself does not look so clear-cut or convincing. One needs to take the thought for the deed to credit *Last Tango* with so much perspicacity.

How representative are these particular sexual antagonists and how significant is their particular conflict? One simply hesitates to draw sweeping conclusions from a relationship that is developed as ambiguously as this one, a relationship that leaves you holding several loose ends of history and motivation.

For example, what is one to make of the mysterious figure of Paul's wife? Evidently, she has been betraying him openly with one of her tenants. From what we can infer, Paul seems to have been in a humiliating, subservient position domestically. What variety of bitch was this woman? What held Paul to her emotionally? Why would she take her own life? Why is a man in such a bizarrely masochistic, dependent situation a definitive symbol of The Last Aggressive Man?

Brando attempts to fill out the character (a role originally intended for Jean-Louis Trintignant) with bits of his own experience and with the force of his personality. He's often fascinating to watch, amusing or brilliantly intense in isolated sequences. The problem is that these isolated moments don't add up to a whole, comprehensible character. Brando remains a uniquely powerful screen presence, but I was never convinced that Paul existed, that he had a life predating the events in the film and an identity separate from Brando's.

One also goes begging for adequately articulated motives in Maria Schneider's Jeanne. The sheer sexual tension in that flat doesn't seem compelling enough to hold her. I think Bertolucci fails to create a persuasive feeling of impending or ongoing sexual activity in these confrontations. Far from achieving a new kind of intimacy and realism, his style of shooting seems peculiarly mannered and solemn. The film is suffused with a heavy, languorous art-film atmosphere, and I think it robs the action of immediacy and tension. If *Last Tango* is an explosive movie, it's inordinately fond of slow fuses and some of the explosions are duds.

Maria Schneider suggests not a *bourgeoise* but a pert, earthy little bohemian (and her interviews revealed that she was the year's most uninhibited bohemian). One doesn't feel that Brando's sexual-power games truly surprise, sensitize, or enthrall her. If anything, the characters seem to be relatively compatible low-lifes, and it's difficult to understand why this girl needs to reject this man after he appears to have pulled himself together. It's not as if Jeanne were a convincing embodiment of a perfidious middle-class girl, like the Jean Seberg character in *Breathless*, and it's not as if her fiancé, an asinine movie nut played by the increasingly silly-ass Jean-Pierre Léaud, were a more attractive and compatible companion than Brando's Paul.

One needs to accept the fatalistic nature of the central relationship on faith, to share the director's sense of gloom and doom about romantic relationships in general. Bertolucci has an unusually awkward time setting up his doleful resolution of the story, dragging the characters halfway across Paris in order to get them in the same room with a murder weapon. This circuitous trip to a despairing finale seems typical of the film's approach, which insists on tragedy without making a credible case for tragedy.

Brando and Schneider often improvise pleasantly, but fully realized and independent characters haven't emerged from these improvisations. The tentative protagonists we get are required to tote a lot of metaphorical weight, but does the failure of an affair between a humiliated expatriate bum and a carnal little bohemian signify so much? The traditional roles may be collapsing in *Last Tango*, but the collapse is not threatening a crucial class of society or a socially significant figure of male authority. It's not exactly like Nora walking out the door in *A Doll's House*. Paul is a pathetic character, and his fate is an item for the tabloids. It's only Brando's personal magnetism that creates the illusion of a major character.

Pauline Kael's review of *Last Tango in Paris* will probably become as famous and legendary as James Agee's defense of *Monsieur Verdoux*. It's another glorious refutation of the notion that criticism can never be a creative form of writing. On the contrary, these pieces demonstrate that our most gifted and dedicated critics may be a little too creative for comfort. Their own imaginative responses to a film may turn out to have more impact, coherence, and emotional reverberation than the film itself. People drawn to *Last Tango* by the Kael review may feel, as I did, that more movie can be found in her appreciation than in the images Bertolucci places upon the screen.

While performing a service for works of art, critics may perform a disservice to the audience by minimizing the flaws and ambiguities in the works, by underestimating the difficulties or presuming common bonds of experience and attitude that really don't exist. One may not share the fatalistic view of sexual relationships expressed in *Last Tango*, for example. But even if you're willing to consider it, the principal characters may appear to be inadequate or equivocal spokesmen for that view.

To some extent the Kael review may have helped to create the impression that the sex scenes are more stimulating and unprecedented than they actually happen to be. She claimed the opening "sex act" had "a boldness that had the audience gasping, and the gasp was caused—in part—by our awareness that this was Marlon Brando doing it, not an unknown actor."

Perhaps the scene carried a special surprise impact that first night at Lincoln Center, but coming to it after the buildup, one feels decidedly detached. The initial coupling is preceded by a tedious stretch of preliminary stalking and staring, and Bertolucci employs a technique that takes the shock out of the sex—he keeps the camera lingering so long that one ceases to believe in the actors' gyrations.

Brando is, of course, pretending to do it rather than doing it, and Bertolucci's camera style tends to accentuate the pretense. The dialogue is frequently profane, and some of the ideas of the sex scenes are startling, but strictly in terms of depiction the scenes are quite innocent of pornographic influence or pornographic appeal. Bertolucci prolongs most of his sex scenes beyond the breaking point of credible eroticism.

I assume most people will remain curious to see *Last Tango* even if they anticipate something less than greatness. Rather than sheer exaltation or utter contempt, the typical reaction may be a sort of respectful confusion or indecision. This is a transparently serious but ambiguously elaborated and resolved work of art. It seems to be getting at something, but you may never know quite what.

People who go with great expectations, particularly great erotic expectations, may come out keenly disappointed. To guard against a letdown, it's advisable to expect an exploratory movie rather than a lucid or intoxicating one. Instead of altering the face of an art form, *Last Tango* seems likely to repeat the fluke success of *I Am Curious (Yellow)*, which attracted a mass curiosity audience, became rapidly passé and inspired no discernible increase in the audience for other foreign films.

Unlike *César and Rosalie*, for example, *Last Tango* is not the sort of import likely to make people glad they went to the movies or inclined to go again in the not too distant future. The film falls far short of becoming a quintessential drama of sexual conflict, but it is a quintessential art movie. That realization could come as an arduous, annoying surprise to many unsuspecting patrons.

April 25, 1973

Brando's Blue Tango

Hollis Alpert

For those who subscribe to the Marlon Brando mystique, Bernardo Bertolucci's *Last Tango in Paris* may not seem as tedious as it did to me. Look at Brando's record for the past quarter of a century, and we find this actor has muddled his way through more unsuccessful films than anyone else of equivalent stature and reputed talent. Yet for his faithful clique—supported by a good many critics—he can do no wrong. Should a film fail, such as the recent *Burn!* or *The Nightcomers*, blame is placed squarely on the director or the material. The canny star chooses the right vehicle, but Brando is patently not canny. Luckily, *The Godfather* came along, and he was rescued once more, although why his cotton-wadded performance should be heralded above those sturdier jobs by Al Pacino, Robert Duvall, and James Caan can only be accounted for by the Brando mystique.

The star whose aura is more luminous than the role itself is bound to pose problems for the serious filmmaker. The personality can dominate, even overwhelm, the film. This clearly happens with *Last Tango in Paris*. Brando's self-absorption, his very acting method, is at odds with the style of the director. On the other hand, I doubt that Bertolucci should be let off the hook. His film is inflated far beyond the limits of the material, for the story essentially is a bitter, erotic melodrama, rather small in outline, and hardly worthy of the symbolic trappings and directorial conceits with which it has been embellished.

Anyway, here we have this aging American wanderer who has settled down in Paris as the husband of a woman owner of a small hotel catering to a dubious clientele. The wife has an affair with an unprepossessing resident and then, for some unspelled-out motive, takes her life by slitting her wrists in a bathtub. (It takes a while before we learn these simple facts.) The mournful widower goes to look at a vacant apartment where he meets a French girl also seeking an apartment, and quickly, animal-like, he ravishes her, although she is firmly engaged to a young French documentary filmmaker who is using her as the centerpiece of his lifelike study of a modern girl. Instead of being flattered, as most girls would be, she rather resents this filmed intrusion on her past and present.

She continues secretly to meet the American in the bare apartment, which he has now rented. They make sex rather than love, and she vastly enjoys the experience. The American treats her nastily, brutishly, humiliates her person in just about every way possible, and thus holds her subject to his will. He won't allow her to tell him her name, he won't reveal his. He insists on making the ultimately personal into the chillingly impersonal. So far, a small idea, and a reasonably interesting one. But on the screen it simply doesn't work out compellingly. To carry on the story, the middle-aged American commits the error of falling in love with the girl. But for *love* she has her boyfriend, and marriage in the bargain. She has wanted only the ruthless, domineering sex from the aging lover; when love enters, out flies the sex, and she rejects him, upon which comes the garish denouement, which, although a cliché, I won't reveal.

Bertolucci originally conceived the two leading roles for Jean-Louis Trintignant and Dominique Sanda (who appeared together in *The Conformist*). Sanda has a delicate beauty, an air of almost mysterious self-absorption; Trintignant is a first-rate film actor with the knack of burying his own personality in the roles he plays. Most importantly, he is French, and thus suited by birth and temperament to Bertolucci's conception of the part. Enter Brando, and of course the script must be modified. The character now becomes that of a wandering American from the Midwest who settles in Paris. Inevitably the story and script change to take account of this literally foreign element.

Brando, according to several well-founded accounts of his working habits, is a meddler during production. And *Time* magazine's recent cover story on the film bears this out. There are usually horrendous results when an actor works out his own dialogue, as happened in this case. The lines often have an amateurish ring as though thought up for the occasion. (Some critics praise this kind of thing by calling it "improvisation.") In particular, his monologue recalling his bucolic Midwestern childhood has a vulgar quality that only a very bad writer could come up with. Bertolucci obviously didn't know the difference. The *Time* story also mentioned that Brando carried the sex scenes further than Bertolucci had intended. One may be sure that Trintignant and Sanda would not have played them. Essentially what happened is that the filmmaker lost control over his material. Brando's personality, along with his foggy conceptions, took over much of the film.

Once a director gets over his head in a project, he struggles to save himself. Bertolucci is by now a cult director, so he caters to his cult. He injects sly cinematic references to his other films and to the films of others. What happens is that the buffs, the director's supporters, will find meanings in the film hidden from the lay members of the audience, but of course the latter will be educated by the director's critical supporters, the film thereby gaining snob appeal: If one doesn't appreciate, he's clearly a dolt. Then there's Bertolucci's political orientation, known to be Marxist. What is happening to the characters is happening to society. So we get more to chew on. If you enjoy these intellectual con games, fine. I don't.

Good films involve and absorb. One responds to them. But the Brando character in no way involves. As a character, he hardly interests, because he is only vaguely defined, and what definition there is makes little sense. Brando simply isn't believable as the husband of a woman who runs a sleazy little Paris hotel; I haven't the faintest notion of why she, whoever she was, would want him in her life, or how he managed to get into hers. If this had been made clear, it might have made for interesting characters, an intriguing relationship. When Brando has his big scene hovering over her coffin, he prolongs spiteful mourning beyond the edge of boredom. It doesn't convince because we have been given no reference to account for the huge, overacted burst of emotion. As they say in acting classes, the motivation is lacking. With Brando it embarrasses.

Bertolucci's previous film, *The Conformist*, contained a remarkable scene in which two women with lesbian tendencies dance a tango in a cabaret. The scene had marvelous ambience, and meaning too, since it was tied in with a general decline in political and sexual morals during the last years of European fascism. And it was rightly applauded. In the new film there is another tango, a reprise of sorts; but this time it is a caricature without point, unless once again Bertolucci is commenting on the decay of bourgeois society. But why the tango? It survives only as campy nostalgia.

Suddenly out of nowhere, we are presented with couples on a dance floor, exaggeratedly, stiffly, doing the outmoded steps à la Valentino in *The Four Horsemen of the Apocalypse*. Enter Brando and the girl; he's chasing her and trying to convince her of his love and the necessity of a life together. It's *his* last tango, of course, but the style, which up to now has been realistic, suddenly becomes surreal. Yet it's not, for we learn that they have stumbled into a tango contest. The silliness is compounded further when Brando lurches onto the dance floor and the lady in charge of the contest chases him off. But there is worse. Brando suddenly lowers his trousers and exhibits his naked backside to the outraged lady. Perhaps there's meant to be some psychological meaning to this, since the American has exhibited some anal tendencies prior to the scene, but by now the character has become so distasteful as to be tiresome. He's not tragic, not pathetic, merely a case.

The film is being handled cleverly by the distributors. First off, a two-page ad in the Sunday *Times* with a reprint of a review by one of our most respected critics, who patently flipped over its unveiling at last year's New York Film Festival. All showings were on a reserved-seat basis, purchasable in advance and at five dollars a head. For those curious to see Brando and Maria Schneider (a girl with a kind of nondescript, unappealing prettiness) in a series of sexual permutations, the film undoubtedly has some voyeuristic appeal. The more clear-sighted will see it as a blend of commercialism and artiness that fails as filmmaking. Bertolucci is young and still experimenting. He's entitled to a failure. The mistake is all on the part of those who are attempting to elevate *Last Tango in Paris* into the forerunner of a new kind of cinema. There's only one answer to that: nonsense.

Meanwhile an earlier Bertolucci film, *The Spider's Stratagem*, has been released in this country. Based on a Jorge Luis Borges short story, it is set in a mythical Italian town called Tara (one hopes we are not supposed to see a connection with the famed mansion of *Gone With the Wind*), the inhabitants of which devote themselves to the worship of the town's dead martyr, Athos Magnani. The town is as somnolent as a Chirico painting. Enter the son and namesake of the martyr, who presumably was assassinated by Mussolini's Fascists. He studies the monuments to his father and looks up the now elderly mistress of the venerated man. She has some secrets to impart. Athos Magnani was murdered, she insists, by one of the townspeople. But whom?

The mystery unravels lazily. Bertolucci infuses the story with misty, poetic moments, borrowing at times the mood of Antonioni's *L'Avventura*. (Young artists are entitled to borrow from their betters.) Flashbacks bring to life the dead hero (played by the same actor, Giulio Brogi), and the circumstances of the murder are fitfully reconstructed. We learn eventually that Athos Magnani, leader of the town's anti-Fascists, was the traitor who revealed to the *carabinieri* a plot to kill Il Duce during a visit to the town's opera house. And that he staged his own violent death by his companions in the plot. Thus the ruse: to make himself a hero through an act of treachery. A sacrifice, in other words, for a higher cause.

An interesting idea, surely, and nicely conveyed on the whole. But faults that appear in *Last Tango* also show up here. Bertolucci is much too dependent on literary means to convey the emotions of characters. They *talk* what they feel, and they *remember* their emotions of a previous time; but we, the audience, are asked to feel for those we don't know and don't essentially care about. The figure of the martyr is cardboard, a conception rather than a person, and an ideological conception at that. By the very nature of the story, the film is an abstraction; and as such it is reasonably successful and beautiful to watch. Bertolucci is obviously a filmmaker to look out for: He had a brilliant success with *The Conformist,* and he will cause no end of talk with *Last Tango in Paris.* But I find dismaying his publicized intention, which is to make his next film here.

Perhaps he ought to bear in mind what happened to Antonioni when he came here to make *Zabriskie Point.*

February 27, 1973

Making America Dance to Last Tango

Joseph Gelmis

If Hollywood gave Oscars for marketing movies, the ad-pub team at United Artists would have to be declared the no-contest winner in 1973 for its masterful selling of *Last Tango in Paris.* A best-supporting award would have to go to critic Pauline Kael, as the fairy godmother who made it all possible.

The distributor, United Artists, is being accused by some observers of hypocrisy and of manipulating the communications industry to make *Last Tango* the most-talked-about picture and hottest ticket ($138,000 advance through March at five dollars a reserve-seat ticket) in New York. But the high-powered promoters can't be charged with the big hype or overkill.

The person who became the chief drumbeater and pitchman for a potentially troublesome foreign movie was the respected critic for *The New Yorker* magazine's small discerning audience of a few hundred thousand readers. And that lady, Miss Kael, is a self-described "propagandist" critic who prefers not to tell her readers about the failures of a film that she hopes to force them to see—so that she can further the career of a filmmaker whom she idolizes.

What prompted her to call *Last Tango* a "breakthrough" in meaningful eroticism? What made her say the film showed the love-hate battle of the sexes more honestly than it had ever been shown before? Why did she call the film the most important one she had reviewed in 20 years as a critic? She is a serious critic who was trapped by her own partisan philosophy into an unholy alliance that made her a willing accomplice to merchandising a picture through an oversell that must inevitably backlash. No movie could live up to her claims. Not even *Citizen Kane* received such a reputation-on-the-line hype from a major critic of that time.

How did it happen?

Last year, when the New York Film Festival program director, Richard Roud, approached United Artists president David Picker to ask for some movie entries to the festival, he was turned down on all but *Last Tango*. Since that was the one picture he really wanted anyway, he was pleased. All of director Bernardo Bertolucci's films had been shown at the festival. United Artists had a condition: *Last Tango* could be shown just once. There would be none of the normal festival screenings—a rehearsal to test projection and acoustics, nor the regular press screening for the festival's 200 or so critics, editors, stringers, celebrities, opinion-makers and hangers-on.

United Artists brought *Last Tango* into the United States by diplomatic pouch (probably Italian), which in itself is not unusual, to avoid red tape. But it apparently also circumvented the required customs inspection, which is rare, and nobody is saying how. By the time the press realized there would be no screening, the world premiere on the festival's closing night was sold out. There were eighteen press seats available through the John Springer office, which handles festival publicity. These were assigned to film writers (no guests invited) who covered the festival regularly, with *Playboy* the only monthly magazine given a precious ticket (which resulted in an extensive nude layout on *Tango* sex kitten Maria Schneider).

The SRO audience was made to feel privileged—by inference, gossip in the press, and the presence of Marlon Brando in his first film since *The Godfather*. United Artists deliberately created an Event, then sat back with fingers crossed, hoping to get some critical nibbles. Miss Kael, who has adored Brando for twenty-six years and has been a fanatical Bertolucci fan since the mid-1960s, took the bait whole.

"It was felt that the New York Film Festival was a perfect springboard for this film," says UA publicity executive Gabe Sumner. "It was felt that the proper reviews, the proper recognition of the film as important and a work of cinema art would be very useful in the handling of the film in Italy, where it was having trouble with censors. . . . Part of the mystique, the magic of *Last Tango* started with that scramble for tickets. Everything followed after that."

Miss Kael outlined her concept of the critic as propagandist in an interview with reporter Jeff Wheelwright on WNET-TV's Jan. 30 broadcast of "Behind the Lines." Critic Richard Schickel of the now-defunct *Life* magazine suggested that she had deliberately exaggerated to make *Last Tango* a *cause célèbre* so that the distributor and the Italian censors would not cut it. She admitted on the program that she felt it necessary to review not only the film itself but also the audience reaction (as she gauged it) to the Event, in her lengthy *New Yorker* piece. In that review, she compared the evening to the riot-provoking landmark debut of Stravinsky's *Sacre du Printemps* in Paris half a century earlier.

"As a critic goes all the way [for a film in danger of possibly being cut]," she said on TV, "then the movie company has confidence in it . . . every good critic is a propagandist. . . . I want people to see it [the film]. That's the thing. And in order to get people to see a European film at all, I mean, first you want to make sure it's released and then you want to make sure that people go to it. And it's hard to get them to go see a foreign film. Until publicity builds up, there is a tendency to find reason not to go. And people look for reasons. So *I often say, if I have any reservations about a film that I think is marvelous and that people should see, I don't discuss those reservations in the review because people will immediately seize on those as a reason not to go at all.*" [Italics added.]

The day that Miss Kael's 3,000-word rave review appeared, UA's top management decided that "the way to launch the film in New York was to use that review in the most unusual and prominent way." The combination of prestige review reproduced in an eye-arresting full double-page spread in the Sunday *New York Times* on Christmas Eve (the *Times*'s critic had not been as deliriously rhapsodic so he had to be bypassed) announcing the opening of the box-office advance sales at five dollars a head worked. Why five dollars? "Where is it written that only a musical or pornographic film gets five dollars a ticket?" replies Sumner. "This is a landmark film and therefore it's not unusual for an entrepreneur to charge a higher price for anything that is superior."

Most front-office editors had not seen the film in New York. But on the basis of Miss Kael's review and the sex angle and all the talk in the press about the Event (news weeklies in particular specialize in national phenomena for their cover stories), as well as the upcoming censorship troubles in Italy, *Time* magazine assigned a cover story on Brando (he had been on *Newsweek*'s cover for *The Godfather* last year) and Bertolucci earned a cover on *Newsweek*. Everything came together. Call it luck, call it timing, call it genius. United Artists had forged an alliance of those who idolized Brando and Bertolucci and filled it in with those who liked and admired them and were not unwilling to give coverage to the filmmakers.

"We decided," Sumner recalls, "that the [preview] screening of the film would be very selective. It would not be an easy picture to see. It would be shown to those people, aside from the critics, who planned to pursue major stories . . . [Why?] to foster the image, the magic of something very special. In our society, the society of advertising, merchandising, and marketing, things that are immediately available and easy to get are usually not important and special." Bertolucci subsequently protested that he wanted the film to cost only three dollars and to be shown at several theaters immediately while it was news. But he said he was told by UA that he wasn't given directions on how to make a film and that he should leave the selling of it to the pros.

Explains Sumner: "Mike Todd taught us long ago that the way to keep the snowball rolling is to have those long lines in front of the theater. That spells success." Asked if they don't regret their exclusive deal with Trans-Lux East Theater now that the film is such a smash at the box office, Sumner is somewhat elusive. But he implies that the film might go into multiple bookings at some not-distant time.

The selling of *Last Tango* is illuminating because it shows how a classic campaign can generate self-perpetuating debate that makes the public curious to see for itself what the fuss is all about. United Artists programed the preview screenings to give everyone involved, including talk show personalities, the feeling of being privy to a major event. They barred several critics, including WNBC-TV's Gene Shalit and syndicated columnist Rex Reed (who already were *persona non grata* at UA for past offenses) and were accused by *Village Voice* writer Clark Whelton and *Cosmopolitan* reviewer Liz Smith of causing unnecessary hardship so that they could spread the publicity over a longer period of time.

Reed was ejected by Sumner from the UA screening room despite his strenuous objections. "I think all they really wanted to do is to stir up a lot of talk about it," Reed says. "And they've succeeded. Every time I talk about it, they're happy, I'm sure." Reed points out that UA is the outfit that usually holds critical reviews in such contempt that its regular policy is not to quote excerpts in ads, as most distributors do. "If they really dislike the press so much," Reed says, "why hold those screenings at all? They say that they don't care what a reviewer has to say. So why take that two-page ad promoting *Last Tango* with Kael's review? Have they never heard of the word hypocrisy?"

Forced to pay his five dollars like the rest of the crowd and see *Last Tango* at the theater, Reed did what Miss Kael had done—reacted to the Event, mixing his review of the film with a review of the audience. But his review came from the opposite emotional starting point: He was a hostile critic. He described in a full page in the New York *Daily News* a riot in which bodies hurtled through the air and beer cans were flung at the screen and there were fistfights all around him until 150 persons rushed outside to demand their money back and the police came to restore order. "They are attracting riffraff," he says, "people who think they're gonna see a dirty movie. The hype, the stories about a breakthrough, about Italian censorship, about Brando's nude scenes, about critics being thrown out of screening rooms, all of this has contributed to a kind of hysteria surrounding this movie. I think it's what UA wanted. And that it's going to backfire."

United Artists has engineered a masterpiece of merchandising for a difficult picture. Friend and enemy alike are polarized and are experiencing what may be purely personal visceral reactions to the Event, rather than to the picture itself. The theater and UA claim that Reed exaggerated a single argument between a heckler and another patron into a riot that never happened. It's pretty funny, really—critical passions raised to fever pitch by astute control of psychological climate.

"There has been some talk of overkill," Sumner says. "But we haven't seen any sign of that at the box office. We're opening the film in Los Angeles in March. The same two-page ad of Pauline Kael's review was run in the Los Angeles *Times*. There was a $38,000 advance sale five days after the ad appeared, which is double what it was in New York."

If you don't think *Last Tango* lives up to its advance reputation, UA is in the enviable position of being a blameless partner to Pauline Kael's salesmanship. Your disappointment will be her fault. What more delicious revenge on the critical community could a tough movie distributor ask than that?

February 27, 1973

THE SPIDER'S STRATAGEM
Labyrinths

Jay Cocks

Made in 1969 for Italian television, this mesmeric film is only now being released in America, in the wake of the wide acclaim for Bertolucci's *The Conformist* and in anticipation of the brouhaha over *Last Tango in Paris*. Perhaps *Tango* may not so much sweep up *The Spider's Stratagem* in its wake as swamp it. *The Spider's Stratagem* boasts no superstars in the cast, no odor of brimstone and no heavy hype. It should not need them. Less exotic than *The Conformist* or *Tango*, certainly more subtle and contained, *The Spider's Stratagem* is Bertolucci's best movie.

Like such otherwise diverse works as Godard's *Contempt* and Peckinpah's *The Wild Bunch*, *The Spider's Stratagem* concerns the workings of myth, the complicity of fancy and legend in history. The screenplay is an extrapolation from a short fiction by Jorge Borges, *Theme of the Traitor and Hero*, in which a historical researcher investigating the death of his great-grandfather, a political martyr, discovers that the man actually traduced his confederates. He collaborated in arranging his own murder at the hands of his allies, choosing "circumstances deliberately dramatic, which would engrave themselves upon the popular imagination and which would speed the revolt." Details of the death scenario were drawn from literature.

In Borges, the researcher becomes an accomplice to the fiction; in the Bertolucci adaptation, he becomes a victim of it. Borges's "oppressed and stubborn country" becomes Tara, a fictional village in the Po Valley, a place of old men and tenacious memories. The great-grandfather becomes a father. The researcher, Athos Magnani (Giulio Brogi), is summoned to Tara by his slain father's mistress (Alida Valli). A statue of the senior Magnani, resting upon a pedestal bearing the legend "vilely murdered by Fascist bullets," stands in the town square, surveying all who pass with unformed, unchiseled eyes.

When Athos finally learns the truth about his father's treachery, he learns, too, that it is irrelevant. History, in a trim irony, becomes the distortion. The myth becomes the vital, seductive reality. Inextricably ensnared in it, Athos cannot leave the town. At the station, successive announcements are made that the Parma train is late. Its arrival will probably be postponed infinitely. Athos kneels to look at the tracks. They are overgrown with weeds.

Bertolucci, like Borges, deliberately omits any explanation for the hero's initial treachery. Author and director both are interested not so much in the act itself as in its effects. The measures taken to mask the incident become a paradigm of the process of myth. Bertolucci suggests the perpetual, inexorable influence of the past by the ingenious expedient of having the characters—the mistress, the father's comrades—look in flashback as they do in the present: the same age, the same aspect, even, at times, a suggestion of the same costume. It gives a disquieting, eerie sensation, like staring into a mirror and seeing everything save yourself decades younger.

In his phenomenal *Before the Revolution*, made in 1963 when he was twenty-two, Bertolucci included a funny, affectionate café conversation during which a film intellectual says flatly that "the dolly shot is a moral statement." By such a playful standard, Bertolucci would be Pascal. No one since the late Max Ophuls (*Lola Montes*) has moved the camera quite so exuberantly, and with such easy, fluid symmetry. Such a luxurious style can sometimes weigh heavily on the material; in *The Spider's Stratagem* it complements the material, indeed reinforces it. Tara, its name recalling

Gone With the Wind and conjuring up phantoms of romantic fiction, is turned into a single huge stage set on which the plot to conceal the treachery is daily reenacted like an eternal pageant. Bertolucci's ornate camera movements, along with the superbly lush lighting of cinematographer Vittorio Storaro, stress the theatricality and artifice of the concept, making Tara a kind of sun-drenched cloister hewed out of time.

The Spider's Stratagem also contains what has become by now a hallmark of every Bertolucci film, a scene of dancing done with a certain intense but stately vigor. Here, the elder Magnani takes a partner and leads her proudly and gracefully round the dance pavilion, demonstrating his contempt for the astonished Blackshirts standing on the sidelines. It is a lovely, graceful scene, and suggests another title for the film, *First Polka in Tara*. Not as apt, perhaps, but probably more commercial.

January 29, 1973

LOVE

Penelope Gilliatt

The old, old lady in Károly Makk's *Love*, nearing a hundred, lives in the here and now as if it were already then. Lying bedridden but dignified in a poor room in Budapest, she has a like-natured son who has been sent to prison for ten years for his politics. She seems to be living in a tower surrounded by water. The goings on at the moment are too much for a normal mind, she seems to feel, with the firmness of being immensely old. The ancient sage with the telescope of a mind is played by the amazing and poetic Lili Darvas, widow of the playwright Ferenc Molnár. In the film, the skin of her face looks as white as her bed linen. The character wears black moire ribbons that remind her of a splendid hat her husband gave her long ago. "She has an unusually strong physique," says the doctor. "She has my respect." Aristocratism survives; steel stands, and this delicate remnant is made of steel fiber. In an era of cringers and tank-shaped politicians, she is a charmed slip of the tongue, with the power to disclose the errors of an epoch. She plucks at the sheet and turns her head. The planes of her face are perfect: a straight line from cheekbone to chin. She is looked after by her daughter-in-law Luca, played by Mari Töröcsik, an actress of equal grace, with the face of a peasant and the mouth-lines of finesse. We are told that Luca has red hair (the film, made in Hungary in 1971, is in black and

white) ; it looks vivid and thick. She is a young woman who catches your
eye for some reason probably to do with character. She seems strong,
wounded, uncomforted, but dispensing ease.

She and the old lady have entered into an unspoken pact. (How much
does each of them know about their joint pretense, and how deeply?) The
daughter-in-law has secreted the fact that her husband, Janos, is in jail. He
is in America, she says. He is going to be a famous filmmaker. He is going
to win the Kossuth Prize. Queen Wilhelmina is coming to see his movie,
and the Soviet Ambassador. Oval pictures of emperors and kings and
queens are shown by Makk in cameo cutouts, like old family photographs.
For the daughter-in-law, perhaps, as for the old lady, the present is no
place to inhabit, and there is more reality in what is over with. As to how
much the old lady believes of the fable, one has to take into consideration
not only the ungovernably clear sight of the aged but also their willingness
to go along with affectionate deceptions and myths that may make life
work when limbs won't. Luca writes airmail letters to her mother-in-law
that are supposedly from Janos, who is actually growing weekly thinner
and thinner in jail. The strain on the girl begins to tell. The old lady reads
the show-business news in the letters through a big reading glass held before her spectacles. This is contact, of a sort, even if she half knows that it is
confected. When she is delirious, she talks of Janos in German. (There are
two sons, seen as children in scraps of flashback that convey the unmistakable mixture of poverty and indestructibility. The family then looks to be
living in one room. Janos turns his face to the wall when his mother is
being unlaced. The other is more curious and ribald. The parents are
unshakable. What has been taken on can't be undermined by circumstance,
however poorly events may turn out.) Near the end of her life, lying in bed
not much more heavily than a tulle scarf, the old patrician seems sometimes
scarcely to be breathing and seldom takes her eyes off the door, waiting for
Janos, celebrity or prisoner, whatever he may be. When the patient has
finally lost consciousness, the doctor says to the daughter-in-law, "Perhaps
I can keep her alive for two or three more days. . . . What is your wish?"
"Whatever would be best for her," the daughter-in-law keeps repeating.

We see Janos suddenly being released from prison. He wears an old
overcoat with the collar furled. He looks tired to death. "Destination?" the
officials ask him. He doesn't know. A doctor weighs him, telling him
sharply to keep his overcoat on. The records have to look healthy,
presumably. The prisoner looks the opposite: dry white skin, anemia, bags
under the eyes. You can see his thoughts going through his mind as if his
face were made of plate glass. Where to go? How is everybody? And what
everybody? The prison authorities give him back his thin fold of money.
He takes a bus, pretending to himself that he has the old energy by leaping

onto it as in better days. He doesn't know Budapest any longer. To keep his spirits up, he heartbreakingly takes a taxi and asks the driver to buy him some Kossuth cigarettes and matches. At all costs, pretend that things are going well. The mime to himself that things are unchanged is one of the most exquisite observations in this picture, which is always exact, sad, and noble. It is a marvelous film, made with a precision of eye and spirit which records real love. Of neurosis and perfidy it knows nothing. Makk's own poise communicates itself. He understands old age and waiting and the possibility of unresentfulness about a political life of knocks on the door in the night. It is a triumph alien to English-speaking cinema to have made a film about these topics without rage.

April 21, 1973

Falling in Love with "Love"

Vincent Canby

Love, the Hungarian film directed by Károly Makk, is very special—precise and moving and fine-grained—and unless you make a point of getting to it within the next several days, you may well miss one of the best films of the year to date. In a season in which excellence has been as rare as snow, it's difficult to understand why *Love* should be leading such a gypsy life. It's now at the Art Theater in Greenwich Village, where it moved from the Beekman, where it played briefly following its initial one-week engagement at the First Avenue Screening Room, where it opened five months after its local premiere at last year's New York Film Festival at Lincoln Center. It still hasn't taken New York by storm, and perhaps it shouldn't. I'm almost inclined to feel protective towards it, as if a lot of people crowding in on it would in some way be an act of rudeness. Which is to deal in a kind of sentimentality that the film consistently avoids. It's also to mistake the respect *Love* shows for its characters for cinematic weakness.

Love is the 13th feature film to be directed by Mr. Makk, who is forty-seven and, as far as I can learn, has never before had a film in commercial release here. It's an adaptation of two novellas by Tibor Dery, one of Hungary's best known writers, and it is, much of the time, a two-character, one-set film, though it covers an extraordinary range of things—psychological, social, political—with a directness and simplicity one seldom finds in a film. The movie image usually conveys too much information, through too many standard details, to allow for the degree of precision one finds in *Love*, and otherwise only in the best prose.

A very old lady (Lili Darvas), whose great beauty hasn't faded but only slightly receded into fine, fragile bones, lies in bed, her life draining away in little fits and starts, sustained by books, old photographs, and memories that cut across one another like telephone wires that mix up yesterday's conversations with ones that took place fifty years ago. Mostly she is sustained by her daughter-in-law, Luca (Mari Töröcsik), who seems to be an entirely different sort of woman: tough, caustic, pretty in the square way of the social realists.

Luca visits the old lady daily, bringing flowers she can't afford and, whenever she feels up to it, letters written to the old lady by her son, Janos (Luca's husband).

Janos, the letters reveal, is in New York completing a film that will open a new, 16,000-seat theater (with an airport on top), to be attended by the President's widow and her best friend, Queen Wilhelmina, the Soviet foreign minister and the Queen of Greece. Right now, he says, he can't send any presents because he won't be paid until the film is completed, and besides, if he sent presents his mother would just have to pay duty. In the meantime, he reports, his life goes on. He's moved from his 100th-floor apartment at the Waldorf-Astoria into a more convenient palace protected by six Secret Servicemen.

The setting of *Love* is Budapest and the time is late in the Stalinist era, and Janos is not in America but only one year into a ten-year term in a political prison. The old lady frets that she won't live to see Janos's return, and Luca points out roughly that the doctor has said she'll probably live to be a hundred. The old lady has bad days and good, and Luca, whom the old lady calls "the young girl," never is entirely certain of how many of the lies the old lady believes.

Luca's love for the old lady is a furious confusion of respect, tenderness, love for her husband, sexual frustration and anger at what her life has been reduced to. The more lies the old lady believes, the more outrageous Luca makes the next ones. When the maid cautions her about them, Luca says curtly that the old lady *wants* to believe them.

The tallness of the stories is just one measure of the younger woman's passion. There are others. She says at one point that she feels the way she did when, as a child, she got lice in her hair and her mother shaved her head. It took a year for the hair to grow out.

When the old lady is having a good day, Luca asks her to tell a story she's told dozens of times before, how, when the family was very hard up and had to live in one room, the old lady, then a young mother, told her two sons to turn their faces to the wall when she undressed. One son, later killed in a war, used to peek. Janos didn't.

"Janos was always honorable," says the old lady. "That's why you wanted me to tell the story, isn't it? He may have one or two affairs when he's away from you, but he'll always come back. . . ." And she remembers—in a confidence that her age makes immensely rueful—her own single infidelity, with a man who may or may not be one of the figures we occasionally see on the screen as her mind goes ricocheting between memory and dream within little pockets of the present.

Miss Darvas has, to date, received the major portion of the critical praise, but both she and Miss Töröcsik are splendid, and so completely complementary that it's almost impossible to tell where one performance leaves off and the other begins. These are not isolated performances, not from each other, nor from the film itself, which recalls the best work of Satyajit Ray in the seemingly effortless way that Makk moves between objective and subjective points of view and creates a world dense with feeling, with echoes, aural and visual, of past and present.

The film has the air of something so modest that it's well along before one begins to recognize it as the tour de force it is. For me that moment comes when Makk suddenly, somehow, makes us all aware of the curious, not always unpleasant, experience of serious illness, when days get muddled with nights, when lights snap on apparently in the afternoon, when solicitous people appear and immediately disappear as if erased by the blink of an eye. The ruts of memory collapse, and there is nothing left to care about.

Were *Love* anything less than a tour de force it would probably be too sad to endure, but although it's moving, it's also hugely satisfying. Some years ago Chabrol wrote that "there is no such thing as a big theme and a little theme, because the smaller the theme is, the more one can give it the big treatment. The truth is, the truth is all that matters."

April 15, 1973

AN AUTUMN AFTERNOON

Robert Hatch

Yasujiro Ozu made *An Autumn Afternoon* in 1962 and died the following year. One cannot be certain that he knew it was to be his last film, but it has the quality of a summing up, the distillation of a life's work, a last thrust of energy, comparable in a way to Matisse's culminating silhouettes. He gave the picture a typically nondramatic title, assembled actors and actresses as closely associated with his career as is Ingmar Bergman's cast with his, and provided a script so redolent of his preoccupations and intuitions that time and again I found myself transported to one or another of his earlier celebrated works.

Ozu grasps so precisely what it means to live a lifetime that he can set a film of nostalgic yearning in surroundings of heart-stopping beauty without ever falling off into sentimentality or the solace of prettiness. His is an implacable benevolence, a love for his fellow beings that embraces their follies while in no sense excusing them. The point is to rejoice that we measure up as well as we do, not to complain because we fall so far short of what can readily be imagined.

And like its content, this film's form seems to epitomize Ozu's approach. He prefers to work in close quarters—the corner of a room, a cubicle in a public house, a courtyard. He does not avoid streets, but neither does he move much along them. Rather, early in a picture he will establish several compositions of gratifying structural elegance, each associated with a particular thread of his narrative. Then, by reverting to these at appropriate moments, using them almost as titles, he establishes his transitions. Scenes filmed in a given location are apt to be almost exact replicas of one another, the effect being to sharpen subtle changes of circumstance. Like most Japanese directors, Ozu is well aware of utilitarian beauty and the aesthetics of bareness, but he is visually sophisticated and does not make a display of his taste.

An Autumn Afternoon is organized around three businessmen, friends since schooldays, now ruefully aware of their years. One of them, a widower, has taken a young wife, and the other two mock him with gentle envy. Another, also widowed, is cared for by his daughter and, his friends tell him, that is an indulgence which may well ruin her life and overwhelm him with guilt. Indeed, they happen by chance on an old teacher, now the drunken proprietor of a noodle shop, who has suffered just that unhappiness. The "action" of the picture (in fact, Ozu pictures have no action, but rather a slow kaleidoscopic rearrangement of relationships) is the emancipation of Hirayama's daughter from her father's dependency.

Since it is Ozu who tells it, that liberation is itself somewhat ambiguous. The girl cannot have the husband she wants (her father was too late setting the marriage inquiries in motion) and accepts the one found for her out of filial obedience, heartache and chagrin at being thought dispensable. The sight of the brusque modern girl reduced to quivering docility by the manikin garb of Japanese ceremony, while the men of her family, dressed in cutaways, stand about her in complacent admiration, is as near to horror as Ozu ever gets. However, her sister-in-law observes that she is a smart girl and will make a go of it. Probably so—making a go of life is the kind of heroism Ozu's people most frequently attain.

The graying Hirayama (Chishu Ryu—I do not list the rest of the magnificent cast because, unhappily, Japanese names do not communicate here in the West) is somehow splendid without being entirely admirable. Like his friends, he drinks too much, and his charming smile is as much a defense as a response. He is, in short, equivocal, and I think it was equivocation that most troubled Ozu. His era might well have induced the concern—postwar Japan was wracked by a culture in upheaval, and underlying his whole work is the struggle between loyalty to old forms and the seduction of modern (Western) progress.

But though the people of his films are uneasy, and he was uneasy for them, the resilience of courage supports Ozu's pictures. He did not expect a great deal from people, but he placed a high value on what he did expect. Like most great artists, he was free both of illusion and of despair.

May 21, 1973

O LUCKY MAN!

Smile and Say Spinach

Penelope Gilliatt

"Once upon a time . . ." Once upon a time, says Lindsay Anderson's *O Lucky Man!*, which has the style of a scabrous but sweet-spirited epic fairy tale, and closes on a magic, quietist end, when balloons float down—well, once upon a time British colonial justice was harsh. In a period prologue shot like a Russian silent, in sepia, Malcolm McDowell's mouth opens in a howl as his hands are cut off for some minor crime or other. The subtitle "NOW" is flashed. Everything is "changed," says the film, which is engrossed in antitheses. Now English institutions may cut off your life itself for not being a lucky one. For two and three-quarters packed hours, we follow Malcolm McDowell through a sort of *Pilgrim's Progress*. No blow on the head, no poisoned paradox can convince him that man is not perfectible. He starts adult life as an apprentice coffee salesman. Rachel Roberts (the widow in Anderson's *This Sporting Life*) officiously teaches him salesmanship and then changes into something loose and orange and does a bit of selling on her own account, inviting the trainee to test the superiority of a particular brew of coffee (a brand imported from Nigeria and then sent back in plastic bags at colossal profit) when drunk from her own lips, which move like a goldfish's. Smile. Smile sincerely. Try this; taste me. McDowell learns the rules of the game as he goes. "Smile while you're makin' it, Laugh while you're takin' it, Even though you're fakin' it, Nobody's gonna know," goes one of Alan Price's affectionate, tough-minded songs, which deserve to be in the top whatever-it-is this week. (Some of them even incorporate Lindsay Anderson's devotion to hymns.) A song called "Poor People" is plangent, ribald, soft, great. Alan Price comes from Newcastle, Northumberland—part of the Northeast that Mal-colm McDowell is given to cover as a salesman. Price used to be one of the group called the Animals. The pieces here—songs and some wordless music, all by him—are the best things he has ever done. He has a witty, intelligent face. We keep going back to him and his new small combo during the film. Their unchanging choric presence is oddly consoling in the splintered form of the picture, which deliberately has a random and pushed-around charac-ter. They amount to one of the things that bind the long movie together. So does the playing of multiple roles by a lot of the members of the cast. Rachel Roberts, for instance, is not only the coffee-public-relations chief but also a grandly lecherous society hostess. The inimitable Arthur Lowe, famous in England as a small-time provincial actor before he came to TV, films, and the London stage, plays a coffee manager hooked on heavy truisms ("You are a failure in catering if you don't know what to do with your leftovers," he says pedagogically), a blandly corrupt and portly North Country mayor, and the coal-black president of an emergent African state, who speaks with a Balliol accent and borrows a dreadful ho-ho line in white imperialists' jokery (we catch him saying about his country's Inde-pendence Day, as the film comes in on a freezing international dinner party, "And, of course, it was your flag that went up and ours that came down, and the extraordinary thing was that the Duchess never even noticed"). Ralph Richardson plays not only a kind old busybody of a lodger in the Northeast, who makes the hero a gold-lamé suit that turns out to be of synthetic fiber and that is one of the boy's totemistic belongings on his Progress (the others include apples and a stick for walking on the moors), but also a smoothly unscrupulous magnate with two mod white telephones in his Rolls, who has staff eulogies ready-printed in bound volumes in his office and intones from them appropriately to the heads of his empire, assembled in one case to observe a carefully clocked fifteen-second silence when a politely sacked red-headed professor of harried brilliance (Graham Crowden) leaps wild-eyed with revenge out of the magnate's heavy plate-glass office window. While the professor has trouble opening the obviously never-opened window, the magnate doesn't move a muscle to stop the catastrophe, but leaves things to his assistant, who falls with the professor's brainy body past thirty or forty floors of identical office windows, from which not a single ordinary rubbernecker is peering out and sullying the symmetry. The sight is ridiculously funny because of the contradiction of its aesthetically beautiful inhumanity, which makes it seem like a view of small boys flinging cricket balls out of a ponderous grownup's window for the sake of mischief.

The film chiefly asserts the icy procedural inhumanity of ambition and modern drive. The Candide hero, called Mick Travis (Malcolm McDowell also played the boy called Mick Travis in Anderson's *If . . .*), is constantly waylaid by thinking he has won and finding he has lost everything. The rich whom he meets—the black president among them, greedy for capital investment and white tourists, and a spoiled glamour puss (Helen Mirren) who is given to Eastern mysticism and champagne for breakfast, daughter of the suave split-second eulogist, who owns half the copper mines in the world—are no more unscrupulous and cruel to him than the poor, who turn on him in a Hogarth circle of leering faces near the end of the picture. (The production, full of grays and browns and the bony, huge-scale beauty of the Northeast countryside, was designed, recognizably, by Jocelyn Herbert, who did *Tom Jones, The Loves of Isadora*, and *If . . .* and dozens of the best Royal Court Theatre productions.) A prison governor (Peter Jeffrey), saying a paternalistic goodbye to the hero at the end of a five-year jail sentence that comes to him out of the blue in his zigzag Progress, tells the boy that he can sense idealism in him: "The world is your oyster. I can see you stripped, building motorways." A judge who has a taste for taking a little light castigation while the jury is out masquerades as a spokesman against frivolity. (In the whole long stretch of the picture, this seems one of the few gratuitous scenes.) Poverty makes reactionaries, says Anderson's modern legend of everyday realism; the powerful are scared; mankind is not at all lucky. A research doctor who appears to be mad (Graham Crowden again, burning of countenance, driven like an early steam engine by the hope that his experiments about turning a man into a pig may prolong the life of the species) throws common thought out of gear by holding that the dinosaur remained extant a great many million years longer than man seems likely to. A Lady Bountiful (Vivian Pickles) who drives a traveling soup kitchen says merrily to hungry people who would certainly rather douse their troubles in a swig of meths than swallow her nourishing scraps, "Remember—only one bun each." A disgusted tramp has written on a wall, "Revolution is the opium of the intellectuals"; Lindsay Anderson, who obviously loves filmmaking, has always been ready to risk the penny-in-the-slot scorn of modish radical talkers in England.

There are snatches of real-life radio speech on the track: about mental health, about Zen. Everything comes full circle at the end of the film, with the difference that Malcolm McDowell has a final new moment of Zen quiescence about taking things as they are. He is up for an audition conducted by Lindsay Anderson. Smile, please. It is like the coffee-public-relations training. No, he says: "I'm afraid I can't smile without a reason." Lindsay Anderson hits him in the face with the script of this film. Acceptance dawns. Zen thinking might recommend "Put your shoes on your head," or "If someone asks an impossible question, say 'Spinach.'"

The film is Lindsay Anderson's most complex, irascible, and contenting feature so far. (His shorts from the fifties and sixties, which doggedly express exactly the same mixture of rebelliousness, Socratic questioning, and affection, have just been showing at the Museum of Modern Art.) *O Lucky Man!* is based on an original idea of Malcolm McDowell's and was written by David Sherwin in a fine vein of the vernacular, as if it were a mod ballad. The script has no great sympathy for particular people in particular dilemmas: probably on purpose. The picture has a clear eye for hypocrisy, but in the casting and direction it finds unfashionable good in, say, the Lady Bountiful character because she believes in what she is doing. The director's reverence for simplicities comes through like a clarion in the long but terse film. His derisiveness is reserved for self-deceivers and fake grandees. The movie has an interesting Brechtian way of signaling the moral of a scene ahead, perhaps inspired by Anderson's feeling for Brecht's peculiar mixture of formalism and charity, which he shares.

June 16, 1973

Robert Hatch

I was disappointed, depressed, and somewhat irritated by *O Lucky Man!* Probably I was expecting too much—it is directed by Lindsay Anderson, who brought us *This Sporting Life* and *If . . .* , it stars Malcolm McDowell of *If . . .* and *A Clockwork Orange* (with Ralph Richardson contributing both a minor and a major part), and the advance word was that it dealt most rigorously with an important contemporary theme. However, I might have discounted those auguries by a good deal and still not felt that the damned thing had collapsed before my very eyes.

The theme, perhaps, is the major problem. It is that success, like happiness, is not a goal but a by-product of life, and I couldn't feel that a philosophical insight that much in the public domain required to be proved in a series of melodramatic episodes that spilled over into fantasy when the script was baffled for escape devices and that ground on for almost three hours.

To this dubious use of time and energy was added the decision that McDowell, in the character of Mick Travis, should play Everyman in modern dress, a part that required him to be innocent to the point of simple-mindedness. Just for an example, Travis happily rents his body for £130 to the patently mad director of a biological research center, without asking what experiments are on the agenda. In general, Travis will sign any document that is thrust beneath his nose, and in particular he sees nothing rash about jumping upon the roof of his car to gaze through binoculars into a super-secret military proving ground. Everyman is a personage greatly honored by time, but he is not effectively resurrected in a script that employs a kind of department store surrealist chic to excoriate current materialism. One gets very tired of Mick Travis's inability to look before he leaps.

Finally, the picture is burdened with a millstone of satire directed at the rapacity, hypocrisy, cruelty, and stupidity of modern society. Anderson and his writer, David Sherwin, have nothing original to say about the evils of our time and they compensate for that lack by inventing grotesque, ludicrous, and horrifying ways of saying it. The result is a very elaborate script, very expensively produced, about the self-evident truth that the world is not, and never has been, a safe place for ambitious halfwits. I'm sure it was not so intended, but this strikes me as a copout. The fact is that simpletons with ambition of the extreme sort here described are exceedingly rare. Parallels will no doubt be drawn with the likes of Vesco and Jeb Stuart Magruder, but they will be false. There is nothing simple-minded or innocent about that sort of drive for power. Such men may well lack an appreciation of history or an ability to figure odds, but they are far from trusting the benevolence of strangers.

What it comes down to is that *O Lucky Man!* aspires to be a serious denunciation of present evils but comes across as an entertainment based on the clichés of social criticism. It smells of opportunism, for, like its hero, it is exposed as being in pursuit, not of a goal but of miraculous success. Unlike its hero, it will probably achieve it.

The best thing in the picture is Alan Price, who wrote the score and who sings his own songs during ballad interludes, inserted in the manner of *The Threepenny Opera*. Price is possessed of the economy of real anger, which he conveys in a tone of mocking good humor that chills your blood. His jingles fatally undercut the ponderous machinery of the main script's pseudo-edifying parables.

July 2, 1973

THE LONG GOODBYE

Charles Champlin

A movie, I keep saying, has to be judged on its own terms. The truth, hard on novelists and playwrights, is that a movie's fidelity to its origins in another medium matters less than whether the movie works as a movie. The origins may provide clues as to why a movie succeeded or failed— some spaciousness gained, some subtleties lost—but it is what's up front on the screen that counts.

That's what I keep saying, and it follows that Robert Altman's movie drawn from Raymond Chandler's detective novel, *The Long Goodbye,* has to be reviewed as a movie. The thing is, I'm not sure I can.

Chandler had a particular vision of the Los Angeles of the very late thirties and early forties, and of a private detective who lived and worked in that city and time. His name was Philip Marlowe and he was a loser who lost everything except his ultimate, stubbornly defended honor. He was not really a hero but not an antihero either; maybe he was a counterhero, a hero who ran counter to the established notions of how heroes operate.

What Altman and Leigh Brackett, his scriptwriter, have done is to invent their own Philip Marlowe, set him in a Los Angeles which is advanced 30 years into the present day and then run him through the adjusted skeleton of Chandler's plot.

The problem is that the Altman-Brackett Marlowe, played by Elliott Gould, is an untidy, unshaven, semiliterate, dimwit slob who could not locate a missing skyscraper and who would be refused service at a hot-dog stand. He is not Chandler's Marlowe, or mine, and I can't find him interesting, sympathetic, or amusing, and I can't be sure who will.

Gould does what he was asked to do with great skill and conviction; the conception, I presume, was not his.

Altman's Los Angeles is part Los Angeles and heavily Altman. A bevy of spaced-out nudes do yoga on the balcony opposite Marlowe's high-rise slum apartment, to take one example. The subsidiary characters all have that kind of hyper-colorfulness you used to find in Peter Gunn.

As a filmmaker, Altman is an unabashed entertainer. His screen is never, never dull and, given the right scripts, what you see often seems to be about something. *The Long Goodbye* is quite, quite sleek, marvelously and inventively photographed (by Vilmos Zsigmond), and full of quaint surprises like dogs copulating in the background as Marlowe crosses a village square in Mexico.

There are some high-amplitude performances, including one by director Mark Rydell as a sadistic gangster and another by Sterling Hayden as an alcoholic novelist. Laugh-In alumnus Henry Gibson brings off a small, sneery role as a crooked doctor, and baseballer Jim Bouton makes his movie debut competently as Marlowe's roguish pal who sets the plot in motion.

At that, the most exciting performance in the movie belongs to Nina van Pallandt, lately Clifford Irving's travel companion. She acts very well indeed, but she also exudes a real-woman vitality which seems refreshingly out of place amidst these mannered and artificial events.

The plot, not that it much matters, turns on whether Marlowe's old buddy really did murder his wife and really did then shoot himself in old Mexico, and why the writer walked into the sea forever and why the widow is so tight with the sadistic mobster and his sadistic henchmen.

There is not much violence but what there is is uncommonly nasty, and there is not much nudity but what there is is gratuitous, and the street language owes nothing to Raymond Chandler except apologies.

Brackett and Altman have made one major plot change, and its effect is to deny almost everything that was honorable about Marlowe.

It is finally hard to know what Altman was aiming for in *The Long Goodbye*. An homage would not have done such violence to the spirit of the original—Chandler's sense of moral indignation in particular. Altman may be suggesting that the realities about private eyes and their world are more sordid and scruffy than Chandler cared to admit.

Maybe. But Chandler made you care and there is no one—including Marlowe—to give a damn about here. If Chandler's hero was amazingly honorable for a man in his circumstances, he was not incredible. And the world in which he moved was recorded with the fidelity which is still astonishing and was interpreted with compassion and insight.

What tones Altman's *Long Goodbye* is a cynical insistence that nothing has value. It is an exercise in style, using a foolish plot and a gaudy, tricked-up world to create effects. But without any real conflict between good and evil, no urgent presumptions that right and wrong exist, the whole thing goes slack and vacuous and finally even the clever images cannot arrest the long difference.

You don't have to admire Raymond Chandler to regret the movie, but it helps.

March 8, 1973

Movieland—The Bums' Paradise

Pauline Kael

Edmund Wilson summed up Raymond Chandler convincingly in 1945 when he said of *Farewell, My Lovely,* "It is not simply a question here of a puzzle which has been put together but of a malaise conveyed to the reader, the horror of a hidden conspiracy which is continually turning up in the most varied and unlikely forms. . . . It is only when I get to the end that I feel my old crime-story depression descending upon me again—because here again, as is so often the case, the explanation of the mysteries, when it comes, is neither interesting nor plausible enough. It fails to justify the excitement produced by the picturesque and sinister happenings, and I cannot help feeling cheated." Locked in the conventions of pulp writing, Raymond Chandler never found a way of dealing with that malaise. But Robert Altman does, in *The Long Goodbye,* based on Chandler's 1953 Los Angeles-set novel. The movie is set in the same city twenty years later; this isn't just a matter of the private-detective hero's prices going from twenty-five dollars a day to fifty—it's a matter of rethinking the book and the genre. Altman, who probably works closer to his unconscious than any other American director, tells a detective story, all right, but he does it through a spree—a high-flying rap on Chandler and the movies and that Los Angeles sickness. The movie isn't just Altman's private-eye movie—it's his Hollywood movie, set in the mixed-up world of movie-influenced life that is L.A.

In Los Angeles, you can live any way you want (except the urban way); it's the fantasy-brothel, where you can live the fantasy of your choice. You can also live well without being rich, which is the basic and best reason people swarm there. In that city—the pop amusement park of the shifty and the uprooted, the city famed as the place where you go to sell out—Raymond Chandler situated his incorruptible knight Philip Marlowe, the private detective firmly grounded in high principles. Answering a letter in 1951, Chandler wrote, "If being in revolt against a corrupt society constitutes being immature, then Philip Marlowe is extremely immature. If seeing dirt where there is dirt constitutes an inadequate social adjustment, then Philip Marlowe has inadequate social adjustment. Of course Marlowe is a failure, and he knows it. He is a failure because he hasn't any money. . . . A lot of very good men have been failures because their particular talents did not suit their time and place." And he cautioned, "But you must remember that Marlowe is not a real person. He is a creature of fantasy. He is in a false position because I put him there. In real life, a man of his type would no more be a private detective than he would be a university don." Six months later, when his rough draft of *The Long Goodbye* was criticized by his agent, Chandler wrote back, "I didn't care whether the mystery was fairly obvious, but I cared about the people, about this strange corrupt world we live in, and how any man who tried to be honest looks in the end either sentimental or plain foolish."

Chandler's sentimental foolishness is the taking-off place for Altman's film. Marlowe (Elliott Gould) is a wryly forlorn knight, just slogging along. Chauffeur, punching bag, errand boy, he's used, lied to, double-crossed. He's the gallant fool in a corrupt world—the innocent eye. He isn't stupid and he's immensely likable, but the pulp pretense that his chivalrous code was armor has collapsed, and the romantic machismo of Bogart's Marlowe in *The Big Sleep* has evaporated. The one-lone-idealist-in-the-city-crawling-with-rats becomes a schlemiel who thinks he's tough and wise. (He's still driving a 1948 Lincoln Continental and trying to behave like Bogart.) He doesn't know the facts of life that everybody else knows; even the police know more about the case he's involved in than he does. Yet he's the only one who *cares*. That's his true innocence, and it's his slack-jawed crazy sweetness that keeps the movie from being harsh or scabrous.

Altman's goodbye to the private-eye hero is comic and melancholy and full of regrets. It's like cleaning house and throwing out things that you know you're going to miss—there comes a time when junk dreams get in your way. *The Long Goodbye* reaches a satirical dead end that kisses off the private-eye form as gracefully as *Beat the Devil* finished off the cycle of the international-intrigue thriller. Altman does variations on Chandler's theme the way the John Williams score does variations on the title song, which is a tender ballad in one scene, a funeral dirge in another. Williams' music is a parody of the movies' frequent overuse of a theme, and a demonstration of how adaptable a theme can be. This picture, less accidental than *Beat the Devil*, is just about as funny, though quicker-witted, and dreamier, in soft, mellow color and volatile images—a reverie on the lies of old movies. It's a knockout of a movie that has taken eight months to arrive in New York because after opening in Los Angeles last March and being badly received (perfect irony) it folded out of town. It's probably the best American movie ever made that almost didn't open in New York. Audiences may have felt they'd already had it with Elliott Gould; the young men who looked like him in 1971 have got cleaned up and barbered and turned into Mark Spitz. But it actually adds poignancy to the film that Gould himself is already an anachronism.

Thinner and more lithe than in his brief fling as a superstar (his success in *Bob & Carol & Ted & Alice* and *M*A*S*H* led to such speedy exploitation of his box-office value that he appeared in seven films between 1969 and 1971), Gould comes back with his best performance yet. It's his movie. The rubber-legged slouch, the sheepish, bony-faced angularity have their grace; drooping-eyed, squinting, with more blue stubble on his face than any other hero on record, he's a loose and woolly, jazzy Job. There's a skip and bounce in his shamble. Chandler's arch, spiky dialogue—so hardboiled it can make a reader's teeth grate—gives way to this Marlowe's muttered, befuddled throwaways, his self-sendups. Gould's Marlowe is a man who is had by everybody—a male pushover, reminiscent of Fred MacMurray in *Double Indemnity*. He's Marlowe as Miss Lonelyhearts. Yet this softhearted honest loser is so logical a modernization, so "right," that when you think about Marlowe afterward you can't imagine any other way of playing him now that wouldn't be just fatuous. (Think of Mark Spitz as Marlowe if you want fatuity pure.) The good-guys-finish-last conception was implicit in Chandler's L.A. all along, and Marlowe was only one step from being a clown, but Chandler pulped his own surrogate and made Marlowe, the Victorian relic, a winner. Chandler has a basic phoniness that it would have been a cinch to exploit. He wears his conscience right up front; the con trick is that it's not a writer's conscience. Offered the chance to break free of the straitjacket of the detective novel, Chandler declined. He clung to the limiting stereotypes of pop writing and blamed "an age whose dominant note is an efficient vulgarity, an unscrupulous scramble for the dollar." Style, he said, "can exist in a savage and dirty age, but it cannot exist in the Coca-Cola age . . . the Book of the Month, and the Hearst Press." It was Marlowe, the independent man, dedicated to autonomy—his needs never rising above that twenty-five dollars a day—who actually lived like an artist. Change Marlowe's few possessions, "a coat, a hat, and a gun," to "a coat, a hat, and a typewriter," and the cracks in Chandler's myth of the hero become a hopeless split.

Robert Altman is all of a piece, but he's complicated. You can't predict what's coming next in the movie; his plenitude comes from somewhere beyond reason. An Altman picture doesn't have to be great to be richly pleasurable. He tosses in more than we can keep track of, maybe more than *he* bothers to keep track of; he nips us in surprising ways. In *The Long Goodbye*, as in *M*A*S*H*, there are climaxes, but you don't have the sense of waiting for them, because what's in between is so satisfying. He underplays the plot and concentrates on the people, so it's almost all of equal interest, and you feel as if it could go on indefinitely and you'd be absorbed in it. Altman may have the most glancing touch since Lubitsch, and his ear for comedy is better than anybody else's. In this period of movies, it isn't necessary (or shouldn't be) to punch the nuances home; he just glides over them casually, in the freest possible way. Gould doesn't propel the action as Bogart did; the story unravels around the private eye —the corrupt milieu wins. Maybe the reason some people have difficulty getting onto Altman's wavelength is that he's just about incapable of over-dramatizing. He's not a pusher. Even in this film, he doesn't push decadence. He doesn't heat up angst the way it was heated in *Midnight Cowboy* and *They Shoot Horses, Don't They?*

Pop culture takes some nourishment from the "high" arts, but it feeds mainly on itself. *The Long Goodbye* had not been filmed before, because the book came out too late, after the private-eye-movie cycle had peaked. Marlowe had already become Bogart, and you could see him in it when you read the book. You weren't likely to have kept the other Marlowes of the forties (Dick Powell, Robert Montgomery, George Montgomery) in your mind, and you had to see somebody in it. The novel reads almost like a parody of pungent writing—like a semi–literate's idea of great writing. The detective-novel genre always verged on self-parody, because it gave you nothing under the surface. Hemingway didn't need to state what his characters felt, because his external descriptions implied all that, but the pulp writers who imitated Hemingway followed the hard-boiled-detective pattern that Hammett had invented; they externalized everything and implied nothing. Their gaudy terseness demonstrates how the novel and the comic strip can merge. They described actions and behavior from the outside, as if they were writing a script that would be given some inner life by the actors and the director; the most famous practitioners of the genre were, in fact, moonlighting screenwriters. *The Long Goodbye* may have good descriptions of a jail or a police lineup, but the prose is alternately taut and lumpy with lessons in corruption, and most of the great observations you're supposed to get from it are just existentialism with oil slick. With its classy dames, a Marlowe influenced by Marlowe, the obligatory tension between Marlowe and the cops, and the sentimental bar scenes, *The Long Goodbye* was a product of the private-eye films of the decade before. Chandler's corrupt milieu—what Auden called "The Great Wrong Place"—was the new-style capital of sin, the city that made the movies and was made by them.

In Chandler's period (he died in 1959), movies and novels interacted; they still do, but now the key interaction may be between movies and movies—and between movies and us. We can no longer view ourselves—the way Nathanael West did—as different from the Middle Westerners in L.A. lost in their movie-fed daydreams, and the L.A. world founded on pop is no longer the world *out there,* as it was for Edmund Wilson. Altman's *The Long Goodbye* (like Paul Mazursky's *Blume in Love*) is about people who live in L.A. because they like the style of life, which comes from the movies. It's not about people who work in movies but about people whose lives have been shaped by them; it's set in the modern L.A. of the stoned sensibility, where people have given in to the beauty that always looks unreal. The inhabitants are an updated gallery of California freaks, with one character who links this world to Nathanael West's—the Malibu Colony gatekeeper (Ken Sansom), who does ludicrous, pitiful impressions of Barbara Stanwyck in *Double Indemnity* (which was Chandler's first screenwriting job), and of James Stewart, Walter Brennan, and Cary Grant (the actor Chandler said he had in mind for Marlowe). In a sense, Altman here has already made *Day of the Locust.* (To do it as West intended it, and to have it make contemporary sense, it would now have to be set in Las Vegas.) Altman's references to movies don't stick out—they're just part of the texture, as they are in L.A.—but there are enough so that a movie pedant could do his own weirdo version of *A Skeleton Key to Finnegans Wake.*

The one startlingly violent action in the movie is performed by a syndicate boss who is as rapt in the glory of his success as a movie mogul. Prefigured in Chandler's description of movie producers in his famous essay "Writers in Hollywood," Marty Augustine (Mark Rydell) is the next step up in paranoid self-congratulation from the Harry Cohn-like figure that Rod Steiger played in *The Big Knife;* he's freaked out on success, L.A.-Las Vegas style. His big brown eyes with their big brown bags preside over the decaying pretty-boy face of an Eddie Fisher, and when he flashes his ingenuous Paul Anka smile he's so appalling he's comic. His violent act is outrageously gratuitous (he smashes a Coke bottle in the fresh young face of his unoffending mistress), yet his very next line of dialogue is so comic-tough that we can't help laughing while we're still gasping, horrified—much as we did when Cagney shoved that half grapefruit in Mae Clarke's nagging kisser. This little Jewish gangster-boss is a mod imp—offspring of the movies, as much a creature of show business as Joel Grey's M.C. in *Cabaret.* Marty Augustine's bumbling goon squad (ethnically balanced) are the illegitimate sons of Warner Brothers. In the Chandler milieu, what could be better casting than the aristocratic Nina van Pallandt as the rich dish—the duplicitous blonde, Mrs. Wade? And, as her husband, the blocked famous writer Roger Wade, Sterling Hayden, bearded like Neptune, and as full of the old mach as the progenitor of tough-guy writing himself. The most movieish bit of dialogue is from the book: When the police come to question Marlowe about his friend Terry Lennox, Marlowe says, "This is where I say, 'What's this all about?' and you say, 'We ask the questions.'" But the resolution of Marlowe's friendship with Terry isn't from Chandler, and its logic is probably too brutally sound for Bogart-lovers to stomach. Terry Lennox (smiling Jim Bouton, the baseball player turned broadcaster) becomes the Harry Lime in Marlowe's life, and the final sequence is a variation on *The Third Man*, with the very last shot a riff on the leave-taking scenes of the movies' most famous clown.

The movie achieves a self-mocking fairy-tale poetry. The slippery shifts within the frames of Vilmos Zsigmond's imagery are part of it, and so are the offbeat casting (Henry Gibson as the sinister quack Dr. Verringer; Jack Riley, of the Bob Newhart show, as the piano player) and the dialogue. (The script is officially credited to the venerable pulp author Leigh Brackett; she also worked on *The Big Sleep* and many other good movies, but when you hear the improvised dialogue you can't take this credit literally.) There are some conceits that are fairly precarious (the invisible-man stunt in the hospital sequence) and others that are waywardly funny (Marlowe trying to lie to his cat) or suggestive and beautiful (the Wades' Doberman coming out of the Pacific with his dead master's cane in his teeth). When Nina van Pallandt thrashes in the ocean at night, her pale-orange butterfly sleeves rising above the surf, the movie becomes a rhapsody on romance and death. What separates Altman from other directors is that time after time he can attain crowning visual effects like this and they're so elusive they're never precious. They're like ribbons tying up the whole history of movies. It seems unbelievable that people who looked at this picture could have given it the reviews they did.

The out-of-town failure of *The Long Goodbye* and the anger of many of the reviewers, who reacted as if Robert Altman were a destroyer, suggest that the picture may be on to something bigger than is at first apparent. Some speculations may be in order. Marlowe was always a bit of a joke, but did people take him that way? His cynical exterior may have made it possible for them to accept him in Chandler's romantic terms, and really—below the joke level—believe in him. We've all read Chandler on his hero: "But down these mean streets a man must go who is not himself mean, who is neither tarnished nor afraid." He goes, apparently, in our stead. And as long as he's there—the walking conscience of the world—we're safe. We could easily reject sticky saviours, but a cynical saviour satisfies the Holden Caulfield in us. It's an adolescent's dream of heroism—someone to look after you, a protector like Billy Jack. And people cleave to the fantasies they form while watching movies.

After reading *The Maltese Falcon*, Edmund Wilson said of Dashiell Hammett that he "lacked the ability to bring the story to imaginative life." Wilson was right, of course, but this may be the basis of Hammett's appeal; when Wilson said of the detective story that "as a department of imaginative writing, it looks to me completely dead," he was (probably intentionally) putting it in the wrong department. It's precisely the fact that the detective novel is engrossing but does not impinge on its readers' lives or thoughts that enables it to give a pleasure to some which is distinct from the pleasures of literature. It has no afterlife when they have closed the covers; it's completely digested, like a game of casino. It's a structured time killer that gives you the illusion of being speedy; *The Long Goodbye* isn't a fast read, like Hammett, but when I finished it I had no idea whether I'd read it before. Essentially, we've all read it before.

But when these same stories were transferred to the screen, the mechanisms of suspense could strike fear in the viewer, and the tensions could grow almost unbearable. The detective story on the screen became a thriller in a much fuller sense than it had been on the page, and the ending of the movie wasn't like shutting a book. The physical sensations that were stirred up weren't settled; even if we felt cheated, we were still turned on. We left the theater in a state of mixed exhilaration and excitement, and the fear and guilt went with us. In our dreams, we were menaced, and perhaps became furtive murderers. It is said that in periods of rampant horrors readers and moviegoers like to experience imaginary horrors, which can be resolved and neatly put away. I think it's more likely that in the current craze for horror films like *Night of the Living Dead* and *Sisters* the audience wants an intensive dose of the fear sickness—not to confront fear and have it conquered but to feel that crazy, inexplicable delight that children get out of terrifying stories that give them bad dreams. A flesh-crawler that affects as many senses as a horror movie can doesn't end with the neat fake solution. We are always aware that the solution will not really explain the terror we've felt; the forces of madness are never laid to rest.

Suppose that through the medium of the movies, pulp, with its five-and-dime myths, can take a stronger hold on people's imaginations than art, because it doesn't affect the conscious imagination, the way a great novel does, but the private, hidden imagination, the primitive fantasy life—and with an immediacy that leaves no room for thought. I have had more mail from adolescents (and post-adolescents) who were badly upset because of a passing derogatory remark I made about *Rosemary's Baby* than I would ever get if I mocked Tolstoy. Those adolescents think *Rosemary's Baby* is great because it upsets them. And I suspect that people are reluctant to say goodbye to the old sweet bull of the Bogart Marlowe because it satisfies a deep need. They've been accepting the I-look-out-for-No.-1 tough guys of recent films, but maybe they're scared to laugh at Gould's out-of-it Marlowe because that would lose them their Bogart icon. At the moment, the shared pop culture of the audience may be all that people feel they have left. The negative reviews kept insisting that Altman's movie had nothing to do with Chandler's novel and that Elliott Gould wasn't Marlowe. People still want to believe that Galahad is alive and well in Los Angeles—biding his time, perhaps, until movies are once again "like they used to be."

The jacked-up romanticism of movies like those featuring Shaft, the black Marlowe, may be so exciting it makes what we've always considered the imaginative artists seem dull and boring. Yet there is another process at work, too: the executive producers and their hacks are still trying to find ways to make the old formulas work, but the gifted filmmakers are driven to go beyond pulp and to bring into movies the qualities of imagination that have gone into the other arts. Sometimes, like Robert Altman, they do it even when they're working on pulp material. Altman's isn't a pulp sensibility. Chandler's, for all his talent, was.

October 22, 1973

William S. Pechter

Is it possible (my pulse races chauvinistically) that 1973 might be the year of the middle-aged? Much as I'd like to believe this, I can't quite blot out the memory of Peckinpah's *Pat Garrett and Billy the Kid*, nor refashion it in my mind, from what remains in its producer-mutilated version, into anything other than a rash adventure in inadvertent self-parody. Nor can I bring myself to join in that happy consensus of those now resurrecting Robert Altman's film of Raymond Chandler's *The Long Goodbye* so as to outfit it according to the latest in New York fashions. A stiff is a stiff, even when propped up by Pauline Kael.

As it happens, I was one of those who first saw *The Long Goodbye* some eight months before its New York opening, during its disastrous run in the provinces when, contrary to legend, it was decently supported by an ad campaign far more in keeping with what is genuinely likable about the film than is the campy-spoofy comic strip (personally selected by Altman) which is seeing it through its second life. Mythology now has it that the film at first flopped because sentimental Chandler devotees found its irreverent treatment of their cherished memories too hard a pill to swallow, a line Altman himself has taken one twist further by declaring, "Audiences are disturbed because it raises questions about their own moral hypocrisy." (Peckinpah, at least, has never gone in for Altman's condescending abuse of his audience to explain away his failures.) But in fact, outside of Chandler himself and a few mystery addicts and film buffs, who exactly does regard with solemn reverence the generic conventions that Altman, with so smug and self-congratulatory a display of boldly slaying dragons, purports to mock? The important difference between Elliott Gould smirking his way through a Jolson impression in *The Long Goodbye* and Bogart turning up his hat brim and affecting glasses and a lisp to inquire after a second edition of *Ben Hur* at a shady bookshop in *The Big Sleep* is that the latter was funny and had comic style and the former isn't and does not. Right or wrong, the out-of-town audiences for *The Long Goodbye* stayed away, but their staying away had as little to do with an attachment to Chandler (not to say moral hypocrisy) as does the fact that the film is packing in the world's most easily intimidated audiences in New York. (In fairness to those audiences, it must be said that even almost all the critics in concert were unable to browbeat them into going to see *The Last American Hero* when there were no hints of campy-spoofy novelty with which to entice them, but only a good movie.)

Is Altman really unaware that much of *The Big Sleep*, and at least parts of several of the other Chandler-Marlowe films, were played intentionally for comedy? (Very possibly he is, given his ability to speak of the novel from which he's adapted his subsequent, as yet unreleased, film as an unknown work, despite the fact it's already served as the basis for a much-admired film by another director.*) As an exercise in flogging dead horses, Altman slamming the menace to our moral awareness posed by private-eye films is like nothing so much as Ken Russell going full steam after the pernicious lies of musicals in *The Boy Friend*. Perhaps Altman is unaware also that the book of *The Long Goodbye* isn't even typical Chandler, but his attempt (rather like Hammett's in *The Glass Key*) to break out of the generic mold (in the book, Marlowe contemplates marriage) and write a "real" novel, and, perhaps owing to this, his least good book. (Not surprisingly, when private-eye films started to be made again in the sixties, it wasn't *The Long Goodbye* among Chandler's unfilmed novels that was turned to first, but his amusing and unpretentious *The Little Sister*, made into the mediocre *Marlowe*.) More importantly, is Altman unaware that the dumb and seedy private eye, the private eye as anachronistic loser, is already (via such little-known but portentous films as *Hickey & Boggs* and

* The novel is *Thieves Like Us* by Edward Anderson; the film was Nicholas Ray's first, *They Live By Night*.

the significantly named *Chandler*) as much a new cliché in our movies as the Last Cowboy? (At least the clichés that *Pat Garrett and Billy the Kid* runs into the ground are largely of its director's own coinage.) When Gould's Marlowe wakes up in the middle of the night and goes through his garbage to find something to feed his cat at the beginning of *The Long Goodbye,* one's thoughts turn not to the audacious changes wrought by the film on the image of the private eye, but rather to recollections of Paul Newman scooping yesterday's used coffee grounds out of the garbage at the beginning of *Harper.* And when you sound echoes of *Harper,* you'd better believe your aim is low. A filmmaker would practically have to be an amnesiac to believe he was breaking ground with this latest Marlowe movie.

In fact, *The Long Goodbye,* with its concentration on issues so peripheral to the private-eye genre as loyalty, cannot, any more than *Hickey & Boggs* or *Chandler,* compare with Robert Aldrich's *Kiss Me Deadly* of some eighteen years ago, which took the genre apart with a sustained savagery on just those live issues where it was really vulnerable: snooping and acquisitiveness. Indeed, were one to attempt to make a case for *The Long Goodbye,* I think it might be better done without regard to Chandler at all, less as a cutting criticism of the private-eye genre than as a shaggy-dog story using the private-eye genre as its jumping-off point. I'm not sure I like this *The Long Goodbye* very much better, but at least it accounts for the fact that, though Altman insists on speaking disdainfully of his Philip Marlowe as a fool and a "goat," the actual sense of Gould's shambles of a private detective that one gets from the film is of a character seen quite affectionately, and of the film itself as a rather gentle farewell to a celebrated detective not so very different in feeling from that life of Billy Wilder's *The Private Life of Sherlock Holmes.* (Altman, who continues to speak of *McCabe & Mrs. Miller* as a critique of capitalism, is probably as unreliable a commentator on his good films as his bad.)

Seen this way, the real issue becomes not how trenchant *The Long Goodbye* is (since it isn't trenchant at all), but how funny. How funny is it? As funny as Elliott Gould wisecracking in blackface, or some buffoonish hoodlums undressing to show they're not hiding anything, or a shot of some dogs fornicating; in humor, as in perhaps nothing else but sexual predilections, there's no accounting for tastes. (To my taste, the funniest moment in the movie is one almost thrown away when Marlowe returns at night to a funny farm virtually all of whose inmates seem to be scurrying about the grounds with their keepers in pursuit.) Like *Mean Streets,* much of *The Long Goodbye* appears to be improvised, though since here getting laughs is the object, the film often suggests the desperately facetious antics of someone putting a lampshade on his head to try to liven up some sagging party. (The most obviously improvised scene, of Marlowe shouting angrily at some cops on a beach at night, is meant to be taken seriously, and, for all its straining to heat up the emotional temperature, the deadest thing in the movie.)

To be sure, there are some beautiful things in *The Long Goodbye*, as in almost any Altman movie: the wash of diaphanous images (photographed as usual by Vilmos Zsigmond) that are almost an Altman trademark, one stunning scene of violence, and, despite the knee-jerk anti-Los Angeles potshots, an almost palpable evocation of the atmosphere of balmy Los Angeles nights. But these are things, at this stage of Altman's career, that one wants to begin with, even to take for granted. What bothers me most about *The Long Goodbye* is not that as spoof or satire it's so much less sharp than *Beat the Devil*, or even *Pulp* or *Gumshoe*, since I think it's not as spoof or satire that it's best taken. What bothers me most is that it's so much less good than *McCabe & Mrs. Miller*, and so backward a step in the career of a director who shows increasing signs of having lost his footing.

January, 1974

LA GRANDE BOUFFE

Robert Hatch

Four men—a judge (Philippe Noiret), an airline pilot (Marcello Mastroianni), a television producer (Michel Piccoli) and a chef (Ugo Tognazzi) —gather for a long weekend at a house not far from Paris that is owned by the judge and there undertake to eat themselves to death. According to *La Grande Bouffe* (The Big Feed) they succeed in this improbable venture, and the progress to their several ends is recorded by the Italian director, Marco Ferreri, in revolting excremental and sexual detail.

No reason is given why this quartet should be bent on suicide, but since they are men who, with little else in common, share an infantile confusion as to the pleasures of the flesh, one may assume that to them the prospect of dying from engorgement is irresistibly alluring. To heighten their transports, they invite three whores to the feast, but these girls—who do not object to being mishandled in various humiliating ways, particularly by the pilot, who is also afflicted with priapism induced by peering under the hood of an ancient sports car—cannot endure the morbid gluttony. Having vomited, they depart. However, a plump, motherly, sweetly bourgeois but nymphomaniac schoolteacher has added herself to the party, and she ministers to her companions, solicitously spooning food into their gaping mouths and attending to their erogenous needs in the manner of the depraved baby nurse of lurid gossip.

From various sources I have heard that *La Grande Bouffe* is enlivened by comedy, and like most people I resent the implication that my sense of humor is deficient. I do recognize that certain scenes might once have moved me to a fit of titters; at one point, for example, the toilet cistern bursts and inundates the company. But it has been a long time since I got a laugh out of contemplating shit. Otherwise, I noticed a great deal of absurdity in the ungoverned preoccupation with swallowing and orgasm, but it seems to me that anyone who could find this melancholy behavior comic would have been well entertained by an eighteenth-century sight-seeing trip to a madhouse.

I must doubt, then, that Ferreri meant to tickle our funny bones, and I cast about for what his motives might have been. It is true, of course, that the French, and to perhaps a lesser extent the Italians, are more concerned about cuisine than some other peoples, and it could be that Ferreri is sermonizing against gluttony. If that was his motive, which somehow I doubt, it fails by reason of overstatement—to be sure, a common fault in dedicated moralists.

Or perhaps there is here a more extended metaphor—a comment on the disposition of modern industrial man to consume more than he needs or the natural resources can thriftily supply. Godard in *Weekend* did something rather effective in that line with respect principally to the motor car, rising by stages from holiday traffic to cannibalism. That comes closer home, but Ferreri gives us the easy out that he is describing some lunatics, not a lunatic society—there is no suggestion that the men's malady is contagious; even their schoolteacher friend keeps her feeding within rational bounds. By no stretch of hyperbole can I find my sins of consumption reflected in the glandular perversions of *La Grande Bouffe*.

So I am left with a couple of hypotheses, neither of which is more than a guess. Ferreri may be afflicted with that revulsion against bodily needs and functions that most frequently strikes one in late adolescence and has chosen this visualization of his preoccupations as a means of exorcising them. In that case, I hope the exercise has been cleansing. Or he may be opportunistically aware that within the past few years there has arisen all over the world a sick rivalry in proving oneself able to assimilate any communication, however degrading. This curious contest is no doubt political in origin—since, willy-nilly, we must know about the Greek

Colonels, the Vietnamese tiger cages, the jackal demagoguery of Nixon-Agnew, an instinct for survival induces a contempt for squeamishness in the context of public affairs. This then slops over into intellectual and aesthetic areas; the hallucinated homosexual novels of William Burroughs enjoy a vogue, architects who adopt the pizza drive-in as their standard of excellence are seriously regarded, graffiti are endorsed as creative achievements, and increasingly one is well advised to attend the movies on an empty stomach. If Ferreri has seized on this aspect of the modern temper he will probably be acclaimed. He has carried the childish pastime of being deliberately disgusting to new heights of adult sophistication, and I have been impressed in the past few days by the number of people who have felt called upon to tell me, somewhat aggressively, that they "enjoyed" *La Grande Bouffe*. It is a form of machismo available to both sexes. Quite frankly, it scares me.

October 15, 1973

Bruce Williamson

Two of the seven deadly sins—namely gluttony and lust—are explored *ad nauseam* in *La Grande Bouffe* (The Big Feast, in literal translation from the subtitled French), probably the most controversial major film since *Last Tango in Paris*. In fact, Italian director Marco Ferreri and a couple of outraged patrons came to blows over *Bouffe* at the 1973 Cannes Film Festival, while festival judge Ingrid Bergman volubly deplored having to sit through such offensive material. Despite the brouhaha, Ferreri's far-out comedy won an International Critics Prize—and deserved it. Vulgar but brilliant, crude but pointedly sardonic, this outrageous no-holes-barred satire co-stars Marcello Mastroianni, Michel Piccoli, Philippe Noiret and Ugo Tognazzi as four affluent gentlemen—respectively, an airline pilot, a TV producer, a lawyer and a restaurateur—who repair to an elegant mansion to commit suicide by overfeeding themselves. The idea of fornicating to death as well comes as an afterthought, and the quartet is abetted thereto by three hookers and a plump schoolteacher (the latter marvelously played by Andrea Ferreol) who evidently embodies some eternal female principle—since she ultimately beats her gluttonous male hosts at their own game. A filmmaker with avowed leftist leanings, Ferreri leaves little doubt that what he has in mind in *Grande Bouffe* is a symbolic celebration of the end of the *bourgeoisie*—a hedonistic consumer society glutting itself to the point of extinction. He tops his statement with a climactic image of raw meat and sides of beef hung over shrubs and trees outside the house, largely ignored by a pack of dogs—creatures too sensible to eat when they're not hungry—though by this time most of the principals have succumbed to their ravenous appetites and have been stashed in a freezer. Explicit references to belching, farting, fucking and defecation are so frequent that it sounds like a contradiction to add that the actors perform their voluptuous rites in the best possible taste, even with flourishes of real refinement. Perhaps the most startling moment is a scene in which Tognazzi, near death but ready to climax, lies stretched on a kitchen table for an exquisitely sensual send-off, simultaneously enjoying a rich soufflé and a hand job. Though Ferreri goes too far—or farther than strictly necessary for the film's avowed purpose—he is a fierce, uncompromising satirist who seldom loses sight of his goal. Like it or loathe it, *Grande Bouffe* delivers a magnum of cultural shock. Better stay home if such dark and heady visions simply repulse you.

January 1974

Go Guiltless into Gluttony

Molly Haskell

La Grande Bouffe is that anomaly peculiar to all the arts but especially to film, where there is a higher number of imponderables: the great, or almost-great, work produced by a minor artist. Made by Marco Ferreri, an interesting but hardly a major-league director, *La Grande Bouffe* approaches greatness by a happy conjunction of idea, casting, and circumstances, and misses it, like other works in this category, by a margin consisting of precisely those flaws and limitations that are present to a more decisive degree in other works—presumably, in all those films that we have never even seen in this country.

Of the six Italian features Ferreri has made (plus episodes in four sketch films), only *The Conjugal Bed* and *The Ape Woman* have been released here—the former, a vicious and funny marital satire of a sexually insatiable wife; the second, a protracted but oddly tender tour de force with Annie Girardot as the hirsute heroine. But whereas the central idea of *The*

Ape Woman finally left us with a So What? the conceit of *La Grande Bouffe* connects with that pleasure in good food that has suddenly become the Esperanto of our times and, in America, perhaps the only common bond between members of different classes, generations, and sex. Show me the radical who wants to see his favorite epicurean haunt nationalized. (Whether the New American Gourmetism is the last gasp of a decadent society or the first accession to taste of a barbarian one, remains to be seen.)

The premise of *La Grande Bouffe*, for those who haven't heard, is that four friends gather in a walled estate on the outskirts of Paris to gorge and die. They are each at the end of tethers whose precise nature we can only surmise, and, reverting back to that point in emotional time (different for each) that the unconscious has never relinquished, they slide guiltless into gluttony, fornication, sodomy, and death.

Ugo Tognazzi, a restaurant owner, is the most obsessively and exclusively gastronomic; Philippe Noiret, a judge, makes his final break with the nurse who coddles and caters to him, only to find in the plump schoolteacher who drops in (Andrea Ferreol) the perfect mother-love death mate; Michel Piccoli, a radio executive with a family, vents suppressed longing in flatulence and pederasty; and Marcello Mastroianni, a commercial air pilot, is the quintessential Italian male, torn between chasing skirts and tuning up his Maserati. He is the first to go. In the chassis of the latter, sitting erect and at attention, he freezes to death.

It is an odd film, mixed in tone like Ferreri's other films and no doubt bewildering to audiences expecting a scandal to go with the five-dollar ticket price (an outrage that does a disservice to any, but particularly this film). For it is not shocking in the more obvious ways. Although we are treated to images of elimination, copulation, engorging, and disgorging, the ultimate feeling is one of sorrow and horror, a metaphysical rather than a physical revulsion. Among the fraternity a certain aestheticism, an observance of gourmet refinements that seems almost to contradict the impulse toward degradation, obtains until the end.

Piccoli's "emissions" sound less like farts than the ones we used to fake, lips to the inner arm, in grade school. And Ferreri's treatment of all the characters, but particularly the lushly beautiful Miss Ferreol, is closer to Rubens or Bernini than to Bosch or Breughel. He gives us neither the warts-and-all close-ups that might indicate a Swiftian loathing of mankind, nor a precisely enough evoked sense of society to suggest Bunuelian indignation. If anything, we are given too little information about the characters—they are so completely defined by their vices that the time between deadly sins is dead time. Hence it is not a psychological study or a satire of the bourgeoisie, but rather a poetic horror film, with a grand, morbid melancholy to it.

The long shots by which Ferreri conveys a detached but sympathetic attitude toward his characters don't really mesh with any fluidity—for Ferreri is visual without being cinematic—but this adds to the horror as images of the four men remain, in all their haunting isolation, to disturb the mind's digestion for some time afterward. We are locked with them, finally, in a parable that refers only to itself, a mystery that is never solved, only preserved in the ghostly images of their deaths. Even more chilling than the spectacle of a frozen Mastroianni is the image of Piccoli, pickled and lifelike behind a glass panel, staring out and waiting as his two remaining friends unhurriedly eat their way to obliteration.

October 4, 1973

DON'T LOOK NOW

Second Sight

Jay Cocks

This is a brilliant film of deep terrors and troubling insights—one that works a spell of continual, mounting anxiety. It concerns the supernatural and has an eerie, dreadful power, but it is not simply a scare show; it is in the tradition of *The Turn of the Screw*, not *The Exorcist. Don't Look Now* uses the occult and the inexplicable as Henry James did: to penetrate the subconscious, to materialize phantoms from the psyche.

Director Nicolas Roeg, formerly a cameraman (*Petulia*) has made two previous films: *Performance*, which he co-directed, and *Walkabout*. Both had a disquieting beauty, a dreamlike sense of dislocation and, most of all, a reliance on the visual vocabulary of the cinema to build and sustain the narrative. *Don't Look Now* is Roeg's best work so far—the most deliberate and contained. Much of the movie's power comes from images that carry a kind of glancing, indefinable threat and remain in some dark corner of the imagination. They are immediate but not quite real, like Pinter's language or a Bergman scene.

The film is being billed as "Daphne Du Maurier's *Don't Look Now*," but a reading of the Du Maurier story from which the adaptation has been made makes one appreciate Roeg and screenwriters Allan Scott and Chris Bryant all the more. Film and story share certain basic elements of plot and an ending of cruel surprise. The story is detached, almost cursory. Roeg and his collaborators have constructed an intricate, intense speculation about levels of perception and reality. Thanks also to the superb performances of Donald Sutherland and Julie Christie, *Don't Look Now* has in abundance what most other excursions into the supernatural lack: rigorous psychological truth and an emotional timbre that is entirely persuasive.

Sutherland and Christie play a married couple, John and Laura Baxter, whose daughter has recently drowned in a pond on their country property. Leaving their surviving son in school, the Baxters depart for Venice, where John is restoring a sixteenth-century church. The movie gives a compelling sense of the city not as a romantic tourist spot, but as a cold, purgatorial place, a labyrinth full of mute threat. It is, as one character describes it, "like a city in aspic at a dinner party where all the guests are dead and gone."

The Baxters meet two sisters, one of whom is blind and psychic. The sisters (well played by Hilary Mason and Clelia Matania) reassure the couple of the happiness of their dead daughter. But they sense danger, too. They tell Baxter that his life is in peril while he remains in Venice. He does not believe them, but he is bothered by strange presentiments, and by the persistent reappearance of a small figure in a hooded red raincoat—the garment his daughter was wearing when she drowned.

Roeg has made this darting figure in red into an embodiment of Baxter's guilt over his daughter's death. Reinforced by Pino Donnagio's fine score, Roeg creates a world where everything seems to have a repercussion. He has composed the film with a series of interrelated visual metaphors—glass breaking under a bike wheel, tiles being crushed under a shoe. He also heightens the suspense by stressing the idea of simultaneity: as simple as a window being closed and a door blowing open, or as complex as water being spilled onto a color slide, making the red dye run, and a little girl in a red raincoat sinking into a pond. Every shot and image is like a tile in the mosaic of the church under restoration. Each fits together, forming at last a picture already prescribed, perhaps fated.

Don't Look Now is such a rich, complex and subtle experience that it demands more than one viewing. Roeg's insistence on the power of the image, his reliance on techniques of narrative that are peculiarly cinematic, remind us how undemanding and perfunctory so many movies still are. Roeg's is one of those rare talents that can effect a new way of seeing.

December 10, 1973

Labyrinths

Pauline Kael

Nicolas Roeg employs fast, almost subliminal imagery in the new English film *Don't Look Now,* and his entire splintering style affects one subliminally. The unnerving cold ominousness that he imparts to the environment says that things are not what they seem, and one may come out of the theater still seeing shock cuts and feeling slightly dissociated. The environment may briefly be fractured; for me ten minutes or so passed before it assembled itself and lost that trace of hostile objectivity. I don't recall having had this sort of residue of visual displacement from a movie before, but it's reasonable if one has been looking at a splintered universe for almost two hours. And one looks at this picture with intense concentration, because here life is treated as a puzzle, and the clues are in visual cross-references that go by in split seconds. Afterward, the environment one moves into holds the danger of discontinuity, as if at any moment something frightening might be intercut. Roeg has an elegant, edgy style that speaks to us of the broken universe and our broken connections, of modern man's inability to order his experience and to find meaning and coherence in it. The style speaks of the lesions in our view of the world; everything on the screen is vaguely incongruous and unnatural. A child outdoors on his bicycle runs over a pane of glass; wherever one turns, there are cracks and spreading stains. But Roeg's modernist style is too good for the use he puts it to.

Taken from a Daphne du Maurier story of the occult, adapted by Alan Scott and Chris Bryant, *Don't Look Now* is about a young English couple (Donald Sutherland and Julie Christie) whose drowned daughter may or may not be sending them messages. The bereaved parents leave their surviving child in school and go to Venice—deserted at the end of the season— where the husband, an art restorer, works at repairing eroded church mosaics. The film, too, is a mosaic, organized on the basis of premonitions. (The present is visually interrupted by glimpses of the future.) The husband is psychic but refuses to admit it; he fails to give credence to the omens that appear to him, and so, misinterpreting them, is destroyed. The material is Daphne du Maurier, but it's treated in the intricate manner of Borges, whose face filled the screen and crowned the murderous climax of *Performance,* the first film Roeg directed (with Donald Cammell as co-director). The atmosphere has too much class for the Gothic paraphernalia: the warnings unheeded, the city plagued by a mass murderer, the worrying bishop (Massimo Serato) with uncanny intuitions, and the ambiguous, dumpy, sub-Hitchcock sisters—one (Hilary Mason) blind and claiming to be psychic, the other (Clelia Matania) a chesty Helen Hokinson woman—who laugh together as if they were swindlers. We've seen all that before—with less style, it's true, but also with more vitality when it wasn't so convoluted and veneered with art. In a less refined picture, one mightn't be so critical of the way Roeg pulls out all the stops in the sisters' creaking, stagey scenes.

When you join the modernist sense of disorder to this canned Gothic mystery, you may satisfy only those who can accept the titillating otherworldly, but you can intrigue the more demanding, too. All that the movie really says to one is that Nicolas Roeg has a modern sensibility without having a modern mind—or, to put it another way, he has the style without the consciousness. And so the lesions are a form of high-fashion chic. It's a great commercial advantage to him not to have a fuller consciousness. Roeg doesn't examine the jaggedness or ask the why of it, or try to find order within it; he uses this shattered vision to bring a Gothic story up to date. Put them together and you have the new international-celebrity look: the boy or girl looking like Bianca Jagger and talking about psychic phenomena. Unisex and ghosts in one smart, high-style package. And there they are on the screen—the modern couple, Julie Christie and Donald Sutherland, with matching curly hair-dos.

The movie has a special ambience: the dislocation is eroticized, and rotting Venice, the labyrinthine city of pleasure, with its crumbling, leering gargoyles, is obscurely, frighteningly sensual. It's a Borgesian setting—the ruins tokens of a mysteriously indifferent universe; Venice might be a reptile-infested Mayan city discovered in a jungle. Roeg, drawn to Borges's tone—the controlled, systematic way in which Borges turns life into a mystical, malevolent nightmare—brings out the sensuality that is hidden in our response to the Borges cool. In *Don't Look Now,* the romanticism isn't of the traditional Gothic variety but a coolly enigmatic sexiness, and though it isn't strong enough to be a turn-on for a large popular audience, it gives the film a reticent, insinuating quality. Nothing in Roeg's style appears to be spontaneous or free-flowing; it's all artifice and technique. And yet the essence of the style is languor. *Don't Look Now* is the newest form of the trip movie. The young couple are at home in this jagged universe; they belong to it, and so does Roeg. He digs it, the way Joseph Losey dug the sunny rot and corruption in *Accident* and *The Go-Between.*

but Roeg doesn't feel Losey's need to condemn the decadence that attracts him. *Don't Look Now* particularly recalls Losey's nutty *Secret Ceremony*, but Roeg isn't confused by a sense of shame. He thinks with his eyes, and puffs up what he sees. Roeg has taken Losey's luxuriant, richly ornamental style into a new domain; he may be the genius of chic that, in movies, Warhol and Morrissey only prefigured. Detached and psychedelic, *Don't Look Now* never touches our sympathies, never arouses any feeling for its characters. Roeg's vision is as impersonal and noncommittal as Warhol's, but with the gloss and craftsmanship of Losey. If the elliptical style says that things are not what they seem, it also says that though they're not as simple as people used to think they were, we don't have to worry about it, because they've all gone out of our grasp. We can relax and accept everything. To tie this together with a du Maurier story of the supernatural is to return to a pre-modernist account of why they're not what they seem. How blissfully, commercially acute to join our anxieties to superstition. And not even honest superstition but superstition used to relieve boredom—superstition as a dead-pan camp. Believed in only as much as anything else is; that is, not believed in at all. This new Gothic of Roeg's is baby talk joined to dislocation. And isn't that just what Warhol was doing? Only Roeg joins the cool indifference to rich elegance. Maybe it's from the tension between the two that we get that faint, erotic vertigo. Roeg seems to say what Losey never dared to but what the audience for Losey was always responding to: that decay among the rich and beautiful is sexy. Actually, Losey's films and this one of Roeg's tantalize audiences in exactly the way that sad stories of the jazz age do; whatever Losey claimed to be doing, he was giving us the beautiful and damned in a fantasy playground for a daydreaming audience. Roeg, I suspect, knows what he's doing (though I imagine people will cook up the usual elaborate deep meanings for this film, just as they do for Losey's moralizing erotic fantasies).

Julie Christie and Donald Sutherland work together wonderfully here— maybe because their sexual differences are so muted. The other actors are merely exploited for sinister effects, and Roeg is crudely derivative in his handling of them, but his treatment of Christie and Sutherland has a highly original awareness. Psychologically, the film barely exists, but Roeg does so much with the two stars' faces—Sutherland's long and thin, Christie's desperately frail—that they become not characters but an archetype of the new couple: sophisticated, gallant, frightened. Sutherland gives a soft, fine-toned performance, and Christie is lovely—with that delicately rapacious jaw and the poignant eyes. She has the anxious face of a modern tragic muse. A key sex scene, with the two nude in bed, intercut with flash-forwards to their post-coital mood as they dress to go out together, is almost the reverse of a strip-tease. The images of their getting dressed—

their bemused, distant expressions, their isolation from each other, and their movements getting into their perfect clothes—have an erotic glitter that displaces interest from their quiet, playfully tender coupling to its aftermath. (To avoid an X rating for the picture, this sequence has been slightly re-edited, but Roeg himself made the changes—substituting a few frames from the outtakes—and they are said to be so slight that someone seeing the English and American versions might not notice the difference.) The sequence is consistent with the whole premonitory scheme of the film, and it also relates to the way eroticism is displaced throughout; dressing is splintered and sensualized, like fear and death—death most of all, with splashes of red.

Roeg, who used to be a writer and director for British TV besides being a famous cinematographer, did the celebrated second-unit work on *Lawrence of Arabia* and was the cinematographer for *A Funny Thing Happened on the Way to the Forum* as well as for a number of Julie Christie's films—*Fahrenheit 451, Far from the Madding Crowd, Petulia*—which have, I think, a close relationship to his work here. It is the assumption in this film that the juxtaposition of images provides instant meaning. Roeg uses the technique, out of Alain Resnais, more effectively than Richard Lester did in *Petulia;* since Roeg doesn't get into complicated feelings or social attitudes, you don't question what he's saying. Despite the surreal portentousness of the atmosphere, the meanings are very simple, very much on a Hitchcock level, and are often organized with that same mechanical precision. But the deliberate mystification is a problem for Roeg that it wasn't for Hitchcock, because Roeg's systematic trickery doesn't quite jibe with the otherworldly. The discrepancy involved in a tightly planned, interlocking *mystery* made me impatient; the preordained can be experienced as the mechanically delayed. (Borges always keeps it short.) The final kicker is predictable, and strangely flat, because it hasn't been made to matter to us; fear is decorative, and there's nothing to care about in this worldly, artificial movie. Yet at a mystery level the movie can still affect the viewer; even the silliest ghost stories can. It's not that I'm not impressionable; I'm just not as proud of it as some people are. *Don't Look Now* gets fairly moldy when the hero confronts his red-hooded fate (seen rather too clearly). The non-believer hero destroyed by his refusal to trust his second sight (that old, old shtick—the agnostic punished because he refuses to believe in the supernatural) gives one such a strong whiff of Hollywood. But the picture is the fanciest, most carefully assembled Gothic enigma yet put on the screen; it's emblazoned in chic, and compared to such Gothics as *Seance on a Wet Afternoon* it's a masterwork. It's also trash.

In Borges, mystery and decadence come close together, and at the picture's consummation the perfect, beautiful couple are split by a hideous joke of nature—their own child become a dwarf monstrosity. Using du Maurier as a base, Roeg comes closer to getting Borges on the screen than those who have tried it directly, but there's a distasteful clamminess about the picture—not because Venice is dying (though this sure is a counter-commercial for Venice) but because Roeg's style is in love with disintegration. A little boy can look at his dead sister with no emotion in his face, but terror and decay are made radiant. Julie Christie is the perfect actress for Roeg, because her feelings are so exquisitely modulated and so small; she doesn't project with enough force to disturb the visual surface with rage or pain. Her jagged face—so extraordinarily beautiful yet not adding up right for ordinary beauty—might be the emblem of his style. She gives the picture a soul—but a soul in a body that's trembling on the verge of breakdown. Roeg is a chillingly chic director. *Don't Look Now* is shallow in a way that I think people are looking for right now; I can practically hear someone asking, "What's the matter with shallow?" This could be Warhol's legacy. *Don't Look Now* is going to be a great success, because it represents the new, high-fashion Gothic sensibility—what the movie audience is just getting into. But it's like an entertainment for bomb victims: nobody expects any real pleasure from it.

December 24, 1973

Two

YOUNG
AMERICAN
DIRECTORS

AMERICAN GRAFFITI
Fabulous Fifties

Jay Cocks

Small towns and the fifties had this in common: many people wanted to get out of both. Then, at a safe distance of miles and years, a certain nostalgia began inching its way into memory like a balm. In recent years several entertainments have distilled that nostalgia—*The Last Picture Show*, for example, and the Broadway musical *Grease*. But none has had the vigor and precision of *American Graffiti*. This superb and singular film catches not only the charm and tribal energy of the teenage fifties but also the listlessness and the resignation that underscored it all like an incessant bass line in an old rock-'n'-roll song.

The movie is cast in the mold of one of those teenage escapade flicks which American International Pictures used to stock the drive-ins with during the late fifties and the sixties. This allows director George Lucas to mock, carefully and compassionately, the conventions and stereotypes of a genre as well as a generation. All the details are here, from the do-whop music and lovingly customized cars to the slang, which hovered between Ivy League and street gang, and the clothes, which seemed, like the time, both shapeless and confining. Even the jokes come straight from AIP: "How'd you like a knuckle sandwich?" inquires a hood of a nervous, bespectacled sad sack outside the local hamburger drive-in. "No, thanks," says the sad sack. "I'm waiting for a double Chubby Chuck."

Graffiti was shot in Techniscope, a wide-screen process that yields the authentic sandpaper grain of the AIP pictures, implying low budgets and quick takes. The vital difference is that *Graffiti* was photographed by Haskell Wexler, that most subtle and agile of cameramen. Most of the action takes place at night under harsh light and neon, a landscape that Wexler turns into extravagantly impressionistic honky-tonk images of glaring, insistent beauty.

Set in a small California town in 1962—the proper, if not the chronological, end of the fifties—*Graffiti* provides a series of vignettes of the last night of summer. On the following day two of the local boys (Richard

Dreyfuss and Ronny Howard) are set to leave for college. Howard and his girl (Cindy Williams) are surrogates for AIP's Frankie Avalon and Annette Funicello, the straight-arrow guy and his girl, the latter a believer in early marriage and eternal obligation. Comic relief is provided by Charlie Martin Smith as the sad sack, and a glimpse into the classic cruising style by Paul Le Mat, who slides down the street in an unbeatable car, his hair in an unruffled d.a., his pack of Camels rolled in the sleeve of his T shirt. The greaser villains, led by Bo Hopkins, have the traditional approach to any problem in interpersonal relations: "Tie him to a car and drag him." The scenes between these young people and the girls they fall in with or fall for (notably Candy Clark and Mackenzie Phillips) are mostly funny, but they leave a lingering melancholy.

The characters seem locked in—to careers, to whole lives. The only one who will break out is Dreyfuss, smarter and more sensitive than the others but careful not to show it. His high school teacher tells him of the time he left town to go to college but came back after only a semester ("I wasn't the competitive type"); the scene captures the slightly anxious self-deceptions that Dreyfuss's contemporaries will soon be using. Dreyfuss climbs aboard his plane for college still carrying a radio tuned to the favorite local station. The radio plays until he is in the air and finally out of range, and the crackle of static is his first intimation—though he does not know it—of freedom.

Lucas is a young filmmaker whose only other feature was *THX-1138,* a cool, cautionary science-fiction tale released in 1970. It established him as a director of great technical range and resource. *Graffiti* reveals a new and welcome depth of feeling. Few films have shown quite so well the eagerness, the sadness, the ambitions and small defeats of a generation of young Americans. Bitchin', as they said back then. Superfine.

August 20, 1973

Roger Greenspun

Mel's Drive-In stands at the center of things. The kids call it Burger City, and at dusk their cars begin to fill the parking spaces, radiating like spokes from beneath the neon-lit canopy where carhops on roller skates carry the orders—burgers, french fries, cherry Cokes—on trays that fit over open window frames. Everyone shows up at Burger City, but nobody stays. There are dates to be made, there will be a drag race to watch, there is the street to drive—the main street, where the cars cruise up and down and everybody exchanges greetings, insults, passengers. A dance is underway at the high school, and, for some, going back there will be like a last look into the past. Most of the kids in this crowd have graduated. Tomorrow, two are supposed to go east for college. It is early autumn, 1962, in a small town not far north of San Francisco.

By now, I think almost everybody has seen or has heard of this movie, *American Graffiti*, and must have a sense of what its world resembles. If Mel's Drive-In is at the center, then at the edges are some very different places: a junkyard where all the old cars go to pass into rust and memory; an overgrown road down by the water for private (or semi-private) loving; a drag strip, Paradise Road, just at the town limits; and somewhere beneath a powerful antenna, the local radio station, where Wolfman Jack broadcasts the favorite hits—like "Sixteen Candles"—all night long. A few seem to worship Wolfman Jack, but absolutely everybody listens to him all the time—his records, his line of crazy patter. If you were to close your eyes and tune out the conversations in the foreground, *American Graffiti* would be like an hour and fifty minutes of unsponsored radio.

Actually, the film covers about twelve hours—from just before sunset one day to just after sunrise the next. It deals mainly with four boys and four girls (more accurately: four boys, three girls, and one dream of a girl), though there are a lot of well-observed minor characters. There is a climax of sorts: the drag race on Paradise Road. There is a romantic plot—a separation and reconciliation between a girl and a boy who finally decides he won't leave the town for college—and even a comic romantic subplot. There are all these things, and more, and yet there is very little purposeful movement in the film. Except for one fellow, Curt, who finally does leave home for college, everybody pretty much ends up where he began—twelve hours older, possibly wiser, but otherwise unchanged. Lack of change is almost a theme in *American Graffiti*, an illusion of course, but an obsession nevertheless. It is like the cars that venture forth on the main street. Fast starts, jockeying for position, temptations, invitations—but nobody's going anywhere; nobody thinks there's anywhere to go.

For John (Paul Le Mat), the over-age drag-race champion whose life, at twenty-two, is all behind him, this is a matter for some despair. For Steve (Ronny Howard), who, without quite knowing it, has already found his fate in the girl he loves, it is a matter for acceptance, for understanding that there is no reason to leave home if home is where you want to be. For Toad (Charlie Martin Smith), whose incompetence makes just getting from one block to the next a full-scale adventure, it isn't a matter at all. As it happens, Toad strikes it lucky. He picks up a good-looking dumb blonde who likes all the trouble he gets into ("and then you got your car stolen, and then I got to watch you throw up . . . yep, I had a pretty good time.") and she turns a night of sustained misery into a kind of personal triumph. But for Curt (Richard Dreyfuss), lack of change is a matter for thought and possibly for terror. Curt doesn't have a girl: he has a vision. And unlike everyone else in the movie, he is presented with genuine choices. He can stay home, like his favorite high school teacher, who chose not to compete back east and is now beginning an affair with a pretty student. He can become a Moose, a good citizen, like the men who provide his scholarship. He can join the Pharaohs, the town hoods who virtually kidnap him and then offer him blood initiation when he proves he's better at juvenile delinquency than they are. Or he can follow his vision.

He runs into the vision on the main street. She drives a white Thunderbird. She is beautiful and sexy, and the very first thing she says to Curt is, "I love you"—except he can't be sure because she says it through a closed car window, and then he never sees her again. But he sees the Thunderbird, in the distance, turning a corner down the wrong street, always there and always out of reach. When he leaves town in the morning, flying off on Magic Carpet Airways, the Thunderbird leaves town on the road below him. It is beginning to keep pace, as it were, for life.

Anyone who is tempted to think that *American Graffiti* is just skillful nostalgia should keep Curt's vision in mind. Its source isn't in the American 1960s. It may be in the films of Federico Fellini (*La Dolce Vita*, 8½, etc.) where a girl, a vision in white, keeps eluding the hero while tantalizing him with memories of lost innocence and innocent desire. There is nothing so specific in Curt's vision, which is all for the future. But I find that vision fascinating because it is so perfectly artificial and because George Lucas, who made *American Graffiti*, had the imagination to stick it in the middle of his realistic movie as if it belonged—and oddly enough, it does.

For all its sense of time and place, for all its marvelously detailed performances and its authentic cars, *American Graffiti* is a powerfully abstract film—as much committed to exploring a country of the mind as to examining any town in northern California. Curt's vision is the most obvious clue to what is going on. But there are other clues everywhere, from the pulsating circle of Mel's Drive-In to the sounds and music of Wolfman Jack transmitted from somewhere out in the night. Before the night ends, Curt actually visits the Wolfman—who turns out to be a kindly loner with a broken refrigerator full of melting popsicles. That visit, as much as anything, seems to convince Curt that he has someplace other than home to go. The Wolfman also has a vision—of another Wolfman, a fantastic world traveler who stops by the radio station from time to time to drop off tapes and tell about his travels. Of course, he's a dream. But so is everything else: the girl in the white T-bird, the drag-race championship, home, security, the girl next door. *American Graffiti* promotes and rather cherishes dreams, which is one reason why it is such a beautiful movie.

George Lucas, who is twenty-eight and not too long out of film school at UCLA, has made only two feature films. The first was a low-budget science-fiction fantasy called *THX 1138*, about a tranquilized future society, a perfectly regulated underground city from which there is almost no escape.

THX 1138 offers a view of Hell, reduced to a kind of antiseptic perfection. *American Graffiti* offers an earthly Paradise diluted into a slightly sweetened self-history. But the Paradise and Hell belong in the same universe—almost mirror images of each other—closed societies, strangely isolated and led by disembodied voices in the night. And because their worlds are so closed, both films end by projecting the idea of escape—overt in the oppressive science fiction; covert, but very real, in the pleasant slice of small-town American life.

Lucas has more on his mind than merely re-creating an ideal image of the past—the sort of thing that goes on in *The Last Picture Show, Summer of '42,* or even in *Bonnie and Clyde. American Graffiti* is more serious than any of these movies because it is centrally about something developing inside its director, a conflict, let's say, between freedom and conformity that is beginning to show itself in rich and complex ways. Anybody can enjoy the movie for itself. But it is even more enjoyable to put it next to Lucas's first movie and to see that between them they make a new kind of whole. It is the difference between just going to the movies and understanding the movies, and it is rare that you can do it so near the beginning of a director's career. I don't know what Lucas's next film will be like, but I'd take bets that it will really matter.

December 1973

William S. Pechter

"Where were you in '62?" the ads for *American Graffiti* ask. Wherever I was I recall doing my best to stay out of earshot of the kind of Alan Freed-style music that washes over the film from start to finish as pervasively as the very air that's breathed. Curiously, that music has become more bearable to me—detoxified, as it were, by my knowledge that it's now (at least outside this picture) escapable, and by the fact that even graduates of the generation that once devoured it now recognize it mainly to have been trash. ("Rock-'n'-roll's been goin' downhill since Buddy Holly died," one of the film's characters remarks, which, along with some speculation on whether a girl looks more like Connie Stevens or Sandra Dee, is about as close as the film gets to open condescension.) But those whose music it once was feel nostalgia for it and for the period *American Graffiti* evokes; I don't. And for them the film's nonstop spectacle of grooving with disc jockey "Wolfman Jack," eating "Chubby Chuckburgers" at Mel's Drive-In, and cruising all night in their cars has an anthropological significance which for me inheres rather in jumping with "Symphony Sid," eating fried soft-shell crab sandwiches in the back of Grant's, and dozing over the Sunday *Times* on the E train at three A.M. on Sunday morning while trying not to sleep past one's stop; and the very fact that I'm as incapable of responding to their cherished memorabilia as they to mine makes me realize that it's all equally without the kind of significance we like to attach to it.

But beyond my not responding to the period ephemera of *American Graffiti*, I don't really quite believe in it. As it happens, Mel's Drive-In, where much of the film was photographed, is not far from where I live, and, in the several times I've passed it since I've seen the film, I've been aware that, from its appearance and that of its patrons alone (excluding only the presence of late-model automobiles), one might not be sure whether one were seeing it in the seventies or the fifties. Surely there must have been something in the summer of 1962 besides d.a.'s and drag races, something which didn't scream "1962!" at you. (I gather from those far more knowledgeable about the period than I that much of the film's music is, in fact, from an earlier period, the songs already "golden oldies" by the time in which the movie is set.) Though I'm susceptible to it, unadulterated nostalgia, at least nostalgia for unworthy objects, seems to me fundamentally an enervating half-emotion, and I soon found cloying, even sickening, the way this film milked it; there was something somehow offensive to my hitherto dormant puritan sensibilities in seeing the lavish expenditure of this film's skill and talent on the meticulous re-creation of such things as a sixties' sock hop. And as the implausibilities of plot began to proliferate (would the cute dumb blonde really have attached herself to the homely jerk as the film has her doing, or the hot-rodder had such difficulty in dumping the underage girl who attaches herself to him, or the owner of a borrowed car be so unperturbed about its being stolen, etc., etc.?), the effect was really rather like that of *Summer of '42*, watching which one had an image of the staff of the art department laboring like Michelangelos to produce Fels Naphtha boxes while everything else—all *essential* verisimilitude—was going awry.

This first reaction gradually gave way to another as it became apparent, if for no other reason than that the film was simply too intelligent merely to be hustling nostalgia, however ironically, that something else must be impelling it. And, for a while, I thought I began to discern in the artful choreography of its characters' apparently aimless comings and goings something of what Susan Sontag may have had in mind when she spoke of works in which "the 'content' has . . . come to play a purely formal role," and even to be reminded of such films as *The Round-Up* and *The Red and the White* by the extraordinary Hungarian director Miklos Jancso, in which what seemed at times to be a purely formal exercise in the grouping and regrouping of characters for rhythmic, textural, and decorative effects eventually took on a distinctive meaning of its own.

But the hope that *American Graffiti* might be anything so audacious also proved short-lived. If, at its best, the film does suggest some of Jancso's rhythmic and textural richness, one nevertheless sees before long that all the work's narrative strands, however freely they've been woven, are going to be gathered, and in the most conventional of fashions. And so each plot line issues in its predictable denouement: the clean-cut class president finds he cannot bring himself to leave his cheerleader girl friend, and decides not to go away to college; the dumb blonde has a good time with the jerk, and promises to see him again; the swaggering king of the drag strip is revealed to be a sentimental softy, and realizes his racing days are numbered; and the protagonist, torn between his ambivalent attitudes about leaving his home town to go away to college, opts finally for the great world outside, though this last, and main, story is left somewhat confused by the conflicting symbols around which it is organized—Wolfman Jack, the mythically hip disc jockey who is reputed to broadcast from Mexico but turns out to be only a very uncharismatic man stuck in the same provincial town as the rest of the characters, and a mysterious blonde in a white Thunderbird who cruises the town and seems to hold out the promise of infinite romance. (The Wolfman Jack material is further muddied by the fact that the real Wolfman Jack, who plays himself, did broadcast from over the border in Mexico, beaming a signal so powerful it was illegal by FCC regulations, and actually was something of a mythic figure if only on the scale of the puny myths of rock culture.)

As if the plot strands weren't thus sufficiently tied up, the film concludes with end-titles, infusing all that has gone before with a lot of unearned and phony poignancy as it reveals how each of the characters ended up years later: the class president who didn't leave town, an insurance salesman; the jerk (who's been as broadly cartooned as "Jughead" in *Archie* comics) killed in Vietnam; the drag racer run down by a drunk driver; the protagonist living in Canada, having become a writer. (This last, while it seems in no necessary way to emerge from the character that the film has depicted, does at least somewhat justify in retrospect the curiously detached air of wry amusement with which Richard Dreyfuss, who's so explosive a Baby Face Nelson in *Dillinger*, plays him.) Indeed, to judge from recent specimens in such films as *The French Connection, Dillinger,* etc., I suspect that end titles threaten to become to the seventies what freeze frames were in the sixties: the new cliché ending, affording filmmakers an opportunity to assert profundities they've been unable otherwise to communicate, and, with this, providing as ingenious a shortcut to artistic creation as any that man has devised since the advent of painting by numbers.

So finally *American Graffiti* turns out to be both something less adventurous than that abstract balletic spectacle I thought I caught glimpses of and of less dramatic impact than such a more conventional work as *The Last Picture Show.* And yet there are things in *American Graffiti* that *are* impressive; it *is* richly textured, fluently cut, and visually handsome. (The photography, which was supervised by Haskell Wexler, seems to bathe the entire film in the pinkish glow of headlights, street lights, and neon.) These were the qualities also of director George Lucas's first feature film, *THX 1138,* if brought here, in his second, to a higher degree; but both films, for all their technical proficiency, seem to me exercises, warmups for work which may yet come. And both films seem to me basically empty, the films of a director working in a dramatic medium whose purely technical skills as a filmmaker are developed beyond any gifts he's yet revealed as a dramatist. If richness of texture alone were enough to make a great film, *American Graffiti* might be the masterpiece some of its enthusiasts are claiming it to be. As it is, Lucas seems to me a director of formidable technique still very much in search of a first work of more than merely technical distinction.

November 1973

MEAN STREETS
Everyday Inferno

Pauline Kael

Martin Scorsese's *Mean Streets* is a true original of our period, a triumph of personal filmmaking. It has its own hallucinatory look; the characters live in the darkness of bars, with lighting and color just this side of lurid. It has its own unsettling, episodic rhythm and a high-charged emotional range that is dizzyingly sensual. At the beginning, there's a long, fluid sequence as the central character, Charlie, comes into a bar and greets his friends; there's the laying on of hands, and we know that he is doing what he always does. And when the camera glides along with him as he's drawn toward the topless dancers on the barroom stage, we share his trance. At the end of the scene, when he's up on the stage, entering into the dance, he's not some guy who's taken leave of his senses but a man going through his nightly ritual. Movies generally work you up to expect the sensual intensities, but here you may be pulled into high without warning. Violence erupts crazily, too, the way it does in life—so unexpectedly fast that you can't believe it, and over before you've been able to take it in. The whole movie has this effect; it psychs you up to accept everything it shows you. And since the story deepens as it goes along, by the end you're likely to be openmouthed, trying to rethink what you've seen. Though the street language and the operatic style may be too much for those with conventional tastes, if this picture isn't a runaway success the reason could be that it's so original that some people will be dumbfounded—too struck to respond. It's about American life here and now, and it doesn't look like an American movie, or feel like one. If it were subtitled, we could hail a new European or South American talent—a new Buñuel steeped in Verdi, perhaps—and go home easier at heart. Because what Scorsese, who is thirty, has done with the experience of growing up in New York's Little Italy has a thicker-textured rot and violence than we have ever had in an American movie, and a riper sense of evil.

The zinger in the movie—and it's this, I think, that begins to come together in one's head when the picture is over—is the way it gets at the psychological connections between Italian Catholicism and crime, between sin and crime. Some editorial writers like to pretend this is all a matter of prejudice; they try to tell us that there is no basis for the popular ethnic stereotypes—as if crime among Italians didn't have a different tone from crime among Irish or Jews or blacks. Editorial writers think they're serving the interests of democracy when they ask us to deny the evidence of our senses. But all crime is not alike, and different ethnic groups have different styles of lawlessness. These Mafiosi loafers hang around differently from loafing blacks; in some ways, the small-time hoods of *Mean Streets* (good Catholics who live at home with their parents) have more in common with the provincial wolf pack of Fellini's *I Vitelloni* (cadging, indulged sons of middle-class families) than with the other ethnic groups in New York City. And these hoods live in such an insulated world that anyone outside it—the stray Jew or black they encounter—is as foreign and funny to them as a little man from Mars.

Many people interpreted the success of *The Godfather* to mean that the film glorified the gangsters' lives. During the Second World War, a documentary showing the noise and congestion of New York City was cheered by nostalgic American soldiers overseas; if audiences were indeed attracted to the life of the Corleone family (and I think some probably were), the reaction may be just as aberrant to the intentions of *The Godfather*, the best gangster film ever made in this country. It's likely that Italian, or Sicilian, Catholicism has a special, somewhat romantic appeal to Americans at this time. Italians appear to others to accept the fact that they're doomed; they learn to be comfortable with it—it's what gives them that warm, almost tactile glow. Their voluptuous, vacant-eyed smiles tell us that they want to get the best out of this life: they know they're going to burn in eternity, so why should they think about things that are depressing? It's as if they were totally carnal: everything is for their pleasure. Maybe it is this relaxed attitude that gave the Mafiosi of *The Godfather* their charm for the American audience. Was the audience envying them their close family ties and the vitality of their lawlessness? Was it envying their having got used to a sense of sin? It's almost as if the non-Catholic part of America wanted to say that *mea culpa* is *nostra culpa*.

Before *Mean Streets* is over, that glow gets very hot and any glamor is sweated off. The clearest fact about Charlie (Harvey Keitel), junior member of a Mafia family—and, in a nonliteral sense, the autobiographical central figure—is that whatever he does in his life, he's a sinner. Behind the titles you see him smiling his edgy, jocular smile and shaking hands with a priest, as if sealing a pact, while the words appear: "Directed by Martin Scorsese." Charlie, you can see in his tense ferret's face, feels he was born to be punished. Like his friends, round-faced, jovial Tony the barkeep (David Proval) and pompous Michael (Richard Romanus), a chiseling dude, he basks in the life. Running numbers, gambling, two-bit swindles: they grew up in this squalor and it's all they've ever known or wanted. To them, this is living it up. But Charlie isn't a relaxed sinner; he torments himself, like a fanatic seminarian. He's so frightened of burning he's burning already. Afraid of everything, he's everybody's friend, always trying to keep the peace. He's a dutiful toady to his Uncle Giovanni (Cesare Danova), the big man in the Mafia, and he fails those he really cares about: his girl, Teresa (Amy Robinson), and his friend Johnny Boy (Robert De Niro), a compulsive gambler—more than compulsive, irrational, a gambler with no sense of money. Charlie is too vain and sycophantic not to give in to social pressure. Teresa isn't rated high enough by his uncle; and his uncle, his king, the source of the restaurant he hopes to get, has told him not to be involved with Johnny Boy. Johnny Boy was named after Giovanni, but the family protects you only if you truckle to the elder statesmen and behave yourself—if you're a good timeserver.

Johnny Boy isn't; he flouts all the rules, he just won't "behave." He's fearless, gleefully self-destructive, cracked—moonstruck but not really crazy. His madness isn't explained (fortunately, since explaining madness is the most limiting and generally least convincing thing a movie can do). When you're growing up, if you know someone crazy-daring and half-admirable (and maybe most of us do), you don't wonder how the beautiful nut got that way; he seems to spring up full-blown and whirling, and you watch the fireworks and feel crummily cautious in your sanity. That's how it is here. Charlie digs Johnny Boy's recklessness. De Niro's Johnny Boy is the only one of the group of grifters and scummy racketeers who is his own man; he is the true hero, while Charlie, through whose mind we see the action, is the director's worst vision of himself.

The story emerges from the incidents without dominating them; it's more like a thread running through. The audience isn't propelled by suspense devices, nor is the cataclysmic finish really an end—it's only a stop. Johnny Boy needs help. He owes Michael, the dude, a lot of money, and it hurts Michael's self-esteem that he can't collect; nagging and spiteful, he threatens violence. But Charlie doesn't save Johnny Boy by going to his big-shot uncle for help, because he just can't risk taking a problem to his uncle. A good Mafia boy is not only subservient; unless something important is happening to him, he maintains his visibility as near to invisibility as possible. Uncle Giovanni, a dignified, dull, dull man, doesn't really see Charlie—doesn't register his existence—and that's what keeps Charlie in his good graces. But if Charlie asks for help for a crazy friend in trouble, he loses his low visibility. So Charlie talks a lot to Johnny Boy about friendship and does nothing. He's Judas the betrayer because of his careful angling to move up the next rung of the ladder. How can a man show his soul to be pettier than that? Charlie, the surrogate for the director, is nobody's friend, and—as the movie itself proves—least of all his own. Charlie knows from the beginning that he pays for everything. Scorsese isn't asking for expiation of Charlie's sins in the movie; sins aren't expiated in this movie. (The director has cast himself in the bit part of Michael's helper; when Johnny Boy makes Michael look so bad that Michael decides to get satisfaction, it is Scorsese who, as the gunman, pulls the trigger.)

It's twenty years since Fellini's *I Vitelloni* planted the autobiographical hero on the screen. Fellini did it in a fairly conventional way: his Moraldo (Franco Interlenghi) was the sensitive, handsome observer who looked at the limitations of small-town life and, at the end, said goodbye to all that. In *La Dolce Vita*, the Fellini figure was the seduced, disillusioned journalist (Marcello Mastroianni) to whom everything happened, and in *8½* Mastroianni, again standing in for Fellini, was the movie director at the center of a multi-ring circus, the man sought after by everyone. In *Roma*, Fellini threw in new versions of several of his earlier representatives, and himself to boot. No other movie director, except among the "underground" film-makers, has been so explicitly autobiographical. But in *I Vitelloni* we never caught a glimpse of the actual Fellini who emerged later; we never saw the fantasist as a young man, or the energy and will that drove him on. Movie directors have not yet learned the novelists' trick of throwing themselves into the third person, into the action, as Norman Mailer does even in his reporting; directors tend to make their own representatives passive, reflec-tive figures, with things happening to them and around them, like Curt (Richard Dreyfuss) in George Lucas's nice (though overrated) little picture *American Graffiti*. Scorsese does something far more complex, because Charlie's wormy, guilt-ridden consciousness is made abhorrent to us at the same time that we're seeing life through it. Charlie is so agitated because he is aware of his smallness.

Scorsese's method is more like that of the Montreal filmmaker Claude Jutra, who, playing himself in *A Tout Prendre*, masochistically made himself weak, like those chinless self-portraits with traumatic stares which painters put at the edges of their canvases. Jutra left out the mind and energies that made him a movie director, and apparently put on the screen everything in himself he loathed, and this is what Scorsese does, but Scorsese also puts in the tensions of a man in conflict, and a harlequin externalization of those tensions. He's got that dervish Johnny Boy dancing around Charlie's fears, needling Charlie and exposing him to danger despite all his conciliatory nice-guyism. Johnny Boy's careless, contemptu-ous explosions seem a direct response to Charlie's trying to keep the lid on everything—it's as if Charlie's id were throwing bombs and laughing at him. When Johnny Boy has finally loused everything up, he can say to Charlie, "You got what you wanted."

While an actor like Jeff Bridges in *The Last American Hero* hits the true note, De Niro here hits the far-out, flamboyant one and makes his own truth. He's a bravura actor, and those who have registered him only as the grinning, tobacco-chewing dolt of that hunk of inept whimsy *Bang the Drum Slowly* will be unprepared for his volatile performance. De Niro does something like what Dustin Hoffman was doing in *Midnight Cowboy*, but wilder; this kid doesn't just act—he takes off into the vapors. De Niro is so intensely appealing that it might be easy to overlook Harvey Keitel's work as Charlie. But Keitel makes De Niro's triumph possible; Johnny Boy can bounce off Charlie's anxious, furious admiration. Keitel, cramped in his stiff clothes (these Mafiosi dress respectable—in the long, dark overcoats of businessmen of an earlier era), looks like a more compact Richard Conte or Dane Clark, and speaks in the rhythms of a lighter-voiced John Garfield, Charlie's idol; it's his control that holds the story together. The whole world of the movie—Catholicism as it's actually practiced among these people, what it means on the street—is in Charlie's mingy-minded face.

The picture is stylized without seeming in any way artificial; it is the only movie I've ever seen that achieves the effects of Expressionism without the use of distortion. *Mean Streets* never loses touch with the ordinary look of things or with common experience; rather, it puts us in closer touch with the ordinary, the common, by turning a different light on them. The ethnic material is comparable to James T. Farrell's Studs Lonigan trilogy and to what minor novelists like Louis Golding did in the street-and-tenement novels of the thirties, but when this material is written on the screen the result is infinitely more powerful. (In a film review in 1935, Graham Greene—a Catholic—said that "the camera . . . can note with more exactitude and vividness than the prose of most living playwrights the atmosphere of mean streets and cheap lodgings.") And though *Mean Streets* has links to all those Richard Conte Italian-family movies, like *House of Strangers*, and to the urban-feudal life of *The Godfather*, the incidents and details are far more personal. Scorsese, who did the writing with Mardik Martin, knows the scene and knows how it all fits together; it's his, and he has the ability to put his feelings about it on the screen. All this is what the Boston Irish world of *The Friends of Eddie Coyle* lacked; the picture was shallow and tedious, because although we could see how the gangsters victimized each other, the police and the gangsters had no roots—and intertwined roots were what it was meant to be about. It was a milieu picture without milieu. In *Mean Streets*, every character, every sound is rooted in those streets. The back-and-forth talk of Charlie and Johnny Boy isn't little-people empty-funny (as it was in *Marty*); it's a tangle of jeering and joshing, of mutual goading and nerves getting frayed. These boys understand each other too well. Charlie's love for Johnny Boy is his hate for himself, and Johnny Boy knows Charlie's flaw. No other American gangster-milieu film has had this element of personal obsession; there has never before been a gangster film in which you felt that the director himself was saying, "This is my story." Not that we come away thinking that Martin Scorsese is or ever was a gangster, but we're so affected because we know in our bones that he has walked these streets and has felt what his characters feel. He knows how natural crime is to them.

There is something of the Carol Reed film *The Third Man* in the way the atmosphere imposes itself, and, like Reed, Scorsese was best known as an editor (on *Woodstock, Medicine Ball Caravan, Elvis on Tour,* C.B.S. documentaries, etc.) before he became a director (*Who's That Knocking at My Door?, Boxcar Bertha*). Graham Greene, the screenwriter of *The Third Man*, wrote a prescription for movies that fits this one almost perfectly. "The cinema," Greene said, "has always developed by means of a certain low cunning. . . . We are driven back to the 'blood,' the thriller. . . . We have to . . . dive below the polite level, to something nearer to the common life. . . . And when we have attained to a more popular drama, even if it is in the simplest terms of blood on a garage floor ('There lay Duncan laced in his golden blood'), the scream of cars in flight, all the old excitements at their simplest and most sure-fire, then we can begin—secretly, with low cunning—to develop our poetic drama." And, again, "If you excite your audience first, you can put over what you will of horror, suffering, truth." However, Scorsese's atmosphere is without the baroque glamor of evil that makes *The Third Man* so ambiguous in its appeal. There's nothing hokey here; it is a low, malign world Scorsese sees. But it's seen to the beat of an exuberant, satiric score. Scorsese has an operatic visual style (the swarthy, imaginative cinematography is by Kent Wakeford), and, with Jonathan T. Taplin, the twenty-six-year-old rock-record impresario, as producer, he has used a mixture of records to more duplicit effect than anyone since Kenneth Anger in *Scorpio Rising*. It's similar to Bertolucci's use of a motley score in *Before the Revolution* and *The Conformist* and to the score in parts of *The Godfather*, but here the music is a more active participant. The score is the background music of the characters' lives—and not only the background, because it enters in. It's as if these characters were just naturally part of an opera with pop themes. The music is the electricity in the air of this movie; the music is like an engine that the characters move to. Johnny Boy, the most susceptible, half dances through the movie, and when he's trying to escape from Michael he does a jerky frug before hopping into the getaway car. He *enjoys* being out of control—he revels in it—and we can feel the music turning him on. But *Mean Streets* doesn't use music, as *Easy Rider* sometimes did, to do the movie's work for it. (In *American Graffiti* the old-rock nostalgia catches the audience up before the movie even gets going.) The music here isn't our music, meant to put us in the mood of the movie, but the characters' music. And bits of old movies become part of the opera, too, because what the characters know of passion and death, and even of big-time gangsterism, comes from the movies. In Scorsese's vision, music and the movies work within us and set the terms in which we perceive ourselves. Music and the movies and the Church. A witches' brew.

Scorsese could make poetic drama, rather than melodrama laced with decadence, out of the schlock of shabby experience because he didn't have to "dive below the polite level, to something nearer to the common life" but had to do something much tougher—descend into himself and bring up what neither he nor anyone else could have known was there. Though he must have suspected. This is a blood thriller in the truest sense.

October 8, 1973

Crime and Punishment Updated

Joseph Gelmis

The hero of *Mean Streets* is a Catholic who believes in hell. He ought to. He's in it.

It's a ten-block-square ghetto bounded by Chinatown, the Bowery, and Greenwich Village. They call it Little Italy.

Charlie is an up-and-coming nickel-and-dime hoodlum in his twenties. His uncle is a local mob big shot. Charlie is being groomed, through an apprenticeship of running numbers and collecting protection money, to take a place within the system. He's got his reward in sight—a restaurant that soon will be his if he obeys his uncle and the code and doesn't make any mistakes.

But Charlie has troubles, including a conscience. The penance of prayers that the priest has him say after confession doesn't absolve the guilt Charlie feels. He knows that his punishment must be meted out in the same streets where he commits his sins as a criminal.

Mean Streets is extraordinarily rich and distinguished on many levels. Everything fits, reinforces, without being merely slick. Charlie's belief in God and in hell makes his friendship for the neighborhood deadbeat/ pariah more poignant. We recognize quite soon that this irresponsible loser, Johnny Boy, has been deliberately chosen by Charlie as the cross he must bear to punish himself.

Before you get the impression that *Mean Streets* is some sort of serious treatise on redemption, let me assure you that it's as funny a film as you'll see this year. But the laughs are inextricably bound to violent conflicts and tragedy that evolves as inevitably as classical drama.

Much of the power of *Mean Streets* comes out of character. And the characters reveal themselves as they should, through action. So you know from the start that Johnny Boy is headed for disaster; he lies charmingly, shows off, buys rounds of drinks and gambles with the little bit of money he gets—instead of paying his debt to the local loan shark, who has threatened to break his legs.

Director Martin Scorsese and co-author Mardik Martin, basing their script on Scorsese's own youth in Little Italy, provide *Mean Streets* with a precise, detailed Italian-American idiom.

Beyond its use of mid-sixties-pop/rock songs, *Mean Streets* itself is like music. Scorsese skillfully orchestrates the performances. Ghetto camaraderie, for instance, is counterpointed by the self-interest role-playing each young man is required to do to survive within the mob-controlled society.

There are so many good performances—most notably by Harvey Keitel as Charlie, Richard Romanus as Michael the loan shark, and David Proval as Tony, who runs the bar—that it seems unfair to single out Robert De Niro, who has the juicy role of Johnny Boy, as the film's most memorable actor.

But De Niro is simply astonishing: cunning, yet playing dumb; anguished, yet always on the brink of cathartic ecstasy; a victim with his back to the wall, yet cracking jokes, insulting those he has reason to fear and victimizing strangers who get in his way. His madness is a violent, self-destructive expression of impotence.

De Niro, as the dying catcher in *Bang the Drum Slowly*, was meant to evoke our pity. That was a tearjerker. The nice-guy pitcher who sacrifices his own convenience in *Bang the Drum Slowly* to assure De Niro one last season of baseball was, presumably, motivated by charitable decency. But it wasn't clear, which made it less convincing. In *Mean Streets*, De Niro is so full of bravado that we may feel concern because we like him, but we never pity him. And the reason that Charlie befriends him—like a missionary adopting a leper—couldn't be more persuasive and moving.

Mean Streets is one of the finest films of the year and was the best picture to come out of the eleventh New York Film Festival. Marty Scorsese is a major talent. His cameras can make a stroll through a garish bar look like a tour of hell, with the damned souls brawling, boozing, even killing each other. Yet Scorsese's art illuminates the experience, makes it an epiphany, rather than a sermon.

October 15, 1973

William S. Pechter

The case for 1973 as a breakthrough year for young American directors can't seriously be argued from such a square little nothing as *Bang the Drum Slowly*, or George Lucas's featherweight *American Graffiti*, or John Milius's derivative *Dillinger*, or Ralph Bakshi's exercise in ashcan Disney in *Heavy Traffic*, or Brian De Palma's rummaging around in Hitchcock's trash pile in *Sisters*. Indeed, excepting only James Frawley's *Kid Blue* and Terrence Malick's *Badlands*, one of the big flops and few hits of the New York Festival, respectively (and both of which I haven't seen), it becomes clear that the case rests almost entirely on Martin Scorsese's *Mean Streets*, and, for a while, the film, a kind of cross between *The Godfather* and *I Vitelloni* set among the petty Mafiosi of New York's Little Italy, looks like it might even be able to shoulder such a weight. Yet in a way the movie begins so beautifully and with such confident control (via a series of vignettes introducing the principal characters) that it establishes a level it cannot itself live up to, and barely ten minutes after it has begun one is aware (during a protracted and at least partly improvised dialogue about some borrowed money which takes place between two of the characters in the back room of a bar) of a frittering away of some of its power. And lively and vital as the film continues to be thereafter, one remains from then on aware of the slow but steady leakage of its power, even, one might say, the ceding of its power by the director, in the name of a quest for that air of spontaneity which the film achieves in abundance, but only at a cost.

Basically, the approaches to improvisation in films have been drawn between those of early Godard, giving his actors their lines but only at the last minute to prevent them sounding worked over, and John Cassavetes (taken up by Mailer), allowing the actors to invent their lines guided by their psychological interpretation of the characters, in hopes that some higher truth will emerge from the unpredictable chemistry of the actor-characters' interaction; the differences are essentially those between a director's cinema, using the actor's unpreparedness as one more tool in the director's creative control, and a cinema in which the actors hold an equal partnership in the work's creation. When the latter method works, miracles can happen, but rarely, unless the director's partner is an improvising actor with the genius of a Brando, can such miracles be sustained for the duration of the picture. *Mean Streets* has some moments touched by this miraculous excitement, and others that simply grind to a halt with that slightly dead, faintly embarrassed sense which always seems to attend actors improvising beyond the limits of their artistic capabilities and waiting for something to happen. (The hallmark of such scenes is protraction and repetition—"What d'ya mean?" [the last line then repeated]—as the actors pass the buck and stall for time, and the characteristic admission of failure comes with the actors going for laughs as the most familiar and trusted escape from their discomfort.) The actors in *Mean Streets* are all good, but none of them, including Robert De Niro (who is to take over the

Brando role in Coppola's sequel to *The Godfather*), seems up to the creative responsibility he's asked to shoulder; though De Niro comes across here as a far more intelligent actor than one might have expected from his work in *Bang the Drum Slowly*, even he falls back more often than he should on such effectively ingratiating things as his crazy grin, and the "hey-goombah" bits of stage-Italian business.

So finally, for all its sharp intelligence in both acting and direction, *Mean Streets* amounts to less than it should. Scorsese has a subject (the conflicting claims of church and street on the soul of his protagonist),* and a main character (who previously appeared in his first feature film, *Who's That Knocking at My Door?* which I haven't seen), and an ethnic milieu which he clearly knows fully and intimately; and he has (as Cassavetes and Mailer basically have not) a director's grasp of the means of his medium. What *Mean Streets* lacks, whether owing to Scorsese's limitations or to the priority he gives to improvisation, is a formal structure, an organizing action; without it, all the film's life seems to seep to its margins, to lie in its incidentals and details. The film is right on target, but goes nowhere, and by the movie's end its spontaneity, which, compared with the operatic heaviness of *The Godfather*, seemed at first the by-product of Scorsese's greater intimacy with his subject matter, seems less telling than *The Godfather*'s measured effects; indeed, apart from its opening, probably the most wholly successful scenes in the Scorsese film are the most conventionally realized ones with Cesare Danova playing a Mafia don. (Perhaps it owes something also to the Scorsese film's reliance on improvisation that such apparent inconsistencies as its religious-guilt-wracked protagonist's blaspheming at a bar have been allowed to stand, and that the impression it conveys of the passage of time is so blurred that one year's St. Anthony's Festival seems to follow on the heels of another.) Given how little sense *Mean Streets* generates of knowing where it's going, it's hardly surprising that the film doesn't so much conclude as simply stop—with a meaningless burst of violence (violence being for a director what laughs are for an actor: an easy way out; and this director seems already to know a little too well how to whip things up with effective applications of violent action).

All of which may seem unduly harsh on a work as promising as *Mean Streets*, though my view of Scorsese has been somewhat jaundiced by my having seen his previous film, *Boxcar Bertha*, and knowing just how pander-

---

* Though he has perhaps an even richer if less articulated one in the way the protagonist is caught up in acting out, with two "mental defectives" under his protection, the fantasy of his being a Mafia godfather.

ingly he can lay on the violence when the exigencies of turning a buck demand it. But in part harshness seems called for just because *Mean Streets* is a work of real promise, with much that is vivid and brilliant in it which the film as a whole fails to live up to. It's just because, at its best, the stakes involved seem so high, that I resent the way *Mean Streets* finally leaves one with such small change.

January, 1974

BANG THE DRUM SLOWLY
Base Hit

Richard Schickel

A. E. Housman did not have Bruce Pearson in mind when he wrote "To an Athlete Dying Young." Pearson, a third-string catcher for the New York Mammoths, is impossible to cast in the heroic Grecian mode. He is a Georgia backwoodsman who can't get the hang of spitting his tobacco accurately, let alone of making his teammates respect or even like him very much. His only distinction is that he has been prematurely touched by mortality, in the form of Hodgkin's disease.

Nobody would write a poem about Henry Wiggen, either. But they do write magazine stories about him, press lucrative endorsement offers on him, ask him to appear on the talk shows. Wiggen is to the fictional Mammoths what Tom Seaver is to the real-life Mets—an ace pitcher with all the right media moves who spends much of his time peddling insurance policies indiscriminately to teammates and opponents alike. The only quirk in his character is his friendship with simple old Bruce.

Wiggen (Michael Moriarty), realizing that a marginal player like Pearson (Robert De Niro) will be released if management gets wind of his illness, ends a spring-training holdout by accepting less money than he is worth—if the owners will agree not to cut Bruce. His efforts to keep Bruce's secret from shrewd Skipper Dutch Schnell (Vincent Gardenia), to get the rest of the club to quit ragging a man they don't know is dying, and to encourage Bruce to play above his half-empty head, form the substance of a funny, gentle, and honestly sentimental movie that is easily one of the best of the year in any category, and very possibly the best movie about sport ever made in this country.

Director John Hancock and writer Mark Harris (adapting his own fine novel) have great, knowledgeable fun with the game, getting in their licks at greedy owners, new-breed ballplayers who practice their pop songs right in the locker room, and old-breed managers and coaches who fail to understand that the game is merely a metaphor for life, not life itself.

But the genius of the movie lies in its introduction of the one subject that superbly conditioned young men rarely think about: death. Their efforts to come to grips with it, to handle it nonchalantly, as if it were an easy pop-up, are shy, deeply touching and completely winning. De Niro's doomed bumpkin is wonderfully exasperating, one of the most unsympathetic characters ever to win an audience's sympathy. Moriarty's Wiggen captures a young celebrity in the moment just before his public persona has iced over his humanity. Gardenia's manager is a perfect study in confusion—the baseball man floundering in existential depths.

The emotional high point comes when Wiggen, groping for the meaning of it all, finally comes up with an explanation that satisfies Pearson and probably ought to satisfy everyone else too: "Everybody knows everybody is dying. That's why people are as good as they are to people." This line, like everything else in this extraordinarily well-made film, is thrown away quickly and casually. But the line, and the movie, reverberate in the memory—not like a slowly, portentously banged drum, but like the crack of a bat drilling a clean single through the visitors' infield on a sweet summer's day in a more innocent time.

September 3, 1973

David Denby

Certain mediocre movies are more interesting for the large-scale response they inspire than for anything in the movies themselves. To my considerable surprise, the soft, mousy *Bang the Drum Slowly*, with its calculated naïveté and sentiment and its small, tentative humor, has received the most ostentatiously warm-hearted reviews of any movie to open in New York this year, and audiences seem to be responding in kind. To be sure, critics occasionally like to relax and reconcile themselves with those readers who complain of nastiness, coldness, and over-intellectual judgments, and everyone likes to cry a bit. But why *this* movie? And why such extravagant praise? Is there something in the response that hasn't been made as explicit as it should be?

Bang the Drum Slowly is still another of those chaste but emotionally charged male love stories in which a strong, resilient man nurses a weaker partner, slowing his inevitable slide toward disaster. Similar in theme to *Midnight Cowboy* and *Scarecrow*, this movie carries an even heavier load of automatic sentiment, for the loser-victim is not an obscure down-and-outer but a young baseball player dying of Hodgkin's disease in the middle of his first decent season. Could anyone imagine a situation better rigged for easy, unearned pathos?

Mark Harris's screenplay, adapted from his 1956 novel, makes little sense as narrative and even less as would-be moral instruction. First we must accept on faith an invincible friendship between two entirely dissimilar men: Henry Wiggen (Michael Moriarty), star of "The New York Mammoths," a glamorous, intelligent young pitcher of the Bouton/Seaver variety who sells insurance, writes books, and will always have it made; and his catcher and roommate, Bruce Pearson (Robert De Niro), an affectionate but alarmingly dumb, tobacco-chewing hick from Georgia, a man helpless in life, erratic on the field, and now mysteriously dying as well. The entire movie turns on Wiggen's concern for Pearson's welfare, but we never know why he's drawn to this man in the first place. Perhaps audiences are moved, in part, because the film touches buried levels of wonder and sentiment: the relationship between the men evokes the awesome mysteries of school or summer camp friendships in which an older, popular boy would inexplicably make a young outsider, a loser, his personal favorite, protecting him against bullies. As kids we never questioned such attachments. As adults, looking at other adults, we might wonder about the motives of the stronger man. Vanity? Love of power? Repressed homosexuality? These are some of the nasty but hardly unusual realities of the moral life that an artist of normal curiosity might consider, even if he intended to dismiss them or mix them with predominantly "good" motives. But for Harris, as far as we can make out, Wiggen's concern is entirely selfless; Pearson simply *needs* him.

Even if we accept Wiggen as an angel of mercy, the story doesn't hang together. He goes to fantastic lengths to prevent the Mammoths' irascible manager from learning of his friend's disease and to stop his teammates from ragging a man they don't realize is dying. His obsessions consume scene after scene, but they're red herrings since (a) the manager continues to play Pearson anyway after he hears of the illness, and (b) ragging in sports is as much a sign of affection as of malice, and nothing could be more patronizing or isolating than protecting someone from it. Wiggen even arranges Pearson's sex life, heading off an ambitious prostitute who wants to get her hands on the dying man's money. We recognize the familiar fantasy structure of the buddy-buddy movie: women, usually poisonous or whorey or both, must not be allowed to intrude on the male relationships. But does Harris realize he's asking us to admire a *sanctimonious* angel of mercy?

In a piece for *The New York Times*, Jim Bouton, an intelligent man, has written that "Basically, *Bang the Drum Slowly* . . . is a story about a marginal catcher named Bruce Pearson, the butt of everyone's jokes, who suddenly becomes one of the boys when his teammates discover that he might die at any moment from a rare disease." But this is *not* what the film is about, and in misstatements like this, one sees the basis of the film's appeal. Wiggen, not Pearson, is the center of the movie and its true subject. The dying man, merely the passive object of Wiggen's goodness, has only a few scenes and remains an utter stranger to the audience to the end. With tobacco spittle hanging from his lips, his hair slicked up in a foul pompadour, Robert De Niro is physically impressive as a graceless, out-of-it, back-country athlete (De Niro studied for the part by traveling with a minor league team and at times he appears to be playing a man too dumb to catch in the majors), but unfortunately he ducks his head away from the camera and never fully opens those dark, mean little eyes, so we can't see what's going on inside the character or even begin to identify. The performance is almost perversely unattractive and selfless. By contrast, Michael Moriarty's wide-open, mock-innocent, blandly ironic blue eyes and conventional good looks hold the camera interminably through scene after scene. Our intended response can only be admiration for Wiggen's intelligence, his guile, his coolly insolent humor, and so forth. It's a relaxed, subtly dominating performance. I think it's precisely this shift in attention from the proletarian slob-loser to the successful athlete-intellectual that accounts for the extravagant emotional response of critics and East Side audiences. Wiggen is their man for all seasons, a perfect fantasy of how they would act in the same situation; through him they can admire their own compassion and generosity—qualities made even more exquisite and self-satisfying in this case because they are directed toward a failing creature who isn't very appealing.

Indeed, I had the same uneasy feeling at *Bang the Drum Slowly* as I did at *Love Story* when people began weeping on cue over the death of Ali McGraw's supercilious bitch. Could they really have cared for her? I doubted it. Why the crying, then? I suppose because we flatter ourselves with tears; no one wants to appear emotionally dead, least of all to himself. But let's make this basic distinction: an honest tearjerker like *Captains*

Courageous or *How Green Was My Valley* moves us by glorifying a good man who dies or a tragic way of life; our emotions, however sloppy, at least flow outward toward some worthy object; dishonest tearjerkers induce us to cry for ourselves, they induce self-admiration and self-pity.

American sports movies used to be strenuous and exhortatory, even patriotic; success in sports was seen as paradigmatic of America's success as a country—at war, in business, anywhere. In line with the anti-mythic, anti-heroic mood of recent years, *Bang the Drum Slowly* lets the hot air out of the "National Pastime." It's a modern film—the aging, unshaven relief pitcher yawns and scratches himself during the singing of the national anthem. Yet the anti-heroism doesn't take the form one might expect—an exposé of the grittiness of baseball life (as in Bouton's book, *Ball Four*). Instead the game is simply reduced in physical and emotional scale. Harris and director John Hancock have successfully captured the special melancholia of baseball—the tedium of the long season; the sad, empty ballparks and rained-out days; the infantilism of men without women. But the mood of resignation and gentleness goes too far, becoming sickly, morbid about personal slights, wanly "sensitive."

It's as if there were something inherently wrong with the competitive swagger and heroic spirit of sports. The actors are mostly too small and cuddly looking (I realize it's a low-budget movie, but since when did large actors cost more?), and Hancock shoots much of the on-field action in slow motion, which, as Andrew Sarris has pointed out, aestheticizes the game in a way that violates its nature, draining it of violence and danger. Baseball, after all, is not as tediously "beautiful" as the Olympic Games (thank God). As I worked on this review the Reds and Mets were struggling through the pennant play-offs, a series which included pitchers throwing at batters' heads, a fistfight, a general melée involving both teams, and a near-riot by New York fans. Baseball has a long and honorable tradition of rowdyism; anyone who has spent time in a major-league dressing room, even as observer or journalist, knows that ballplayers aren't sweet fellows, that their solidarity and affection for one another is likely to take the form of lunatic pranks. Asking them to stop "ragging" because a man is ill or because we are all mortal and therefore should be nice to one another is not the life-enhancing impulse that Harris implies it is; if anything, it's the opposite.

Perhaps Harris and Hancock calculated that the post-Vietnam art-house audience *needed* this diminution of American heroism and physical force. In his updating of the book, Harris includes several references to Vietnam, as if to say *"That's* what happens to American boys when they get overly competitive and violent." Yet his baseball is so feeble that it's hardly a moral equivalent to war, and anyway, without its violence and anger sports would cease to interest most of us for very long. One wonders how this inappropriately soft view of baseball will go over with the mass audience.

Can this really be a movie with a *sports* setting? Apart from the baseball ballet on field, *Bang the Drum Slowly* has virtually no movement or flow, narrative or pictorial energy. The actors sit stock still and talk slowly, imprisoned in flat, unresonant, super-tight close-ups; most of the film is as banal in style as an afternoon soap opera.

Because of the phlegmatic TV-drama ambience we may be puzzled by the quasi-absurdist turns in the script. In the first scene with Vincent Gardenia (as the exasperated manager) the over-tight close-ups don't allow the comic declamation to claim any space, and comedy needs space, it doesn't play in tight. At first we may think that the character is putting us on, a deception that the close-ups are designed to penetrate, but in fact the director has simply miscalculated the scene. Gardenia has an accurate and funny manager's walk—hands in back pockets, gut thrust out—and blazing hawk's eye and general irascibility evoke Edward G. Robinson and occasionally Zero Mostel. But he's badly used. The tirades Harris has written for him fluctuate between Casey Stengel surrealism and ordinary Jewish monologue humor, Catskills division, and we never do get a handle on the character. There are repeated gags, like Gardenia's tossing a burning cigarette into a toilet (we hear the sizzle) that are too cheap to use more than once, and some aimless caricaturing at sub-TV level (e.g., the blonde-bitch club owner and her sycophantic assistant) that should have been thrown out altogether. I suspect the comedy is inconsistent and scattered because it's not intended to make any satirical point, but only to distract us from the dismal pathos of the story.

Hancock is mainly a New York theater man (his only previous feature: *Let's Scare Jessica to Death*), and he may improve with experience. To be fair, there are some very simple images that will stay in memory: the credits sequence of the two men loping around the outfield green, which establishes an appropriate mood of pastoral friendship; a slow pan across the players' faces—bored, sleepy, forgetful—as they sing the national anthem on opening day; and best of all, a single, long-lasting shot of Wiggen, Pearson and other players performing an asinine pop song on television that becomes increasingly hilarious and sad as Pearson—forever the tool—tries to dance but can't stay in rhythm. This intimation of what might have been—a comic elegy for a man who could do no right—makes us regret all the more the smug tearjerker we have before us now.

Winter, 1974

PAYDAY

Bruce Williamson

A fine, funky little movie called *Payday* charts the last day or two in the life of a country-western singing star whose chauffeur-driven Cadillac whips him through the southland on a barnstorm tour. As Maury Dann, actor Rip Torn has his best screen role to date and performs it with furious conviction, whether singing (words and music by Shel Silverstein), swearing, or "hauling ass" down the open road. In the brief but erratic trajectory described by the film, he commits vandalism against his former wife's home, puffs grass, pays off a dee-jay, kills a man in anger, leaves a flunky to take the rap, picks up a hicktown chick (Elayne Heilveil) and mounts her in the back seat of the Caddy while his regular bimbo (Ahna Capri, a sexpot who can act as well as simmer) pretends to be asleep. Canadian-born director Daryl Duke filmed *Payday* on location in Alabama and obviously felt at home amid the clutter of roadside honky-tonks and streamlined motels that are built to be seedy while still brand-new. Ever thumb through a trashy novel and find you can't put it down? That's *Payday*. Small, jagged bits of Americana comin' atcha with a real sting to them, rather like the effect achieved by some smart-ass throwing beer bottles out a car window at 80 miles per hour.

February 1973

HEAVY TRAFFIC
An Attack on the Drabs

Penelope Gilliatt

In Ralph Bakshi's *Heavy Traffic*, a full-length cartoon about Manhattan that is made with the love and rudeness of an intimate of the city, a Harlem black says about a caged bird that won't move, "He don't fly unless you open the cage, and he got to come back again, because he's trained to." The lad he is talking to, named Mike, is an innocent, hesitant white who takes shelter from his squawking mom in drawing. (Later on, he hopefully describes himself as "a religious-strip cartoonist" to a geriatric hospital patient in an oxygen tent who still, in his toothless dotage, has an excitable regard for himself as a talent spotter.) Mike lets the bird out onto the rooftops of Manhattan, hoping perhaps for a signal that liberty is more possible than it seems to be to him. But the bird merely hops from TV aerial to TV aerial, because he is trained not to escape, just as *Heavy Traffic* is full of human New Yorkers trained not to escape. This is what gives the funny, boisterous, ill-bred film its underlay of melancholy. The characters are indoctrinated to stay inside the bars of their types: Mike's bossy mother, who must be the prize maniacal client of every beauty parlor she obviously goes to, grumbling about her sexually battered husband; bands of luckless, head-tossing, plum-thighed girls without a nickel; a black who mournfully repeats to himself routine abuse about being a crazy nigger; a tough girl in a bar who allows herself to voice regret only that hassles aren't what they used to be; homosexuals scared or belligerent; fashion models in bikinis posturing for a photographer who treats them like slices of salami; a plump naked girl who has caustically tried flirting with Mike and fallen off a tenement roof to hang like a billowing piece of laundry from a line running across the street. The characters know their limitations as well as the hopping bird does. Mike says uncertainly to a rumbustious black girlfriend who is dressed in a fake-fur coat and red pants to which she gives the shape of a light bulb in a sleazy part of town, "I'm really not too big with the girls. Mick Jagger I'm *not*." The girl is furtively nice to him and doesn't mock when he says, about her proposition that they move in together, that he could sleep on the floor.

Heavy Traffic was written by Ralph Bakshi as well as directed by him. Before it he made *Fritz the Cat*, which started on the same path. This new and obstreperous farce in honor of people who beat urban doldrums is a giant stride ahead in technique and seriousness. The graphic work consists sometimes of pure animation, sometimes of drawn figures against photographed backgrounds that elide now and then into stills doctored in the darkroom to have the look of etchings or of black-ink drawings splashed with a thick brush onto white paper. Or sometimes a whole scene will be realistic, and the voices that have been doing the dubbing of the drawn characters will turn out to belong to visible actors wearing naturalistic versions of the cartoon clothes. The sound track always seems to be spoken by a cast in motion, wandering away from the mike whenever a drawn event moves to the edge of the screen. We are all so inured to dubbing that might as well have been done by a row of bored reciters immobilized on ranks of chairs that the technical energy coming from the sound track is a wonder in itself. So is the point of view of the film, which chooses to disguise its intelligence and charity under garishness. If the film goes too far, it is only like Manhattan. If the film is exaggerated, showing us characters who have no steadiness and events that seem without cause, again it is only like Manhattan. The demotic, buffoonish film has the same eruptive gaiety and fits of temper as the city, and the same coarse beauty. The photographed backgrounds of the city treat tenements and garbage cans with the gravity that a grander photographer would give to Paestum. The bums, the boozers, the down-at-heel, the fluorescently dressed girls who make up the population of the film are out to get a rise out of you, since life has taught them you are unlikely to give them a wage; the movie practically taunts you into the slip of dismissing it as "offensive," which it isn't, though it is full of double-dares. It even shows us the beginning of deceiving religiosity, and of God's being created out of garbage. There is a sequence that shows Man being crucified. "It hurts," he says. It does.

The film comes back again and again to a shot of a pinball machine in an amusement gallery. It is as if the machinery of fate will toss your life about willy-nilly for your money. Mike is seen naturalistically at the end of the picture; he can do nothing to make the gadget let him win, because there is no definable reason for winning or losing. So teleology is a con trick, like religion. A Manhattan dweller's history rockets about in the cheap machine with no power over itself and no power exercised by the person who put in the dime. It is a sober and genuinely felt conclusion for a gaudy film to come to. The content of *Heavy Traffic* is cheeky, disjointed, comic, very dark. But the effect of it afterward is buoyant, as originality is. The feeling of commotion and disquiet caused by what goes on in the film is drained away by its talent and nerve.

August 20, 1973

Morals Through the Shudder

Andrew Sarris

The moral issue with *Heavy Traffic* is complicated; Ralph Bakshi's animated cartoon seems less concerned with beguiling its audience in the manner of *Cops and Robbers* than of bestirring it in the manner of *Last Exit to Brooklyn*. By any standard, Bakshi's achievement is spectacularly uneven. But then he is just about the only X-rated cartoonist around, and thus there is really not too much basis for comparison. As with *Fritz the Cat*, the uniqueness of the genre puts the captious critic in the uncomfortable position of hunting down an endangered species. Bakshi's artistic alibi seems to be that he is a conscious antithesis to Walt Disney. He has even accelerated Disney's unfortunate evolution from pure animation to a melange of animation and live-action, but whereas Disney's clinical orientation was anal, Bakshi's seems to be genital, and whereas Disney's fantasies did not exclude children, Bakshi's seem designed to exclude even squeamish adults. But as Stuart Byron has noted in *The Real Paper*, Bakshi's urban hero flashes all kinds of Bambi expressions when confronted with the absurdism of his existence. And it is still an open question whether Bakshi is any more ruthlessly Darwinian in his big city confrontations than Disney was in his so-called "nature studies."

The notion of the hero's being afflicted with both a Rothian Jewish Mother and a machismoid Mafioso father may have been suggested by the peculiar casting of parents in an Andy Milligan very-soft-core-and-hard-yell sexploitation opus of some years ago. Having thus disposed of the ethnic anxiety of the Jews and the Italians, Bakshi is free to cash in on much funnier but more sensitive targets, mainly raffish blacks and drag queens. Indeed, the sound tracks of both *Fritz the Cat* and *Heavy Traffic* tend to indulge occasionally in dialect humor only a few obscenities removed from *Amos 'n' Andy* and Disney's black crows in *Dumbo*. At what point does Bakshi exploit the very horror he says he has set out to expose? This is an especially difficult question to ask of cinema with the built-in hypocrisy of its sensuous spectacle. Hence, most anti-war films glorify war, anti-crime films glorify crime, anti-rape films glorify rape, or if they don't glorify these evils, they at least celebrate them, and thus make them more thinkable.

What is especially confusing in *Heavy Traffic* is the extraordinary exhilaration with which evil is committed. If audiences can laugh at the buffoonish spectacle of a girl being knocked accidently out of a high-story window by her would-be lover, and then being suspended grotesquely on an intervening clothesline, well then it begins to seem that the last exit to Brooklyn may be leading instead to a kind of downbeat Disneyland. But these are peripheral matters. As I watched the cartoon, I did become involved with the desperate adventures of the hero, and I followed the narrative on its own terms. And then about halfway into the plot, the hero and black girlfriend decide to rip off a john. The girl lures the john to a hotel room, and the hero cracks the john's skull open with a piece of lead pipe, and we see all the blood streaming out, and the john plopping down dead, and I said that's all folks because you can't put Humpty-Dumpty together again by treating mugging and murder as mandatory courses in a ghetto education and the picture can't go on as if nothing happened. The same thing happened to me when the pool shark died in *Fritz the Cat*. I simply turned off the movie and let the images float freely to oblivion. But even on the most abstract level, *Heavy Traffic* collapses completely when it shifts from animation to live action for its soft-headedly scenic finale.

September 20, 1973

SISTERS
Half Hitch

Richard Schickel

Sisters is being promoted as a routine shocker of the kind that has made its distributor, American-International, rich and infamous. But it is something more—and more interesting—than that. It is a homage by a gifted, if erratic, young director Brian De Palma (*Hi, Mom* and *Greetings*) to one of cinema's genuine masters, Alfred Hitchcock.

The theme is Hitchcockian: a demonstration of the way private sexual obsession has a way of spilling over into public, with murderous consequences (*Vertigo*). There are innocent bystanders drawn dangerously into a closely woven criminal web (*The Man Who Knew Too Much*). Even the murder that is the film's central incident—a perhaps too ghastly knifing— reminds us of the famous shower-bath murder in *Psycho*, as does a splendid, spooky score by that film's masterful composer, Bernard Herrmann. More important than these specific references to glories past, however, is the Hitchcockian discipline De Palma brings to his storytelling, the delicate balance between humor and horror with which he permits it to unfold, the suspenseful way he lets the audience in on the plot's secret before his characters tumble to it.

De Palma's story is about a woman who survives an operation that separates her from her Siamese twin. She turns schizophrenic in an effort to keep her dead twin's spirit alive, then is allowed to roam dangerously free by the doctor who performed the operation. He in turn is both guilty about and possessive of the human accident he created. It is a weirdly plausible and marvelously original plot. So are the parodies that enliven the film: a lunatic TV game show that caters openly to voyeurism, an earnest and dimwitted documentary explicating the medical and psychological problems of Siamese twins. De Palma's New York location work, as it has in the past, reveals facets of an overfamiliar urban landscape untouched by other filmmakers.

There is an appealing performance by Jennifer Salt as the investigative journalist whose cries of "Wolf, wolf!" go unheeded until it is almost too late, and Margot Kidder is touching and frightening as the most thoroughly split personality in movie history. Above all, however, *Sisters* reveals De Palma as capable of moving from the esoteric fringe of the movie world to its commercial center without sacrificing the exuberantly anarchic spirit that first marked him as a director worth watching. *Sisters* provides moviegoers with the special satisfaction of finding a real treasure while prowling cinema's bargain basement.

April 30, 1973

Three

AMERICAN
THEMES

THE NEW LAND

Gary Arnold

The New Land completes the narrative and resolves the themes begun so magnificently in *The Emigrants*. I don't see any reason to be cautious about evaluating the achievement of the Swedish director-cinematographer Jan Troell. *The Emigrants* and *The New Land* are new classics. Individually stirring and engrossing, together they comprise one of the great, indispensable moviegoing experiences of recent years.

I have no doubt about the durability of the experience either. Five 'or ten or twenty or fifty years from now Troell's epic will stir audiences anew. One simply doesn't forget passages like the ocean voyage in *The Emigrants* or Liv Ullmann's exquisite, breathtaking death scene in *The New Land*. Aesthetic experiences this intense and transcendent become an indelible part of one's own history.

Karl Oskar and Kristina Nilsson, the Swedish farm couple played by Max von Sydow and Liv Ullmann, settle with their family and a small band of fellow emigrants in a fertile Minnesota valley in 1852. Their pioneering community grows and prospers. We see that the Nilssons and their compatriots do indeed form the nucleus of a new society, still rural and pious and still circumscribed by many Old World customs and sentiments, yet clearly less restricting and frustrating than the impoverished, theocratic society they fled.

The Nilssons take root in the new land, Karl Oskar far more readily than his wife, who will never be able to commit herself emotionally to their American homestead or think of it as "home." The promise symbolized by America is fulfilled in certain lives, but we also see the casualties and victims of emigration and westward expansion. Robert (Eddie Axberg), Karl Oskar's restless and naïve younger brother, leaves for the California gold fields with his oafish friend Arvid and returns three years later wasted and swindled, a ravished human being at the age of twenty-two. As the new emigrant society prospers and expands, it forces the native American society—in this case the Sioux tribes—into decline. The Indians, remote but peaceable in the early stages of the film, have grown desperate and threatening at the climax.

100

It's ironic that we had to wait for a Swedish director to give us a comprehensive, clear-eyed vision of the nineteenth-century settlement of this country, a vision that recognizes both the fulfillments and tragedies of the so-called American Dream. Troell, working from a popular cycle of four novels by the late Vilhelm Moberg, which were published in Sweden between 1949 and 1959, shows us the dream and the nightmare impartially. There's no cant or sentimentality in his image of American history. We're allowed an accurate accounting of things, an accounting that doesn't gloss over the debts and losses in order to celebrate the profits.

Jan Troell has a uniquely beautiful and liberating movie vision, and one feels immensely grateful for his lucid, humane, and disinterested view of the American past. Troell is blessedly free of the self-congratulation and self-hatred that customarily distort American treatments of American history. It's conceivable that Fred Zinnemann might have achieved something like *The Emigrants* and *The New Land* if he had been able to film Michener's *Hawaii* the way he wanted to, but that remains one of the great unrealized movies of the sixties.

Troell's epic *exists*, and perhaps it will have a profound, exemplary influence on the way epics are made in the future. I wouldn't be surprised if the decision by Francis Ford Coppola and Mario Puzo to retrieve the emigrant period of Vito Corleone's life in their upcoming sequel to *The Godfather* were inspired to some extent by Troell's work, which demonstrates the dramatic advantages of tracing American social problems back to some of their European sources.

The Emigrants and *The New Land* were ambitious, expensive productions for a studio like Svensk Filmindustri, but they cost only a fraction of what conventional American epics (or many American potboilers) would cost. Troell has mastered the difficult, crucially important technique of rendering epic story material intimately. He contrives to use a small group of characters expressively and representatively, inferring widespead longings and social movements from their particular aspirations and struggles. Troell has restored dramatic involvement as the primary element in epic storytelling. In the typical epic of recent years the human beings were usually on the periphery, dwarfed by spectacle.

Troell's wonderful feeling for the sensuous potentialities in color photography and editing enhances his narrative style. The images are concise and evocative, and so are the best scenes. When Troell is at the top of his game, his movies have a beautiful, unhurried rhythm. We keep accumulating new impressions of the setting and the characters without lingering over any single impression. Troell keeps us very close to the people, observing their labor, apprehension, suffering, and happiness. The photography helps us feel closer by catching the textures of clothing, furnishings, and tools and the very atmosphere the characters breathe—one can almost taste the smoky haze in a log cabin or feel the bite in a blizzard. Even when Troell uses visual symbols for the characters—like the golden leaf suspended in the air for poor disillusioned Robert or the needle-and-thread stuck in the muslin curtain for the dying Kristina—the images are so apt, discreet, and lovely that one barely registers the artifice and certainly doesn't resent it. Troell's lyrical imagery isn't merely pretty; it's also dramatically expressive and emotionally transporting.

Troell has such a masterful sense of movie technique that it comes as a jolt when he does stumble. For example, he suddenly overdramatizes the camerawork in a scene where Robert fears he is being stalked by an Indian. There's also a structurally awkward section in *The New Land*—the flashbacks dealing with Robert's experiences in the Far West. I don't think we need this material. It's already apparent from the boy's haunted face and rotted teeth that something awful has happened to him, and it might be more effective if we simply heard him confide in his brother or sister-in-law. The flashbacks interrupt the flow of the story and give us information we can easily infer. While they're unreeling, the movie seems to stop, to mark time, and it's a relief when Troell finally gets back to the present tense.

One also misses a sense of the Nilssons' children in the later stages of the film. They're quite visible as infants or little kids, but they do an inexplicable disappearing act later on. It seems a peculiar oversight. One of the traditional strengths of this type of historical saga is the depiction of what changes and what endures from one generation to the next.

As Karl Oskar and Kristina, Max von Sydow and Liv Ullmann become a little like members of one's own family. Contemporary filmmakers seem to have a terrible time making any characters believable for six seconds at a stretch, but Troell and his stars leave us with the remarkable, gratifying impression of knowing the central characters intimately, of having gone through so much with them that we feel like companions and confidants. Does one need to add that this is a quality of illusion that used to make people positively eager to attend the movies or the theater?

Ullmann's performance is especially striking. As an actress Liv Ullmann possesses the same economy of means and richness of expression that distinguish Jan Troell as a photographer and director. She doesn't have a long speaking part or protracted dramatic scenes in *The New Land*, but she's so completely in character that she can move and delight you even in brief, fleeting moments. Modern directors tend to deploy actors more sparingly and abstractly than film directors used to, and Ullmann can evidently accommodate her acting to this change (which is not necessarily a change for the better). Without ever overemoting she gets the maximum emotional communication out of her time on the screen.

There's no wasted motion in Ullmann's style of acting. Having imagined the essence of Kristina's feelings in a given scene, Ullmann gives us that lucid, expressive essence. She has a knack for touching you to the quick very concisely, and three scenes in *The New Land* provide especially wonderful examples: the wave of homesickness that suddenly overcomes Kristina when the other settlers are talking about how glad they are to be out of Sweden; her changes of expression when she tries on a fancy hat; and Kristina's lyrical death. It's a radiant performance in a fine tradition—Jane Wyman in *The Yearling* and Cicely Tyson in *Sounder* had comparable intensity and impact as peasant mothers—and it's only part of the enduring satisfaction that awaits moviegoers in *The New Land*.

November 2, 1973

PAPER MOON

Judith Crist

The world, let alone Watergate, is so much with us that amid a clutch of "thesis" movies one opts for the simple, the sweet, and the pleasurable.

And the last, happily, comes from Peter Bogdanovich in beautiful, relaxing and appropriate black and white. *Paper Moon*, his fifth and most recent film, is exactly what we have in mind when we talk nostalgically of what movies "used to be"—meaningful rather than metaphorical, engrossing rather than exploitative, humanistic in their comedy and their sentiment. Indeed there will be those cinéastes who will declare that this is a used-to-be movie, with shades of *The Kid*, *The Champ*, *Little Miss Marker*—if not *hommages* to the makers thereof. They're right as far as genre goes—a basic theme is, of course, that of the waif and the con man, the child up against the hard heart and larcenous leanings of the adult. But as Bogdanovich has shown in the progression of his films, along with a steady growth of professionalism and ripening of talent, through *Targets*, *Directed by John Ford*, *The Last Picture Show*, and *What's Up, Doc?*, he is artist enough to make his personal mark upon a genre.

Based loosely on *Addie Pray*, a novel by Joe David Brown, with a screenplay by Alvin Sargent, *Paper Moon* is the story (a love story, perhaps, or a story of love) of a nine-year-old orphan and a small-time confidence man making their way through a Depression-bleak Kansas en route to her aunt's in St. Joseph, Missouri. The Panama-hatted slick-suited gent is a Bible salesman, working the widow racket, and they meet at her mother's graveside. Since he's on his way to St. Jo, why not take the girl to her only surviving relative? He agrees—and in no time has gently black-mailed a chap in town into giving the child $200 in compensation for her mother's death and spent a chunk of it on refurbishing his roadster; he's about to put her on a train for St. Jo with $20 cash when suddenly he sees the child plain. "You owe me $200," she declares. And he has met his match.

Moses Pray's match is about four feet tall, a hideous cloche pulled down to her eyebrows, sexless in overalls, firm-jawed and bass-voiced, clutching a cigar box packed with her treasures, chief among them a bottle of perfume and a snapshot of her mother, a posturing, cheap and pretty belle in the same cloche. And Addie has a perceptive eye, a mind like a calculator, a bent for smoking in bed, a passion for Jack Benny and Fibber McGee, a cool head for business, and a yearning for tenderness. But in eternal-woman fashion, she's up against a total stinker, a foolish, cowardly, petty crook without an honest instinct or a non-egocentric emotion. He'll earn and repay the $200—if he won't, Addie will scream—but not an iota more will he give.

And so the two set out and before you know it, Addie's running the business. True, there's a bit of a setback when Moses gets himself besotted by Trixie Delight, a carnival dancer of good family, and near-disaster when he gets into bootlegging. But you can bet on Addie all the way.

Addie is portrayed by a nine-year-old named Tatum O'Neal—and only a father would be willing to co-star with this technically amateur but actually top-pro picture-stealer. And indeed, it is her father, Ryan O'Neal, who not only cooperates in her large case of larceny but in the course thereof proves himself a first-rate character actor.

Bogdanovich's basic triumph is in keeping the film unsentimental, unslapstick, and unstrained. Laszlo Kovacs's camera has captured so completely a sense of time and place, of a poverty-stricken Midwest and a Depression era whose hopes are fed by Addie's idolized "Frankie Roosevelt" and of an age of relative innocence, that one is transported in the watching. And the casting is impeccable, beyond the O'Neals, with Madeline Kahn, that deliciously nasal fiancée from Iowa in *What's Up, Doc?*, sheer delight as the whorish and pathetic Trixie with highfalutin talk of bone structure and a bitter awareness of her shaky holding power; P. J. Johnson as Trixie's stolid slave who accepts the burdens of hard times and the joys of emancipation with equal patience; Burton Gilliam as a gamy desk clerk—and lots more, with every face a part not only of the scene but of the era. And again Bogdanovich has used period music within its context as the final seal on our nostalgia. We can revel in *Paper Moon* as a reminder that the good things of film not only used to be—but are.

May 21, 1973

Gary Arnold

Paper Moon may prove a disappointment if you go with sizable expectations. At its best the film is only mildly amusing, and I'm not sure I could recall a few undeniable highlights if pressed on the point.

Several supporting and bit players are enjoyable for the brief moments they occupy the screen: John Hillerman in the dual role of a bootlegger and his sheriff brother; Burton Gilliam as a lecherous desk clerk; Dorothy Price and Dejah Moore as swindled saleswomen; P. J. Johnson as the teenage maid of a prattling trollop, a would-be hilarious role that has been grotesquely overplayed by Madeline Kahn, evidently at the insistence of director Peter Bogdanovich.

None of these performers happens to be critically important, indispensable to the action and appeal of the story. The problem with *Paper Moon* is that it's hollow at the center. The central relationship, involving a small-time con man and a tough little girl who practice a Bible-selling racket in the Midwest during the Depression, remains undeveloped and unaffecting.

Having tried without success to maintain some interest in the source of material, Joe David Brown's novel *Addie Pray*, I was prepared for certain inadequacies in the story. *Addie Pray* seemed like a synthetic imitation of *True Grit:* Brown affected Charles Portis's vernacular style but failed to reproduce the charm and originality. The tone was reminiscent, but the kick was gone. Apart from its literary charms, *True Grit* was also an exciting adventure melodrama. Nothing particularly compelling happens in *Addie Pray.* It's an episodic account of some negligible-to-pathetic swindles, scarcely comparable to Mattie Ross's relentless pursuit of the men who murdered her father.

Alvin Sargent's screenplay retains the episodic structure of Brown's book, and the film suffers from a lack of either strong episodes or a strong line of dramatic development. The truly surprising weakness is the failure to create a touching, ongoing relationship between the country con man, played by Ryan O'Neal, and his orphaned kid accomplice, played by

O'Neal's nine-year-old daughter Tatum. The substance is so thin and the movie treatment so superficial that nothing emotionally lasting takes hold, not even an implicit sense of affection between father and daughter.

O'Neal, adorned with a mustache and garbed in thirties duds, bears an occasional agreeable resemblance to Warner Baxter and Clark Gable, but his performance has no style or authority. He acts rather uptight and flustered. There was never a moment when I believed that his character had either the gall or the charm he would need to have to survive.

The press material for the film includes a comment by Bogdanovich that O'Neal wanted to do the role with a Southern accent but was dissuaded, because Bogdanovich felt the accent would "soften" the character and fail to convince the audience. But O'Neal is not convincingly tough as it is, and perhaps an accent would have given him a useful handle on the role, a ready means of stylizing his character. It's now apparent that O'Neal desperately needs some method of individualizing the role.

An actor like Gable would surely have been a little playful and ingratiating when impersonating a con man, and one would like to see Ryan O'Neal take a similar tack. I suspect that O'Neal became too concerned with Tatum's level of performance to concentrate on having a good time in his own part. A harmless device like an accent might have helped to loosen him up.

Considering the box-office success of *What's Up, Doc?* and the probable success of *Paper Moon*, it sounds rather preposterous to suggest that Peter Bogdanovich and Ryan O'Neal may not be right for each other, but I don't think they are right for each other. O'Neal has not been at his most attractive doing humorless derivations of old Cary Grant and Clark Gable assignments, while Bogdanovich, extraordinarily capable with the straightforward dramatic material of *The Last Picture Show,* is inclined to strain and miscalculate when he undertakes the breezier forms of motion-picture entertainment. Bogdanovich's luck will probably hold: If *What's Up, Doc?* can be mistaken for a heady revival of screwball comedy, *Paper Moon* can be just as easily mistaken for a heartwarmer. It isn't, but it should be, so audiences may feel like making the necessary allowances.

I wanted to be more impressed and affected by Tatum O'Neal than I was. The most disappointing aspect of the film in my opinion is the lack of anything noticeably original or moving about either her personality or performance. Perhaps the reviewers who have been raving about her should take a look at Hayley Mills in her first movie, *Tiger Bay* (a little girl-loves-outlaw story that has the kind of conflict, suspense, and sentimental appeal *Paper Moon* could use), or Margaret O'Brien in *Meet Me in St. Louis,* or Butch Jenkins in *The Human Comedy,* or John Howard

Davies in *Oliver Twist* and *The Rocking Horse Winner*, or Jean-Pierre Léaud in *The 400 Blows*, etc., etc.

Miss O'Neal has a pleasantly round, tomboyish mug, and when she smiles, she suddenly becomes an endearing spittin' image of her father. She's obviously meant to recall Jackie Coogan in *The Kid*, but she doesn't project remotely as much expression or intensity. Tatum O'Neal has a surprisingly reserved screen presence. One enters the theater anticipating a terrific new image of a tough, lovable kid, but this little girl acts unusually subdued and self-conscious, as if she were trying hard to remember her lines and deliver them precisely on cue.

The script doesn't give Tatum O'Neal the opportunity for much variety. Most of the time she merely acts a little stubborn or belligerent. The camera catches her far too often with the same slightly pouting, tight-lipped expression on her face. If there's something more exciting or vibrant or uninhibited in her personality, Bogdanovich has failed to bring it out. P. J. Johnson, the unheralded supporting kid in the cast, is more interesting to watch, because she looks and sounds like an original—a somewhat lumpy, big-boned girl with an offbeat vocal delivery. While I'm sure Tatum O'Neal is a good, lively kid, I hope she doesn't believe her reviews, because those raves have been more than a little premature.

June 15, 1973

THE WAY WE WERE*

Joseph Gelmis

As a boy at the movies, kissing scenes sent me ducking out of sight. The violence got my attention.

Now I prefer the love stories and the comedies. I watch the kissing and I avert my eyes when the violence starts.

Lately, I seem to be forced to spend more of my time looking away from the screen than at it. So the arrival of a good love story becomes a cause for celebration. It means being allowed to look uninterruptedly at a movie again.

The Way We Were is a love story. For adults. Meaning it deals with life

* See also Molly Haskell's piece in the section "Women"—Editors.

as it is. Not to be confused with sex in the raw. Lovers will recognize the truth of the emotions.

The movie is about attraction and loss. The lovers—played by Robert Redford and Barbra Streisand—are opposites. He wants to breeze through life, have fun, avoid hassles. She's serious, committed, champions underdog causes, feels responsible for wars and injustice everywhere. She also believes in his writing gifts more than he does and she makes demands on him that he finally feels he can't fulfill.

They love each other, but are incompatible. The qualities of grace and charm and vivacity in him and of integrity and passion and commitment in her, which are the basis of their appeal to each other, are ultimately the reason they can't live together.

Based on Arthur Laurents's novel (he also wrote the script), *The Way We Were* is part of the current period-movie trend. Yet it doesn't succumb to showing off the ambience of the late thirties, early and late forties and early fifties for its own sake, as nostalgia. The looks and sounds of the periods are used as they should be, to establish authentic details within which the characters can play out their drama.

There is one major flaw in the film that I am told didn't exist in the novel. The hero's insecurity over his own abilities is twisted into outright cowardice in a terrible scene in the movie. He virtually begs and whines and crawls to his director to keep him on as a screenwriter in the adaptation of his first novel in Hollywood. The scene would have made sense only if the Hollywood establishment were holding over his head his wife's outspoken leftist politics. (She defends the blacklisted Hollywood ten before the House Committee on Un-American Activities.) And that is, in fact, the way the scene is written in Laurents's novel, *The Way We Were*—he must either force his wife to stop or else become a casualty of her militant politics.

It's a regrettable lapse in the movie version of the story. Because there aren't supposed to be heroes or villains in the romance. Just different styles. This way, Robert Redford is made to seem a coward for the wrong reason—that he's a failure as a writer. The scene, as it's written in the novel, shows that it's not a question of cowardice, but of style. Simply, Redford is not willing to take responsibility for his wife's commitment, because he is not willing to believe in anything, so they necessarily have to break up.

I haven't been kind to Robert Redford in reviews of anything he's done except for *Butch Cassidy and the Sundance Kid*. By co-starring with him and giving him the sort of heroic role he ordinarily would have been typecast in himself, Paul Newman helped transfer to Redford much of his own status as the nation's leading male sex symbol. Since then, like

Newman had to do before him, Redford has been trying to find movies that continue to exploit his popularity while giving the chance to expand his medium-range acting talents to prove to himself and us that he's not just making it on his looks.

The problem is that Redford's looks *are* his fortune, while his co-star in *The Way We Were*, Barbra Streisand, is beautiful because she is so talented. In his earlier movie career (*Barefoot in the Park*, etc.), Redford was the graceful ingenue. Later, in the movies since *Butch Cassidy* (including *Big Fauss and Little Halsey* and *The Candidate*), Redford has been the ambivalent antihero. He hasn't had a screen persona, other than that of the handsome, insecure (and therefore, often, defensively smug) façade in search of an identity.

In *The Way We Were*, Redford is perfectly cast as the too-handsome character for whom everything comes so easily he never develops confidence or maturity. It's a splendid film because, instead of being told things, we watch them happen, share the experience—of Streisand swooning over him (funny, touching, sad), chasing him, getting him, losing him, calling him back in a profoundly moving telephone sequence, then finally losing him for good—though they still love each other. The film's best moments are those days the married couple spend together in a beach house, each making those necessary adjustments that marriage and commitment require.

The movie is, in effect, a record of Redford giving one of the best performances of his career—playing himself—while Streisand does an acting job that consolidates her position as the foremost American movie actress of her generation.

October 21, 1973

Miss Left and Mr. Right

Paul D. Zimmerman

The Way We Were begins as the classic American fable of the ugly ethnic who wins the Protestant prince. With Barbra Streisand and Robert Redford as the culture-crossed couple, it couldn't be otherwise: Streisand, the spectacularly plain Jewish girl whose stardom serves as surrogate for the daydreams of millions of ordinary girls; Redford, a handsome, golden hero in the grand Hollywood tradition. This is one of a vanishing breed of movies in which the stars, by their very presence, alter the story. In a way, they *are* the story.

As long as director Sydney Pollack and screenwriter Arthur Laurents keep mining the mythic properties of their scenario, this tale of the Young Communist League Cinderella who marries the orthodox American hero-prince delivers the generous, glossy pleasures of pulp fiction. Redford's Hubbell Gardner and Streisand's Katie Morosky are the kind of ripe, overdrawn figures from popular novels that allow room for great stars to move around in. But they are poor vehicles for social commentary, and, when Pollack and Laurents push them into the era of Hollywood blacklisting, the film falls to pieces.

When Katie first meets Hubbell at college in the late thirties, she is a poodle-haired leftist trying to change a world that has barred her from its highest reaches. He accepts that same world because it has paid off for him. Like most revolutionaries, she is committed, humorless, inflexible, earnest. He is detached, skeptical, accommodating, easygoing. In one sense, their romance puts adjustment itself on trial.

Hubbell is a novelist, a proposition we can never entirely buy because he seems so perfectly adjusted to his surroundings. What in the world can he write about? It is Katie who should be the writer; instead, she knocks herself out goading the laziness out of him, because she believes in his talent even if he doesn't. She is content to win by losing—their first love-making happens during the war when he is on Navy leave and is too pie-eyed to know who he is sleeping with. She studies "Protestant cookery" to please his palate; once, when they quarrel, she begs him in tears to return to her as a "best friend"—a slow tour de force of weeping that character-izes Pollack's willingness to provide his stars with acres of acting room.

Once Katie wins Hubbell in marriage (and that's the only way to put it), the stars and their myth have played themselves out. Perhaps sensing this, Pollack and Laurents rush through the final chapters, mostly by leaving them out. One moment, Hollywood has bought Hubbell's novel. An instant later, Hubbell is busy declaring "I'm not a novelist. I like to think of myself as a screenwriter," in what must be history's fastest sellout. Despite the smug, patronizing tolerance with which the film treats Katie's radi-calism, the characters have been delicately calibrated—Katie's doctrinaire political passion balanced by Hubbell's colorless common sense. Suddenly, this equipoise veers drastically in Katie's favor. Hubbell is co-opted by the system. Hubbell is caught sleeping with an old girlfriend. Hubbell stands for neutrality in the struggle to support the blacklisted Hollywood writers. Hubbell is the real loser when the marriage dissolves.

Pollack and Laurents are so busy working on the dubious proposition that politics can kill a good marriage that they barely have time to establish the political atmosphere that is meant as a catalyst to the connubial collapse, sketching it in hurriedly in bits of cocktail gossip and snippets of radio reports and newspaper headlines. Meanwhile, we watch this luxurious vehicle founder and finally crack apart. Superb performances by Redford and Streisand are not enough to sustain our hopes for the kind of glamorous, big-star romance that Hollywood rarely attempts anymore.

October 22, 1973

SAVE THE TIGER
The Good Life Crumbles

Charles Champlin

In recent years a tight handful of films, each markedly different from the others, has made strong impressions on American audiences, because, like lightning rods catching thunderbolts out of the uneasy air, they have isolated and given voice to ideas, questionings, anxieties that were abroad in the society and waiting to be said.

The Graduate, farcically particularizing a new generation's restless dissatisfaction with the material goals of the parent generation, was one of those films. Another was *Easy Rider* with its inchoate but impassioned look at the hatreds crevassing the country but also with its dawning perception that you can't opt out of all responsibility. *Five Easy Pieces* and its dropped-out hero, who seems to prefer not trying to trying and failing, caught a larger, later uncertainty about goals. On the other side, part of the success of *Love Story* can be explained by its wistful insistence, endorsed by its audiences, that we are really still romantic idealists at heart.

To this small company of movies which have found their time can now be added Steve Shagan's *Save the Tiger*, a profoundly unsettling portrait of an early middle-age American businessman, simultaneously compassionate and corrupted, likable and full of self-loathing, moved in a day of crisis to wonder where have all the values gone and what became of the nice guy he was.

In its study of disillusion and the erosion of values, Shagan's story, which he wrote and produced, becomes in a sense an extension of *The Graduate,* brushed with sardonic humor but closer to tragedy. The point of view now belongs to the graduate's father and his contemporaries, whose certitudes about plastics and the good life at poolside have unexpectedly and bafflingly crumbled.

Harry Stoner grew up on the 1939 Brooklyn Dodgers and Bunny Berigan, radio and the movies and the great boxers. He was drafted and fought at Anzio and would have said he did well. He came back confidently to pursue the American dream of the good life.

When we meet him he has made it, at a price. He lives in Beverly Hills splendor and is partner in a dress firm in the Los Angeles garment district.

It costs him, he reckons, $250 a day to get out of bed. The firm has had a catastrophic season; his partner has had to cook its books to stay afloat. The nice guy from Anzio pimps for important buyers and is negotiating with an arsonist for insurance money to get the firm into one more season.

Unattractive, all of it. What gives the film its power and its disturbing ability to touch those a world away from Stoner's demoralized life is the extraordinarily affecting and sensitive portrayal of Stoner by Jack Lemmon.

It is much the best thing Lemmon has ever done, which is saying a great deal if you remember only *The Apartment* and *Days of Wine and Roses.* The tenderness, the intelligence, the likability, the distraught innocence which have been denied to Lemmon in *The Out-of-Towners* and *Avanti!* and were supplanted by an unattractive and abrasive clangor are all restored here and they are crucial. It is not necessary, not possible, to admire the man Harry Stoner has become, but it is urgent to understand him and to realize that his disillusion and his captivity within aspirations that once seemed reasonable and even admirable are not his alone.

"If we were making missiles and got in this kind of trouble," says his partner, played with dour and sympathetic naturalism by Jack Gilford, "the government would write us a check. But we make dresses."

Everybody fiddles with taxes; computers have removed the human element and the possibility of compassion from everyday life. The virtues and the values begin to go, and how does a man know where to stop the changed world and get off, assuming he can? The partner stops at falsifying the books (only the impersonal government is victimized). Lemmon stops at borrowing from the mob, although that's self-preservation, not morality.

The only refuge for Harry is the past, the seemingly simpler past of Harry Walker and Cookie Lavagetto, Marcel Cerdan and the Goodman Sextet. The recollected past gives the movie its texture and its sadness, because the past fails as refuge and its echoes merely confirm Harry's awareness of irretrievable loss.

John Avildsen, who directed *Joe*, was the director here, and he again demonstrates his considerable ability to get social reality on film. *Save the Tiger* was shot in sequence and entirely on locations: in a garment loft, a Malibu beachhouse, a Chinatown restaurant, in a downtown sexploitation house where Harry talks terms with the cool arsonist ("It's technology, not morality, boy"). The difference is that *Save the Tiger* is as quiet and internalized as *Joe* was shocking and melodramatic.

Shagan, translating a state of mind and a point of view into story terms, has built his structure carefully and the devices sometimes reveal themselves as devices. A long coincidence brings Lemmon together twice with a hitchhiking hippie chick (Laurie Heineman) who is too neatly prototypical of a later generation lost in its own way without ever having had, as Shagan says, the chance to be innocent. What saves the sequence is that it achieves its ends of illuminating more of the Stoner character and of the beguiling Miss Heineman's times.

Similarly, an old Jewish pattern-cutter in the factory is almost too neatly symbolic of a still older generation which has held on to traditional, simpler values of love and work. The sequence comes off, again, because of the careful and affecting playing of Lemmon and William Hansen as the old man.

The delicate problem of avoiding any inference of anti-Semitism Shagan has handled, effectively, by his considered balancing of Gilford's indignant rectitude against Lemmon's reluctant criminality and again by the inclusion of the chiding old cutter.

It remains possible to argue that Shagan's indictment of the times is too harsh and that the American middle class does not universally share Harry Stoner's disenchantment nor his corrupted willingness to hang on to what he has by any means. And yet Harry's litany of laments about a world whose values have been misplaced and whose capacity for human contact has been grievously reduced is all too obviously not his alone.

At that, if it seems too late for Stoner to reassess his own aspirations and set some new rules for his life, Shagan suggests that there is still hope for a younger generation who can learn from both the past and the present without being captives of limited goals, or the lack of any goals.

Like the earlier touchstone films, *Save the Tiger* is a small and intensely personal work, carrying the concerns of Shagan (who fought for two years to get it financed), Lemmon (who did it for no salary) and Avildsen (whose sympathetic response to the material is evident in every frame).

The performances are uniformly stunning, centering inevitably on Lemmon's and Gilford's but including as well Miss Heineman in the difficult role of the girl, Norman Burton as the lecherous visiting buyer, Patricia Smith as Lemmon's weary wife, Thayer David as the confident arsonist, and William Hansen as the old man.

Harvey Jason is the firm's waspish designer and Lara Parker is a call girl and both take their roles beyond the cliches.

Marvin Hamlisch's excellent score also incorporates a good deal of actual big band era sounds, and Berigan's "I Can't Get Started," which closes the film, is not less than heartbreaking.

Ed Feldman was executive producer.

In the force and conviction of its social commentary, *Save the Tiger* stands alone among current American films. My guess is that we will see no more controversial movie this year, for like it or not, Shagan has caught some currents from the present uneasy air.

February 11, 1973

William S. Pechter

From the moment Harry Stoner wakes up in his palatial house, and, via his remote controls, turns on his television set to hear in rapid succession news of Vietnam, of a freeway accident (or was it a building collapse?), the smog report, and a dog-food commercial, you know it's going to be another bad day in Los Angeles, America. As it happens, this will be the day (give or take a few hours) in which Harry will decide to commit arson on one of his factories (because declaring bankruptcy of his ladies' sportswear business would reveal that the previous year he'd done "a ballet with the books"), and veer further toward a nervous breakdown and complete withdrawal into some simpler past. Along the way, he'll pimp for a buyer, visit a porno theater, sleep with a hippie, and generally wonder what this country is coming to.

Spiritually, in *Save the Tiger*, we are in Arthur Miller country, from the sludgelike prose and sledgehammer subtlety to the pulpy abstractions and earnest tone of high moral seriousness. The telltale signs abound. Despite his big house and remote controls, Harry is unhappy; he has built his life on the evanescent standards of commercial enterprise, while the old-world cutter in his shop, though poor, remains happy because he "has his craft." Attempting to overcome his partner's objections to the act of arson, Harry speaks of a country in which "there are no rules anymore, only referees," and declares, "If we were making missiles and flat on our back, we'd get a certified check from Congress in the morning." (Well, yes, one may assent, but the man who will commit arson to cover up his previous juggling of his books will find his rationalization for doing so, another if not that one.) No point is made that's not italicized and underlined. In one scene, with a hint at nuances of perverted pleasures beyond human ken, a prostitute unpacks her wares, among them a variety of oils including baby oil, olive oil, and just about every other kind of oil except banana oil, which nevertheless is elsewhere to be found in profusion throughout the film.

And yet, while I have no doubt that *Save the Tiger* is a bad movie (though Jack Lemmon, after a shaky start and despite a few impossible scenes, does manage to break out of the comic marionette mold he's adopted for so many years), its disaffection does finally generate a crude power. As in *Death of a Salesman,* though the superstructure of social criticism (the we-are-all-salesmen metaphor, the business about being "well-liked") may totter, beneath it is some kind of bedrock (the failures we've all experienced between fathers and sons); so, too, is *Save the Tiger* propped up by an idea which, however bad, is surprisingly forceful. A few years ago, I was addicted to Rod Serling's television series, *The Twilight Zone,* and noticed in it the recurrence of a theme which, whether developed by Serling or one of the program's other writers, was always treated with an intensity of feeling far in excess of the series' norm: the appeal of a simpler past, of a lost innocence. In one of the shows, a man embroiled in the rat race of modern-day toy designing returns to his childhood neighborhood to find it has remained unchanged and its inhabitants haven't aged; in another, an actor, harried by the clamorous importunings of agents and his alimony-hungry ex-wife, literally escapes into the happy family life depicted in the movie in which he's acting; in yet another, an ulcerous advertising executive, dozing on his commuter run to Connecticut, continually dreams of the train stopping at an idyllic, turn-of-the-century small town, redolent of county-fair Americana, and one day he actually disembarks there.

In *Save the Tiger,* as the accumulating complexities of his present life urgently press in on him, Harry Stoner increasingly turns toward thoughts of a happier time in a happier land: when everyone was united in the desire to defeat Hitler, baseball was played on dirt rather than plastic, one could listen to Benny Goodman instead of rock, and everywhere there was "craft," quality, and people doing what was honest and right. What is wrong with this idea, so dear to television and movie writers and producers (and the writer of *Save the Tiger* is its producer), is not that it has no validity, but that its focus is so self-indulgently misplaced. One responds to the idea, and I do: the feeling of a loss of innocence is an experience vaguely shared by everyone, and, even if one knows better, it's easy to sentimentalize old times. But it's not the times, or a country, that are any more or less corrupt; the innocence lost is not America's but one's own. Harry Stoner dreams of years gone by in a better America when he wouldn't have to set fire to his factory. But this year Harry Stoner burns down a factory, because last year he did a ballet with his books.

May 1973

PAT GARRETT AND BILLY THE KID
Outlaw Blues

Jay Cocks

It is a story that has been told many times over: how Pat Garrett hunted and shot down Billy the Kid, who was his friend. It was never told so strangely, however, with such a weird, stern sense of beauty and of fate, as it is here by Sam Peckinpah. He is one of the most prodigious of all American filmmakers, and perhaps, as well, one of the most prodigal.

Peckinpah and the scenarist Rudolph Wurlitzer (*Two Lane Blacktop*) transform Garrett and the Kid into the kind of uneasy antagonists who test and challenge each other with every inflection. Like Randolph Scott and Joel McCrea in *Ride the High Country,* like William Holden and Robert Ryan in *The Wild Bunch,* Garrett and the Kid have become estranged by ungovernable coincidence, made enemies by the casual intervention of circumstances. Billy (Kris Kristofferson) had his chance at settling down, building a respectable life working for the cattle interests. He chose instead to run free. Garrett (James Coburn), older, feeling threatened by age, takes a lawman's job. The marshal's badge means he is to protect everyone in the territory, but the men who pinned it on him—the ranchers and the politicians in Santa Fe—are really the ones he serves. It is their star, their job, and they want Billy out of the way. Garrett rides down to Old Fort Sumner to give him the warning and a few days' head start. "The electorate," he tells Billy, "wants you out of the country," but Billy isn't fooled. He makes an ironic toast: "Sheriff Pat Garrett sold out to the Santa Fe ring. How's it feel?" "It feels," Garrett tells him, with unmistakable finality, "like times have changed."

Billy doesn't run very far or especially fast, and Garrett, true to his word, brings him in. But it is almost as if the two are living through some elaborate ritual of myth. "You're in poor company, Pat"—Billy smiles at Garrett, who grins back. "Yeah. I'm alive, though." "So am I," says Billy, still smiling. Garrett leaves Billy in jail, guarded by a couple of deputies, while he goes off to collect some taxes. Billy, seeing his chance—maybe even given it outright by Garrett—makes his escape. For the next couple of months, Garrett tracks him. He gives Billy as much time and distance as he can, but keeps closing on him all the same. Garrett stalks him, circles him. Billy rides for Mexico, but turns around, surrendering to inevitability and paying his price.

It is never clear enough exactly why Billy does go back. When he does, though, the movie wobbles and goes lame. Some men working for Chisholm, the cattle baron, have tortured a Mexican friend of Billy's who, dying in his arms, murmurs existential folk wisdom like "You will go back. You will say it is because they kill me. But it is because you are afraid to change." It's all fudging, of course, last-minute editorializing to get over a rough transition. It is careless and clumsy, but the real reason it doesn't work is that Billy's relationship to and affection for the Mexican has only been dealt with briefly once before. Peckinpah and Wurlitzer are on much surer ground dealing with the dubious morality of Garrett's decision to hunt Billy. In previous Peckinpah films, the reasons for similar actions are stated and accepted, if not honored. Here they are closely questioned. Garrett, unlike Peckinpah's other protagonists in *High Country* and *Wild Bunch*, is no hero, however reluctant. As played, superbly, by Coburn, he is a dead-eyed sadist, a man who can slither neatly from one moral position to another. "It's just a way of staying alive," he says at one point. "Don't matter what side you're on. You're always right."

There is a severe irony in all of this, because Pat Garrett was killed some twenty years later by the same Santa Fe cattle interests who hired him to hunt Billy down. This irony frames the film. At least, it framed Peckinpah's original version of the film, which has been altered, shortened, and generally abused by MGM, a company which treats filmmakers with the same delicacy and understanding that the Inquisition reserved for infidels. Garrett's killing of the Kid was only a moment on the way to his own death; he made Billy a futile hostage to fortune. This dimension is almost entirely lost because MGM decided to remove the scene of Garrett's death, which originally began the film.

There have been other major excisions: a scene between Garrett and his Mexican wife in which his ruthlessness was first revealed; a long, crazy, and very funny interlude at a trading post, featuring such reliable character actors as Elisha Cook, Jr., and Dub Taylor; and a crucially important scene between Garrett and John Chisholm, the cattle baron (played by Barry Sullivan), in which Garrett's and Billy's friendship was more strongly delineated, and in which their history of working for Chisholm was more clearly defined. In all, 16 minutes have been excised. Peckinpah, who has a history of running afoul of studio executives, calls it "my worst experience since *Major Dundee*," from which approximately one quarter of the running time was removed.

The changes ordered up by the studio—according to Peckinpah, by MGM President James Aubrey and Production Vice-President Daniel Melnick—are mostly stupid, and certainly substantial, but they are not disastrous. Even in the maimed state in which it has been released, *Pat Garrett and Billy the Kid* is much the richest, most exciting American film so far this year, a cause both for rejoicing as well as regret. There are moments and whole sequences here that stand among the best work Peckinpah has ever achieved: a raft moving down a muddy river, a ragged family huddled on board, watching a grizzled man standing near the edge taking shots at a bottle with an old rifle; a slow, merciless humiliation in a trading post, with Garrett relishing the violence he quietly deals out; the final meeting of Garrett and Billy back at Old Fort Sumner, at night, with men moving like apparitions and dust blowing like a rasping fog. The whole film has a parched, eerie splendor that no one could really destroy. The cast is sometimes confusingly large but uniformly excellent, featuring—besides Coburn and the exceptional Kris Kristofferson—Jason Robards, Richard Jaeckel, Slim Pickens, Chill Wills, R. G. Armstrong, Katy Jurado, Luke Askew, Richard Bright; and Bob Dylan, who furnished the music and plays a character named Alias ("Alias what?" "Alias anything you please"). Dylan is quirkish, and appropriately enigmatic, shifting on his feet, shrugging and smiling by twitching the corners of his mouth, always threatening to go a little out of control. He always manages to keep control, though. Peckinpah lost his, courtesy of the executives at MGM. You're in poor company, Sam.

June 11, 1973

Michael Korda

I don't myself believe that your average adult can be corrupted by a movie, not one about sex, at any rate, but due to the vagaries of our laws and national morality it is possible for children to accompany their parents or other adults to see *Pat Garrett and Billy the Kid*, and that, I submit, is truly an obscene notion. Most of the audience in Westwood consisted of UCLA students, who treated each act of violence as a piece of high camp, a kind of stylized ritual like the mayhem in Kung Fu movies. I am not at all sure that this was the case with the children in the audience, who were mistakenly concluding, if anything, that it's all right to laugh when a man gets his guts blown out. In Peckinpah's movies, the violence is both endemic and universal: horses are shot or crippled; the hero practices his marksmanship on live chickens by shooting their heads off. A child can be forgiven for assuming that it's heroic to kill people and good sport to be cruel to animals. Everything in Peckinpah's world is bloody and cruel, except for his women, who are always soft, compliant, forgiving, and sexually attracted to the most effective killer. The proposition is a simple yet revolutionary one: Men love killing, women love and give themselves to men who kill, the hero is the man who kills fastest, and he gets the prettiest women. We are a long way here from Gene Autry, Tom Mix, and The Lone Ranger, but of course equally far from the real West, where killers were looked upon as social nuisances, not heroes. Peckinpah would like us to believe that Billy the Kid was a handsome Robin Hood, beloved by the poor and hated by the rich cattlemen, but in fact the Kid was a squinty-eyed, runty, murderous and cowardly psychopath who was born, of all places, in a New York tenement. Violence has its own radical chic, and Peckinpah has enlisted some major talents for this excursion into the history of the Old West as seen through the eyes of the Marquis de Sade: Kris Kristofferson, the Nashville answer to Bob Dylan, plays the Kid with unlikely charm, as if an A&R man from Columbia Records were waiting for him around the next arroyo instead of Bob Dylan himself, who plays the Kid's mumbling, knife-throwing sidekick, or James Coburn, who plays the Kid's ex-friend and nemesis, Sheriff Pat Garrett. The script is by Rudolph Wurlitzer, a minor novelist specializing in visions of violence, who has found in Peckinpah perhaps the only person who shares his vision of violence as a kind of beauty, an intellectual attitude that comes easily to those who have forgotten or never known what the true face of violence is.

I'll grant Peckinpah a stunning visual sense, but beyond that any excitement in his film consists of waiting to see how and in what new way he will handle the bloodshed. When his characters are shot, great gouts of blood spray out, explosions of gore flash like firecrackers. In fact, on the rare occasions when I have seen people shot, nothing much happened that was visually exciting. But then Peckinpah's movie is to real violence and death what Radio City Music Hall's Easter pageant is to the crucifixion. It is the ultimate obscenity, because it corrupts in the name of entertainment, and because we allow children to see it and congratulate ourselves because they can't after all see movies like *Deep Throat*.

June 1973

THE LAST AMERICAN HERO

Roger Greenspun

Lamont Johnson's *The Last American Hero* has a source in an *Esquire* article Tom Wolfe wrote several years ago about a stock-car racer and automobile customizer named Junior Johnson. The source isn't very close, however, and the film, with its hero, Junior Jackson (Jeff Bridges), hasn't too much to do with the subject of Wolfe's famous article. It hasn't too much to do with the mystique of automobile racing either—though it is full of automobiles and races. It does have to do with human relations, with the choice between a private and a public life, with the meaning of imprisonment, with the ways in which a souped-up hot rod is like a Carolina moonshiner's still.

Junior's dad (Art Lund) makes the moonshine. Really committed to his trade, by now almost friends with the revenue agent who keeps tossing him in jail, he is a man of great character and gentle sadness whose way of life is pushing him into an extreme of privacy literally hidden down inside his native earth. Junior's spirit of independence, equally fierce, has no such luck. In a sense he must rise, taking nothing with him—not his friends, not even his own car—as success encloses him in its own forms of isolation.

The outline of this progress is conventional. But the terms developed for it in *The Last American Hero* are serious and rich and sometimes very beautiful.

Strictly for its car racing, the film isn't so exciting. But you might say the same for Howard Hawks's stock-car movie, *Red Line 7000* (1965), which from this distance begins to look like one of the important films of the last decade. But Hawks did care about the world of the drivers and their women, and he used car racing to express the stoical pessimism typical of his later work. Johnson withdraws from all that to concentrate on individual solutions and moments of personal exploration. In this he is aided by stunning performances from Bridges, from Lund, from Geraldine Fitzgerald as Junior's mother, from Ed Lauter as the factory-team manager to whom Junior must finally sell himself, from Valerie Perrine as the girl for Junior—and for any other driver in the circuit.

Miss Perrine—known only, and rather spectacularly, for her performance in *Slaughterhouse Five*—has an interesting role. Quite obviously cast as the fickle prize of fame, she becomes humanly more appealing as she is revealed to be more tawdry, more helplessly disloyal—to just about everybody, even herself. *The Last American Hero* is a film of many regrets but no great bitterness. And its freedom from easy ironies and from any kind of condescension is one clue to its value.

The movies of Lamont Johnson (*The McKenzie Break, The Groundstar Conspiracy*, etc.) continue to impress me for their intelligence, their good B-movie toughness, their care and grace in performance.

July 28, 1973

BLUME IN LOVE

Roger Ebert

Paul Mazursky's *Blume in Love* is the best American movie so far this year—the best movie this year, in fact, after *Cries and Whispers* and *Last Tango in Paris*. And that's not easy to pull off when your material isn't an agonizing confrontation with life and death, but just a busted-up Southern California marriage.

The marriage belonged to Blume, divorce lawyer, and his wife Nina, a social worker. It busted up all of a sudden one weekday afternoon when Nina came home with a cold and found Blume in bed with his secretary. Why, you may ask (Blume certainly does), could his wife not forgive this indiscretion—especially as Blume is madly in love with Nina and must have her back or die? ("And I don't want to die," he reasons, "so I have to get her back.")

Well, maybe Nina was sort of halfway ready for the marriage to end. She's into her own brand of self-improvement and women's lib, and isn't sure she approves of marriage anymore. She takes up with an out-of-work (for 12 years) musician who lives in a VW truck with his dreams. She gets into yoga and learns to play the guitar and to rely on herself instead of men.

Little good that does Blume, whose love for her becomes a consuming passion. It is complicated by the fact that he gets to like the musician, too: thinks, in fact, that the bearded Elmo is the nicest man he has ever met. Blume even goes so far as to start a beard himself. But nothing will work for him, because of the fact he refuses to accept: Nina simply does not love him anymore. Does not. Period. Blume is driven into a frenzy of love, desire, frustration.

You see what I mean. This material, so far, doesn't exactly sound like the stuff of a great film. It sounds more like the brainy, funny dissections of California dreamin' that Mazursky carried out in his three previous films: *I Love You, Alice B. Toklas; Bob & Carol & Ted & Alice;* and *Alex in Wonderland.* Those were all fine films—Mazursky is one of the best directors of comedy in Hollywood today—but they were all more concerned with the laugh than with reality.

With *Blume in Love,* however, he seems to have pulled off what everybody is always hoping for from Neil Simon: a comedy that transcends its funny moments, that realizes we laugh so we may not cry and that finally is about real people with real desperations. He's done that in a number of scenes, and yet somehow even during the movie's gloomiest moments he keeps some sort of hope alive.

That's probably because Blume is played by the charming George Segal, who here more than ever before gives promise of becoming the first star since Cary Grant to be able to give even the grimmest scenes a light touch. Segal seems intrinsically optimistic. No matter what Nina says, he cannot quite give up on her, because he knows she must eventually love him again—because he loves her.

He carries this hope with him on a trip to Venice, which is where the film opens; she's asked him to go away somewhere for a couple of weeks, while she thinks. They had their first and second honeymoons in Venice, but now Blume wanders through Piazza San Marco in the autumn, stranded with a few other lonely tourists looking for love. The story is told in flashbacks from Venice, and it ends there. It ends with a note so unashamedly romantic that Mazursky gets away with *Tristan and Isolde* as his soundtrack music. He's right. The ending would not be believable at all, except as hyperbole.

Nina—thin, earnest, determined to do the right thing and no longer be mastered by mere emotion—is played with a very complex charm by Susan Anspach. We have to like her even though she doesn't like Blume, whom we're cheering for. We do, and we like her boyfriend as much as Blume does. The itinerant musician is played by Kris Kristofferson, who gives evidence once again that he has a real acting talent. He was excellent in the neglected *Cisco Pike,* and here he's more than that—particularly in the scene where he hits Segal and then bursts into tears, and in the scene where he tells Segal he's hitting the road again.

Blume in Love (which, somewhat to the astonishment of everyone, is doing land-office business) has a quality that's hard to analyze but impossible to miss: It sets up an intimate rapport with its audiences. In the theater where I saw it (and where it set a new house record), the audience was alive, responsive, and even relieved, in a way, to be given an intelligent adult movie instead of banal "sophistication." I've felt this electricity in audiences before, with movies like *The Graduate, Bonnie and Clyde* and *Z.* Now *Blume in Love* draws it, and deserves it.

July 10, 1973

William S. Pechter

"Of course, I've nothing against adultery; some of my best friends are adulterers," one may soon find oneself saying of yet another oppressed minority demanding its due. Times have changed; one needs to be broadminded. And the movies, where the wages of fooling around were once likely to prove fatal, have done their best to keep up, their changing scruples reflected in one recent movie's title: *I Could Never Have Sex with Any Man Who Has So Little Regard for My Husband.* Or as George Segal remarks to Glenda Jackson in *A Touch of Class,* one of two recent films in which he portrays a participant in an extramarital affair, "I've never been unfaithful to my wife [while we're] in the same city."

In the other of these films, *Blume in Love,* Segal's philandering does have serious consequences: not death, but divorce (or to put it precisely in California legal parlance, "dissolution of marriage"). This is serious not because of divorce itself—like adultery, divorce has long since been divested of dramatic shock in our movies as in our culture—but because Stephen Blume, the character Segal plays, loves his wife, Nina, or at least thinks he does. In any case, he's obsessed with winning her back, and his efforts to do so constitute the film's story.

Blume is, in fact, an affluent divorce lawyer in Los Angeles, a locale in which the film's writer-director, Paul Mazursky, has specialized to the point of its being his subject. Mazursky's two earlier films as a director were *Alex in Wonderland* and *Bob & Carol & Ted & Alice,* both written in collaboration with Larry Tucker, with whom he had previously collaborated on the script of *I Love You, Alice B. Toklas* for another director. (Before entering films, the two had been involved with the Second City improvisational theater company.) There's an echo in *Blume in Love* of the scene in *I Love You, Alice B. Toklas* in which two men sit in an outdoor café, and one of them anguishedly asks, "Where do they come from?" as they watch the endless numbers of long-haired, mini-skirted girls stroll past, a scene which memorably captured the bewilderment and frustration of those the so-called "sexual revolution" had passed by. The only explicit explanation we are given for Blume's infidelity (which, at the time his wife catches him, consists of a single afternoon home early from the office with his lush black secretary) is his exclamation to his law partner that ". . . you see it there, everywhere . . . no brassieres. . . ."

Fragmentary as this may be, it's at least more of an explanation than we're given for Nina's bitterly intransigent refusal of any reconciliation, and one searches the glimpses that we see in flashback of their six-year marriage (ended before the film begins) for some fuller understanding which doesn't really come. Facts are there, but somehow don't add up. Their meeting at a benefit dance for the striking Delano farmworkers. First and second honeymoons in Venice. He at his job, and she at hers as a worker for the Venice (California) Department of Welfare. Regular sessions (at least by her) on the couch. Some dabbling in such California-isms as encounter groups and yoga. His sarcasm after their attendance at a class in the latter in fact occasions what is probably the most fully articulated expression of the anger which one senses seething within her and which his infidelity seems more to "legitimize" than to provoke. He's "always putting people down," she berates him; they have "everything anybody could want," and still they're "both miserable." When he protests he's not miserable, she belligerently declares, "We're not committed!" "I don't need a guilt trip about money on top of everything else!" he tells her. "You're full of shit, just like the rest of America!" she replies.

Cut loose from the moorings of their marriage, the two drift into new liaisons (he with Arlene, a divorcée friend of theirs, she with Elmo, an unemployed hippie musician whom she meets when he applies for welfare) across a Los Angeles setting, filled with unmoored people, which Mazursky explores with an attentiveness to cultural forms approaching that of an ethnographer investigating some hitherto undiscovered society. It's a society in which all communication is colored by the jargon of the "human-potential" movement. Blume and Arlene openly discuss their "using" each other, and she remarks of his ex-wife, "She's the only girl I know who doesn't have any ego hangups. She's very giving." Nina, donning love-beads with her easygoing musician, tells Blume, "I want to be free and open and clear in all my relationships," and, when he asks if she hates him, replies, "I don't have time for that," even as she's obviously still choked by it. Elmo, the mellow, "together" musician with his "good vibes" is the model aspired to, but though Blume and Nina desperately try to sing along with him they are hopelessly mired in their "uptight" feelings (at one point, she plays her guitar and sings "You've Got a Friend" at the very moment she's rejecting Blume's clumsy attempts at rapprochement). And permeating all is the omnipresent authority of the "shrink," the guru-sphinx occasionally dispensing some pseudo wisdom but to be depended on mainly for the refrain of "We'll discuss it on Thursday." Between sessions, the characters flit hopefully from one panacea to the next: singles bars, swinging, communes, etc. In this world, it's the parents who are dropouts and runaways, their kids the ones who have to send them money.

And perhaps what's most remarkable about Mazursky's observation of that world is its freedom from malice or ridicule. These people may behave ridiculously, but they aren't ridiculed; we are too aware of their vulnerability for that. In part, this owes to the performances, but surely these, too, are partly attributable to Marzursky, given that Segal has never been better (one has only to compare his frenetic, mechanical work in *A Touch of Class*) and that scarcely a trace of the tremendously appealing personality Kris Kristofferson (playing Elmo) reveals here was visible in his two earlier films. (Much as he seemed miscast in *Pat Garrett and Billy the Kid*, Peckinpah must surely have been asleep at the wheel to have got so little out of him.) But though Susan Anspach as Nina, Marsha Mason as Arlene, and Shelley Winters as one of Blume's clients are also excellent, the film's generosity of feeling goes beyond performance to characterization. The portrait of a psychiatrist (played by an actual psychiatrist) in *Bob & Carol & Ted & Alice* is probably as vitriolic as any that recent movies have given us, but the psychiatrist in *Blume in Love*, if not exactly evoked with affection, is nevertheless seen chiefly from the aspect of his pathetic helplessness. "Sometimes it doesn't help. Sometimes it helps," he replies to Blume's doubts about the efficacy of psychotherapy; "Until we find something better, what else is there to do?" Working with the materials common to all his films, Maursky has this time got more deeply into those materials than ever before; he's got all the way down to the pain.

And yet, though *Blume in Love* is Mazursky's most assured and fleshed-out film by far, something vital is missing from it, something more important to the movie than the misfirings of its would-be aphoristic wit at the beginning, or its dramatically weak ending (a weakness the endings of all of Mazursky's films have shared) of Blume's and Nina's reconciliation. We believe in Blume's obsession with regaining his wife, but we don't understand it; the suggestions that he (and she) may need their emotional violence for his (and her) sexual satisfaction remain only suggestions. (After his divorce, Blume goes through an episode of impotence dramatically cured when he engages in sexual relations while the television is tuned to scenes of combat, and his reconciliation with Nina takes place only after he rapes her and she becomes pregnant.) And though we believe in Nina's anger, we don't understand that either; if in fact it stems from a liberal's guilty conscience (as her outburst about America might suggest) or from a nascent feminism of which there are hints, then surely her return to their life together ought to be seen as a kind of defeat rather than the heart-warming hokum it seems here. And that reconciliation itself is something we neither understand nor believe in; and, despite the film's attempt to keep tongue in cheek as a nine-months' pregnant Nina waddles into Blume's arms across the Piazza San Marco while the orchestra plays the "Liebestod" from *Tristan and Isolde*, the result is as flagrant a serving of *schmaltz* as any we've had since Joan Crawford sacrificed herself for love of John Garfield while he fiddled the very same music in the 1947 *Humoresque*.

Or to bring the comparison up to date, it's as dishonest as George Segal ending his affair with Glenda Jackson in *A Touch of Class* in the name of his wife and children, characters for whom, throughout the film, he's demonstrated no hint of fondness, if not actual distaste, and who are depicted as no more than lifeless icons of middle-class respectability. Of course, in *A Touch of Class*, which is just machine-tooled junk, this is only one dishonesty among many; long before its pious embrace of domesticity, the film has falsified the reality of the adulterous affair by glossing over such details as the apparent accessibility to Miss Jackson (who plays a divorcée with children) of instantaneously available, marathon baby-sitting, and the seeming ease with which, in stolen moments, the couple convert a slum apartment rented for their meetings into a *House Beautiful* showplace. In a way, compared with *A Touch of Class*, the lack of conviction in *Blume in Love*'s ending could even be considered a form of honesty: the film's admission, despite its reluctance to say so, that, though it can believe in the sexual antagonism of Blume and Nina, it can't convincingly imagine the reality of their happy marriage, and perhaps even, by extension, of happy marriage itself. It seems to know (as we had better know) that, if we want to believe and to continue to believe in the viability of marriage, we're going to have to imagine something more compelling than moribund obligations, pregnancies, the "Liebestod" and these films' other variations on string and chewing gum with which to hold our marriages together.

November 1973

Odd Coupling, Strained Interlude

Molly Haskell

The star casting of the old days had certain advantages. If you saw a close-up of Katharine Hepburn and Charles Boyer, or Ingrid Bergman and Cary Grant, you felt they belonged together by divine mandate, by the strength of the feelings you had for them as well as theirs for each other. You willed their coming together and helped to charge the magnetic field of their attraction. This movement toward the final embrace gained impetus also from social conventions favoring marriage.

But with George Segal and Susan Anspach in *Blume in Love* or George Segal and Glenda Jackson in *A Touch of Class* their "rightness" as lovers is by no means so overwhelming. The burden is no longer, as it was with the gods and goddesses, to devise means to keep them apart for an hour and a half, but to show good reason why they should stay together for five minutes, a difficulty that is compounded by the lack of social pressure to do so. (Or *not* to do so: the marriage that, in *A Touch of Class,* is invoked to end the Segal-Jackson affair, has no moral or social weight, and its use is shabbier than any presumed immorality in the affair itself.) George Segal, whose two love stories opened almost simultaneously in East Side theaters, thus making him the matinee idol of 1973, is hardly in the Valentino–Gable–Boyer tradition. Although he has more sex appeal, he is closer to Jack Lemmon's charming schnook, the born victim in whom the combination of sweetness and stupidity makes too inviting a target to resist. Far from suggesting the heroism or inevitability of love, he is the very embodiment of its improbabilities.

The feelings that Paul Mazursky, writer-director of *Blume in Love,* and Melvin Frank, director and, with Jack Rose, writer of "That Touch of Class," hope to evoke are those of love and of the lover, but with the heroism of one who is not the vanquisher of obstacles like class or economic barriers but merely the survivor of his own limitations. I am not sure that either succeeds, but Mazursky comes so much closer (and skirts greatness and misses it so disappointingly) that it would certainly be my choice in the Segal sweepstakes.

Mazursky, the man who gave us, in part or in toto, *I Love You, Alice B.*

Toklas, Bob & Carol & Ted & Alice, and *Alex in Wonderland,* is here dealing with the same breed of overanalyzed, underintrospective, middle-aged hippies, food-sex-and-everything faddists of California, but he is trying to plunge beyond comic observation into the depths of a *grande passion.* Everything is there but the passion.

The film's assets are those we have come to associate with Mazursky, particularly the instinct for, and direction of, minor characters. Kris Kristofferson, better used than he has ever been, is a gentle, slow-moving, slow-talking musician living off love and welfare, a foil to Segal's over-achieving divorce lawyer. Marsha Mason, an Ellen Burstyn type, is marvelous as the friend-mistress who takes up with Segal after his divorce, especially in the guiltless spontaneity with which she embraces a friend, turns him into a lover, and continues to love him like a friend. Interludes like this, and moments of intimacy between Segal and Anspach, reach out for a directorial vision that is more than just a collection of the sketches Mazursky does so well, but that is not fulfilled by the too carefully framed, artificial memory structure Mazursky has given the film.

Like so many of his characters, Mazursky seems to be looking for some panacea, analysis, yoga, causes, and never knowing when he's got a good thing right before his eyes. His chief asset, and continuing liability, is his sense of irony. But he never manages to fully integrate into it his main character, so that Segal alternates between being its near-victim and its vehicle. He seems a thoroughly credulous dupe of analysis, and when making love to Marsha Mason, honesty bids him report (and insist, when she doesn't break down in tears) that he was thinking of Nina the whole time. And yet when he meets Nina at a farmworkers' union charity garden party, he seems to share the slightly ironic perspective of the camera viewpoint, and certainly his attitude toward Nina's yoga—from the de-risive way the scene is shot, and from Segal's comments afterwards—is profoundly skeptical.

In many ways, Susan Anspach's Nina is the most fascinating charac-ter—not very likable, totally humorless, stubborn with middle-class guilt, evangelical, embracing every new cause in a desperate effort to find herself, closed in, suspicious, and yet curiously touching. I am not sure that Mazursky understands her any more than I do, and yet I have seen her, oh I have seen her, and read her, and been subjected to her rhetoric, without ever quite grasping her faith. I wish Mazursky had gone into her more, or at least explored the dialectics of her relationship with Segal. Is he in love with her humorlessness or is he himself humorless? Does his condescension disappear as she emerges, and how have they changed? On one side passion, on the other hostility, and we are asked to believe that the two suddenly fuse and are reconciled. But how? With any serious confrontation or discussion or alteration, no. By the magic of motherhood! As Nina walks pregnant across the Piazza San Marco to rejoin her husband where several varieties of Love are on display (including an old-man–young-boy, *Death in Venice* parody) her fierce mysteriousness and his unyielding passion are drowned out in a phony reconciliation, an unearned and unwelcome hymn to life.

Perhaps the problem—for drama—is that there are too few conventions to react against; people are floating free in space able to alight whenever and for as long as they wish. Mazursky's framing device and reconciliation are no substitute for a real framework, but at least his characters recognize a kind of personal morality which is beyond the characters of *A Touch of Class*. Glenda Jackson and George Segal are nothing less than expert— Glenda Jackson is particularly delightful in a change-of-pace role—in a situation comedy whose every gag springs from a failure to abide by the "keeping up appearances" ethic that went out with Queen Whatshername. There is also the conflict between Segal as the blustering American and sexual boy scout (which doesn't quite fit) and Jackson as the wry, wise Englishwoman. It is good for a few laughs, particularly his anxious quizzing, after their first bout, if it was "great" for her too. But the antagonism seems to conceal no real affinity, and one wonders what it is that's keeping them together. Then what it is that drives them apart. They try to conjure up a sense of tragedy by a reference to *Brief Encounter*, but it is precisely the sense of limited options that these characters lack. He works, she works (although in good old woman's film fashion she hangs around and waits over her cooling stews while he goes to concerts and the theater with his wife). The sense of duty and resignation that activated the sacrifices in the old tearjerkers may not be our favorite qualities today, but they strike me as a more satisfying reason for ending an affair than those dangers to the constitution represented by eating two gourmet meals and servicing two women in a night.

July 12, 1973

Four

POLITICS

MEMORIES OF UNDERDEVELOPMENT
Thought's Empire

Penelope Gilliatt

Cuba, 1961. The small island that every big power would like to take over. The past Havana, now running out of both the old European grace and the less old American spare parts for refrigerators, cars, radios. The new Havana, looking a little like the razed and rebuilt Warsaw, full of cheer, short of food, replete with fun and progressives. The airport: reactionaries saying goodbye to their relatives and leaving for Miami; babies crying; a man who looks rather like Paul Scofield, and whom we recognize to be the hero of the film that is starting. Not meaning to be callous, probably, he wipes the mark of his departing wife's lipstick off his face after she has kissed him goodbye. The piteousness, the concealed loneliness, the irrevocability of farewells at airports, cloaked in the stabbingly practical hospital bustle of such places. The sequence makes you wonder how people ever leave the loved.

The hero, called Sergio, is marvelously played by Sergio Corrieri. The film is the Castro Cuban *Memories of Underdevelopment,* from a novel by Edmundo Desnoes called *Inconsolable Memories.* It is one of the very finest, subtlest of Latin-American pictures. Sergio's memories are indeed inconsolable. They have a bitter passing sting that seems more European than anything to do with Fidel. Things inflict pain that is nearly unbearable, and then the pain almost goes. On the bus back to his apartment, where he makes a living as a landlord, the hero obviously remembers the parting with an intensity that he can barely manage, but then it makes him yawn. Everything happens to him at a distance. He has a telescope on his terrace. He almost seems to be looking at himself through a telescope, too. He is also a writer, and his prevailing sense of stasis will probably prevent him from ever being a good one. Camus's Stranger was *engagé* by comparison. In a revolutionary society, Sergio has only one role to play psychically. It is the role of witness. The pinched nature of the part he has allotted himself shows in his work (we see a fragment of it, eloquent but

132

tinctured with complaint, rolled into his typewriter), and in his way of saying goodbye to intimates, and in his refusal of spontaneity, and in his comically self-absorbed love affairs. When he is coming away from the airport, his voice, over an image of him sitting in the bus on his way back into Havana, says chillingly about his wife, whom he has seen off to America, "She'll have to go to work there until she finds some dumb guy who'll marry her." He is glad to be on his own and away from all the people who "loved and nagged me to the last moment," as he taps on his typewriter; sometimes his writing voice has the note of Dostoevski or Goncharov being farcical.

He peers through his telescope at Havana. Everything seems the same to him, except that it has the look of a set. So what about the revolution, you can catch him thinking. No imperial eagle? "Where is the dove that Picasso was going to send?" He plays with his own birds, in a cage on the terrace. He has a moment of admitting that the country is falling behind. Havana is no longer the Paris of the Caribbean. To his mind, Cuba is an island collapsing into desuetude and neglect, caught between Russia and America, ruled by hunger, inhabited by people who seem to him to be getting more stupid. His conservative friends' crassness irritates him, until one of them suddenly says something discerning. The conservatism depicted is Freudian. It is an ethic of everyone returning to his own individuality when he wants to get away from the infection of communal misery.

Three times a week, a Baptist maid comes in to clean up the spotless bachelor apartment. Her being a Baptist strikes him as buoyantly sensual. But his self-consciousness always stops him short of real eroticism. People on a diving board make him think of defenseless and almost hairless animals absurdly managing on two legs. He has sex in the head (as the gamekeeper in *Lady Chatterley's Lover* had, for all Lawrence's railing against such a thing). What exerts power over him? Nothing public or revolutionary, certainly. Personal change? He likes an actress for enjoying being able to be someone different, though repeating the difference every evening baffles him: he feels surrounded by lives that are scratched records. Even books look dead. Why didn't he go to New York with Hannah, his German ex-girl friend? he asks himself. She was the best thing that ever happened to him. He wished to be a writer. She believed in him. They wanted to go to New York. What was missing in him? this wonderful, tangled, risky film asks. It doesn't suggest that it might be the impulse of history. Sergio has chosen to stay, to try to merge into Castro's Cuba, and he even amusedly tries to educate a culturally "underdeveloped" girlfriend called Elena by taking her to museums and writers' conferences, but salon

Socialists strike him as irredeemable asses. He agrees with New York's own left-wing writer Jack Gelber, who funnily and seriously says as much at an actual conference in Cuba that is shown in the film.

The director, Tomás Gutiérrez Alea, was born in Havana in 1928. He studied film in Rome and then got involved in revolutionary filmmaking in Batista's time before helping to found the famous Instituto Cubano del Arte y Industria Cinematograficos (ICAIC). This is a beautifully organized picture in its technique, with the most skillful possible use of voice-over, of newsreel footage of the Bay of Pigs, and of leaps backward and forward in time. The note is sardonic and also immensely affectionate toward effort. It is a startling combination in a film made in a revolutionary country, even such a surprising one as Cuba. The film has the lightness of a bird coasting, and a humorous gravity that makes it a piece of work without burden, extending much charity to the stoic hero's hidden distress.

May 26, 1973

STATE OF SIEGE

Notes on Reporting and Fiction

Penelope Gilliatt

PART I

Remarks made to me lately in answers to questions about Latin America, quoted because of the new Constantin Costa-Gavras film, *State of Siege*, which is nominally about Uruguay but concerns the whole continent, and also paternalism, foreign investment, questions of public responsibility, processes of change:

Brazilian Unpublished Novelist of Seventeen, Just Arrived in North America with a Bad Cold: South America needs strong governments, because it is underdeveloped, and we have to wake up from our primitivism. Military governments are strong governments. They are the only ones strong enough to fight big powers who have education.

Uruguayan Laborer: The Tupamaros are our guerrillas. They come from the middle-up class. They come from universities.

Wife of a Millionaire Plastic Surgeon in Venezuela: We're going to leave Caracas. There are no more patients for my husband to treat. The lepers? Oh, the poor don't care what they look like.

Brazilian Intellectual in His Forties: Brazil is the most imperialist country in Latin America.

Argentine Waiter and Shop-Owner: Brazilians have never seen anything, so they expect nothing.

Argentine Café-Owner: I don't think the Peronist government is good, or the best, but I like a change. The military did nothing for Argentina.

Young Argentine Mechanic: Yes, the military did nothing for Argentina. What the Peronists are trying to do is become more Socialist, but they have no plans. The unions are very strong, and the Peronists control the unions. The military asked for key positions in the Peronist government. If it doesn't get them, it may overthrow the government as before, and perhaps that would be civil war, because many members of the military are for Peronism.

Brazilian Boy of Eighteen, Butcher's Assistant: Under the military we have always been very much a colony of the United States, but now the people are enlightened by our boom. Brazil will soon be the biggest country in the world.

Latin-American Economist: The boom is from American investment and American markets.

Brazilian Coffee-Boy: Military governments tend to be leftist. Strong governments are leftist governments.

Young Uruguayan Translator: We are a very small country between Brazil and Argentina, but our guerrillas are serious. They know the truth about charity from big countries. Charity is guns. We would rather have choice.

Scottish Nursing Sister in New York: A.I.D.? Assistance for Industrial Development, isn't it? Of course, in Scotland it means the Artificial Insemination Donor Plan, for cattle and so on. I don't know why a beautiful country like America needs to inseminate anyone. Look at the mess England's made of converting Ireland ever since Cromwell. Wicked waste, all that I.T.T. money.

George Stevens, Jr., Director of the American Film Institute in Washington, about the Cancellation of Showings of State of Siege *at the New Kennedy Center Movie Theater:* I canceled the showings entirely on my own judgment. Nothing to do with losing Nixon's money for the Institute. Though there were a lot of congressmen getting ready to support me on the cancellation. It was a question of taste, not of censorship: this picture rationalizes political assassination. I'm not against pictures people might call anti-American. I took *West Side Story* to Moscow. If it had been *The Ugly American* the Institute staff had picked, that wouldn't have been an ideal choice but one could have lived with it.

Costa-Gavras: There is no connection between the assassination of the Kennedy brothers and the assassination of Dan A. Mitrione in Uruguay by the Tupamaros—Mitrione was the head of the public-safety division of the A.I.D. mission—because there is no evidence of concerted effort and political thinking by an intellectual group in the terrible Kennedy killings. As to what the film shows about A.I.D., my fellow-conspirator is a European— Franco Solinas, the writer of *The Battle of Algiers*—and you know more than we do, because you are in America. It is for all of you here to judge whether we did right in using the facts we have found out about Mitrione when he was supposed to be representing A.I.D.—his knowledge of Brazilian torture cases when he was in Brazil, the F.B.I. card he carried, the Uruguayan police card he had undercover in Uruguay, the police training he went through in North America—and then whether people will understand us when we personify his story in our hero, who is by nature not such a bad man at all. It is not the facts of Mitrione's private life that are reproduced in our character. Only the public ones that we could be sure of by research.

A Colombian Who Drives a Taxi to Earn the Money for College Tuition: If there is a revolution in my country with people like the Tupamaros in it, I will leave New York and join it. And if there isn't one, when I finish my education I will go back and try to make one.

In the thoughtful new political film by Costa-Gavras, the third of a near-trilogy with *Z* and *The Confession*, the character based on the assassinated Mitrione is called Philip Michael Santore. He is played by Yves Montand. Especially since *La Guerre Est Finie*, Montand has contained exactly the nature of a certain kind of jaded, intelligent left-wing European. Hopes unfulfilled by events seem to be lying emptied in the dead air of his head. Montand can make idealism and radicalism look like habits of long ago. Nothing new here, he seems to be feeling, but still nothing to be given up. Life is full of a taste like sour wine, and of sleep lost on the undertaking of missionary tasks with vanished purposes. Whether Montand's quality has anything much in common with Mitrione's seems doubtful, for Montand is such a European. (So was Mitrione, actually, in a pedantic sense that is not to the point: he lived in Italy until he was two.) The experience of watching the film is like looking at the story through a prism. A Frenchman is playing a Latin-American-trained United States immigrant who is in naïve servility to a big proselytizing power that only could be America or a Communist force or an embattled Vatican. The prism does nothing unhelpful; in fact, it puts any propaganda content of the film at a useful distance. This picture is much less dizzying than the earlier ones. But it has the same narrative energy and the same whipping cuts; unless you see a Costa-Gavras picture two or three times, and if you naturally respond to more reposeful filmmaking, it is easy to find things in his movies glib. Terrifying political topics go by with a swiftness that seems meant not to trouble, and to make the problems look soluble. I don't think these bits of crabbiness are deserved, though, especially about the new film. One is simply in the presence of a director and a writer who prepare slowly for production but who value speed on the screen, and who are more interested in the sweeps and causes of events than in character. The Brechtian anti-typecasting of Yves Montand speaks for the director's and the writer's priorities. The chunkily debonair Renato Salvatori here plays no one to swoon about. He is a goonish A.I.D. hireling of forty called Captain López, flawless in hypocrisy, evasive under journalists' catechisms, and impeccably sad at official funerals.

It is August "in Latin America," says the script, but obviously Uruguay, though the place isn't stressed. The weather is wintry. One feels the particular chill of a flunkey nation. Police barriers everywhere. A man is frisked on a bus. The computer voices of messages transmitted on car radios control police movements. A man with the look of a foreigner peers into López's room. Then the corpse of Yves Montand is seen in a hospital. Medical notes are barked out. The body has been brought in from the back of a Cadillac with Montevideo license plates. The car was reported stolen the day before. Parliament votes for a national day of mourning. The Santore whom Montand plays was an A.I.D. "functionary." There is a pompous funeral procession. Courage sometimes prevails in the obsequious circumstances: "It is regrettable that the places reserved for the university president and faculty are empty," says the voice of a TV reporter, unseen. And the archbishop has refrained from giving the funeral oration for a man whom he knows to be another country's hireling. Cameras study the face of the widow. Her husband happened to be a likable man. It was his job, including training in torture, that made him humanitarianism's enemy. How much did his wife know about his job? Was she ignorant? Or his ally? Or even an accomplice? Perhaps she didn't ask questions. But one is at fault not to ask questions, suggests the picture.

Already, even before we are party to any of this, the utterances of officialdom have the ring of lies. What is meant by calling Santore in his eulogy "a victim of terrorism and violence"? It sounds like a don't-ask sign. Flashback to the kidnapping. The Tupamaros have been appropriating cars for it. Journalists question officials. "Will the terrorists demand ransoms?" "Or, as in Brazil, the release of political prisoners?" "We have no political prisoners here," a representative of law and order answers with dignity. "Only common criminals." "Don't you think the terrorists must have had huge numbers of supporters?" says one journalist. And another: "Is Brazil massing troops at our borders?" The state of affairs is said by still another journalist to be intolerable to the government. It is more intolerable to the country, retorts a correspondent with a wider view.

We see something of the city: ordered, ducal-looking official mansions with guards and quick escape routes; thousands of poorly dressed people going to work. Emergency powers are in operation, voted to last sixty days, now two years old. The word "Tupamaros"—the recognition that a guerrilla force even exists—is officially banned. Linguistics to deal with overwhelming reality. The journalists weren't aware of Santore. He had no official position. Everything is clouded. Costa-Gavras has a growing respect for ambiguity, like the scriptwriter Solinas. Santore is described by the lofty A.I.D. director as "a specialist in communications." Captain López says to weary-looking, sage journalists, "Yes, A.I.D. collaborates with our police. . . . Safety measures affecting traffic." No, says the picture, it collaborates on coercion and torture.

Flash to another place. Santore is being questioned by young Tupamaros with gray-brown masks over their heads, showing only tired eyes and mouths that look oddly made-up and pretty in the petrifying surroundings. Santore admits he was in Brazil and Santo Domingo, yes. His smile is not unsympathetic, and his ironies are unaggressive; he feels himself to be in command. "In 1964, Goulart's Brazilian democracy was overthrown by the military," says a young Tupamaro. "Parliament was abolished, political parties, freedom of the press, trade unions. But you, you still stayed. . . . Johnson even sent congratulations a few hours before the putsch." "Political expediency," answers Santore casually, to which the inquisitor says, "And morality was guarded by Spellman's blessing." Another Tupamaro, very young, unmasked, intervenes, and simultaneously wishes he hadn't thought of the remark: "The American God is *putschiste*." The interruption is over in a second, but the Tupamaro's regret stands for the film's benign over-all eye for muddle, for mistakes, for brave measures wrongly undertaken, for the paradox of a privately kind man like Santore countenancing torture by the Brazilian police, which he suavely calls Communist propaganda.

One begins to sense a curious intimacy built up hour after hour between Santore and the Tupamaros, like the tie that can bind torturer and victim as it was located by Sartre in his introduction to *The Question*, Henri Alleg's book about Algeria. Now and then in the film there is an offer of a cigarette, an exchange of current news when the inquisition for the day is

over. Stretchers are used gently for wounded hostages threatened with
assassination unless demands are met. A seized Brazilian diplomat in a
little next-door room marked off by a curtain is less frank than Santore
about his role as torturer. And there follows a dogfight in Parliament about
foreign influences, foreign investment, the right to use the unmentionable
vital word "Tupamaros." We are in a small country with colossal problems, tenacity, and will—a place where cops are often produced by hunger,
and not only by some richer nation's masquerade of having a vocation for
peace. Other people, out of the same hunger, become thieves. Hunger
doesn't leave people many choices. Even Santore, who thinks he is the boss,
is the flunkey of his own catch phrases. His situation becomes piteous
through the compassionate vision of the film. He realizes all too well the
truth that, once captured, he is more useful to his government dead than
alive. The local Minister for Foreign Affairs is concerned to protect what
he calls "sovereignty," which is like the sovereignty of "other interested
countries"; the diverse countries are all of the same stripe when it comes to
the question of individualism.

State of Siege is not about morals so much as about politics. It is not at
all a romantic film but a grievous one. Cant kills. The picture deliberately
hacks away all possibility of plot suspense. The grip of the story is in the
possible twists and turns that casuistry can take, and it has two fine,
inquiring minds controlling it.

Electrician from Uruguay: Ech, you have heard of the Tupamaros? But
you have not been to Uruguay. Well, you know what is a peon? The
Tupamaros are necessary because we are a peon country.

April 14, 1973

PART II

Cloaked Identity

Constantin Costa-Gavras, director of *Z* and *The Confession,* and Franco
Solinas, writer of Gillo Pontecorvo's *The Battle of Algiers,* have lately
made a movie called *State of Siege.* It was unwisely banned by the
American Film Institute for its Kennedy Center opening after being officially invited, but it is now in theaters all over the country and they are
packed to the gunwales. Costa-Gavras's whipping cuts probably play more
part in its popularity than Solinas's levelheaded traditional Marxism,
which shows us a Uruguay that believes itself to depend on United States

aid but that actually contributes vitally to the United States economy every time a Uruguayan uses American toothpaste or swallows American aspirin.

The central character, an A.I.D. worker whose actions are villainous in the picture's terms, emerges as more hero than sinner, because he is played by Yves Montand, who irreversibly seems a rather exhausted good guy, carrying the sour taste of a jaded Europe on his tongue like cigarette fur on an all-night driver's. He doesn't seem to belong at all to the clan of energetic good-lookers who carry out the late President Kennedy's plan for benevolently collaring underdeveloped countries before Communism gets its foot in the door. His name in the identifiable affairs depicted was Dan A. Mitrione: an A.I.D. man assassinated by young Tupamaro guerrillas in 1970. But his name in the film is Santore. Why the change, when Solinas and Costa-Gavras insist on the social veracity of their sources? Shakespeare's *King Lear* obviously couldn't be accurately biographical, but there are verifiable cases, like Mitrione's, where future students are apt to be vitally misled by the bequests of artists. *Hamlet* and *King Lear* merely pose as biographical; fiction of this sort has a freedom that journalism can't properly allow itself. The result of the name change in *State of Siege* is that a knife-blunting job is done on A.I.D. and on the involvement of big powers in the sovereignty of little powers. The casting of Yves Montand further dulls the blade. One is looking at Uruguayan events across reflecting cutlery: In what is specified only as "a real South American country," though it is identifiably Uruguay, one sees a very European and benign Frenchman playing a wicked American. It is like casting, say, Henry Fonda as Neville Chamberlain. The edges of the story don't bite. The Pentagon Papers would have meant nothing if they hadn't been about what turned out to be documented historical facts. *State of Siege* allows itself not the liberty of art but the cloaked name-calling of the New Journalism.

The Vehicle of Urgency

Any journalism is a powerful engine. Daniel Defoe—son of James Foe, a tallow chandler who lived in Cripplegate—often used the classic form of journalism for fiction. He used it in his *A Journal of the Plague Year,* which is written as if it were a contemporary chronicle. No one would believe from its sober, factual, brick-on-brick style that Defoe was actually only four when the Great Plague broke out, in the winter of 1665, and that he was using the instinct of a novelist in electing to end the book not with the real, purging climax—the Great Fire of 1666—but with citizens praising God for an abatement of the plague. Chekhov, greatest fiction writer of all the Russians, chose to work instead as a reporter in his "The

Island: A Journey to Sakhalin," which gives a firsthand account of the Czarist penal colony on Sakhalin Island. As for *State of Siege,* you wonder why Solinas, in particular, didn't use the method of reporting, which implies not the Olympian omniscience of fiction but the "there are things we don't know" element in newspaper stories, which helped to make *The Battle of Algiers* so remarkable. A work using journalistic methods is a quick nail to drive into a subject, not a slow fuse, like a novel. The intellectual technique of *State of Siege* gives it an inapplicable stately look of factual dependability, for all the whirring style of the editing.

The Half-Nelson of Semi-Biography

Cinéma Vérité about real people—*Salesman, Marjoe,* the Leacock and Pennebaker films, *Chronicle of a Summer*—often tells semi-truths, because the unadmitted presence of the camera forces more or less unreality on behavior, depending on how native the style of showoff is to the characters. Entertainment hucksters and, indeed, salesmen thrive on it; subjected to it, perfectly nice children tend to turn into little Shirley Temples. Girl models and ballet dancers, who are anyway used to inspecting themselves in looking glasses all the time, aren't modified by the presence of the camera, but most ordinary people are. So what seems to be truth—a housewife with a shopping bag being interviewed on TV in the street—actually has less veracity than the same chronicle would probably have if it were played by an actress. Even drum majorettes get shy of a camera in a way they don't of a football crowd. In the Maysles brothers' *Salesman,* the scenes of the Bible peddlers in people's front rooms ring sometimes dead false. The Richard Leacock film about the police at a convention in Hawaii, called *Chiefs,* itself and for the same reason, has some of the hollowness of the backslapping he is trying to show us. In Howard Smith's and Sarah Kernochan's *Marjoe,* the young evangelist of the title thrives on exhibitionism but seems—correctly, as it turned out—to be taking part in a story of conversion which is being told with hindsight. On the other hand, Jean Rouch's and Edgar Morin's interviews in *Chronicle of a Summer* are done in a probing, psychiatric style that forces confidences out of their subjects by pressing questions and cameras so close to them that sometimes they almost cry. Vanessa Redgrave's Isadora probably comes closer to the truth of Isadora than the real Isadora would have done if she had been trying to draw herself; it is a difficult thing for nonprofessional actors to convey an essence of themselves, as the cast of Straub's dramatized and slow, slow *Chronicle of Anna Magdalena Bach* did. If *State of Siege* had veered more from Uruguay, Mitrione, and the concrete-looking but unknowable facts (who can tell what Edward IV or the Duke of Clarence actually thought about when he was alone?), it might have come closer to the vividness of fictional truth, instead of giving us the passing color of fake reporting flashily done.

Primers of Revolutionary Method

Even more than Godard, Brecht was the master of revolutionary handbooks. In *Galileo*, for instance, we are shown an unscrupulous man of the senses who claims credit for the invention of the telescope when it has already been invented (by a Dutchman). The Pope's own astronomer confirms Galileo's round-earth findings, but the Inquisition forbids their publication. So for eight years, to the chagrin of his worshipful apprentice Sarti, Galileo remains mute, then recants after breaking silence, and meanwhile writes his great *Discorsi* in secret. He ends by knowing himself to have been a traitor to his profession, a man who has made science the servant of authority, a criminal whose cowardice has been signal. Yet he stands on the central plank of Brecht's revolutionary platform, the plank of the antiheroic. ("Unhappy the land that breeds no hero." "Unhappy the land that needs a hero."—Brecht's *Galileo*. And, from his *The Exception and the Rule*, "Next to you someone is thirsty: quickly close your eyes! Plug up your ears: someone is groaning next to you!")

Brecht is energetic, sardonic, a writer of broadsheets in urchin poetry. In his didactic plan of things, though not in his often sweet-spirited and gentle view of people, the poor are stingy and the rich are ruthless. After an increase of income, the sufferers immediately turn into rapacious businessmen. Like Brecht's *The Mother*, freely adapted from Gorky, *State of Siege* intentionally neglects the psychological and particular. It is about the theoretical and communal, and it is written in an arid style with a rasping eloquence. Even so—as with Brecht's plays, in spite of himself—the central figure emerges potently as a dignified, sly human being. But there is an essential difference between Brecht's work and *State of Siege*. Play after play of Brecht's shows us the horror *before* revolution, whereas *State of Siege* happens *during* what is very nearly a successful overthrow of a stolidly brutal government by students, trade-union leaders, professional men and women, and workers conjoined in learning to master the mechanics of revolution, as the people of Dubček's spring were. The repeated wording of a referendum that is conducted in an undertone on a bus has the echoic effects of poetry. Like Defoe's prose, the film can perhaps best be understood by people similarly placed to the ones depicted: by people like the Uruguayan rebels, who are shrewd, matter-of-fact, philistine, to whom the methods of the pamphlet are natural.

The Biographer Polemical and Presumptuous

Costa-Gavras and Solinas would have done better to call the Mitrione character by his real name, and to come clean about where the events happen. After all, the writer and the director are dealing in polemic. Why not use the zest and liberty of the form? They could have held up Brechtian placards when they were talking about unknowable things if compunction kicked. What really stopped them? Misplaced respect for a dead man who is anyway besmirched politically by their story? A hope that a quasi-fictional method would look less patently anti-monopolistic (seen in America as anti-American)? It merely seems hole-in-the-corner.

Pratfalls of Commitment

Like High Tories depicting butlers and charwomen, Communists drawing the rich are likely to take headers. Brecht's stock-exchange intrigues in *Saint Joan of the Stockyards* present a grotesquely naïve picture of capitalism. So does the procession of corporation owners and bankers in *State of Siege*. Only Brecht's furious comic muscularity wards off the objection to Hitler's being represented as a Chicago gangster in *Arturo Ui*, with its careful parallels to Shakespeare's *Richard III*.

Blackening the Enemy

The most cogent pamphleteer and fiction writer of them all, George Bernard Shaw, knew the wisdom of giving good arguments to the other side. The Inquisitor in his *Saint Joan* debates brilliantly. So does the Church in Brecht's *Galileo*, and so does the existing order in his *Days of the Commune*, in which the pull between violence and discipline is stated but not resolved. *State of Siege* has to deal with the same problem and doesn't quite make it intellectually vivid, though it sometimes successfully shows the Tupamaros as creatures of surprising wit and whimsy, who catch by infection their totalitarian government's brutality and capacity for committing torture. They are dressed in hoods that make them look like Ku Klux Klansmen, with nothing but pairs of eyes and alarmingly pretty pink-lipsticked mouths showing through their brown wool masks. The armed guerrillas are mostly escorted by girls carrying handguns. (The abundance of pretty girls equipped to kill seems to make the hackles of the film's detractors rise.) But when the young men take off their masks they look tired and scared. We have the sense, after their kidnapping of three officials in an attempt to overthrow the government, that they hadn't counted on the cold-bloodedness of A.I.D. Nor had the Montand character, who wrongly reckoned that he was more valuable to authority alive than dead. The decision of the government to let the ultimatum about his execution go past without a move is shocking to the Tupamaros. Their position is suddenly and rather piteously impossible. If they give in, they will seem impotent through weakness; if they hold out, they will seem impotent through cruelty. This Marxist understanding of the characters' predicaments is one of the best things in a coolheaded picture, written with gravity and seriousness. If the big-power opposition had been less caricatured—in the scene where American diplomatic wives are indoctrinated and warned against local water, for instance—*State of Siege* would have been comparable to Shaw, though still culpable for lack of biographical truth. In two hundred years' time, one wouldn't like putative students of our benighted period to find this film in the biographical file about Mitrione; its shrewdness about A.I.D. is a different matter.

May 12, 1973

Andrew Sarris

PART I

If *State of Siege* had happened to arrive in America under ordinary circumstances as a commercial enterprise seeking a payoff and a playoff in a capitalistic country, a political analysis of the material would have seemed supplementary if not indeed superfluous. A movie is a movie is a movie and all that. Unfortunately, *State of Siege* has been rather conveniently converted into a cause célèbre under the auspices of the allegedly American Film Institute. The issues have become George Stevens, Jr., and Freedom of Expression rather than the images, sounds, and alleged "facts" of *State of Siege*. Ever since George Stevens, Jr., disinvited *State of Siege* from the opening series of screenings at the AFI Theatre at the Kennedy Center, we have had alarums and excursions and pronouncements and perorations. Indeed, people were busy signing petitions and striking moral poses in support of freedom of expression even before they had seen the movie. As Nichols and May once reminded us in their classic skit on the quiz-show scandals, moral issues are ever so much more fun than real issues. And especially when the culprit is such an easy, harmless, safe target as the infinitely vulnerable American Film Institute. For the record, however, my own position on the moral issue of freedom of expression has never varied by a hair's-breadth over the years. I am flatly opposed to all censorship, be it applied to *State of Siege* or *Deep Throat* or *Birth of a Nation* or *Triumph of the Will* or every last racist flicker of the old cowboy-injun flicks. My commitment to cinema and all other forms of artistic expression is unconditional.

As it happened, I had submitted my resignation from the Board of Directors of the American Film Institute a few days before the controversy over the Costa-Gavras movie erupted. As only one out of 37 members of the board, I hardly intended to overdramatize my departure. I have too often criticized others for grandstand plays not to feel uncomfortable over one of my own. Also, I have always been very careful to make a distinction between reasons and excuses. My basic reason for resigning? I had too many other obligations. That's all, folks. I did not resign because George Stevens, Jr., had the temerity to ignore my political predilections by inviting Richard the Third to the John Ford dinner. I did not resign because *State of Siege* was disinvited, and I did not resign because George Stevens, Jr., had refused to resign or even relent.

My role at the AFI was always too marginal for any administrative megalomania to take hold. I enjoyed my association with Roger Stevens and George Stevens, Jr., and all the other members of the board and the staff. I must confess also that sitting on the board with such star eminences as Gregory Peck and Charlton Heston always gave me a Through-the-Looking-Glass feeling of being a villainous character actor in a movie about Greg or Chuck as an idealistic executive looking right through my darkly circled night-school CPA eyes into my evil corporation-raiding soul, and thus foiling all my nefarious plans. I mean that I was suddenly on the wrong side of the movie screen, and my muse beckoned me back into the creative and critical sanctuary of that darkness in which I had always been destined to function in my proper role.

Nonetheless, I still stand behind the American Film Institute and its objectives, particularly in the crucial area of archival preservation. I believe also that the Institute should assume more responsibility in the encouragement of film scholarship, a domain that has been shrinking in the AFI budget ever since the ouster of Jim Kitses, Estelle Changas, and Paul Schrader from Greystone. After all, it is a community of film scholars we can thank for the continuing interest in John Ford's career through the sixties and the seventies, and not the assembled Hollywood and Washington stuffed shirts at the Ford dinner. But I shall have more to say about that Ford dinner after I have disposed of all the questions connected with *State of Siege*.

I have talked with both parties to the dispute: George Stevens, Jr., and Roger Stevens for the AFI, and Costa-Gavras for the film. I have now seen the movie, and checked the reviews of Vincent Canby, Judith Crist, Kathleen Carroll, and Archer Winsten. I have also benefited from some instant research on the subject. But it is very hard to know where to begin, and so I will just sort of spill all over from Rome and Paris to Montevideo, from New York to Washington, from *The Battle of Algiers* to Z, from fact to fiction all the way to dialectical distortion and the poisonous poetics of partisanship.

First, I can understand why George Stevens, Jr., was upset when he saw the movie and thought of it being screened a few yards from a bust of John F. Kennedy. As a Kennedyite and Washingtonian (and McGovernite too, let us remember), Stevens remembers too many flag-draped coffins, and too many widows' weeds and grieving children to accept the murder of an American on the screen as a parable of Marxist justice. Even an American like Daniel A. Mitrione, for whom few tears were shed around the world at the time of his death. An ethnic police chief from Richmond, Indiana, on a dubious mission for the A.I.D. first in the Dominican Republic, then Brazil, then finally and fatally in Uruguay, is hardly the stuff of which memorable martyrs are made.

Costa-Gavras and Franco Solinas have concentrated on Mitrione as the focal point of all American foreign policy, and indeed of all social evil in the world. However, the film is fictionalized to the extent of using assumed names. Hence, Mitrione is called Philip Michael Santore, but the American flag and the Alliance for Progress, and every aspect of American involvement with Latin America is tied up with Mitrione in a Montevideo cellar. Of course, *State of Siege* was shot not in Montevideo or in any part of Uruguay, but in nearby less chilly Chile. One senses the steep topography of Chile in the early shots of police roadblocks snarling traffic. For the Marxist sensibility, all of South America and indeed all the world is governed by the same laws of oppression, exploitation, and expropriation. The well-publicized statement of Franco Solinas, screenwriter of *State of Siege,* is clear enough:

"We haven't sought to make a suspense film. We wanted to ask the public a question—not in the classic sense, will he die? But is he or is he not responsible? Guilt not in the traditional sense—he has killed, he has robbed—but much greater. A responsibility of a political nature. Our point of view is not romantic. We are not giving a discourse on morality. We do not seek to establish whether Santore is good or bad. Santore interests us because he represents a system which is bad for the majority of men."

In his telegram to the members of the Board of Directors of the American Film Institute, George Stevens, Jr., declared: "Sometime ago we announced plans to premiere *State of Siege* in the AFI Theatre at the Kennedy Center. Though I had not, at that time, seen the film, I made the decision based on my respect for the filmmaking abilities of its creators. I have now seen the film and discovered it deals with a theme which makes it an inappropriate choice for the showing that has been planned for it as part of our opening at the Kennedy Center.

"*State of Siege* deals, according to published statements by the authors, with an event which actually happened in 1970, the political assassination of an American A.I.D. official, Daniel Mitrione, at the hands of guerrillas in Uruguay. Our decision to provide this film with its U.S. premiere in the opening days of the new motion picture theater in the Kennedy Center was a serious mistake, particularly in the wake of recent events which saw the assassination of the American Ambassador and the chargé d'affaires in the Sudan by Arab terrorists.

"Moreover, it appears to me that this film rationalizes an act of political assassination; and I think it undesirable to initiate programing at the John F. Kennedy Center with such a film. I hope any disappointment Costa-Gavras might feel over this will be balanced by the knowledge that his film and the statement he makes within it will be available to the American public in theaters throughout the country of which the film is highly critical."

Stevens later told me he had first been alerted to a possible problem with *State of Siege* when he was having dinner with Max Palevsky, the film's financial backer. Palevsky reportedly remarked that he was surprised to see *State of Siege* go into Kennedy Center. Stevens then made his request to see the film. I first learned of the cancellation when a reporter from the Washington *Post* called to ask my reaction, first to the cancellation, and then to the fact that Stevens had substituted for *State of Siege* one of my alleged "faves," Jacques Rivette's *L'Amour Fou,* as if I had engineered the whole thing to pay off Jacques Rivette. For just an instant, I felt a twinge of Nixonian nastiness toward the *Post,* but it passed, and I pleaded ignorance of the whole dispute.

When I attended the press conference given by Don Rugoff to explain his own position and that of the film's director and screenwriter, there were several interesting plays on words, first as to whether Stevens really meant "rationalization" or "justification." Costa-Gavras and Solinas insisted on making a distinction between the former, which they considered a valid approach to the subject and the latter, invalid. Don Rugoff then made the distinction between assassination and "reluctant" execution, and I popped up to ask what the difference was as far as Mitrione was concerned, and I felt waves of hostility surging over me from all over the auditorium. Mitrione was a non-person that morning, even though an unreasonable replica is now serving as mayor of nearby Philadelphia, and another may be in City Hall come 1974.

My curiosity over the film now thoroughly whetted, I went to see *State of Siege* at the Beekman at its first public performance in New York. At first, I felt the kind of documentary diffuseness I associated more with *The Battle of Algiers* than with *Z*. I was thoroughly familiar with both Costa-Gavras and Solinas, having seen all their work with other writers and directors, and thus spotted the tensions between them. Costa-Gavras flashy, intuitive, fatalistic, almost tragic; Solinas solid, theoretical, dialectical, almost lucid. With Costa-Gavras there was the swirling public occasion with the sardonic Greek Marxist chorus, on this occasion O. E. Hasse as the raisonneur. With Solinas there was the documentary authentication of fictional detail, the torture gadgets shipped in diplomatic pouches from Disneyland training ground in Texas. Step by step, Solinas will instruct us in all the picturesque details of an American conspiracy to enslave the world. It is the same story everywhere, one of the guerrilla interrogators declares: Algeria, Cuba, Vietnam.

Of the reviewers thus far, only Vincent Canby has expressed any reservations about the factual background of the narrative. One would never know from this picture that Uruguay was in a state of civil disorder largely because of the malaise induced by a rampaging inflation, the same kind of inflation which brought Hitler to power in Germany. However, Costa-Gavras and Solinas cannot be faulted for neglecting the bread-and-butter issues of economics. Nothing would be more effective in keeping audiences away from the theater. American complicity in South American torture is a much more effective ploy for the box office, and there is undeniably American complicity in our support and recognition of regimes which torture their citizens, but I really wonder if Algeria, Cuba, and North Vietnam are exempt from the distressingly long list of countries whose dictatorial regimes practice some form of repressive torture. Where does the guilt begin and where does it end, and do Costa-Gavras and Solinas really mean to imply that repressive torture is exclusively the mechanism of capitalistic countries? Why is Mitrione any more the logical product of capitalism than Stalin is the logical product of Marxism?

When I spoke with Costa-Gavras and Solinas, they countered my objection that there was a tendency nowadays to attack the evils of one country's regime against another country's landscape. Thus, I argued, the film versions of the Solzhenitsyn novels were shot in Norway (*One Day in the Life of Ivan Denisovich*) and Denmark (*The Ninth Circle*), *Z* was shot in Algeria, *The Confession* in France, and now *State of Siege* in Chile. But, they responded, the purpose of ideological cinema is not necessarily to convert the enemy, but to enrich the consciousnesses of one's supporters. Why shouldn't the left have its own entertainments?

I can't find much to quarrel with in this unusually modest statement of intention. I could even agree with Costa-Gavras and Solinas that all cinema is ideological either by commitment or default. In this sense, *The God-father* may well be Nixonian by default as *Sound of Music* is Eisen-howerian by evangelical zeal. Why then should I quibble over the discrepancies and distortions in *State of Siege* when there is so much in the film that does attest accurately to the state of the world in our time? I suppose it is because I don't like it when a film tries to outsmart me by juggling its categories between fact and fiction. And also, I feel that Costa-Gavras and Solinas have chosen to exploit libertarian ideas in which they do not really believe. Hence, there is in *State of Siege* a recurring reference to the supposedly sacred Constitution, to the principles of democracy and judicial restraint and parliamentary pluralism, and to the rights of nations to govern their own affairs without outside interference. However, the Tupamaros were a small group of middle-class intellectuals who rejected democratic methods of persuasion. They hardly served as examples of capitalistic exploitation, being closer to our own Weathermen than to Fanon's *Wretched of the Earth*. But from the moment they first appear on the screen, they are romanticized in a way that can only be called Holly-woodian. They seem to travel perpetually in pairs, virile young man with pretty but idealistic young girl. No overt macho here. The Theodorakis percussive rhythms accompanying the capers of the Tupamaros are sympa-thetically pulse-stirring. There are flashes of comedy relief and humor. It's all such a lark to "expropriate" cars by luring dumb drivers with pretty decoys, and then brandishing guns all over the place. It *is* funny to wrap a middle-aged American in a rug so that his bald pate is sticking out. I could hear the audience giggling. It wasn't quite as exciting as blowing up French men, women, and children in *The Battle of Algiers*. That was really an orgasmic thrill. Perhaps Costa-Gavras and Solinas are not quite ready to rationalize the "reluctant" execution of the Jewish athletes in Munich, but Mitrione, alias Santore, alias Yves Montand as dialectical antagonist for the hooded inquisitors of the left, will do for the moment.

Yves Montand's casting is the movie's biggest coup. Montand gives Santore more gravity, dignity, lucidity, and moral stature than any mere police chief from Richmond, Indiana, would ever dream of demanding from central casting. And it is this inspired casting which gives the movie the tiniest semblance of the objectivity and ambiguity granted to it by those reviewers who have chosen to swallow it whole. Otherwise, every frame of the film is loaded with one-sided propaganda. Indeed, the frames them-selves are often gilded with obtrusively oversized officer's hats left over from *Catch-22*. Renato Salvatori, who is especially adept at playing the fascist buffoon for Costa-Gavras, acts more with his ridiculous hat than with his sympathetically primitive face. The fascists are often distorted through the mercilessly derisive lenses of grotesque caricature; the Tupamaros are almost invariably seen in modestly heroic middle shots.

What then of the double layer of the film? It serves merely to imply a causal relationship between every manifestation of the American system and Mitrione. But is it Mitrione as an American, or is it Mitrione as a policeman in any society in the world that is at issue here? Let us say that we comfortable Manhattanites prefer not to know what our Mitriones are doing in the back rooms of station houses throughout the city, the country, and even the world. The order which we seek and which perhaps we now even crave cannot be purchased cheaply. But how much terror would it take in our own immediate neighborhood for us to call Mitrione back from his grave to save us?

Costa-Gavras and Solinas can mince all the words they want. If they do not rationalize or justify assassination by the Tupamaros, they certainly romanticize and sentimentalize it. For example, we see the atrocities of the repressive regime in all its graphic (almost pornographic) detail, but Costa-Gavras never shows us the Tupamaros actually killing Yves Montand. Why not? We saw Montand clobbered again and again in Z when he was the good guy being assassinated by the bad guys. Why not now when he is the sympathetically bad guy being "reluctantly" executed by the good guys? Were Costa-Gavras and Solinas afraid that their "rationalization" of leftist terror would leave a bad taste in the viewer's mouth if the viewer were treated to the spectacle of a breathing human flame being snuffed out in the name of a principle?

In Z, if you remember, a postscript told us of subsequent developments in Greek politics, all depressingly bad and reactionary. Strangely, there was no postscript to the activities of the Tupamaros. The American fascists go on as before under the watchful Eye of the People, but of the Tupamaros what? Normally, a movie ends when it chooses to end, and the critic has no business pushing it forward in time. Unfortunately, no one thus far seemed interested in checking out what ever happened to the other two officials kidnapped along with Mitrione, namely, American agronomist Dr. Claude L. Fly and Brazilian consul Gomides. On the bus in which the various guerrillas meet in turn to vote on the execution of Santore, the leader is asked about the fate of the other two captives, and the leader answers that they are innocent and will be released in a few days unharmed. The audience is left with the impression that this is precisely what happened. Both men *were* released, but only after a million-dollar ransom was paid for the Brazilian, and only after Claude L. Fly suffered a heart attack during his eight-month captivity. Eight months, not three days. Meanwhile, this same group of Tupamaros had kidnapped the British ambassador to Uruguay, and later another group kidnapped a French woman journalist. A million-dollar ransom was asked for Fly also, but his family couldn't raise the money, and they severely criticized both the Nixon administration and the Uruguayan government for not negotiating with the Tupamaros. The Tupamaros later kidnapped the attorney general from Montevideo, released him after two weeks, and then kidnapped one U. Pereira Reverbel, President Pacheco's confidant and director of the state-owned telephone company for the second time in three years, while he was sitting in a dentist's chair. He pulled a gun but was beaten unconscious and taken out of the building bundled in a blanket.

The British ambassador, describing his ordeal upon arriving in England, said that the kidnappers looked like Ku Klux Klansmen in their masks and that they were about university age. He termed conditions of his imprisonment "abominable," but added that the kidnappers gave him books to read. In that respect, Claude L. Fly wrote a 600-page diary which the Tupamaros delivered with him when he was released. I have not been able to determine whether or not Fly died a short time later as a result of his ordeal, but it was a chance comment of Roger Stevens's that led me along this line of inquiry. There is at once a comic opera aspect and a note of prophetic horror in the full story of the Tupamaros. *State of Siege* does not begin to tell this story in all its historical, sociological, and psychological complexity. But if Costa-Gavras and Solinas had not come along with their provocative movie, I would never have bestirred myself to brush away all the cobwebs from the Mitrione affair. They have thus made me rethink much of my politics and poetics.

What upsets me most in *State of Siege* is not the anti-Americanism, and certainly not the anti-capitalism, but rather the dramatized deliberation of a group of idealists as they prepare to kill an ideological enemy in cold blood. If I believe in anything as a matter of unyielding personal principle, I believe in the total abolition of capital punishment everywhere in the world, and especially in the United States. I don't believe premeditated political murder can ever be sanctified by a poll of the murderers, and, consequently, I cannot participate vicariously in the murder of Mitrione when we have seen already that even Eichmann's execution failed so dismally as psychological retribution that there seems to be an unconscious fear in Israel of another Nazi war criminal doddering into the dock with traumatic irrelevance to the horror of history.

I am willing to believe Stevens rejected *State of Siege* more for its imagery than for its ideology. Still, Stevens was ethically wrong in first inviting and then disinviting a film, the makers of which never sought the honor of an AFI screening in the first place. The feelings of an honored filmmaker should be considered of more import than the feelings of official Washington. Even on the most tactical level, Stevens would have lost nothing by having allowed official Washington to be outraged a bit. So far New York doesn't seem to be outraged at all. Our national self-hatred seems so insatiable that the ideological disapproval of America shared by Costa-Gavras and Solinas seems mild by comparison. There is at least a part of me wondering why Costa-Gavras and Solinas don't go home to take pot-shots at Pompidou and the Pope. It is that same part of me that warms to Jane Fonda, but gets turned off by Vanessa Redgrave. Social criticism should begin at home, and if America has had a bad habit of exporting its presumed virtue abroad, Europeans have an equally bad habit of thinking they can diagnose all America's ills with a quick course in Berlitz and a very short interview with Allen Ginsberg. The strange thing is that *State of Siege* is a great deal more fun as a movie-movie than I seem willing to give it credit for, and both Costa-Gavras and Solinas are a great deal more sympathetic than I seem willing to concede. Perhaps it is the critical and audience reaction that has turned me off from this very skillfully wrought spectacle. So go see it without fail while I prepare to plunge more deeply into its curious paradoxes in Part II, now that I have discussed some of its surface aspects.

April 19, 1973

PART II

All Greeks are exiles at heart. When they are not in flight from their impoverished geography, they are in retreat from their glorious history. They are officially the most beloved of all minorities, and emotionally the most beleaguered. After all, the rocky, arid, unproductive soil of Greece is hardly the ideal terrain for a national pedestal. Being of Greek descent myself, I believe I have as much right as any non-Greek to have a theory about Greeks.

All my life I have heard condescendingly kind words about Greeks and Greece from non-Greeks. These kind words seemed always to have been designed to make me feel like an unfortunate orphan who had lost his illustrious ancestors a very long time ago. It was therefore in character for the so-called civilized world to repay its debt to Greece by looting the country of almost all its art treasures. There is consequently more of the glory of Ancient Hellas in New York, London, Paris, Berlin, and other museum metropolises than there is in the barren wastes of Greece itself. In this respect, we might say that Lord Elgin loved Greece with the dreadful efficiency of Genghis Khan.

But then who could expect Hellenophiles around the world to entrust modern Greeks with the heritage of Ancient Greece? Even Byron was supposed to have become disillusioned with the brawling Balkan tribe he found foraging on the sites of his romantic visions. He journeyed in quest of nineteenth-century Pericleans, and all he found was a procession of pushcart vendors, who can be found nowadays on any streetcorner in New York beginning the very tedious task of amassing great fortunes.

However, I do not profess to be a professional Greek even in this supposed year of the ethnics. I have very rarely socialized with my ancestral compatriots unless their cultural interests happened to coincide with mine at any given moment. And although I have visited London and Paris fairly regularly since 1961, I never managed to make it to Greece until 1968, and even then and in the following year I never bothered to venture beyond Athens with its open-air cinemas at the walls of which young Costa-Gavras used to leap up and down to get a free view of the screen. The respective birthplaces of my father and mother are not too far from where Costa-Gavras was born, but I have little desire to visit these ancestral locales. Somehow I don't want to repeat Byron's mistake by forcing a pathetic patina of rot and ruin and poverty to fulfill the heroic fantasies my father left behind as his only legacy. Besides, my roots and memories are in Brooklyn and Queens and Manhattan, and not in the Peloponnesian ports from which Greek kings once sailed to reclaim Helen from the Trojans. Still, there were moments in 1968 and 1969 when I sat in the syntagma in Athens with the ghostly feeling that I had been sitting there always in spiritual harmony with my true people, and that some part of me would never leave again.

Perhaps it is true that you can't go home again, but it may also be true that you can never entirely escape the ghosts from the grave. Modern Greece has been politically and often bloodily divided ever since King Otto assumed the throne in 1830. The Monarchists and the Republicans have struggled for power ever since. Nowadays they call each other Fascists and Communists. Even the language has reflected this division with the Cretan dialect of Venizelos and Kazantzakis contending with the Constantinian Katharevousa in which I was instructed by a succession of very genteel Greek-American teachers.

From everything I have read of the early life of Costa-Gavras in Greece, I know instinctively that his mother and my mother would never get along. I have had many affectionate arguments over Papadopoulos with my mother, but in the crunch I don't think I could turn her over to revolutionary or even reformist authorities for political rectification. Nor would I be particularly overjoyed to see my bourgeois relatives in Athens butchered or even badgered in an "objectively" justified revolution. I don't argue their case or their cause, but there is enough of them in me, and of me in them, to keep me effectively apathetic about the political situation. If the alternative to Papadopoulos and the coarse colonels were some ideal democratic Eden which combined economic justice with political and intellectual freedom, and which excluded the influence and domination of Big Powers, East or West, I would have no problem making the sentimental choice Costa-Gavras has suggested in his last three movies. But I find it naïve to think that any small country (except possibly Switzerland) can find happiness and prosperity in the Big Power–Multinational Corporation maelstrom of today's power politics. Hence, Greece, Czechoslovakia, Uruguay—each in its own way is a pathetic anachronism, a clucking victim of those Big Power Predators: the Eagle and the Bear.

But what of the tortures and arbitrary imprisonments Costa-Gavras complains about in his movies? Of course, I'm opposed to torture and arbitrary imprisonment. Who isn't? But is it more important to condemn a wicked system in which torture and arbitrary imprisonment are possible, or to single out wicked men at random in a melodramatic fashion? If indeed the late Daniel Mitrione practiced torture in Central and South America, and I notice now that that fact is in some dispute, would not a concern with habeas corpus and due process be relevant to the situation? But such a concern applies only if we are talking about politics rather than poetics. When we shift to poetics, the problem is of a different order. Then we must ask if the melodrama surrounding Mitrione is a valid pretext for indoctrinating the audience with a Marxist view of American economic imperialism in South America and the Third World. Most reviewers seem to think it is. Look at the ITT scandals and the Watergate follies, they say. Look at Daniel Ellsberg and Ray Dirks in the dock and on the carpet for exposing chicanery in high places while the worst culprits get off scot-free. Certainly, the most morbid Marxist would be hard put to think up a plot as sordid as Watergate or the Equity Funding Corporation with a computer actually programmed for fraud.

We are ready to believe the worst about anyone and anything. Thus, Costa-Gavras and Solinas do not have to prove their case against Mitrione alias Santore. They merely have to shout: *"J'accuse!"* and the mob will do the rest. For some reviewers, the daily headlines fill in the blank spaces of *State of Siege.* Judith Crist, for example, considers the machinations of ITT in Chile as full confirmation of what Costa-Gavras and Solinas impute to Mitrione in Uruguay, Brazil, and the Dominican Republic. Now, no one can accuse Judith Crist, Archer Winsten, and Kathleen Carroll of being systematic Marxists or anti-Americans. None of these critics has ever been unduly enchanted with Jean-Luc Godard's brand of Marxist-Leninist cinema in recent years. It isn't really a movie, they complain of just everything Godard has done in the past five years, and even before. Godard seems boring and self-indulgent whereas Costa-Gavras seems exciting and entertaining. But if anything, Godard's politics are more radical than Costa-Gavras's. Having recently interviewed Godard and Jean-Pierre Gorin at the Algonquin, I retain an image of two field-jacketed fugitives from Mao's Ninth Army walking across the media-hardened indifference of the dining room. By contrast, Costa-Gavras and Solinas at the relatively palatial Pierre evoke the elegant middle-class leftism of the brightest salons in Paris and Rome. And yet in the esoteric reaches of world structuralism, Godard is still regarded as a stylistic force, and Costa-Gavras merely as a manipulative entertainer with a weakness for sacrificing form to effect. It is this perverseness in the structuralist scene in Paris against which Mary McCarthy was reacting when she declared in a recent symposium in the *Partisan Review* that she did indeed enjoy Z, as if the topmost towers of Tel Quel, Cinethique, and the newly structured Cahiers du Cinema would topple in shock from such vulgar impudence. My own reading of Costa-Gavras from his films has always been that he was nothing if not passionately pragmatic.

But when I finally did meet him, I found that my previous insights were only partially confirmed. In a sense, we both belong to a multinational firm of film sensibilities and we are both limited in our power, our choices and options, he as a filmmaker and I as a film critic. On the gut issues, he is probably closer to radical anarchism, and I to liberal skepticism, and this is perhaps the widest chasm possible between two sensibilities in the modern world. I state my bias openly so that my instinctive resistance to his movies may be taken by the reader as a personal idiosyncrasy. I have read elsewhere that Costa-Gavras's father fought on the EAM or losing side of the Greek Civil War, which in its way was as traumatic a struggle between left and right as the Spanish Civil War. One could not expect a direct victim of the Truman Doctrine to grow up with a warm feeling for American Manifest Destiny anywhere in the world. But have the movie-movies of Costa-Gavras radicalized the world any more than has the anti-cinema of Godard? Or do they serve, as Luis Buñuel suggested to Carlos Fuentes of all subversive movies, merely as a means of expressing a margin of dissent from established authority?

It is significant that violence and/or torture figure very centrally in all three Costa-Gavras political films. Costa-Gavras told me that he had imported a tragic vision of life into the French cinema from both his Greek background and from the American movies he always admired. Orson Welles once remarked that tragedy in the English-speaking world since Shakespeare had become inseparable from melodrama. By contrast, French tragedy since Racine is locked in the mind, the will, and the language. Thus, as Shaw once noted, whereas English-speaking intellectuals tend to disguise their feelings as ideas, French intellectuals tend to disguise their ideas as feelings, the difference precisely between Shakespeare and Racine.

Curiously, the most feeling I ever sensed in a Costa-Gavras came through in his very first movie, a nonpolitical exercise entitled *The Sleeping Car Murders*, particularly in the relationship between the wisely world-weary detective played by Yves Montand and his surrogate son played by Jacques Perrin. There was an odd sweetness and intensity to this relationship, which, in retrospect, takes on an autobiographical coloration. I am beginning to understand Costa-Gavras's feeling for tragedy as I have always understood his image of himself as an exile. It is a feeling that is evidenced in the looks people give one another in flashbacks as if they already know that things are going to end very badly. With a natively somber artist like Costa-Gavras, life does not really begin until someone has died. But tragic feelings and tragic looks do not constitute a tragic vision. There is more of a tragic vision in Mizoguchi and in Ophuls and even in Sergio Leone than there is in Costa-Gavras. And least of all is there a tragic vision in *State of Siege*. Why not? Simply because Costa-Gavras and Solinas do not display the slightest interest in Daniel Mitrione as a human being. Time and again, the recurring images of memory and celebration threaten to break through into personal reverie, but they always stop safely on the other side of congealed politics. What was it really like for a police chief from Richmond, Indiana, to await death in a Montevideo cellar? For that matter, what was it really like to be a police chief in Richmond, Indiana? Costa-Gavras doesn't really care. He has convinced himself somehow that life is a collective experience within certain prescribed ideological limits, and the Enemy is invariably vulgar, corrupt, perverted, and, when Yves Montand plays the lead, pathetically deceived. But tragic feelings divorced from individual, idiosyncratic personal destiny result only in sentimental politics.

Hence, *State of Siege* reminds me of nothing so much as those old Warners historical allegories like *The Life of Emile Zola* and *Juarez* with a touch of *Watch on the Rhine*. The assassinated pacifist leader in *Z* was a combination Zola, Dreyfus, and Juarez, and the "reluctant" execution of Maximilian in *Juarez* bears more than a passing resemblance to the "reluctant" execution of Mitrione in *State of Siege*. It remained for Lillian Hellman's *Watch on the Rhine* to dramatize how some murders were less evil than others, and how the end sometimes justified the means, especially when Mother Russia was being menaced by fascist Finland. But then why shouldn't the left have its own John Wayne–type genre entertainment? I prefer to see left and right as arbitrary points on a circle of human illusions rotating endlessly around lonely, alienated exiles from Eden in search of a meaning to life before the darkness of death. My poetics are therefore even less in tune with *State of Siege* than are my politics. However, it is possible that Costa-Gavras may have decided that to let his tragic feelings come through all the way in his political films would make him tactically guilty of the Sin of Despair. Art and Revolution. Choose One. I choose Art.

April 26, 1973

THE DAY OF THE JACKAL*

Roger Ebert

Fred Zinnemann's *The Day of the Jackal* is a fiction, and an enormously clever one. It's based on the Frederick Forsyth best-seller about a mythical attempt on the life of President Charles de Gaulle in 1963. The attempt didn't happen, but Forsyth's compulsively readable book makes it seem real by surrounding the fiction with fact.

Almost all his names and places are real. His descriptions of European police and security techniques are accurate and informed. He uses de Gaulle's name in the book, and the movie employs a man who looks so uncannily like de Gaulle that he must be stopped on the street all the time. There is even a moment in the film when de Gaulle, fired upon, misses death only because he happens to lean forward. The bullet hits the pavement behind him.

How has the movie been received? With reviews that could also have been about a superb new film by Hitchcock or Chabrol. The ads are filled with raves from many critics. My own reviews of the two movies are revealing; unconsciously, I accepted the polarity between the "real" film and the "fiction" film. My review of *The Day of the Jackal* called it exciting and spellbinding, while in the *State of Siege* review I felt constrained to deliver myself of several portentous remarks about Watergate, International Telephone and Telegraph, democracy and so on.

The whole business of "reality" in movies can be totally confusing. Even in documentaries, the truth is largely a matter of selection. The editors and director, faced with a mass of material, are tempted to go for the more

---

* This discussion is excerpted from a longer article about *The Day of the Jackal* and *State of Siege* which contrasted movies made from fiction and those based on real events.

entertaining footage if the "truth" is boring or uneventful. *An American Family* would have been no less true if it had consisted of several hours of the Louds passing the salt and pepper to one another.

Why is it that *State of Siege* is real, and *The Day of the Jackal* is fiction—apart, of course, from the fact that the event in the first allegedly happened? Both employ professional actors and screenwriters. Both use the techniques of narrative filmmaking to build dramatic tension. Both are made up, in the sense that we're seeing records, not of actual events, but of events staged for a camera.

Imagine, for a moment, what our reaction might have been if *State of Siege* were simply an anti-American fiction film, but *The Day of the Jackal* was based on a real attempt on de Gaulle's life. Assuming both films remained in their present form, frame by frame, wouldn't we be describing *State of Siege* as a thriller, and analyzing *The Day of the Jackal* for its political orientation?

These considerations are interesting because they underline so conclusively the magical nature of film itself. Film is the truth 24 frames a second, Godard said, because that's the number of frames passing in front of the light. But Bergman is sometimes given to describing film as a tissue of lies: Even when we think we're watching a moving picture, he says, the screen is actually black a third of the time, because that's when the lines separating the frames are going past. In his *Persona*, Bergman was so concerned to show us the insubstantiality of his images that he actually made the film seem to tear and burn in the center. Then, to gear up for his story again, he repeated a montage (introduced at the beginning) recapitulating the history of film itself.

I used to think there was a gulf between fiction films and documentaries, but I'm no longer sure how deep that gulf is, or whether it might not be crossed on occasion. Most documentaries are structured to look like coherent stories. They have their scenes and their narrative flow. And some fiction films are so true to the .underlying nature of human experience (even if they're only made-up stories) that they get closer to what's real than documentaries sometimes can.

Since the presence of the camera inevitably influences what goes on in front of it, in fact, it's just barely possible that actual documentaries are more fictionalized than not.

The subjects, even while acting "naturally," are editing their dialogue and responses to present a favored persona to the camera. And then the cameraman must select what to photograph and the director and editor must order the material, often according to their own perception of what it means.

In a fiction film, on the other hand, the camera is not an intrusion into life, but the rationale for the entire effort of the movie. In very good films, the screenplay is the writer's considered distillation of what he observes life to be, and what he thinks about it. The director imposes his own vision of reality onto the story, and the actor realizes it. Truth about human experience as it's actually lived may be far easier to achieve in fiction than in documentary. And does it really matter, anyway, whether the events in a film actually happened? Should that be the overriding consideration in how we look at movies?

If we want "truth" about political assassins, terrorists, police practices and contemporary politics, we might just as well go see *The Day of the Jackal* as *State of Siege*, actually. And if we want truth about the more forlorn reaches of the human soul, why don't we turn away from *An American Family* and toward *Last Tango in Paris?*

Movies are always fiction, in a way; all we see are light and dark shadows that pretend, for a time, to be human beings. Whether they really lived or not—whether the people on the screen have names that are also in the telephone book—is insignificant when registered against our own instinctive recognition of truth about the human condition.

June 3, 1973

I. F. STONE'S WEEKLY

Vincent Canby

It's only 62 minutes long. It was photographed in black and white with a religious austerity. It has no theme music. It is a documentary, and its title sounds like something glimpsed on an index card at the Public Library.

Yet Jerry Bruck, Jr.'s *I. F. Stone's Weekly*, which opened yesterday at the First Avenue Screening Room, is such a thorough delight it left me feeling the way other people said they felt after seeing *The Sound of Music*. That is, quite high.

I should admit that *The Sound of Music* depressed me. It evoked civilization's imminent collapse. It made me think of the Chinese Communists and suspect that they'd be taking us over sooner rather than later. What was the use of thought or reason? Our minds have already turned into mashed potatoes.

Or have they?

Not, I think, as long as Isadore Feinstein Stone is on the American scene, passionately exposing the fallacies, double-talk and ignorance of the various rascals in government, elected, appointed, or there simply because of being someone's friend.

I. F. Stone, now sixty-six, has been a maverick all his life, a Communist anarchist in his youth, once described as "a strident voice of illiberalism" by Spiro T. Agnew, and now self-defined as a counterrevolutionary.

Through it all, he has been the ferocious conscience of American journalists and those American citizens who would listen to him in person or who subscribed to his newsletter, which he started in 1952 and finally folded in 1971, when he moved his often dumfounded prose to the *New York Review of Books*.

I. F. Stone's Weekly is no dopey paean to a great man. Supplemented by a modest, informative commentary spoken by Tom Wicker, the film presents Izzy Stone straight, with all his eccentricities and enthusiasms intact, in interviews, in public speeches and even walking down to the corner to stuff a week's issue into the post box.

We listen to Izzy describe a hilarious early confrontation with the Atomic Energy Commission (about underground testing), requiring him to make a visit to some seismology experts in the Commerce Department's Coast and Geodetic Survey. "They were so glad to see a reporter. I don't think they'd seen a reporter since there was a tremble from Mount Ararat, when Noah's Ark landed."

He describes the danger for Washington correspondents who become pals with statesmen ("You begin to understand there are certain things the public ought not to know"). He talks about his own lean years as a blacklisted reporter and the genesis of his weekly, through which he taught all the rest of us how to find stories within stories, through inconsistencies, through information inadvertently made public but unnoticed by other reporters.

The film brilliantly succeeds in communicating Stone's near-obsessive interest in truth and his optimism. The war in Vietnam, he suggests, and the survival of the Vietnamese people through years of bombing have reestablished "the primacy of man in an age of technology."

Toward the end Stone tells a group of students: "I really have so much fun I ought to be arrested." There is more to that statement than sentimental fondness for his profession. A cub reporter, he says, may get so excited covering a big fire that he forgets that something really is burning.

As Jerry Bruck, Jr. is lucky to have a subject as dynamic as Stone, so is

Stone lucky to have a young filmmaker as persistent and as obsessed, in his way, as Bruck. *I. F. Stone's Weekly* has been three years in the making, on a shoestring, and in bits and pieces. The result is a rare film, a fitting tribute to a man who never gives up.

October 18, 1973

TOUT VA BIEN
He, She, and Godard

Vincent Canby

No matter how austere and didactic and boring his revolutionary films may be from time to time, Jean-Luc Godard has maintained his genius for titles—which may be the real clue to the well-being of this most passionate and nervy and irritating of artistic temperaments. Work backward from *Vladimir and Rosa,* through *Wind From the East, One A.M., Le Gai Savoir, La Chinoise, Two or Three Things I Know About Her,* and *Vivre Sa Vie,* all the way to *Breathless,* using the original French titles or their English translations, and it would be difficult to tell exactly when Godard became converted by the radical left, when he elected to make only revolutionary teaching films for audiences of an ever dwindling number of supporters.

Yet as the poetry remains in his titles (it's less difficult to renounce an income, a wife, or even an ideology than it is to shuck off a particular talent), the poetry also remains in the films as a signature that cannot be easily disguised by any amount of production chaos (*One Plus One*), Marxist mannerisms (*Wind from the East*), or collaboration (*Vladimir and Rosa,* made with his young political mentor, Jean-Pierre Gorin). The poetry is something immutable. It can't be used up or denied. It remains constant even while the body and the mind that contain it suffer all sorts of physical and spiritual ravages. It separates the great directors, who, I admit, can make awful films, from the competent directors, who often make some of the excellent ones.

Tout Va Bien (freely translated as "Just Great") is his newest film (written and directed in collaboration with Gorin), and although I like the title immensely, it might have been better as *Un Film Comme Les Autres* (which I would translate as "A Film Like Any Other"), the only problem being that Godard squandered that title on an apparently impossibly aggressive, political-lesson film shown here just once, with a garbled English soundtrack, at Philharmonic Hall in December, 1968. It's not really a film like any other, but it does recall the preradicalized Godard, the Godard who was experimenting with revolution (aimlessly, he seems now to think) with films like *Two or Three Things* and *La Chinoise*, before the Paris riots in May, 1968. Actually its casting style goes even further back, to 1963, when he made a film, *Le Mepris* ("Contempt") with such stars as Bardot, Piccoli and Palance.

Tout Va Bien stars Jane Fonda and Yves Montand, who are—in spite of their loudly proclaimed leftist (but hardly radical) political views—symbols of the bourgeois film industry on which Godard turned his back five years ago.

It is Godard's first revolutionary film for the bourgeoisie and, unless audiences are more indulgent than I credit them to be, it may well be his last. Although I find Jane Fonda most appealing (and very funny) as a solemn American political correspondent who becomes radicalized after being trapped overnight in a strike in a Paris sausage factory, I suspect that most people who go to movies would prefer to see her as the unhappy hooker for which she won her Academy Award.

Tout Va Bien is two stories, sort of. It's about the making of a movie these days—about the things you have to put into it, supposedly, to attract the conventional audience—and it's about She (Miss Fonda) and her lover, He (Montand), a former New Wave director who has chosen to step out of that rat race and, instead, to make television commercials. The dramatic line, such as it is, is one of self-discovery.

He and She find themselves prisoners at the Salumi sausage factory, where she has gone to interview the manager on the problems facing management today. They are caught when the Maoists usurp a nice, genial, one-hour work stoppage, planned by the conservatively Communist C.G.T., and turn it into a leaderless rampage. The sit-in describes the workers' frustrations in mostly comic actions. The plant manager is locked in his office and not allowed to go to the bathroom. The personnel files are destroyed. One woman striker argues with her husband over the telephone: "You'll have to heat it yourself . . . *You* stayed at *your* factory during *your* strike. . . ." Another woman paints her nails. Occasionally they revive themselves with a revolutionary song.

As the actions describe the frustrations, typical Godardian monologues define them—some are broadly funny, some pious and just a little foolish. All, however, are photographed with that particular Godard eye for finding beauty in the most banal shapes and colors. If red and yellow were the predominant colors of *Weekend,* dusky blues, and greens and beiges of the sort Braque used, are the colors of *Tout Va Bien.*

To the extent that Godard has any interest in allowing us emotional involvement with He and She (Him and Her?), *Tout Va Bien* is both moving and witty, but these are qualities that slip through in just three or four scenes.

In two sequences, one shot at a TV studio and another at a Paris construction site, Montand, talking directly to the camera, describes the weariness with which he came to direct his fiction films and how he finally preferred to make commercials, which allow him to participate in the system without hypocrisy.

When at last he was offered his chance to direct a David Goodis novel he'd always cherished (a rather nasty reference to Truffaut's "bourgeois" adaptation of Goodis's *Shoot the Piano Player*), he says he no longer cared. It's not necessary that you believe the character (characters in Godard have always been slightly implausible and unreal in any conventional way), you believe the passions expressed, you believe Montand, and you believe the world in which Godard, at the beginning, has carefully set his film, a world, he has told us, in which "farmers are farming, workers are working and the middle classes are middle classing."

Jane Fonda has some equivalent sentiments near the end of the movie. She and He have been freed from the sausage factory, they sit having breakfast in their flat, the liberated She now furious with He who, though politically aware, remains impossibly chauvinistic where She's concerned. When we last see He and She, each is, says the narrator, rethinking himself in historic terms.

Tout Va Bien looks a lot like the earlier Godard films (the opening of the breakfast scene mentioned above is taken directly from *Vivre Sa Vie*), and it talks the committed radical line of the most recent films. Though it does both with great style and a surprising amount of humor, it's neither the look of the film nor its politics that I find most fascinating about Godard at this point. Rather it's his courageous and quite mad persistence in trying to evolve a film form to match the intensity of his political and social concerns. In the last five years he's tried to do without everything except, perhaps, film itself. He got rid of the narrative, actors-as-performers, and anything resembling emotional suspense—all techniques of the bourgeois cinema that, he thinks, have helped enslave the capitalist world. The results have been films that have bored almost everybody, most especially the masses that he would politicize.

Tout Va Bien, with a few graceful if minor concessions to conventional cinema form, shows Godard getting ever closer to a new kind of film that makes most other politically and socially concerned movies seem like sentimental garbage.

Take, for example, *Save the Tiger*, the new Jack Lemmon film directed by John G. Avildsen and written by Steve Shagan, about the decline and fall of a Los Angeles garment manufacturer played by Lemmon. I've no doubt that Avildsen, Shagan, and Lemmon are very concerned about the moral breakdown of a system that supposedly allows a once-nice guy (Lemmon) to juggle books, to pimp for clients, and to employ arsonists in order to continue his existence in a rotten world. Yet their method (realistic, full of attempts to engage our sympathies, and full of references to simpler, more decent times past) is to bathe real horrors in the kind of self-pity that precludes meaningful action. When we go to see movies like *Save the Tiger*, we're invited to watch the spectacle of decadence. We aren't— heaven knows—asked to do anything. We aren't even asked to think very much, just to feel sorry for a poor slob who made it big and feels lousy about all the rotten things he has to do to stay on top.

This is the kind of cinema that Godard sneers at, rightly, I think. And although I find his politics as muddled and self-indulgent in their way as the sentimentality of *Save the Tiger*, I admire Godard's willingness to use his talent so extravagantly, so recklessly, in the pursuit of a goal that may forever elude him. *Tout Va Bien* is a film of true political importance, whether you believe its politics or not.

February 25, 1973

THE MATTEI AFFAIR

Andrew Sarris

Francesco Rosi's *The Mattei Affair* lingers in my mind as the most fascinating political film of the year thus far. It was relatively well received by the local reviewers and was granted a reasonable run at the Little Carnegie, but the audiences simply didn't turn out for it. I caught it during the end of its run in a virtually empty theater. I didn't brood about this circumstance particularly. I have enjoyed some of the greatest films of all time in virtually empty theaters. Quality and popularity have a very erratic relationship in any art. Very recently, however, a political journalist of my acquaintance pointed out to me the ironic coincidence of a film's being at one and the same time dialectically opposed to the American oil companies, and yet officially distributed by the movie company arm of Gulf and Western. The journalist in question is clearly not to be classified as paranoid in terms of the overwhelmingly conspiratorial times in which we live. Still, he wondered why the studio had not backed up *The Mattei Affair* with a bigger publicity campaign. Could this lack of support be interpreted as a devious maneuver by Gulf and Western to keep audiences away from the biography of a man whose mission in life was to pour oil on troubled waters and who may have been assassinated by a conspiracy of multinational interests?

I'm not that sure that a bigger publicity campaign would have gotten that many more people into the theater. It's been my experience over the years that political people talk a good game of political cinema, but when it comes time to go out at night they line up for *Last Tango in Paris* or *The Last Picture Show*, and not for the latest exclusive *cinéma-vérité* interview with Eldridge Cleaver. "Where are our movies on Vietnam?" we were asked rhetorically for years and years. And yet when a local theater owner showed antiwar documentaries for free, hardly anyone showed up. Of course, the Movement as a mass phenomenon has turned out to be one of the biggest pipe dreams of the sixties and seventies.

But I am not arguing now about the futility of preaching to the converted. I am suggesting instead that even the converted stay away in droves from the cinematic ceremonies of political revivalism. This is especially true of intellectually complex reconstructions of the ambiguities of history and biography such as Rosi's *The Mattei Affair,* and, before that, *Salvatore Giuliano.* Rosi's cinema does not cajole his audience with sentimental certitude in the patented Costa-Gavras manner. Nor does it cater to the voluptuous helplessness and pseudo-innocence of the audience in the face of obvious evil. Rather, Rosi chooses to pose political mysteries for our contemplation, and he is aided in *The Mattei Affair* by the dynamically unsentimental performance of Gian-Maria Volonte as Mattei, that curious eruption of recent world history, that odd blend of bluff, bluster, idealism, insecurity, and intransigence, that volatile mixture of grown-up self-discipline and childlike wanderlust. Above all, Mattei is a creature of global economics, a would-be magician trying to fly around the earth on a cheap mixture of Italian methane and hot air, floating from Lenin's tomb to the Arabian sands in search of oil and power for his own people. But there are no easy answers for Mattei or for Rosi or for us, and power of any kind and in any cause can be perilous.

The Mattei Affair is a masterful political biography, and I very much doubt that Gulf and Western would pass up a dividend to discourage

American audiences from seeing it. It is more likely that even the most cultivated moviegoers prefer to use the screen for escape rather than for elevation. And what could be more irritating for a supposedly knowledgeable New Yorker than a cinematic reminder that he is a mere babe in the woods when it comes to international economics. Whereas *The Mattei Affair* indicates that a course in high (and lowdown) finance might be in order, *State of Siege* contents itself with a rousing chorus of "The Internationale." And as a New Yorker cartoon of ancient vintage suggested, if you don't know the words, you can just hum.

October 4, 1973

Five

WOMEN: THE MISSING PRESENCE

MEN WITHOUT WOMEN, WOMEN WITHOUT MEN

David Denby

A short time ago, when critics wanted to dismiss American movies as trivial and artless, they could always point to Hollywood's mania for working romance into practically every picture. Our love-struck cinema often deserved to be snickered at; convinced that the public would feel cheated without a little smooching every half hour or so, the pioneering studio tyrants forced a "love interest" into desert adventure pictures, sci-fi, Westerns, mysteries, Marx Brothers' comedies—you name it. And yet, even if "love" occasionally slowed down a nifty melodrama or raised false issues, American movies offered one of the most engaging romantic myths in the history of popular culture—men and women working, competing, playing, or suffering together out in the great world and falling in love while doing it. Companionship between the sexes was once a genuine ideal in our movies.

Today, that norm seems remote and peculiar. Romance is just about dead in our movies; there's plenty of sex, of course, but movies in which male and female equals meet, fight, fall in love, have an affair, get married or don't get married have just about disappeared. And when you do see a love affair at the center of an American picture, the picture is nearly always terrible. Romance has become the province of a sickening and retrograde commercial sentimentality, the genre in which mind and ambition and style are relinquished. (Moviegoers will doubtless be able to come up with exceptions, but I'm trying to get at a general trend.)

Our filmmakers seem to have lost the ability to make ordinary heterosexual behavior interesting. In the past the American in love was an inspired wise guy; now he's simply blander than other movie characters. A few scenes of Sidney Poitier's mush in *A Warm December* were enough to make me grateful for the most scabrous black exploitation movies. The divorced husband and wife (George Segal and Susan Anspach) in Paul Mazursky's *Blume in Love* are both so nebulous that the movie never gets off the ground; since the flashbacks show they were bored with each other during their marriage, why should we spend two hours rooting for the wife to give in and take her husband back—aren't they better off divorced?

A Touch of Class tries to revive the old thirties magic, but it stumbles badly. Following the convention that has been standard in romantic comedy since *It Happened One Night*, writer-director Melvin Frank gives us a couple whose mutual insults cover an irresistible attraction until finally, after a variety of adventures, the mask of antagonism drops away and their love is that much stronger for having emerged out of anger. It's a charming formula, but it requires a certain delicacy to work. Here, in a misbegotten attempt to be modern and knowing, Frank turns the comic insults into vicious name-calling and competition. Thus, when George Segal and Glenda Jackson fall into bed after a bit of "healthy" violence, only the crassest assumptions about the healing powers of sex would allow us to think that these two could swallow their pride and anger and immediately become idyllic lovers. Yet this is what Frank is up to; he wants us to think they might live happily ever after if it weren't for Segal's rotten marriage, and in the second half of the picture the inhuman, pseudo-"smart" dialogue gives way to a conventional pathos of lost opportunities.

It looks as if *A Touch of Class* has become a moderate-size hit, but anyone can see that the real action these days isn't in romantic comedy. Most of the big hits as well as the movies that have earned critical raves and awards in recent years have done without romance, and an amazing number have dispensed with women. In the important new movies the main emotional relationships are between men; more and more, women are forced out to the periphery as men's whores, sisters, or stay-at-home wives, or they are excluded altogether. (Of course a few movies are dominated by women—those starring Barbra Streisand or Liza Minnelli, for instance— but, as I'll explain later, these pictures are peculiarly sexless and unromantic.) Since 1966, with *A Man for All Seasons*, and including, year by year, *In the Heat of the Night, Oliver!, Midnight Cowboy, Patton, The French Connection,* and *The Godfather,* the Academy Award for best picture has gone for seven consecutive years to a movie without a major female role. To this list we could add another group of films, equally successful, all of them male competition/companionship epics, all of them indifferent or hostile to women: *Easy Rider, M*A*S*H, The Wild Bunch, Husbands, Butch Cassidy and the Sundance Kid, Deliverance, The Candidate, The Friends of Eddie Coyle,* and *Scarecrow.*

The two men, drifters, meet at the side of the road somewhere out West and quickly become friends. The older has done six years in the pen and is on his way to Pittsburgh to get some money out of a bank and start a car wash; the younger has been at sea, avoiding the responsibilities of fatherhood—he carries a lamp in a little white box for his child in Detroit who may be a boy or a girl, he doesn't know. Together they travel east, hitching, riding on freights, dropping in on relatives, whoring, fighting, getting drunk in bars, always moving across the country in one of those movie journeys that is less an experience of an actual landscape than a metaphorical test of American ideals and liberties. And we aren't surprised when the ideals are shown to be an illusion and the liberty impossible; the journey ends in madness and defeat.

What I'm describing is the recent Gene Hackman–Al Pacino film, *Scarecrow*, yet, apart from specific details, it sounds suspiciously like many other serious-minded American pictures of recent years—*Easy Rider, Midnight Cowboy, Two-Lane Blacktop, Five Easy Pieces*, etc. This negative picaresque, the journey through corrupt, betraying America, has become a major new movie genre, and *Scarecrow* has all the familiar elements: fancy, bleak photography; an elegy for a simpler land; forlorn little "sensitive" moments, repeated over and over until they become clichés; and, most important, those two demoralized male characters at the center. In these films, despite the dithering, aimless quality, defeat is built into the basic structure; we know from the beginning that the two heroes of *Scarecrow* aren't going to make it, and we know the same about the other down-and-outers who have recently become the ironic models of American ambition and idealism in our movies. These men are all harmless enough and their dreams are innocent, yet America is too much for them, America does them in. Some of these movies have been very affecting, yet the condemnation of America comes too easily: The country may be corrupt, but films like *Easy Rider* and *Scarecrow* haven't begun to comprehend the complexity of American life. Despite all the adventures, all the experience, these movies take place in a vacuum, an America more mythical and metaphysical than actual. Their reality isn't our reality, at least not centrally, and one of the principal reasons is that women are never allowed to intrude on the masculine relationships; the movies take place in a land where women barely exist.

It's probably the contrived absence of women that allows these films to indulge in pretentious, vacuous attitudinizing about America; women would turn the films back toward the center, back toward a consideration of work and sex and love, and they would also tighten up the films dramatically and make it easier for them to find a more plausible resolution. As it is, this type of ambitious buddy-buddy movie has nowhere to go except toward death and madness—the sudden apocalyptic ending that always seems so phony—or toward homosexuality.

So far, any suggestion of sexual attraction between the principal characters has been avoided like the black death, but as one after another of these movies is released, certain critics have begun to discern a subtext of *repressed* homosexuality; this "insight" is accompanied by an attack on the filmmakers for refusing to face up to the obvious implications of the material. But this is a line I would be wary of taking. Pointing out homosexual motifs in movies gets to be a nasty, invidious game, particularly if the charge is that these are closet-queen movies. Calling someone a repressed homosexual is far more damning these days than merely calling him a homosexual, and the same is true of movies—the charge implies not only incompetence and ignorance but a cowardice that is no longer quite plausible, even for commercial movies. Homosexuality is now good box office, and there's no compelling reason for movie companies to avoid it.

Critics look for homosexual explanations because they are uncomfortable with the content of movies like *Midnight Cowboy* and *Scarecrow*—men learning to take care of each other, learning that friendship is more important than anything else, and so on—and because these movies seem to carry an excess of emotion. It's true that *Midnight Cowboy* was out of control at times and that *Scarecrow* lacks focus and becomes repetitive and silly, but refusing to come to terms with homosexuality isn't necessarily the reason; dozens of movies are plagued by artistic failures of this type. Moreover, there's nothing distinctly homoerotic about the relationships in these movies as there was, say, in movies like *The Servant, King Rat, Performance*, and many others. Movies like *Scarecrow* inhabit a sexual limbo (despite all the whores), and dramatically they're irresolute and irritating.

Leaving aside the question of homosexuality, I think the men who write and direct these movies are guilty of a kind of sentimental fraternalism that downgrades or simply ignores women—the feeling that women aren't as *fine* as men, not as spiritual, not as noble, or as sublimely pathetic. In this view women are practical, earthbound, reality-oriented creatures, friendly and sexual and generous, but on the whole rather trivial; in the larger, "mythic" American experiences that Hollywood loves so much, they don't count for a thing.

In fact, whores are virtually the only women to appear in the current male-action films. In his recent *Pat Garrett and Billy the Kid*, Sam Peckinpah, who is something of a connoisseur in these matters, brings back the grateful, adoring Mexican types he used in *The Wild Bunch*. Like so many of the semi-anonymous women in recent American movies, they are there only to be screwed, quarreled over, and slapped around.

The picture is still another of those elegies for the Old West; the two heroes, posed nonchalantly against a variety of Mexican landscapes, lament the good old days when gunslingers lived the free life. This sappy male fantasy has become a central American experience—not by virtue of its truth, not because anyone outside Hollywood deeply cares about it, but because it is forced on us in one form or another about six times a year. One after another, the male professionals offer their swan songs: gun-slingers, gangsters, pimps, cops, rodeo stars—each in turn takes his last ride, makes his last run, sustaining his style and courage right to the end (our cinema succumbed to Ernest Hemingway's sentimental side in the late forties and may never come out of it). What we've got is a cinema of male dithering and gracious male nostalgia—a crackpot cinema.

Let's examine the other side of the coin. American movies are terribly diminished at the moment by the almost total absence of *heroines*. Every movie period had its great female stars and archetypes, its heroines of love and adventure and suffering. There were the exquisite, trembling Griffith virgins (Mae Marsh and Lillian Gish), fiercely struggling against violation and death; Mary Pickford, the more sentimental vision of purity in white; Theda Bara, the heartless vamp who "ruined" men by the dozens; Gloria Swanson, the over-dressed society adulteress; Garbo as the complex, neurotic modern woman; Constance Bennett, seduced and abandoned by wealthy men in picture after picture; Jean Arthur, the thirties working girl—man's companion and equal; strident, exasperated Carole Lombard; Jean Harlow, the good-hearted loudmouth, and Claudette Colbert, the tease; Katharine Hepburn and Bette Davis, exemplars of heroic striving and feeling in role after role; Joan Crawford, Lana Turner, and Barbara Stanwyck as the sexually overpowering murderesses and adulteresses of the forties, and so on.

I indulge myself in this list partly out of longing for some of the old actresses, partly to show the necessity of creating truly contemporary women in the movies. Most of these roles reflected asinine ideas about women, and no actress of today is going to get very far playing embattled virgins or poisonous husband stealers. Stanwyck, for instance, was exciting as the wicked woman of the forties, but that image makes sense now only as a reflection of male paranoia. Still, sexist or not, those were parts that a woman could sink her teeth into. Today such parts are rare; if she's lucky an actress can get a *major* role as a hooker rather than one of those nominal parts in a male-dominated film. The hooker seems to be about the only type of modern woman that male directors and writers will allow themselves to admire, the hooker movie being the only interesting exception to the blight on romance. Jane Fonda in *Klute*, Barbra Streisand in *The Owl and the Pussycat*, Julie Christie in *McCabe and Mrs. Miller*, Karen Black in the atrocious *Portnoy's Complaint*—these are the funny, tough women who are the descendants of the heroines of the thirties. The hooker has benefited from a reversal of male fantasies—strength of character is now widely associated in the movies with sexual generosity, weakness with sexual inhibition. The hooker is available and she is good at what she does (yet she is the only woman professional now appearing in the movies—is it because she doesn't compete with men?), and she won't gum up a relationship with conventional romantic talk and nagging demands.

Jane Fonda, who was so brilliant as the hooker in *Klute,* is the only major contemporary actress to carve out a persona for herself in the old manner—the tough, bruised, resourceful girl who's a little more aggressive than she need be because she's been pushed around too much. But what kind of a future does Fonda have as an actress? Half the time she gives the impression that acting is a rather trivial occupation for a grown woman (although, unlike Brando, she doesn't draw on that self-disgust when she performs); and her radical activities are gradually making her unemployable in large-budget films. All over America there are theater owners and TV station managers who won't play her pictures. It would be a shame if her career collapses, because the movies desperately need her. She obviously likes men, and she plays well with them, so she's uniquely qualified to act out the new conflicts in feminine roles, the new, necessarily tension-ridden styles in romance that have developed since women's lib began putting such extraordinary pressures on young women. And any mass art form even halfway alert to the times would provide her with such roles (it provided comparable roles for Hepburn, Jean Arthur, and Davis thirty-five years ago—why not now?).

But what about superstars like Barbra Streisand and Liza Minnelli? These actresses certainly are getting good roles and carrying them off, but they may be too powerfully energetic and individualistic to team up with men successfully; the actors appearing with them try to stay cool and usually get left behind; there's no sexual equality and no real connection. Streisand has more natural vitality than any other performer now working in the movies, but it has its destructive, wall-slamming side—she can make your head hurt. She ran right over Omar Sharif in *Funny Girl* as well as Ryan O'Neal in *What's Up, Doc?* and bypassed Yves Montand altogether in *On a Clear Day You Can See Forever* (as nearly everyone said, they hardly appeared to be acting in the same film). A surly, withdrawn Walter Matthau looked at her suspiciously out of the corners of his eyes in *Hello, Dolly!* and they never made contact. (This may have been more his fault than hers; Matthau was bored and resentful in almost all his roles a few years ago.) George Segal did achieve a very pleasing sexual parity with her in *The Owl and the Pussycat* when she calmed down in the second half of the film, and so did newcomer David Selby in *Up the Sandbox!* but, unfortunately, the film was disastrously misconceived and they had only a few scenes together. At her worst she increases the tempo of her lines until the words become gibberish (something she'd never do when singing), and kills her partner's timing by reacting to the next line before he's even said it. But her talent is overwhelming, and if she would only forgo the nonstop attack and relax a bit, she could easily become the leading romantic heroine of the American screen.

Liza Minnelli has a giddy, perverse, almost masochistic vulnerability that makes her fascinating and also a little nerve-wracking to watch. Perhaps too jumpy to be sensual, she seems drawn to bizarre sexual roles. In *Charlie Bubbles* she offered herself to a comically indifferent and baffled Albert Finney; staring at her breasts, he could hardly conceal his dismay, and as she moved down on his body, her wig fell off and sat on his chest like a giant spider—surely one of the most grotesque love scenes ever played by two major talents. In *The Sterile Cuckoo* she was very affecting as Pookie Adams, the screwed-up, hyperactive teen-ager who overwhelms the conventional college boy played by Wendell Burton, but eventually her self-laceration destroys our interest in the romance. *Cabaret* was her first non-masochistic role, and of course she was marvelous; this conception of the material softens the hard-bitten, sexual-opportunist side of Isherwood's Sally Bowles, gives her some genuine performing talent, and leaves her in full glory on stage at the end, all alone but doing what she wants to do more than anything else. The film thus becomes a bittersweet celebration of show-biz drive, a force that obliterates mere romance.

Perhaps female superstars need to work with a different kind of actor than is now available; the cool, self-effacing style that has been fashionable in leading men for some time simply isn't enough for these prodigies of energy and talent; in picture after picture they propel themselves into orbit, leaving their earthbound men far behind.

What happened? How can we explain the general dominance of men, the relative exclusion of women, and the eclipse of romance? A few points:

• Violent action-adventure movies continue to be trustworthy at the box office while other genres fail. So as not to slow down the slam-bang stuff, women aren't being written into these movies anymore. In many cases we can accept this exclusion as properly realistic. Would *The French Connection* or *The Godfather* have been better movies with larger roles for women in them? There's no reason to think so.

• To a considerable degree popular culture has lost its affirmative character. Television remains goody-goody, but sometime during the sixties movies caught up to the negative temper of modern literature and began to assume a distaste for conventional relationships and happy endings. Marriage is now seen as a trap or at best a perilous, exhausting compromise; thus the sort of romantic comedy whose actual or implied end is marriage becomes harder to justify, and it becomes more hip to make a film about a disintegrating relationship than about one that works.

• The sixties, unlike previous decades, did not develop a new style of romance that could be useful in the movies. Grass may be a better aphrodisiac than alcohol but it doesn't do much for conversation; "sensitivity training" probably makes banter seem phony, and sexual liberation doubtless makes it unnecessary, but in American movies romance thrives on jokes, wisecracks, and insults, not on good vibes, "openness," and a willingness to touch. Extreme sensitivity is charming only if you are receiving it or expressing it; as entertainment it's banal and boring.

• Women's liberation has paralyzed the movie companies. In New York and Los Angeles, where movie projects are hatched, relations between the sexes are a battleground on which all previous rules of warfare have been thrown out. What's happening between men and women is now so charged-up, improvisatory, and bewildering that the movie companies are afraid to touch it. They ask, won't any movie about what's happening be out of date by the time it appears? If we make a film about the sex life in the urban centers and the suburbs, won't it offend the rest of the country, where sexual protocol remains traditional? Of course it's chicken-hearted questions like these that kill movie projects at birth.

So far, the movies have responded to women's lib only in oblique ways; instead of contemporary stories, we get two simultaneous versions of Ibsen's *A Doll's House* (with Claire Bloom and Jane Fonda); instead of movies with strong-willed, mature women who know what they want or at least know that they must look for something new, we get movies that respond to the masochistic side of women's-lib writing and portray women as victims. In Frank Perry's *Diary of a Mad Housewife* and *Play It as It Lays* and Otto Preminger's *Such Good Friends* the heroines suffer passively at the hands of boorish husbands and lovers. We are meant to be sympathetic, although many of us probably want to give them a kick: Why don't they fight back? Women are also being raped more often and more viciously than ever before, not just in grind-house shlock, but in classy movies like *A Clockwork Orange* and *Straw Dogs*. Sometimes it looks as if woman-as-victim is a very useful option to people who want to be high-minded about exploitation.

American movies aren't much fun anymore, and I suppose if you wanted to be solemn you might say they aren't very healthy either. The violence stuff goes on and on and will probably never end or even slacken off. At the same time there's a trend toward an increasing isolation of the sexes, and that means no comedy, no joy, no lyricism, and no myths that are fun to believe in. Movies like the working-girl comedies of the thirties or the

Astaire-Rogers or Tracy-Hepburn series are remembered so vividly because they made people feel better about their own lives. Our movies don't do that anymore. Sometime in the sixties we decided we no longer deserved to feel good and romance died.

September, 1973

SISTERHOODWINKED:

The Bitter Tears of Petra von Kant, Year of the Woman, The Way We Were

Molly Haskell

Sexual politics invaded the New York Film Festival late this year: a group from Lesbian Feminist Liberation picketed the two showings of Rainer Werner Fassbinder's *The Bitter Tears of Petra von Kant*, a highly stylized "chamber film" (literally, since it takes place within one room) concerning the convulsive passion of a lesbian dress designer for a young model. The outcry was presumably sparked by the title (since the demonstration was planned before anyone could have seen the film) with its politically unacceptable implication that lesbians are unhappy, and by the advertising, which was indeed exploitative.

As the lesbians marched and chanted outside Alice Tully Hall, they looked every bit as joyful and healthy as their leaflet proclaimed, and the vibes were good. But once inside, they were, like all the other hissers that have come to plague the festival, a pain in the ass. They pounced on a funny little comic-erotic short about an artichoke, in which that vegetable becomes to the female anatomy what the banana has traditionally been to the male. And they proceeded to hiss intermittently during the Fassbinder, although the very randomness of the hissing proved that when confronted by a work of art of any complexity, the political reflex is unreliable and the knee is apt to jerk at the wrong moments.

I don't mean to pick on the lesbians, but their action raised once again the whole thorny question of judging, or possibly prejudging, a work of art by the slogans and criteria of an ideology that posits a progressive—"correct" and wholesome—view of human nature.

Film, perched on the dividing line between art and commerce, has always presented a more inviting target for political protest than the arts/media on either side. As pure commerce, television is almost immune to cries of sexism; and poetry and fiction are too private and personal, and, in a sense, "irrelevant" to such assaults. Who pickets the publishing offices of Philip Roth or Thomas McGuane or James Dickey for their treatment of women? What gay groups would sign petitions, were their authors alive, against the homosexual "humiliations" suffered by Aschenbach in *Death in Venice* or Olive Chancellor in *The Bostonians?* But there is a lingering feeling that film, despite the highly, almost exclusively personal nature of movies nowadays, is still enough of an expression of our collective unconscious that it is accountable to the kind of sociological/political analysis from which the "pure" arts are exempt. And there is just enough validity to this view, although less than there has ever been before, that it can't be completely dismissed.

The problem is that by the pure precepts of a feminist aesthetic, a filmmaker who deals with women at all is more likely to be attacked (for presuming to understand their sensibility) than one who simply ignores them. Hence, the Festival, with its heavy preponderance of European filmmakers (and their traditionally woman-centered vision) provides more grist for rhetorical attack than the American cinema, which blithely ignores or brutally downgrades women. (In preparation for an encyclopedia roundup piece, I recently made a list of the hundred or so main films of 1973 and discovered that, not counting the freak genre parodies like *Cleopatra Jones* and *Lady Kung Fu,* only three American films dealt centrally with women—the number was slightly higher if you counted "couple" films like *Blume in Love* and *The Man Who Loved Cat Dancing.* The rest—*The Hireling,* the two productions of *A Doll's House, Love and Pain and the Whole Damn Thing, A Touch of Class,* etc.—were all English, and most American films were either men's cops-and-robbers films, men's middle-America films, men's weepies, or men's Westerns.)

The idea, of course, is to have more women filmmakers, but I wouldn't count on that solving all our problems. As I've been forced to conclude from a viewing of Sandra Hochman's *Year of the Woman,* which I'll get to shortly, we should not necessarily expect to see reflections of "ourselves" in the films of other women.

I thought the Festival was especially rich in good women's roles this year: Chabrol's two Stephane Audran-starrers, *La Rupture* and *Juste Avant la Nuit,* but particularly the former in which a woman's natural goodness and strength of character turn, under duress and in defiance of her stripper stereotype, into an almost supernatural strength, with a power to repel evil that is as strong as Doktor Mabuse's to create it; or, in Lang's

1922 masterpiece, the marvelous countess (Gertrud Welcher) who goes incognito to nightclubs to escape her dreary marriage, but who finally rejects the "ecstasy and damnation" of Mabuse in a belated appreciation of lost companionship with her husband; or Joelle, the production assistant (Nathalie Baye) in Truffaut's *Day for Night,* who is horrified at the script girl's running off with the stuntman: "I can understand leaving a man to work on a film, but leave a film for a man . . . never!"; or Janice Rule as the forthright prostitute in *Kid Blue,* who makes Hopper understand that she would like to turn away the sheriff (one of her best customers) because he is Hopper's enemy, but that such principles are a luxury that she, as a working woman, cannot afford; the intriguingly individualized women and wives in *Rejeanne Padovani,* who without being involved in crime, seem to key the film's atmosphere of hot and cold running power and sexuality; Jane Fonda as an extraordinarily glowing and growing Nora (in Losey's production of *A Doll's House* that is, curiously, more emotional and less militant than the one with Claire Bloom).

Nor would I want to ban Jean Eustache's three-and-a-half hour, three-person monologue, *The Mother and the Whore,* because its hero (Jean-Pierre Léaud) is a sexual fascist who sees women as biologically and ontologically subservient to men . . . but as holding his fate in their hands. The movie is a paradigm of that division of woman into virgin and whore that underlies Christian (particularly Catholic) culture. But its appeal for me is that it captures, far more than Godard's or Truffaut's or even Rivette's more romantic fantasies, the atmosphere of the Left Bank in the early sixties when I did time there: the whole ritual of meeting Frenchmen—intellectuals and would-be lovers—in cafés, talking about books and film, an atmosphere in which conversation was the food of life, not just because the French were brilliant conversationalists, but because they were too cheap to buy you a dinner (except once, as prologue to an affair). And finally there is a matter of the performances of the two women, Bernadette Lafont and Françoise Lebrun, who invest their roles with something that takes them beyond the bare bones of the director's attitudes and allows them to steal the show, as they are meant to, from the dominant male/intellectual figure played by Léaud.

No less striking are the performances of the six females in *The Bitter Tears of Petra von Kant,* featuring some of the regulars of Fassbinder's repertory: Margit Carstensen as the droll, imperious Petra, Irm Hermann (the skinny, puffy-eyed woman from *The Merchant of the Four Seasons*) as her mute slave-apprentice Marlene, and Hanna Schygulla (from *Recruits in Ingolstadt*) as the sluggish, stunningly sensual Karin who comes to live with her, make her name as a model, and then break the heart of her benefactress.

Of the three Fassbinder films I've seen, this one is his most artificial in design, a tragi-comic love story disguised as a lesbian slumber party in high-camp drag. The elaborate, studied compositions and camera place-ment, the single set (Petra's bedroom-studio), the comic pop-cultural references (the conjunction of Verdi and the Platters, Miami and Joe Mankiewicz), mannequins carefully placed in visual counterpoint, and the use of a dialogue and delivery that, like the mannequins have a familiar shape but are empty of meaning, all contribute to a theatricalized, highly controlled world that appears devoid of the kind of passion that is its subject. A pageant of feminine display, of suffering, abuse, insinuating glances, is acted out in front of a Titianlike painting whose free, poly-morphous, bacchanalian carnality seems to make mockery not just of the angular, desiccated emotions of Fassbinder's women, but of his own "bloodlessly" modern *mise-en-scène*. But it is through just such distancing devices, the grand gestures and the comic routines, that the clichés of love (and art) are exhausted and reborn. Fassbinder does not really believe in the ideal of unfettered sexuality portrayed in the painting (Karin, the woman who most resembles the lush late-Renaissance figures, is the most passionlessly mediocre), and knows that the sixteenth-century painter was as neurotic as his twentieth-century counterpart. And just as Titian's or Rubens's art was a reaction in the name of realism to the overidealized subject matter of early Renaissance, Fassbinder's cinema of artifice and agony is a new kind of "realism."

Like his other films, this one is a study of exploitation, greed, medioc-rity, stupidity, redeemable by love (or death) and by a principle of alternation by which the victim turns into the victimizer, and the victimizer turns into victim.

Petra describes, to a countess-friend who is about to introduce her to Karin, her relationship with her ex-husband, expressing a disappointment that they were not able to achieve what she holds as an ideal—a free, honest, nonpossessive love. These admirable Lawrentian sentiments, so easy to maintain when the heart is uninvolved, are quickly forgotten in the love affair with Karin. But far from being "defined" by her misery, the irony comes in the disparity between her intelligence and talent and success on the one hand, and her abjection on the other.

The scene of ultimate degradation occurs when, in a paroxysm of drunken grief, she confesses the unwelcome news of her lesbian attachment to her mother and daughter (an adolescent just home from boarding school, and full of her first love). It is a scene of unbearable cruelty and high comedy—on one level, it is an evocation (and duplication—life *is* a cliché) of those Hollywood films like *Joy of Living*, when the career woman (Irene Dunne as a singer) finally discovers that the members of her freeloading family are basically selfish, and kicks them out on their ear—for their own good.

Similarly, Petra has "broken through," liberating her mother and daughter, perhaps more than herself, by forcing them to recognize the less-than-ideal side of *their* daughter, and mother. Our first reaction, and it is the first strong emotion we have been permitted, is fury—"How can she do this to her daughter?"—but it is an emotion that even as we feel it is called into question. Petra is purged, her mother is restored to her womanhood. But in the final irony (there is, for Fassbinder, no ending, only another twist of the screw) she loses Marlene, who is willing to play masochist or sadist, but not equal.

Nothing is intrinsically wrong with the accusation by the Lesbian Feminists that *The Bitter Tears of Petra von Kant* is a *man*'s sadomasochistic vision of the universality of dominant/submissive power relationships, acted out by six *women*. (Except that it's not the vision that's sadomasochistic—Fassbinder doesn't abuse his women, if anything he exalts them—but a vision of sadomasochism.) But the same could be said of many another director, and particularly the Germans. *Mabuse* can hardly be understood without an appreciation of the irrational will to power and that joy in the manipulation of people which reduces them (as characters so often appear in Lang's films) to stick pins on a campaign map or draws from their lips their own death wish. Fassbinder's is perhaps a more modern view, in that he sees, in the shifts and reversals of status, the interchangeability of the two terms, the secret yearning for self-abasement of the sadist, and the stranglehold of guilt in which the masochist grips him.

But the implication that women are only incidental to the vision of the film is absurd. Lesbianism is no more incidental to *Petra* than blackness is to *Othello*. The women are in an extreme, womblike situation, and form master-servant relationships existentially, with an operatic purity that is more stylized and less physical than male homosexuality, and that is less complicated than a heterosexual coupling, where the man's dominant role is always a social given, whether or not it reflects the true division of power. In addition, the attraction of the brilliant aging Petra for the young, simpleminded girl contains that element of self-hatred that has inevitably characterized homosexual relationships. In fact, any attraction of opposites, heterosexual or homosexual, is predicated on an element of self-hatred—a rejection, or oversufficiency, of that part of oneself (social background, age, intellect, metabolism) to which the other person is the antithesis.

Such an antithesis animates (or tries to) the heterosexual dialectic in *The Way We Were*, between Barbra Streisand as a humorless Jewish politico

and Robert Redford as a gorgeous all-American Wasp writer. She is supposed to be attracted to the fascist decadent in him, he to the Jewish mother
in her in this Hollywood fairy tale about Hollywood sellout. The story of
their impossible romance is taken from Arthur Laurents's novel (adapted
by the author amidst rumors of difficulties) of life and political styles in the
late thirties and forties. As directed by Sydney Pollack, there is a great deal
of glamor surrounding the two stars, but so little real sense of struggle, of
decisions made or not made, friends abandoned, tastes altered, so few
environmental details (and I don't mean the laboriously re-created forties
look, but a sense of past, of being born into one kind of family or another)
that they are merely archetypes in some kind of morality play pitting New
York against Hollywood, Integrity against Sellout. They are chic torsos on
which to hang the styles and ideologies of a nostalgia trip (making this,
not the Fassbinder, the movie that really treats people as mannequins), and
both they and the issues are trivialized in the process.

Part of the problem is that something quite obviously has happened on
the way to or from the cutting room. There are huge gaps in time and
motivation, and we never know how many minutes, months, years have
passed between important events. But it is not the structural flaws as much
as the absence of any idiosyncratic reality within the scenes that makes the
film seem so "unlived" in, and its characters untouched by all the up-
heavals they undergo.

Those changes that do occur are magical: Streisand goes with Redford
to Hollywood and presto! she sprouts a sense of humor, learns to play
tennis, and actually makes some friends (although one of them is the
Uncompromising European, played by Viveca Lindfors). She keeps her
political activities within bounds (except for one excursion to Washington
to demonstrate against McCarthy), wins over Redford's recalcitrantly
Wasp friend (Bradford Dillman), and, except for Redford being forced by
his producer (Patrick O'Neal) to make mysterious cuts in his screenplay
(and thus does Hollywood imitate Hollywood), everything seems to be
going along fine, when the next thing we know Redford is leaving her. She
seems to know all about it, but it came as a shock to me.

Well, at least she doesn't run after him, I thought (although she can't
very well, since she's lying in bed after delivery), or use the baby to lure
him back. Let's grant the film a few points for treating her political activities half-seriously. She is not the figure of ridicule that crusading women
in movies like *Susan and God* used to be, but her sense of political purpose
does not really counterbalance the pull of romantic attraction evinced in a
single close-up of Robert Redford. As Hubbell the doomed Wasp, Redford
is too controlled to be self-destructive; as a writer, he's not terribly convincing, rating somewhere between Gary Cooper in *The Wedding Night*

and Humphrey Bogart in *In a Lonely Place;* but as a heterosex object, he's ineffable. Streisand's wrongness is more subtle. She's too self-aware, too much of an ego to be an Eleanor Roosevelt or a Dorothy Thompson type (and can you imagine either of them with F. Scott Fitzgerald or Gatsby? And if she were really as ideological as she says, wouldn't she have found his writing hopelessly decadent?) and so we are brought by that ineluctable star magic, unchallenged by a contrary pull, to wonder why in the hell she doesn't run after him. It's the early fifties now, and she's parading in front of the Plaza with some ban-the-bomb posters and he arrives with his new Tricia-type girlfriend and he stops and talks to her and gives her this long look, so lost and attractive and appealing, and obviously wanting her back. And I felt this pang like I hadn't felt since *The Umbrellas of Cherbourg* that she had really made a mistake, only she didn't know it. I knew it, but what I don't know is how a moment of pure exquisite movie-movie agony can come like that out of nothing and nowhere.

Throughout the movie, I kept feeling Streisand would be happier in some other role, something freer and more footloose, just as Sandra Hochman (I kept thinking through *Year of the Woman*) would be happier in the silver shoes of Liz Renay, the stripper with whom she spends considerable time in the film, and with whom she seems, perhaps unconsciously, to identify. The two women even discuss the possibility of "playing" each other in films, and when Sandra parades Liz, attired in a gold sequin "second skin" dress, through the convention floor, purportedly to expose male lechery, she is obviously getting a vicarious thrill from the looks and catcalls lavished on her protégée. (Evidence for this is provided in early snapshots of Hochman as a little girl, more physically developed than her playmates, and her remarks that she always wanted to be a "sexpot.")

Neither Hochman nor Streisand seems comfortable with the first person plural, which would be fine except that their roles as Stalinist and feminist require such poses of solidarity. Both play Jewish princesses committed to something larger than themselves, and both manage to reduce world issues to toys in their sandbox and make their male adversaries look like paragons of wit and charm and understanding. (No ethnic slur intended— some of the women in *The Women* make me feel the same way.) If anything, Streisand seems more committed to her left-wing programs, possibly because she's the better actress, than does Hochman to the matriarchal ones in the "fantasy" she herself has written, directed, and starred in as an observer at the 1972 Democratic Convention.

"I am a poet, a spy, a fool, I am Everywoman," she announces at the outset, and one has to be disarmed by the degree to which she allows her footage to substantiate at least the middle two claims. A poet she may be. Everywoman she is not.

The movie consists of interviews with (in descending order of length and emphasis) male celebrities, male noncelebrities, women celebrities, and women noncelebrities, interspersed with fun and games among the women in Miami, skits (they descend on the CBS news team and harangue them for treating women as freaks), Ms. Hochman's musings about her childhood, thoughts on Miami, and recitation of her own poetry, some previously published, some freshly minted for the occasion.

Next to Ms. Hochman, Art Buchwald has what might be called the second lead. He appears in the beginning, middle, and end, first shooting pool and deploring the loss of the hurdy-gurdy atmosphere, and at last in a planetarium on the moon where he has been consigned after the woman takeover. He is a sort of male chauvinist mascot, performing a function similar to that of the pig that Billie Jean King gave Bobbie Riggs, but to transpose Billie Jean's remark, he's "too cute."

Hochman's tendency to gravitate to the men is easily explained: she is putting together a collection of "male chauvinist remarks." Warren Beatty tells her she's changed quite a bit, has gotten more forthright, since the time she came to interview him at the Beverly Hills Hotel when she was constantly doing "little numbers." She is definitely aggressive in her dealings with men now, especially when it comes to one who is less of a celebrity than she is and might need the publicity like the electronic poet (Edmund Skelling?), rather than a bigger name (Mailer) whom she cuddles up to as a "sister" and is repaid by being called a "bitch."

Skelling she accuses of male chauvinism because of a song he does in which he reduces the mating game to two phonemes "now" and "no," for male and female, which he elongates electronically. But here, as elsewhere, she draws the wrong conclusion. Surely if the two responses are to be compared, it is the woman's desire to prolong the experience rather than the man's for immediate satisfaction that is "superior."

The movie contains some splashes of the humor that Ms. Hochman, in interviews, has claimed for it, but somehow it is more often at her expense than at her instigation. Her refusal to take politics or politicians seriously only limits her view of what is going on and the film's ultimate value as a record. Michele Clark, of one of the major networks, makes what even then should have been recognized as one of the sounder observations: that McGovern couldn't have a woman on his ticket because he already had "too many packs on his back," but Hochman dismisses this as media-compromise nonsense.

Flo Kennedy offers some gloriously acerbic remarks (on motherhood:

"You got to love this kid to keep from killing it, you're so pissed!"), but I would have liked to hear more from Gloria Steinem (whose only contribution is a quote from Mayor Daley for Sandra's "collection"), and from some of the unknown members of the Women's Caucus.

For me the moment of truth came when a group of Hochman-led militants thinly disguised as "freaks" descended on the empty auditorium where the CBS crew was talking things over and began yelling at them, at Dan Rather and Mike Wallace and Roger Mudd with his bewildered blue eyes (anyone who hassles Roger Mudd will have to deal with me), and I experienced the same pang of disloyalty that I had felt when I wanted Barbra Streisand to abandon politics for Robert Redford. But it was not just my own shameful atavism, I suddenly realized, but something in the women themselves, perhaps a sexual self-hatred (a hatred, that is, of their own sex) that made them defer to male power and, in attacking men, ennoble them. My only response was to want to run for the nearest patriarchy, or at least as far as possible from the prospect of a matriarchy—a course that Hochman herself takes, escaping to the moon with Buchwald at the first opportunity.

The idea of a matriarchy is no less oppressive (or absurd) than a patriarchy (Jill Johnston wrote eloquently to this point several weeks ago), and to promote it is to insist on primitive female roles and the kind of fixed, hierarchical power structure that we are supposedly trying to destroy. The fact that Hochman doesn't really believe in it, is acting in bad faith, makes it even worse. By exaggerating the barrier between men and women, she plays on extremes (like the counterculture-establishment charades in *Billy Jack*), and reinforces those sex definitions by which men retain their nominal superiority. Like those women who write funky "angry" letters to Norman Mailer in *The Voice*, she is turning on to the male celebrity-power stud and panting lustily for the signs of that sexism she pretends to be routing in the name of Sisterhood. (Even Buchwald is surprised when she asks him to devise an ending for the film. "But it's your fantasy, Sandra," he says.)

I tend to think, like Fassbinder, that there will always be hierarchies and inequities and oppression of one person by another, as long as love, intelligence, ego are distributed in unequal proportions. Our only hope is that power structures shift, today's celebrity is tomorrow's forgotten man, new loves are born, and things even out a little bit in the long run. But beware of women crying "we, we, we" all the way home—they may be pigs in disguise.

October 25, 1973

SUMMER WISHES, WINTER DREAMS

Judith Crist

Summer Wishes, Winter Dreams is a lovely, intense, and deeply affecting drama of emotional crisis, deep in the tradition of *Rachel, Rachel* (sharing its star and screenwriter) and *I Never Sang for My Father* (sharing its director). It boasts another fine performance by Joanne Woodward, in a searing portrait of a middle-aged woman forced, on her mother's death, to face her own pattern of living, and an equally impressive one by Martin Balsam as the understanding husband who helps her break through the web of self-deception we weave out of the past to protect ourselves from present truths. It is more than the *Death of a Snow Queen*, its original title.

Gilbert Cates, who made his screen debut with *I Never Sang for My Father* in 1970, has brought the same universals of everyday detail to the realization of Stewart Stern's original screenplay in an appreciation of the immutabilities of the middle years, our refusal to accept and, even stronger, even to voice the regret that eats at us. Ms. Woodward and Mr. Balsam are the embodiment of all of us who have let central relationships atrophy while we hurry through the routines of living. A haunted, harried woman, a supportive but inarticulate husband, children who love but are alienated, siblings seething with the angers of childhood—and a sudden death in the midst of life's tensions is the catalyst for the purgation we must have to survive. It's a shocking drama—told in terms of upper-middle-class living, the large perpetually-being-decorated apartment, the baby-sitting and do-gooding. It is the exploration of the very heart of Stephen Sondheim's ladies who lunch—and the key scene, in fact, is ladies lunching, Miss Woodward the impatient daughter, Sylvia Sidney (of the still-stunning eyes and dramatic intensity) the mother at the root. This isn't a blockbuster; it is the small movie that caring men venture on without a box-office eye. But it is a film that matters and that will remain in your heart.

October 29, 1973

Paul D. Zimmerman

Along with Barbra Streisand and Liza Minnelli, Joanne Woodward is one of the few American actresses to consistently put the stamp of her personality on the films she makes. Parts are tailored to suit her enormous talent because she is a star, and she remains a star because roles are written to suit her. From *Rachel, Rachel* to *The Effect of Gamma Rays on Man-in-the-Moon Marigolds* to her most recent *Summer Wishes, Winter Dreams*, she has specialized in sensitive, emotionally undernourished losers seeking to love and be loved.

Her Rita Walden is such a figure: the well-off wife of a successful New York ophthalmologist (Martin Balsam). Rita has inherited from her dyspeptic, querulous mother (Sylvia Sidney) a legacy of lovelessness that she has passed on to her dumpy, resentful daughter (Dori Brenner) and her homosexual son, who has taken up residence in Amsterdam to escape her.

This is one of those movies that thrive on their fidelity to a world we immediately recognize. We have met Rita's mother a thousand times, heard her complain about the decline in courtesy as she behaves rudely to a waitress, or listened to her bicker with her daughter over the way lemons are sliced in London hotels. We have seen Ritas at little restaurants for rich ladies, functioning on a third of their intelligence, dabbling in charity to give their lives an illusion of meaning, channeling their feelings into caustic cadences of complaint about a world they have made for themselves. But Joanne Woodward, through her ability to get inside her sterile heroine, makes us care about Rita. As we watch her boss her daughter or push away the tentative embraces of her ineffectual husband, we recognize in the lines of her aging face the pain of a woman without real malice struggling in an emotional straitjacket.

We know who knitted her that jacket in the scene where Rita holds her dying mother in her arms and receives as last words a command to "cancel my appointments." We understand why Rita relives dreams of her childhood on her grandparents' farm and why her husband mines the memory of the battle of Bastogne as a cherished moment of "freedom" before falling into the quicksand of a muddled marriage.

But director Gilbert Cates (*I Never Sang for My Father*) and screenwriter Stewart Stern find no way of dramatizing Rita's eventual breakthrough to feeling. When the caged couple fly off to Europe as an antidote to the death of Rita's mother, the movie atrophies into what Hitchcock calls "photographs of people talking." And talk they do, in London, revisiting the Bastogne battlefield, in their hermetically sealed hotel rooms, about the peace they have found, her new freedom to say "I love you" and their hopes for a fresh start. All this talk accentuates the inadequacies of Cates's ponderous, pedestrian and utterly humorless style and leaves us with nothing to look at but Gerald Hirschfeld's drab-ugly cinematography. The film finally becomes soap opera, and even Ms. Woodward's Rita, a touching mixture of strength, suffering and self-awareness, is buried in a bathos of big, sad bubbles.

November 19, 1973

A DOLL'S HOUSE
Two Dolls

Molly Haskell

I was most anxious to see Joseph Losey's version of *A Doll's House* with Jane Fonda [at the Cannes Film Festival] in order to compare it with the Claire Bloom film, directed by Patrick Garland. Claire Bloom and her husband-producer Hillard Elkins had been forced to open the film ahead of schedule because of the Losey film, and when I saw her briefly in London, the only harsh words she could be induced to utter about anything or anybody were for the underhanded maneuver of a certain London money-man who after promising to back the Elkins-Bloom production had turned around and offered the project to Losey.

I was an early admirer of the New York production and Bloom's perfor-mance and, like so many others, astonished at the timeliness of the play and Ibsen's prescience. But by now, perhaps, some of the bloom has worn off. While the action of a mother leaving her children is no less radical, we have absorbed the shock in the intervening months, and must agree that *A Doll's House* is one of Ibsen's lesser plays. It is nevertheless a strong feminist statement, and for this reason I had serious reservations about Losey, one of the screen's most elegant and insidious misogynists, directing it. It had been preceded by rumors of *mauvaises vibrations* between the director and his two actresses, Fonda and Delphine Seyrig, and reports that they had formed a women's lib enclave on the set.

But now the verdict is in and Losey's is unquestionably the superior film. It is, first and foremost, a real movie, with an acute sense of period and place (it was shot in a breathtakingly beautiful snowy-serene town in Norway), while Garland's is a literal transvisualization of his stage version.

Garland has "taken it outdoors" in the catch phrase that connotes the manner of a minor alteration, like letting out a hem. Losey, on the other hand, remodeled the material. With perhaps less help than might be expected from screenwriter David Mercer, whose dialogue too often underlines Ibsen's imagery without enriching it, Losey adds a prologue that establishes the relationships between Nora and Christine, Christine and Krogstad (Edward Fox) before the action begins. In the opening shot, the camera pans along a bank of snow and fir trees, glides across a lake of skaters, takes in a fire on the far side of the lake that is the first indication of color in the film and travels with Nora and Christine only as far as the door of the tea house where they go for chocolate. The camera rests for a moment outside, peering at them through the frosty pane, setting up the controlling visual dialectic of the film: a sense of external chill and internal warmth and light, a warmth that gradually gives way to gloom and darkness as friends and lovers flee each other, flee their instincts, and take refuge in obligations. Physical coldness and repression and above all class structure weigh more heavily in the motivations and evasions than they have before. At the expense of a concentration on Nora, who is the *raison d'être* of the Claire Bloom production, Losey creates a continuous world which the characters seem to have inhabited with varying degrees of compliance, long before we are introduced to them. Krogstad, the real idealist of the play and the exception to the rule established by Torvald and Nora that men rarely sacrifice honor for love while "millions of women do it all the time," emerges as something of a hero, and his final reconciliation with Christine in a glorious union of wisdom and faith becomes a positively weighted counterbalance to the disintegrating Helmer marriage. In a distinctly drawn class dialectic, Krogstad and Christine are seen, in the Losey version, as superior to Torvald and Nora, while in the Garland version, Denholm Elliott and Anna Massey never achieve this transcendent value. When she pleads with him to stay with her rather than go for the letter, Anna Massey does so in the interest of sexual desire rather than saving truth.

Claire Bloom's exquisitely wrought Nora has been preserved intact and, ironically, what seemed intimate and sensual on the stage seems cool and impenetrable under the prying eye of the camera. Each character in the Garland version is surrounded by an invisible screen, shielding them from us and one another. By contrast, in the fluid and architecturally expressive Losey version, the characters relate to each other and to the space they inhabit. Fonda and David Warner's Torvald seem to have lived with each other forever. The emphasis in Losey's *Doll's House* is on the *house*, a masterpiece of thematically expressive set design, rather than the *Doll*. In the long, narrow vista from the parlor through the dining room to the playroom, Nora's world is seen, in the reduced perspective of deep focus, as a doll's house in an optical as well as dramatic delusion. Fonda is a glowing Nora—vibrant, impulsive, a transitional figure between past and present, between Victorian pretense and lonely liberation. We don't get "inside" her any more than we do Claire Bloom's heroine, because ultimately Nora is not a creature whose soul we are invited to explore. Krogstad's ethical deliberations are more interesting than hers because he has a more complex relationship to the world, contradictory ties which she is only beginning to discover when the play ends. She is a before-and-after figure, with none of the mystery and resonance of Ibsen's other heroines, Hedda, Rebecca West, Hilde Wangel. She hasn't the emotional complexity to interest a "women's director" like Bergman, and yet she is solid and intractable enough that she can't be subverted by a misogynist. (Conversely, Ibsen's straightness seems an excellent anchor and antidote to Losey's tendency to stylistic perversity.) To this emblematic feminist, Fonda brings her own reverberations, the evolution of an actress-and-woman from Papa's (and Vadim's) little girl to up-front militant, but a militant who, from the evidence of *A Doll's House*, remains an actress first and a feminist second.

May 24, 1973

SUCH A GORGEOUS KID LIKE ME

Penelope Gilliatt

François Truffaut's *Such a Gorgeous Kid Like Me* is a story of love and infatuation veiled as a tale about tracking down murder clues. The beloved object, in a story told entirely in flashback apart from the beginning and end, is morally speaking a multi-murderer, though she manages eventually to slither around all factual culpability. She is played by Bernadette Lafont to the hilt of sleaziness, with a hairdo like an Afro wig that has slipped. She finds a credulous supporter, who thinks for a long time that she has been wrongly accused, in a sociologist (André Dussollier). She bemuses him. At the start, he arrives in prison with his tape recorder to do a study of her as a specimen of criminal woman, and earns the scorn of the wardress for his choice. "Why not the giant who strangled her husband with one hand?" she says. But the luckless sociologist, a thin pedant in spectacles whose profession has unfortunately tutored him to approach the particular from the general and to back into it from the wrong end, is determined to turn up a prisoner to prove his thesis that a rotten childhood will always lead someone to be a rotter. The girl is a patent liar, who says that she is a singer though she has a voice like a nutmeg grater, and who earlier pretends offhandedly that her moon-faced husband is her brother when she happens on a good soul who speaks to her dank eroticism. Man after man falls for her, including an absolutely charming and very religious exterminator with the soul of a troubadour. The exterminator's name is Arthur. Nice name for a white mouse. He is played by Charles Denner, whose upright, good, alertly stupid face looks very like an exterminator's when you come to think of it. He drives a large truck with sky-blue sides announcing his Christian name and profession. His chief weapon against the evils of the animal kingdom—the evils of man overwhelm him, and he has decided not to take·them on—seems to be a rusting gadget that puffs out fatal gases and looks much like some treadle sewing machine invented by James Watt when he was trying to arrive at a perfected version of the steam engine.

The story comes from a book by Henry Farrell, and the screenplay is by the director and Jean-Loup Dabadie (who has also worked with Claude Sautet and Philippe de Broca). The movie has more in common with Truffaut's *The Bride Wore Black*, even to a plainly intentional reminiscent scene about a church tower, than with most of his other work. Truffaut is generally more absorbed than he is in this film by the spectacle of someone's muddle of criminality and solemn, absurd love. Most of the people in *Gorgeous Kid* are glad to be friendless. There are few of Truffaut's affectionate odd pairings (though I suppose a whore using an exterminator as her taxi driver is not to be sneezed at). "I adore other people's parents; that's about the size of it," says someone who is clearly speaking for Truffaut in *Bed and Board;* but there is no character here like this. Instead there is a central figure whose presence heavily says that, for all her sluttishness, she doesn't like haziness or the ambiguous or the equivocal, whereas Truffaut's more natural subjects are in league with ambiguity, although they often think themselves into insisting on a preference for the *définitif*. The crafty slob who is the gorgeous kid succeeds with a firmness that people seldom have in Truffaut. She is a fearsome mixture of the tawdry and the precise. Her choice is for the clear-cut. Her lies and machinations are razors. She ends up the winner at her macabre sports of seduction, false-trail-laying, and murder. We see her singing her unbeautiful larynx out in a nightclub, wearing jewelry handcuffs, and surrounded by more admirers. Perhaps it is because Truffaut finds her charmless and implausible that the audience does, too. You wonder why anyone in the picture is taken in.

A victory for the ambitious figure in a Truffaut film leaves it without a hero or heroine. I think the movie would have had more of his usual conviviality, drollness, and feeling for earnest alliances between tacit people (as in *The Wild Child*, for instance) if the huge part of the girl had been played by someone who seemed either more hapless or to have more of the stylishness in amorality of, say, Catherine Deneuve in *Mississippi Mermaid*. It could have been much cut, as well, to leave room for the more complex Truffaut small parts to flourish and expand. One likes the exterminator greatly. One also responds a lot to the secretary called Hélène. She is played by Anne Kreis, a long-faced, straight-haired, obviously bright and uncompetitive girl. The secretary is crazy about her misled sociologist boss, but she has to type the transcript of the prisoner's testimony without blinking, though she can smell mendacity and showoff in every line of it. The credulity of her employer is wounding to her as well as amazing. She is a very appealing character, beautifully played by Miss Kreis, who is still a student. And there is a scene with an infant film buff that seems purest Truffaut. Hélène and the sociologist are on the trail of an amateur photographer who may have a vital piece of evidence. They come to a doorway and ask for Mr. Farrell (also the author's name—in-joke). "Mr. Farrell," says a nice bourgeoise at the door, "is dead." "Oh, excuse us, our condolences; your husband dead . . ." "No, not my husband," says the housewife, inexplicably brightening up a little at the red herring, "my son." "But such a fine *photographer*," the interlocutors plug on. "Ah, that would be my nephew," says the housewife, and she yells for an extremely small boy in an Eton collar, who reaches up to the amateur detectives' waists but nonetheless holds with dignity that he doesn't like showing his rushes before they are edited. Perhaps the most typical Truffaut flash in the whole of this film, in which he seems often to be marking time and sometimes to be quite off the track, is a scene in a prison yard when a wrongly accused prisoner with a neat turn of mind finds a bit of paper; sweeps it up; can find nowhere to put it, because prisons specialize in useless, Sisyphean jobs; and furtively shoves the scrap down a grating, as though that were a much worse crime than the murder he has been accused of.

Truffaut has always been delicately rueful on behalf of the gulled. This would have been twice the film it is if it had been more open about Truffaut's standing topic, which is the mixture of comedy and damage that can lie in the train of perfidy. Now and then the idea sticks out of the rather gaudy structure of the film like bones in the sun. There are scenes of disruption that are some of Truffaut's most perturbed since *The Soft Skin*.

March 31, 1973

MAILER ON MONROE

Andrew Sarris

Norman Mailer's book on Marilyn Monroe is shaping up as the book industry's most scandalous event since the Clifford Irving hoax with Howard Hughes. As it happens, *Marilyn* is largely a critique and cannibalization of earlier writings on the subject, and much of the controversy seems to have arisen from Mailer's belittling of his predecessors as if they were his research assistants. It would certainly be too tedious for anyone but a lawyer or a judge to compare Mailer's copy word-for-word with the full texts of Fred Lawrence Guiles's *Norma Jean* and Maurice Zolotow's *Marilyn Monroe*, the two most-quoted sources for the book in question. It would be even more tedious to accuse Mailer of sins to which he has confessed freely in a series of self-scourging interviews with the media magistrates of CBS, *Time* magazine and *The New York Times*. In this very lurid context, confession may be as good for sales as for the soul.

But what may have been lost sight of in all the confusion is that Mailer has manfully transformed a tackily commissioned coffee-table project into a personal crisis. We have been told that Mailer received a $50,000 advance from a photographer named Schiller to write a 10,000-word "preface" for a picture book on Marilyn Monroe. If all that had mattered in Mailer's mind had been the hard cash he needed to support two homes, five wives and seven children through Phase Four, he could have ground out a 10,000-word "meditation" on Marilyn Monroe in his sleep; and then spent his waking hours toiling on that white whale of a novel his more tiresome admirers keep demanding from him. But it would never do for a writer of Mailer's magnitude to be dropped lightly on a coffee table, to be demeaned by the literati as the glib librettist for the visual music of a horde of lens-hounds. By expanding the 10,000-word preface into a 90,000-word "novel biography," Mailer now lands on the coffee table with a heavy thud, but he has become the master of his own book, and Marilyn Monroe, in death and in dreams, has become his mistress, a moonlike mystery to be penetrated by his literary astronaut's projectile.

Since there is no writer maler than Mailer, the cultural coupling of two sex symbols, one a prisoner of sex and the other a hostage to Hollywood fortune, makes a certain amount of mythic sense. The built-in publicity value alone is beyond measure, and Mailer's professional talent is virtually beyond dispute. To say, therefore, that Mailer's latest venture is more readable than admirable, and that it displays more charisma than character, or charity, or even courtesy is to say that it is the least we might have expected under the circumstances.

Of course, Mailer is an old hand at confounding his critics by confusing their categories. What is Mailer's "novel biography," after all, but the New Journalism transported to those outer limits of perception where the lies of art whore around with the lies of gossip. If Tom Wolfe with his invisible white suits and his chastely uncommitted persona embodies the voyeuristic branch of the New Journalism, Mailer with his mauled machismo thrusts upward and outward as New Journalism's most extended exhibitionist branch, veritably its Lenny Bruce of letters. The problem here is that movies and movie stars are more fitting subjects for voyeurs than for exhibitionists. As the glaring illumination of New York City's skyline obliterates the luster of the Milky Way, so does Mailer's own superstar status dim the flickering glow of Marilyn's milky screen incarnation. And being a man closer to politics than to poetics, he is obsessed more by the Machiavellian processes of power and publicity than by the magical idiosyncrasies of her image. The book is therefore richer in intrigue than in insight as the Marilyn we all knew dissolves in a mist of fresh metaphors and stale anecdotes, the latter mostly borrowed and mostly blue. Much of Mailer's locker-room language cannot be reprinted in family newspapers like *The Washington Post*, and so there is that extra dividend for X-rated readers of books.

In the midst of all these commercial considerations is the ever-elusive ghost of Marilyn Monroe, who died of an overdose of sleeping pills during a lost August weekend in 1962. She had been born Norma Jean Mortenson on June 1, 1926, not far from where she was to be eventually incarnated and ultimately entombed as the American sex goddess of her era. Her mother actually lived for a time in Hollywood and worked at the processing laboratories of Consolidated Film Industries. The identity of her father always remained a speculative question, and Norma Jean ran the gamut of orphanages, foster homes, madness in the family and the savage, rootless religiosity, then as now, of southern California. However, Mailer's effort to drag in Richard Nixon's boyhood in Whittier as a broken-mirror reflection of Norma Jean's girlhood seems to be strictly a post-Watergate conceit to make the book more relevant. At times Mailer conveys the impression that everything west of Elaine's is malignantly Middle American and that anything Far West is especially far out. This kind of presumptuous New York provincialism has more to do with Mailer's own disorientation from the non-intellectual middle class than with the life story of a pretty girl who wanted to get into the movies.

At eighteen Norma Jean marries James Dougherty, whose story now is that his bride was a virgin on her wedding night. Ergo, virgo. Mailer chooses to believe everything Dougherty says because this relative nobody is such a humble, cooperative witness, such a fountain of information for the otherwise parched biographer. By contrast, Maurice Zolotow and the late Ben Hecht are not to be trusted. They are in the myth-making business along with Mailer, and they have already covered most of the terrain. Mailer seeks to dislodge them by suggesting that their anecdotes on Marilyn are too symmetrically mythic, too meaningfully psychoanalytical. Mailer recounts their anecdotes just the same, but he is too much into tarot cards, word games, karma and the afterlife to play Freud with Freudian fan-magazine material. Still, Aquarius refuses to liberate himself from the Robbins-Susann drugstore rack formulas for fictionalized biography. Instead of pinning down the beautiful butterfly of Marilyn Monroe, he crawls back to the cocoon from which Norma Jean Mortenson wriggled like a carnal caterpillar to womanhood and stardom.

But, irony of ironies, it is now Norma Jean Mortenson who is the fabricated myth and Marilyn Monroe who is the authentic reality. For Norma Jean to become Marilyn, she must discard Dougherty and take up with a succession of producers, photographers and agents. She will engage make-up men and masseurs for her body and her mind; she will marry and divorce two mythic consorts—Joe DiMaggio of Yankee Stadium, Fisherman's Wharf, Toots Shor's, and then Arthur Miller of Brooklyn Heights, Connecticut, Karl Marx, Reform Judaism and *Death of a Salesman*. From the crowd to the crucible to the grave, and in between some thirty movie appearances, thousands of photos, millions of words of publicity copy and reported affairs with Marlon Brando, Frank Sinatra and Yves Montand, to mention only the most mythic. Indeed, the most striking picture in the book is Bruce Davidson's harshly lit three-way confrontation of Simone Signoret and Marilyn Monroe with Montand, his back to us and presumably to the wall as well. Mailer is singularly unkind to most of the men in Marilyn's life: Montand he dismisses as a pushy Italian peasant (right out of an

Arthur Miller play about the little people) who merely uses Marilyn to get some needed Hollywood notoriety; Miller he ridicules for the pontifical pipe with which Miller hopes to puff his way into becoming the first Jewish Pope; DiMaggio degenerates into an ethnic joke as an over-the-hill-athlete-turned-saloonkeeper; and Sinatra is rather conventionally maligned as a Mafia singer right out of the pages of *The Godfather*.

It is to Mailer's credit that he at least goes through the motions of discussing Marilyn's movies as artifacts apart from her sex life. He claims to have screened twenty-four of her thirty movies, but that's precisely the trouble. He's had to catch up on movies the authentic Monrovians caught at the time they came out. Hence, there is no historical resonance or icono-graphical perspective in Mailer's account of Marilyn's career. After all, it isn't as if Marilyn were the first sexy blonde Hollywood had ever seen, or the last. Fox, the studio that first found Marilyn and finally cast her aside, was noted for its blonde succession, from torchy Alice Faye to tip-tappy Betty Grable, and from Betty Grable to June Haver (through their sibling act in *The Dolly Sisters*), but poor June couldn't cut the mustard and betook herself to a nunnery. Way back in the thirties, of course, there was the classically bawdy blondeness of Jean Harlow and Mae West, and also soulful Carole Lombard, snazzy Ginger Rogers, snappy Joan Blondell and sloe-eyed Ann Sothern. Even the bosom build-up wasn't new. Forget about Jane Russell's publicity H-bomb in *The Outlaw*. Lana Turner as doomed jailbait in *They Won't Forget* (1937) enters and exits in a sweater which helped pull the wool over the eyes of the proletariat during the Depression.

The dumb-Dora blonde who can't type, or act, or say anything intelligent but oh-watch-her-hips-and-other-protuberances (essentially the ethos for the eye-popping walk-ons Marilyn did in *Monkey Business, All About Eve, The Asphalt Jungle, Love Happy*) happened to be a staple of comic strips, movies and television. Barbara Nichols, Marie Wilson, Joi Lansing and Dagmar were around at about the same time doing the blonde archetype bit. Kim Stanley executed the definitive Method interpretation of Marilyn in Paddy Chayevsky's *The Goddess*, and Lola Albright crossed the erotic frontier of film in *Cold Wind in August*. Jayne Mansfield became the first prominent Monroe imitator, but went so far into harsh, Westian self-parody that she marked the beginning of the camp female impersonation of the Warhol era. Through the sixties and seventies, camera magic endowed Stella Stevens with some of Marilyn's fleshy phosphorescence, and Tuesday Weld with some of her luminous nymphet's soul. Which is not to say that there could ever be another Marilyn, but her ineffable uniqueness hardly qualifies her as Mailer's "Napoleon" of the medium, a conqueror with no need of a context. She had severe limitations as an actress, particularly with her voice, which, fortunately, we don't have to endure in a picture book.

However, it just so happens that Marilyn was in the business of talking pictures. Yet she could never do any of the wise cracking Lombard, Rogers, Arthur, Harlow, West roles of the thirties. She was all marshmallow, with perpetually moistened, quivering lips, and males of a certain sensibility in search of sexual redemption worshipped her for her divine compliance with their fantasies, but most women despised her for throwing the game to the boys in the locker room without making a fight of it. Nowadays, of course, women's libbers try to transform her into a Joan of Arc who died because of the sins of men, but Marilyn was really done in by the women who stayed away in droves. That is why Fox was paying her only $100,000 for her last movie while Elizabeth Taylor was raking in a cool million from the same studio.

Mailer underrates Marilyn's more interesting cult movies like *River of No Return* and *Don't Bother to Knock* and even *Niagara,* while overpraising her laboriously chic performances in *Bus Stop* and *The Misfits.* Worse still, Mailer either ignores or demeans the contributions of other players to her most successful movies, particularly in *Some Like It Hot,* a Billy Wilder classic of transvestism which Mailer describes bizarrely as a Marilyn Monroe comedy with support from Jack Lemmon, Tony Curtis and the late Joe E. Brown, when it is precisely the other way around. Marilyn is winsome and winning, and gives her part something extra. But even her biggest scene in which she seduces the supposedly impotent Tony Curtis would have made audiences uncomfortable if it had not been intercut with the Last Tango in Drag of Jack Lemmon and Joe E. Brown, with one wild rose between them to switch from mouth to mouth.

As for Mailer's "theory" that Marilyn was murdered by a right-wing conspiracy to embarrass Bobby Kennedy, even the author finds it hard to believe. Indeed, it is somewhat disingenuous of Mailer to catalogue all her pills, sores, wrinkles, abortions and tubular pregnancies, to describe all the scars of her soul and all the muddle of her mind, to drag us through all her bitchy days and lonely nights, and then tell us with a straight face that this thirty-six-year-old sex goddess on suspension from her studio in hostile Hollywood had everything to live for. Perhaps she sensed intuitively that her most devout admirers would never forgive her for getting old (*vide* the sad, lonely death just recently of Veronica Lake). Perhaps also, she could look into the future to see the blowsy screen image of Diana Dors in middle age. At the end she needed friends more than she needed worshippers, and she didn't really have enough of either. In the East, the elitists were savoring Jeanne Moreau in *Jules and Jim* and Emmanuele Riva in *Hiroshima, Mon Amour* and Jean Seberg in *Breathless* and Monica Vitti in

L'Avventura and Bibi and Harriet Andersson in the Bergman films. In the West, the Fox and the other species of studio were dying before her eyes. Look at the last pictures of Marilyn in the book, and you will see her gazing very gallantly at the angel of death.

August 12, 1973

Molly Haskell

It's enough to make you believe in divine destiny, or at least that great publicity agent in the sky. The highest paid New York outfit couldn't have planned it better. Her career was going downhill faster than the stone of Sisyphus. *The Misfits* was a flop, her marriage was over. She had lost her leverage in the industry, been fired from her latest picture. Except for *Some Like It Hot* (1959), she had made her best films in the early and mid-fifties. It was now 1962. Marilyn Monroe's death by an overdose of sleeping pills was, as they say in the business, a shot in the arm of her career and probably the best thing that could have happened to her myth. Instead of drifting into that penumbral world between stardom and oblivion, a quaint artifact of the fifties, she became a national monument. With her death, her youth was preserved in formaldehyde; she was turned into a work of art—"forever young, forever fair," a narrative with a beginning, middle, and end.

Let us not weep and call it a tragedy or even untimely. At age thirty-six-going-on-thirty-seven Marilyn may have been young as a human being of the female sex, but as a sexual fantasy she was over the hill. For what does a sex symbol do when it stops being sexy? It retires, like Brigitte Bardot, to St. Tropez to grow herbs. It refuses mother roles, as Mae West is reported to have done at age sixty-five, because "my fans would never believe I don't get the man." And Marilyn's career expectancy was more ephemeral than most. Her Venus emerged half-clothed in the most repressed decade of the twentieth century, in veils it could never shed. Her appeal was peek-a-boo prurient, braless under gauze, not (nude calendar to the contrary) total exposure. Once topless came into movies and braless came onto Fifth Avenue, Marilyn's number was up.

There is a kind of hypocrisy endemic to all writing on Monroe that is hard to avoid (except by silence, and who among us will choose silence?). To mourn Marilyn's death is to wish to eliminate the major source of our interest in her; to deplore it in terms of victimization by the industry is to deny her its significance; and to pretend it could have been otherwise is to ignore, as Mailer does in *Marilyn,* the evidence of those photographs beside which his text sits in uneasy alliance. In the later ones she is undeniably a woman in the shadow of death: flouting it, perhaps, as the garish whore of Bert Stern's semi-nudes, but succumbing to the lure of nothingness in George Barris's wintry, black-and-white beach shots where Mailer unaccountably finds her "not unsturdy" and "wistful and tough."

And now I, too (who can resist?), prepare to feed on the cornucopia of her corpse, or rather on its recent, juiciest blood-filled diner. (The metaphor is not inapt: characteristically ignoring the distinctions between the edible and inedible, Mailer has invaded her very womb and intestines, extruded himself with each abortion, dozed into inanity with each Nembutal, risen with the full moon on her blood; his book sends off odors as bad as those attributed to Marilyn, and catches us up suddenly with her sweetness.)

But if I am going to add to the graffiti on her tombstone, at least I will not dishonor her by pretending I loved her while she was alive. Although I have come to like many and love some of her films, I more than resented her at the time. To me and most of my friends growing up in the fifties (I was thirteen in 1953, when *How to Marry a Millionaire* and *Gentlemen Prefer Blondes* came out, fifteen when *The Seven Year Itch* was released), she was an almost traumatic confirmation of everything I didn't know and feared to be true about sex. She called forth the ugliest side of the male libido—that part of desire that was not even animal lust, which at least expects to give as much as it gets, but the passive, leering demand for painless titillation. Cheaper than a whore, she gave men what they wanted: sex free of charge; free, even, of discharge. The sex she offered had nothing to do with love or even, as far as she was concerned, physical pleasure. Her joy was not in the calibrated response of her body to a man's touch but the power it gave her over them. Her body was a commodity, its packaging a masterpiece of American technology, rendered human by the small, incongruous voice that whispered out of it. It was a body that made me want to abjure mine, not out of jealousy but out of shame. I would have gladly bound my breasts (had there been anything to hide) as the Chinese women bind their feet. She, of course, was the reverse mirror image of my repression, the unleashed flesh of my "taped up" sexuality. We both paid a price. To the extent that we were equal victims of the sexual polarization by which society divides women into virgins and whores, I can now feel a "sister's" solidarity with her.

But to canonize her as a martyr to male chauvinism, the line recently adopted by some members of women's liberation, is at best incomplete. (Her relevance to the women's movement and woman's "dilemma" is better seen in that absence of an ego, that lack of a strong central sense of self in which the orphan's void is a paradigm of the female child's. Except on the screen, and perhaps even there, she was a hyphenated personality. When problems arose, her husbands and associates ran interference for her, and the people in her shifting entourage became a kind of aggregate ego.)

For real martyrs, look to the women who never made it or were powerless to change the direction of their careers, women who never had the temerity to run along the streets of 20th-Century Fox in a negligee in order to capture the attention of Darryl F. Zanuck, women who were unskilled in the art of self-display or unwilling to transfigure themselves with make-up or adjust their whole beings to the camera's presence, so that there would be no moment too intimate for the photographer, and no photograph of the "private" woman that did not belie the term.

Decidedly, Fox never made the most of her, never gave her the opportunity to become a normal, intelligent woman in the sense that Harlow was. But dumbness was as much a part of her persona as blondness: her voice could never have curled with irony or spat with anger and wit. And more than anything, verbal definition—wit, eloquence—is what separates, in the naturally sensual medium of screen, women from sex objects; that is, women as agents from their function as objects of contemplation. Because she cannot "prove herself" in action like a man, a woman's stature is based far more on dialogue, on a sharp line here or there, than his. Hence the success of Marilyn's performance in *Some Like It Hot,* where she has funny lines, and *Gentlemen Prefer Blondes* where she is doubly blessed, not only with funny lines (even if they are dumb-blonde funny lines), but with the stature of a "professional" in the heroic Hawksian sense.

Let us assume that she was not entirely a victim of circumstance or male concupiscence and had a hand in shaping her career: a hand that the women's movement denies her for ideological-political reasons; and that Mailer denies, almost inadvertently, by introducing so many root causes and fateful connections, from Valentino's footprints to her pet dog's "murder," that she drowns in a sea of determinism.

One story Mailer passes over quickly seems more significant than all the orphanage "horrors." In describing her passage through Van Nuys High School, he gives us the recollection, courtesy of Zolotow, of a staff member who states, eighteen years after Marilyn, "We are proud to claim Jane Russell, but we do not claim Marilyn Monroe. She didn't learn anything about acting while she was at Van Nuys High." "No," Mailer explains, "she was not forward." Although during the same period, she was "wearing her bathing suits smaller" than the other girls, and "was delighted at the result." Marilyn could have chosen power or art, or conceivably both. She chose power.

When a woman gave her her first make-up job, she later reported (Zolotow again), "This was the first time in my life I felt loved—no one had ever noticed my face or hair or me before." We cannot fail to note the priorities. From then on, the face and the hair (and the body) became the "me," almost interchangeably. But there was always the little voice, and with it she bequeathed us her identity problems, namely, the teasing idea that there was some hard-core, irreducible "real" Monroe, or that it would be of any interest without the mythic Monroe that makes such a dialectical notion possible. To try to extract the "real Monroe" is like trying to reduce Frankenstein's monster to human size. Her essence is monstrosity. Who, really, cares about the "real Monroe," the one with dirty blonde hair and a shy little voice, the one whom nobody recognized when Norman Rosten took her to a Brooklyn party, the one who gained weight and had insomnia and wrote poetry and loved cats and possibly never had an orgasm. For anyone interested in this Monroe (minus the sex data), Norman Rosten's memoir is the thing to read. It is a tender, modest account of a rather mediocre human being, the one that Rosten befriended, the one, no doubt, that Joe DiMaggio loved. (Marilyn's voice coach, Natasha Lytess, was always complaining that DiMaggio loved his wife for herself and not for her career.) But who can help but be suspicious of the "human being"—"the precise phrase actors employ," writes the other Norman, "when referring to that small part of themselves which is without a role." So it is fitting that Rosten's book, about those few inches of humanity untouched by the camera, is only 125 pages long, while Norman M.'s about the fabulous, factoidal, factitious, facial and faecal Marilyn is, with acknowledgments, quotations, information and assorted insights, 90,000 words, and with photographs, 271 pages retailing at seven cents a page, a bid for attention comparable in its blatancy to her own.

While there have been a number of movie people who could exercise their talents in other areas, Marilyn is one of those (Keaton and Hitchcock are others) who are unthinkable without the medium of cinema. Something magical happened to Marilyn on the screen, and yet it is the only act of alchemy to which Aquarius, with all his dabbling in necromancy, seems resolutely blind. But then, perhaps he has a grudge against movies. He came to them late, thinking he could shake film up formally as he had literature. But cinema has never been as susceptible as the other arts to the charm of the romantic ego. Mailer leaped in, thrashed out some films and some theories, and jumped out, and film, like ole man river, just kept rolling along, repaying his arrogance by nearly obliterating his traces. And so, perhaps in revenge, he has tried to bring Marilyn into existence apart from film, to accomplish in wide-screen, technicolor prose an act of magical magnification equal to that of film, and owing it nothing.

For one who was once contemptuous of "the capital of cinema" (see *The Deer Park*), he out-Hollywoods Hollywood in vulgarity, excitement, hype.

It is hard to grasp hold of, this jumble of arms and fingers, a hydralike embrace between Mailer's various selves and Marilyn's. And since hers will be determined by his, it may be appropriate to try to sort out which Mailer personae have been drawn into combat by the lure of necrophilia, money, anagrams, and hard-core Americana.

1. Mailer, the lustful male. The m.c. who introduces the book and speaks of Marilyn as "every man's love affair with America" and "the sweet angel of sex," Mailer's surrogate middle-American playboy, a Hugh Hefner with imagination and the one I least believe. Marilyn is the antithesis of the raunchy and earthy women who populate Mailer's life and novels, and if he really believes in this chocolate box, ice-cream idol of sex "who was not the dark contract of those passionate brunette depths that speak of blood . . ." then he is painting a darker picture than he imagines.

2. Mailer, the competitive male-Jewish author, competitor with male-Jewish Arthur. Although his insights into her relationship with Miller (in fact, into all her relationships) comprise the best writing in the book, he is gratuitously cruel to the playwright. Is he contemptuous because Miller did not stand up to Olivier for her, and would Mailer have done better? (Or isn't it the fate of the artist, the eternal voyeur, to be unable to give the kind of support that DiMaggio could give—and vice versa?) Or is it merely the rankling irritation of having to experience sexual jealousy of one's literary inferior?

3. Mailer the showman, copywriter supreme. This Mailer is not above extracting the last flavor of scandalous tidbits in the quotes of Guiles, Zolotow, and Ben Hecht even as he is denying their reliability. The prose ranges from bubbling blurbery, disguised by obscenity ("she had never looked so fuckable"), to the usual extraordinary analogies ("Her mind, at its worst, is in ways analogous to a basket-case who seethes with desires to move but has no limbs"). But the line between hype and art has never been so faint.

4. Mailer as novelist/dramatist/self-styled cabalist. This Mailer must avoid Freudian (too middle-class) insights, and find karmic explanations for phenomena as common as a split sensibility (one that was given a quite satisfying physiological account in a recent *Times* magazine article on the two halves of the brain); must set up symbols and cross-references that will resonate through the cultural wasteland of southern California (Marilyn plus Nixon equals ?); and must in every instance prefer the farfetched and exotic explanation to the commonplace one. Thus Marilyn's insomnia, which is hardly unusual for any woman under pressure, must be traced back to the unproven story of the grandmother who tried to smother her, for "if there is nothing to the story, then there is also no dramatic explanation for her acute insomnia."

The underlying fear (which cannot be indulged, or the book would not be worth writing) that the subject is not very interesting betrays itself in the overdramatization and overdetermining of events. It's not that the emperor is wearing no clothes . . . it's that he is wearing too many.

5. Mailer as Marilyn. This Mailer, an offshoot of the last one, invests Marilyn with his own sensibility, expands her spiritual horizons to the point where she will justify his love and the book—and, coincidentally, will be dissatisfied with other men. In emphasizing her insanity, Mailer falls into its trap: that of identifying oneself with the universe and succumbing to megalomania. He fills her void with his own ego, and redeems—or destroys?—her with his novelist's art.

Having infused her with so much of himself, the one role he never appreciates is that of a woman. He sees her as an orphan, an actress, a madwoman, but never just a woman, and he traces her death to all manner of conspiracies, and even admits the possibility of accident, but never sees it as the logical expression of the despair of a woman growing old.

But perhaps the sex symbol will always override and preclude the woman. In *The Misfits*, written by the man who loved her and directed by the culturally fashionable Huston, when she was not just sitting around being mythic she was turned into a shrew, a sentimental harpie in an all-male world. And yet in *Gentlemen Prefer Blondes*, made by an "action director," Howard Hawks, she is a creature of awe, with a sensuality at once delicious and perverse. In what can only be a shift in emphasis towards the sexual theme from the Broadway version with Carol Channing, Hawks explores the depravity inherent in Monroe's ooh-la-la image and our own implication in it, but with the same ambivalence as Wilder in *Some Like It Hot* (the ambivalence not just of a male but of a filmmaker, for who could fail to respond to that blonde image on the screen?).

We are meant to feel real admiration for Monroe and Russell, who, as Andrew Sarris has pointed out, are like Western heroes, with the biggest knockers instead of the fastest guns in the West. But who are the men in their lives? A precociously lascivious little boy, a dirty old man, a sexless millionaire, and a group of body-building studs so intent upon their exercises that they fail to notice Russell in their midst. And the one "normal" man, the one who apprears to love Russell for her "self," turns out to be a spy. The fusion of love and sex, which Russell herself represents, is as futile as their isolation! The humor cannot conceal in current revivals as scathing a picture of American society and sexuality as we are likely to find—and in a musical comedy. Perhaps we can dismiss it as "uniquely fifties," but perhaps not. Is Marilyn different from the rest of us in kind or in degree? and are we destined forever to divide ourselves into inner and outer selves, our (real or metaphorical) blonde hair and unlined faces separate from our lined, lived in, dirty-blonde souls, and are movies, in their everlasting attraction to surfaces, a prime instrument of this division?

Norman Rosten cites a letter to him in which Marilyn, misquoting Yeats's famous line, writes: "Love me for my yellow hair alone." He assumes her intention is ironic, but I wonder. Perhaps she managed the fusion better than the rest of us in becoming her myth, her outer self, her yellow hair. At any rate, only God and Joe DiMaggio could have loved her for herself alone and not her yellow hair. And I'm not so sure about God.

October 10, 1973

Six

MASCULINE REVERIES

SCARECROW

Bruce Williamson

Of his *Scarecrow* role, a total departure from the virility and toughness he showed in *The Godfather,* Al Pacino has said: "I play this little guy who's sort of lost—more of a follower and kind of funny, because he doesn't know who he is or where he's at." The description is apt, and Pacino's open, vulnerable, tragi-comic performance turns out to be only one plus mark for a movie filled with the kind of gutter magic that made *Midnight Cowboy*'s losers so winning. *Scarecrow* stands up even better in several respects—more accurate in studying the growth of a relationship between two men, less given to theatrical sham or a patronizing attitude toward its underdogs. Pacino and Hackman play a pair of drifters who meet out West on a dusty, deserted stretch of road, thumbs up. They decide to travel in the same general direction, which turns out to be fine logic, since both are going nowhere fast but don't yet know it. After five years at sea, Lion (Pacino) is headed back to Detroit to see whether a girl he left pregnant will offer him a boy-child or a girl-child or any hope for the future. After six years in San Quentin, Lion's irascible friend Max (Hackman, doing his grittiest job of film acting since *Bonnie and Clyde*) has piled up a little money in jail, and means to spend it on his pitiful lifelong dream of opening a car wash in Pittsburgh. Their odyssey comes to naught, of course, for they are voluntary exiles from a world scarcely worth conquering. Such essays on stunted human aspirations tend to become depressing, usually, but *Scarecrow* is saved by its rambunctious vitality and credible detail. Written by fledgling scenarist Garry Michael White, the episodic story provides director Jerry Schatzberg (who directed Pacino's screen debut, *Panic in Needle Park*) with a rare opportunity to explore nuances of character at close range, and he manages to make the seedy milieu his misfits inhabit not just a background, but a crippling state of mind—all junkyards, gas stations and honky-tonk bars, as well as the tidy county work farm where Pacino is beaten to his knees by a homosexual thug (Richard Lynch). The first-rate supporting cast at various stops for bed-and-broad includes Dorothy Tristan, Ann Wedgworth and Eileen Brennan; and all concerned owe the usual debt of gratitude to cinematographer

Vilmos Zsigmond, who makes of *Scarecrow*'s exhausted landscapes a visual tour de force comparable to his work in *Deliverance, Images,* and *McCabe and Mrs. Miller.*

May, 1973

THE STING

Judith Crist

The Sting is pure gold, the kind of movie that dreams of sophisticated entertainment are made on, one that is as good to look at as to listen to—and you can also hear, via the superb Scott Joplin piano rags that provide the score, the burble of laughter on the part of all involved in their sheer enjoyment of their work. It demonstrates what can happen when a gifted young screenwriter—David S. Ward, whose *Steelyard Blues* showed little more than offbeat invention—has the good fortune to fall among professionals his second time out. And what professionals are here! George Roy Hill, Paul Newman, and Robert Redford, the triumphant director-and-star triumvirate of *Butch Cassidy and the Sundance Kid,* are reunited, but *not* in the Hollywood do-it-again-to-milk-the-box-office tradition. They've been joined by a co-equal, Robert Shaw, in the great entertainment tradition—to con the people and make 'em love it.

For *The Sting* is a con, in story and effect, a tale of grifters and their mark that not only makes a sucker out of you but also makes you love every minute of the game and, after the climactic twist, delight in being proved pure chump. (Some switch for us victims of the Big Con that seems to have become a way of life in this Watergate world of ours!) And even as I, I suspect that you'll want to see the movie again to find the red herring or false clue that fooled you (we game-players don't take submissively to losing)—and sorry, folks, you can't call the cops. They play fair every step of the way.

To be equally fair, you should be given only the setting and situation in advance. The scene—and how beautifully it is set with old *Saturday Evening Post* design for the titles and visual cast introductions—is Chicago's underworld of the thirties, the lush loot of the rackets a contrast to the Depression drear of the world around them. Redford, an apprentice con man from Joliet, has come to the big town for help in avenging the

mobster murder of his beloved mentor after one of their marks turned out
to be a runner for a major syndicate; he's on the lam too, not only from
the mob but also from a grafting cop whom he paid off in counterfeit
money. For vengeance—and its tools for con men, those "aristocrats" of
the underworld, are brains, not bullets—he seeks out Newman, king of the
Big Con, an aging king gone to seed while hiding out from the FBI. And
their target is the big gun, Shaw, New York head of the syndicate, a
vicious Irish mobster with social aspirations and a passion for gambling—
so long as the cards are stacked and the wire is rigged in his favor.
Newman mobilizes the fraternity and the Big Con is on, with brain-tickling
machinations and breathtaking suspense and lots of laughter and a touch at
the heart in every twist and turn of the action-packed plot. That the
gamesmaster John Scarne served as technical consultant is not irrelevant.

Redford is at his peak as the quick-to-learn grifter who doesn't lose his
barefoot-boy sweetness as he operates in big-league crookery. He serves as
apt foil for Newman, never better than as the world-weary old master
whose gusto for the game is as winning and as controlled as the poker hand
he plays. And Shaw stands at the apex of the triangle as the mark worthy
of their complex (but never overcomplicated) scheme, a stolid, seething
figure whose very presence radiates malevolence, his silence as menacing as
his softly brogued speech, his passivity as threatening as his outbursts. It's
the head, not the heater, that rules plot and performances alike.

Perception and intelligence emanate from the actors and the director. As
has been his style since *Period of Adjustment,* through such fine films as
The World of Henry Orient and *Slaughterhouse-Five,* Hill has filled his
stage with equally fine performers in supporting roles. Eileen Brennan, the
original Little Mary Sunshine, comes into her own at long last in a beautifully low-keyed performance as the madam who is Newman's lady. Jack
Kehoe, as Redford's Joliet pal, Robert Earl Jones as his teacher; Harold
Gould, Ray Walston, and John Heffernan as top con men; Charles Durning as the crooked cop, and Dana Elcar as an FBI agent are all first-
rate. And Dimitra Arliss, as a short-order waitress, makes a middle-of-the-
night encounter with Redford an exquisitely romantic and memorable
interlude.

For the overall blend, Hill has reached for nostalgia and touched it with
the hand of the artist, reaching anachronistically to Scott Joplin's pre–
World War I rags for the tinkle and rhythms that are so amazingly right,
filling his background sets with the minutiae of memory, his stage with
underemphasized characters and minor moments that parody the gangster
movies of the thirties. Credit Henry Bumstead's art direction, Robert
Surtees's cinematography, Edith Head's costumes, Marvin Hamlisch's
music adaptation, of course—but it is the ultimate mixture in Hill's hands

that makes the film so completely satisfying. It's a no-problem movie that has movie stars, a fascinating plot, and a whiz-bang pace to please the mind. It's a joy to look at and has that rarest of present-day ingredients, Hill's hallmark—taste. What glisters here is pure movie gold.

December 31, 1973

Bernard Drew

What would be more natural than for Paul Newman and Robert Redford, the superstars of the super *Butch Cassidy and the Sundance Kid,* to team up again, along with its director George Roy Hill, in a slambang ripoff of Chicago gangster movies of the thirties called *The Sting.* Right?

Wrong, *The Sting* is not a ripoff at all. As written by David S. Ward, it is a nest of Chinese boxes, wheels within wheels, and a highly convoluted plot of two Chicago con men who hope to fleece a big New York gang lord (Robert Shaw) because he has killed their friend, and who are themselves followed by a vicious Chicago cop on the take, maybe the FBI, and God knows who else, each conning the other. Here and there is a chase, here and there a murder, here and there a twist.

There is a nifty one toward the end, and the final one is good, and genuinely surprising, but it takes too long to get there.

It is set in 1936, and there are some amusing *Saturday Evening Post* type of illustrations which look as if they were drawn by Clarence Buddington Kelland for the opening titles and these are retained throughout the movie along with ricky-tick music on the track. And that is indicative of what is wrong with the film.

What is piquant and even nostalgic used once, becomes precious and cutesy if repeated endlessly, and *The Sting,* which runs for more than two hours, has no more than three or four good jokes in it and settles the rest of the time for shticks, gimmicks and twists which reach a point of diminishing returns before the movie is half over.

Thus Robert Redford is the innocent young con man who gets into trouble with crooked cop Charles Durning and New York racket boss Shaw, and so he must flee to the hideout—a deserted merry-go-round which doubles as a whorehouse—of older, big-time con man Newman, who is hiding out from the FBI.

On the Twentieth Century Limited, they fleece Shaw in a cleverly arranged poker game, and then set up a phony gambling house there to entice him and finish the job while the cops are knocking at the door.

There is little comedy and fewer thrills in this, much movement but little action. At its best it is stylish and clever; at its worst, interminable.

Redford is his boyish self and don't we always root for him, as well as Newman, who is moustached and plays Clark Gable playing in *San Francisco* and *Manhattan Melodrama*, and Shaw, who has not only a moustache, but a limp and an Irish brogue.

Such other good people as Durning, Eileen Brennan, Harold Gould, Ray Walston and Dana Elcar flit in and out, but a bunch of shticks, even clever ones, do not a 130-minute movie make.

December 26, 1973

PAPILLON

Stuck on an Island

Paul D. Zimmerman

Papillon offers torture as entertainment but winds up making entertainment a form of torture. For two and a half hours, Franklin Schaffner guides his stars, Steve McQueen and Dustin Hoffman, through an obstacle course of degradation, betrayal, and lurid violence based on Henri Charrière's best-selling account of his incarceration in the prisons of French Guiana.

It is a tournament of brutality unrelieved by imagination. Schaffner catalogues all the standard indignities of the prison genre—convicts knifing one another, mutilating themselves to get into the prison hospital, rushing out on abortive escape attempts. Prison films of the 1930s, such as *I Am a Fugitive From a Chain Gang*, were animated by reformist zeal. Here there is only a lurid delight in topping one atrocity with another.

This is meant to be another male love story in which McQueen, as Papillon, protects Hoffman, as a convicted counterfeiter, in return for Hoffman's financing his escape. But their camaraderie seems artificial and their growing affection remains unconvincing. Despite this, McQueen is marvelous, especially during his extended period of solitary confinement, transforming himself from a defiant, sardonic loner into a crawling, stammering gray thing, living on insects and laboring with the strength of Hercules to utter a single cogent sentence. Hoffman seems uncomfortable and constricted under Schaffner's direction, building his timid counterfeiter out of pinched mannerisms and tricks, deprived of the imaginative sweep that is his hallmark.

McQueen's determined series of prison break-outs, his ordeal of survival and his eventual flight from Devil's Island are intended to show man's ability to hold together under the worst conditions. But the dispiriting grim tone of the film and its sensational interest in atrocities speak only of the futility of rebellion. By the time McQueen makes his getaway, he is old, gray, and broken, a victim of his own courage in a world where debasing acquiescence to authority or futile revolt are the only options.

December 17, 1973

DEEP THROAT

Vincent Canby

Trying to write honestly about pornographic films is like trying to tie one's shoe while walking: it's practically impossible without sacrificing stride and balance and a certain amount of ordinary dignity, the sort one uses with bank tellers who question a signature. Almost any attitude the writer adopts will whirl around and hit him from the other side. The haughty approach ("It's boring") has long since been suspected as evidence of a mixture of embarrassment and arousal. The golly-gee-whiz style ("They've gone as far as they can go!") is patently untrue, while to make fun of pornography is to avoid facing the subject at all. To call it a healthy development is another vast oversimplification that refuses to acknowledge that it may be fine for some people, and quite upsetting for others.

Then, too, to suggest that pornography degrades the audience as well as the performers assumes a familiarity with all of the members of all audiences that I, for one, do not have. It even ignores what little evidence I do have about the production of the films. Not long ago, a director of several porno films, a seriously bearded young man with an interest in Cinema, told me he was never aware of any of his performers' feeling degraded. "They do it because they enjoy it and because it's an easy way to make money—I think in that order. They're also exhibitionists. The camera turns them on. The women as well as the men. Sometimes, at the end of the day, they don't want to stop."

It's difficult to write honestly about pornographic films, but it's getting easier, largely, I think, as a result of all of the publicity given to *Deep Throat*, including the recent, widely covered Criminal Court trial here to determine whether or not the film is obscene. With an early assist ("The very best porn film ever made") from Al Goldstein, the editor of *Screw* magazine who isn't exactly stingy with his superlatives (a few months later he was quoted as saying that "*Bijou* tops *Deep Throat*"), *Deep Throat* has become the most financially successful hard-core pornographic film ever to play New York. According to *Variety*, which now regularly reviews porno films as a service to the film trade and gives weekly box-office reports on their business, *Deep Throat*, made in Florida on a budget of $35,000, has grossed more than $850,000 at the New Mature World Theater here since it opened last June. (The New Mature World Theater is, incidentally, the former World Theater, on 49th Street near Seventh Avenue, which, in its old immature days, used to play films like *Open City* and *Shoe Shine*.)

For reasons that still baffle me, *Deep Throat* has become the one porno film in New York chic to see, and to be seen at, even before the court case, even before Earl Wilson wrote about it.

When I went to see it last summer, mostly because of the Goldstein review, I was so convinced of its junkiness that I didn't bother writing about it. Still uncertain, I went back to see it again last Sunday. The large afternoon crowd sat through what seemed like at least a half-hour of porno trailers (which may be better pornography than narrative features since they're nothing but climaxes), plus Paul Bartel's fairly amusing non-porno short, *The Naughty Nurse*, as well as an old Paramount cartoon, a G-rated, absolutely straight, violence-without-sex cat-and-mouse thing, in order to experience the dubious achievements of *Deep Throat*, which runs sixty-two minutes. Although the audience last Sunday was a good deal more cheerful and less furtive than the one with which I first saw it, the film itself remains junk, at best only a souvenir of a time and place. I'm sure that if *Deep Throat* hadn't caught the public's fancy at this point in history, some other porno film, no better and maybe no worse, would have.

As for *Deep Throat*, its pleasures—its powers to arouse—are not inexhaustible, or, at least, they are very exhausted once one gets over the wonder and surprise at the accomplishment of its heroine, Linda Lovelace. The frame of the film—Linda's search for sexual fulfillment once she learns that fellatio is her thing—provides little room for the kind of satire that some critics have professed to see in the movie. Its few dumb gags, not including a rather funny title song, cannot disguise the straight porno intent of what has been reported to be the film's "seven acts of fellatio and four of cunnilingus."

At the risk of sounding like the usual bored critic (which I certainly wasn't the first time around), I must say *Deep Throat* is much less erotic than technically amazing. How does she do it? The film has less to do with the manifold pleasures of sex than with physical engineering.

It's possible—but only if one really tries—to make *Deep Throat* sound more significant than it is. You can argue that Linda in her way is a kind of liberated woman, using men as sex objects the way men in most porno films are supposed to use women. But that's straining to make a point that is very debatable. You can also argue, as Arthur Knight did at the trial here, that Linda and her friends show us that there's more than one way to have sex. It's almost as if he saw the film in the position of a missionary.

All of these arguments can be made—and, I suppose, they should be made—to defend the film against censorship laws that are, academically speaking, wrong. I say academically because I'm about to put myself in a corner that can't be reasonably defended: the laws are wrong but the film isn't worth fighting for. The necessity to prove a film totally without redeeming social value in order to get an obscenity conviction is, to my way of thinking, absurd. Everything created in this era—good, bad, and pornographic—is or will be of social interest (my definition of social value), hence it's rather idiotic to have adults arguing this point back and forth in court. Expert witnesses, who defended *Deep Throat* against the charges made possible by fuzzy laws, wind up, in effect, by acknowledging the validity of the laws. In defending the film the way they do, they become parties to the foolishness of the established order.

They've been co-opted, which is, I understand, the only way to fight the laws, but I think they might have second thoughts about attempting to prove their points by citing *Deep Throat* as "more professional, more cleverly and amusingly written" than others. Professor Knight even went on about the "clarity and lack of grain" in the photography.

We are living on the other side of the looking glass. Bad films are correctly defended for the wrong reasons. *Deep Throat* is described in terms that would not demean Henry Miller.

What may be worse, the film is prompting a whole new flood of inexpert, very biased writing about pornography, including this piece and other rather tortured articles elsewhere. *The New York Review* headed its recent contribution "Hard to Swallow," and at least two writers I've read have made bad puns on the fact that while most people are curious about porno films, they're too yellow to see them, in reference, of course, to the Swedish film of 1969 that a lot of hysterical people said was pornographic and went as far as films could go. Both claims turned out to be false.

The only possible way to write about porno films, I suspect, is to be so autobiographical that the reader gets a fair idea of the sexual orientation of the writer, of his each little quiver during the showing of the film. This, however, makes necessary a kind of journalism that few of us are equipped to practice well. When it isn't practiced well, we are apt to get the dopey film critic-confessionals that reverse the usual way of doing things. They intrude the critic's privacy upon the public.

January 21, 1973

LIVE AND LET DIE

Joseph Gelmis

What is there to say about the eighth in the series of James Bond pictures except that we miss Sean Connery if we do have to continue to suffer through these things without him.

Roger Moore has the broad shoulders and finely chiseled features to be credible as a lover. But he's a creampuff as a tough guy.

I was never thrilled with the 007 series. But Connery did somehow project a sublimely arrogant self-confidence along with a muscular kind of zest for countering or initiating violence. Moore has the look of a man who'd prefer more languid roles, a British Dean Martin. He goes through his 007 paces smoothly yet blandly.

Now, as for the new Bond flick, *Live and Let Die*. It's standard in the action formulas and rather below par in the quality of plot and nemesis.

I'm not aware if the Ian Fleming novel that gives the movie its title had anything to do with the story as presented. Because *Live and Let Die* is not only sexist, as the adolescent fantasy had to be, it is also racist, evidently to cash in on the black exploitation trend.

In the new picture, 007 is, in effect, the antidote to the get-whitey *Shaft* and *Superfly* black catharsis movies. James Bond battles a tough black mob and, unlike the white gangsters or cops in the typical black exploitation flicks, he single-handedly liquidates them. In the process, he makes love to, among others, a luscious black girl, and he seduces and steals the virginal white ward of the black kingpin. Insult to injury.

The black big shot is played without distinction by Yaphet Kotto. Tom Mankiewicz's screenplay makes Kotto too weak to be interesting as a villain. There's a subplot that might have been worth one laugh but instead goes on *ad nauseam*. It involves a tarot card reader (Jane Seymour) who serves as fortuneteller and adviser to the black mob boss. She is always right about the future, so long as she remains a virgin. Bond, naturally, intervenes.

There are the obligatory chase scenes: Bond taxiing around an airport being chased by gangsters' cars, a land and bayou pursuit by police patrol cars and speedboats that hurtle out of the water across lawns and paths. Bond's escapes are part of the few pleasures this sort of flick affords the more discriminating moviegoer, so I won't reveal how he gets away from crocodiles coming for him on a tiny rock where he has been stranded.

A Bond movie is not made. It is packaged. Like an Almond Joy. So much coconut to this much chocolate and just a dash of almonds. Thus, it is no great surprise to find Paul and Linda McCartney writing (and Paul and Wings recording) the title song for *Live and Let Die*. The McCartneys are just another ingredient: Big Name with a shimmery, heavy beat, nondescript song. An expensive ingredient in the package. But with an $8,000,000 budget, you can find out anyone's price fast enough. That's why Sean Connery's apparent retirement as 007 shows integrity. He made the last Bond movie for United Artists on condition that he be allowed to produce (and star in) two less-commercial pictures to be made for about $1,000,000 apiece. Maybe Connery will never find a role he or the critics think does justice to whatever talent he has. But he will have covered himself with glory for having tried.

June 28, 1973

KUNG FU CRAZE: FISTS OF FURY

David Denby

A few years ago, Woody Allen came out with a film called *What's Up, Tiger Lily?*, a takeoff on those violent, stupid Oriental quickies, which the comedian parodied simply by doing his own English dubbing. Well, the genre has returned, but it's the real thing now, and the hottest thing in town. And not only in New York City, but in South Carolina and Texas and the West Indies (where a recent outbreak of Asian flu has been named Wang Ya Flu in honor of the star of *One-Armed Boxer*). I missed *Five Fingers of Death*, which topped *Variety*'s box-office chart several weeks running but have now gratefully taken in *Fists of Fury*, a product of the Golden Harvest movie factory in Singapore. It features Kung-Fu superstar Bruce Lee, who doesn't seem very bright but who is a lot more fun to watch than Clint Eastwood or Richard Roundtree.

Fists of Fury, which was shot in blurry, washed-out color, and dubbed by fifth-rate American actors who sound like they're dying to break into soap opera, is so blissfully inane that you can't take your eyes off it for a second. How can I convey to you its wonderfully lifeless style? Lovers of trash, the most discriminating and categorical of all moviegoers, may now rest in peace: the search for the true primitive has ended. *Fists of Fury* is a movie in virginal comic-book style, unpolluted by a trace of sophistication or self-consciousness. The elements are perfect: on the one hand an intense Boy Scout atmosphere of virtue, loyalty, and fraternal love; on the other, an unremitting and quite fantastic dependence on gratuitous violence, with vicious fights starting up as regularly as sexual events in an adolescent daydream. With their sideburns and black hair worn in bangs, and blue jackets turned up at the collars, the Chinese youth in this picture look like teenage American gangs of the fifties. But while the kids in shlock movie-making of that period only wanted to dance or play rock music, here fighting is their only desire, and, from all evidence, virtually their only activity.

The hero, Cheng, lives with his six cousins and works in an ice factory run by dope smugglers. ("Dope in ice?" he says at one point, the truth slowly dawning.) Cheng loves the gentle Chow Mein (can that really be her name?), but submits to a good-hearted prostitute with cigarette burns on her breasts who is content to fondle the hero's beautiful chest after he's passed out on a drunk. Having promised a philosophical uncle that he won't get into fights, Cheng stays on the sidelines at first, but he is taunted once or twice too often, and finally his cousins are killed and frozen into blocks of ice—what you might call the last straw.

His great antagonist—an evil boss-man who might be considered a bit much even for *Terry and the Pirates*—sits in his large house blowing dope through a hookah while innumerable teen-age girls (brought to him by a pimping son) continuously massage his aching joints. Boss-man is also a great fighter and Kung-Fu master, and dozens of disciple-thugs lounge on his front lawn, having at each other from time to time, and casually chopping up anyone who dares approach the front door.

Now I won't pretend that Bruce Lee isn't hair-raising when he finally jumps into the fray, feet whirling through the air like scythes, lips curled into a terrifying sneer. Lee is a Chinese-American raised in California, and although he's done quite a lot of TV work (ever see the *The Green Hornet?*), he is totally unconscious of the art of acting, which is just fine for us lovers of helpless trash. I can't vouch for the correctness of his fighting style, but he's pretty scary when he gets going, and legends abound. (A junkie outside the theater told me that six hoods once set on Lee in L.A. and he killed two of them on the spot.) With his smooth, doll-like face and body, and his fierce sexual narcissism laced with hints of fetishistic cruelty à la Elvis Presley or Mick Jagger, Lee could reduce the teenage girls in this country to jelly, given half a chance.

During the fight scenes, tricky cutting covers a variety of feats that are clearly impossible, but still, the stop-and-go action, with its periods of quiet stalking followed by savage chops and kicks, is continuously exciting to watch. And there are pleasant surprises for the uninitiated, such as when a group of men rush the hero and his cousin and the two simply jump up in the air and let the attackers pass underneath. These movies, ridiculous as they are, possess something authentic, a genuine love of fighting and a glory in prowess, and no matter how upset we may get about movie violence, there are probably few of us who won't respond on some level to the gleam in Bruce Lee's eye when he goes in for the kill. Violence is the bedrock of mass culture, and each new fad, whether an advance or a regression, only confirms this inescapable fact.

May 24, 1973

Seven

COPS
AND
QUARRY

MOVIE COPS, PURE AND CORRUPT:

Serpico, Magnum Force, The Laughing Policeman, The Seven-Ups

David Denby

Moral Heroism—positive virtue carried to heroic lengths—is a very unusual and discomforting human quality, so it's not surprising that the movies have rarely portrayed it. If you look at the big hits of recent years it's clear the public prefers openly brutal and amoral heroes—Malcolm McDowell's jocular thug in *A Clockwork Orange;* the racist bully Popeye (Gene Hackman) in *The French Connection;* Clint Eastwood's procession of impassive killers; the pimps, pushers, and private eyes of the black exploitation movies; the family monsters of *The Godfather;* Robert Redford's glamorous WASP washouts; and many others. The public has responded not only because these were some of the better-made and heavily publicized movies, but also because there has been a great change in the mood of popular culture. The nihilism that twenty-five years ago occasionally broke through the complacent surface of mass entertainment (in a movie such as *The Third Man*) now has become the equally complacent surface of the mass entertainment of our own time; idiotic myths and unbelievable heroics have given way to cynical new myths and ritual antiheroism, praise of courage to praise of brutality.

   Given this atmosphere, how can you make a movie about a man like Frank Serpico—a man with a righteous passion—and get the wised-up audience to accept it? Frank Serpico, the New York cop who exposed wide-scale police corruption in the city, combined physical courage and moral intransigence in a way that frightens and infuriates many people (not just police officers). Instinctively honest himself, refusing even the most trivial bribes, he was at first astonished, then sickened, then consumed with fury by the instances of graft and complacency he encountered at all levels of the police department. As he began to talk to grand juries and the Knapp Commission, he suffered from exclusion, contempt, threats on his life; and in February 1971, less than a year after his revelations were made public, he was shot in the face and nearly killed by a Puerto Rican dope pusher in what may have been a setup arranged by fellow officers. Not an easy man to make into a movie hero.

The solution found by the screenwriters, Norman Wexler and Waldo Salt, and executed efficiently by the director, Sidney Lumet, was to combine the strategy of the sixties youth movie with the street-wise gaiety and obscenity that's become popular in movies of the seventies. The youth movies depended on the generation-gap principle, which held that moral differences could easily be conveyed by an invidious contrast of cultural styles; the same trick works here, even with officers no older than Serpico. The hero lives as a free spirit in his *House and Garden* hippie pad in Greenwich Village with his girlfriends, plants, and pets, slouches around in old clothes, and grows a variety of beards and moustaches. On the other hand, his opponents—virtually everyone else in the movie—are all abnormally square middle-class types who seem corrupt *because* they belong to the middle class (or want to get into it); they include vicious young cops, grabbing as much money as they can; older administrative bigwigs, stuffy and weak, protecting their reputations and the department's image; Ivy League smoothies hanging onto the Lindsay administration, all flash and no substance; young women who think they want careers but really want marriage and babies ("Come back to bed, honey") and haven't got the guts to stick it out with Serpico otherwise.

In other words, the only incorruptible person is the only one who's loose and open and hip. Al Pacino, with his shambling physical presence and beautiful immense actor's eyes, gives an ingratiating star performance that obliterates everyone else in the movie. The actors playing the other cops, for instance, appear to have been picked for physical clumsiness and unattractiveness, and at times they don't even seem like men; photographed in close-up with distorting wide-angle lenses, their leering ugly faces come right out of a fifties comic book. The evil shows in their thick necks and tasteless clothes.

Serpico certainly pulls no punches about police corruption, but it's so eager to establish its hero as the only human being in a world of swinish sellouts that it becomes offensively single-minded and uncharitable. Is integrity simply a matter of style? I doubt it, but this sort of identification always seems to work commercially. I saw the film a second time with a young audience in Times Square, and it loved the joke that Pacino's goofy hippie was working with all these superstraight jerks, doing the same job, only better and more honestly. The kids roared every time Serpico reported to the precinct house dressed like an Eighth Street dropout and again when he expertly lit up a joint during a solemn lecture on the basics of marijuana detection.

I laughed too, but this kind of cultural jeering (much of it at the college-revue level) tells us nothing about Serpico's character, which I hoped to understand. Exactly why is he made physically ill by corruption while everyone else feasts on it—because he's cool and doesn't worry about his status? Because he wears funny clothes? In lieu of any other explanation, that's what the audience may come to believe. Salt and Wexler offer few clues to his motives or to what makes him so different from the others. His monologue recalling how he admired the police as a child explains nothing: many of the other cops in the movie also came from working-class neighborhoods where the police were revered and where joining the force was seen as a means to respectability, steady employment, and upward mobility, yet they all became corrupt bastards and he didn't. While turning Serpico into a martyr and pop icon, the filmmakers ignore the possibility for genuine moral drama. After all, Serpico the crusader went way beyond the traditional ethics of the "honest cop" (look the other way and keep quiet). As a graduate of the street gangs of Bedford-Stuyvesant, where betrayal of a buddy is the ultimate taboo, how did he get to the point where he could blow the whistle on his peers without any guilt or even a twinge of ambivalence? Did his rapid passage from Brooklyn street kid to Manhattan ballet-lover fill him with a distaste for his police friends that was aesthetic and social as well as moral?

One turns for enlightenment to Peter Maas's *Serpico*, the book on which the script was based, but to no avail. Although he's good at narrative highlighting and anecdotes, Maas makes no attempt to penetrate Serpico's character. The trouble with Maas, actually, is that he thinks like a cop. Whether describing Serpico's struggles and sufferings, his sexual and cultural choices, or the knick-knacks in his Village apartment, he writes in the same tone of gruff "masculine" neutrality, and at times the book reads like a long-winded police blotter. For each of the moment-of-decision vignettes there's just enough information to lend dramatic plausibility to Serpico's acts, yet the complex, tortured man implied by all the scene-fragments never emerges as a coherent personality.

Why do these men—Maas, Salt, Wexler, Lumet—refuse to look inside their hero? One suspects that they know how troublesome moral heroes can be for the audience. For many people there's something inhuman or, at the least, ridiculous about men and women who estrange themselves from community and friends in adherence to an ideal of morality, honor, or faith; it's much easier if we can think of such heroes as fanatics or freaks. The movie Serpico isn't exactly a freak, but since we don't understand the roots of his behavior or the steps by which he arrived at his commitment, he doesn't challenge us to puzzle out the relation of his acts to our own. The filmmakers let us off the hook by transforming their hero into a wondrous, inexplicable creature—both martyr and holy fool.

Because they are unwilling to threaten the audience's cynicism and complacency, they concentrate on Serpico's sense of isolation and futility rather than on the real Serpico's achievements (an immense shake-up in the NYPD). Thus at the end of the movie, rather than appearing ennobled by his ordeal, he seems diminished—a rejected man of honor, a schlemiel rewarded with a detective's shield for allowing himself to be shot. The printed epilogue that informs us he has exiled himself to Switzerland evokes the clichés of "ironic" defeat familiar from the epilogues to *Z, The French Connection,* and many other movies. It's as if his extraordinary rebellion meant nothing.

Serpico is a film that indirectly confirms the cynicism of the audience. *Magnum Force, The Laughing Policeman,* and *The Seven-Ups,* more typically, are films that pander to it. In these recent cop movies, we get the familiar ruthless bastard, a hero by virtue of his daring and efficiency and nothing else. When a movie genre becomes this successful (other recent examples include *Bullitt, The French Connection, Dirty Harry, The New Centurions, Badge 373*) it's not just a series of images on the screen, but something we are doing to ourselves, a form of self-scrutiny; so it's worth examining this new hero in some detail.

Formerly so mild and reassuring (a cross between a high-school coach and a priest), the police detective has evolved in recent years into a relentless avenger whose commitment to "legality" has become ever more tenuous. Indeed, it has become harder and harder to tell him apart from the criminals he pursues. He has the same furious zeal, the same devotion to his task. Estranged from friends, family, and leisure—a normal life in the society he defends—he has no identity apart from his work. If we see his home at all, it is likely to be a conventionally bland suburban-tract house or a furnished room consisting of bed, refrigerator (with only a beer or two inside), and telephone. If married, he will be at odds with his wife; otherwise, he drags himself through a hopeless love affair with a pleading, sullen woman who doesn't understand him, or he's alone, his solitude only occasionally interrupted by a young girl whose advances he accepts without pleasure or comment; sex seems to be one of the more tedious aspects of his life, like filling out forms.

Even though he's a denizen of the city, he doesn't talk often or easily; he is taciturn and suspicious, a man without gaiety or warmth, and his curiosity about people goes no further than discovering what kind of filth they're into. And they are all into something, for he lives in a society where literally everyone is a criminal or a creep or both. Prowling the city in his car or waiting—sleepless, cold, unshaven—through some grim stakeout, he works in a state of bitter discomfort. (Gone forever is the glamorously corrupt night-world of the thirties and forties private-eye movies, in which the hero moved through sinister, shining streets on his way to some mansion or nightclub, there to meet gangsters in evening clothes and a beautiful woman whom he would save, or perhaps kill, cradling her in his arms as she slid to the floor.) He is familiar with the worst and most dangerous parts of the city—ghettos, bars, topless joints, junkyards, and obscure, rotting piers. Through his eyes, the whole town is a jungle. If he lives in San Francisco, that city's brilliant light and unmistakable aura of generosity and hope mock his grim concentration on evil and his devotion to work; if it's New York, the center of power and status, his confinement to the raunchier sections of Brooklyn and the Bronx (Manhattan's conquering skyline is often seen in the background), where it's gray, heavy, dirty and always raining, reminds him that he's a nothing, a loser in the city of winners.

Apart from sheer dogged persistence, his methods are intimidation and violence, and he doesn't need any provocation to use them; at any moment he may lose control and beat up someone, torment a prisoner, smash furniture and dishes, endanger the lives of innocent people. The Western hero, private eye, or old-style police detective worked under a standard of honor; the new detective shoots first and aims for the stomach or back. Above all, he exists in a state of bitter, constant, self-serving rage at everyone—at the criminal who eludes him, the public that "misunderstands" him, and at his immediate superiors—invariably gutless phonies and hypocrites—who hamper his freedom to operate. This hostility to superiors lends a vaguely rebellious cast to his instinctive authoritarianism and helps to disguise his true purpose from himself and from us.

His purpose, it now becomes clearer with every movie, is not to uphold the law, but to kill criminals; not to bring them to justice, but merely to eliminate them. It's worth noting that the violent new police films, with their thrills, chases, and shootouts, have almost entirely replaced the type of movie in which a detective searched for clues and leads, trying to penetrate a mystery to its heart; the detective's desire was basically for knowledge and clarity (which was even true of Mike Hammer). In the new genre, however, clues are unnecessary because the identity of the criminals is usually known early on, and the action consists of tracking down the beasts in the most exciting way possible. Movie traditionalists like to point out that the new cop films have restored the chase to its earlier primacy, but there's this major political and moral difference to consider: in the silents and the films of the thirties and forties, one was usually supposed to identify with the person trying to escape, while in today's chase scenes, one is always forced to identify with the pursuer.

I am not concerned with the reality of the new hero (although anyone who's tried to get some action out of the police in many cities knows the absurdity of this notion of the detective as a man consumed by zeal) ; the question is, How could such a son of a bitch—a man without any of the *romance* of heroism—how could he become a major pop-culture figure? It's as if the public had entered into a kind of uneasy deal, an understanding, with the image on the screen. Our attitudes toward authority are probably ambivalent at any time, but given the events of recent American history, that ambivalence has been exaggerated; we need authority, we miss it, we also hate and fear it, and the conflict in our feelings is embodied right there in that policeman. On the one hand he has become a sort of publicly subsidized vigilante, with a license to kill the various undesirables, the *others*, popularly perceived as a threat during recent years; he fights for us on the front line against cultural disorder. On the other hand, because we allow him to fight dirty (and we know it's dirty), we require his degradation and misery, his radical dissatisfaction, his lack of style or grace. He becomes our hostage, a sacrifice to our conflicting desires.

If the movie police detective is a product of the paranoid, avenging spirit of the Nixon-Agnew years, it will be interesting to see what happens to him as that spirit declines. Some uneasy changes may be occurring already. Earlier, in Don Siegel's *Coogan's Bluff* and *Dirty Harry*, Clint Eastwood went after the hippie scum of New York and San Francisco; *Dirty Harry* also included angry muttering against recent Supreme Court decisions protecting the rights of the accused. In the current sequel, *Magnum Force*, the filmmakers respond to those critics who complained of fascism and vigilantism in *Dirty Harry* by setting Eastwood against a police department "death squad," a quartet of rookie patrolmen who go about eliminating gangsters and pimps. Thus Eastwood is forced to defend a system of legality in which he admittedly has little faith. ("There's nothing wrong with shooting as long as the right people get shot.") And how does he protect society against these murderers? As you may have guessed—by killing them. And in case you still thought the film was a statement against vigilantism, Eastwood shoots a hijacker and a couple of robbers (more hippie scum) in incidents that have nothing to do with the plot (but everything to do with the filmmakers' double-dealing bad faith). An arrest in one of the new police films would be a rare occurrence indeed.

These atrocity and mass-murder films require lots of anonymous corpses. What's creepy about these deaths is that one rarely feels anything about them: the victims are dispensable bodies, neither villains nor innocents but mere abstract counters in the police-movie game. In *Magnum Force*, there's an ugly attempt to imply that they deserve what they get: a prostitute who flirts with a taxi driver, for instance, is killed by her pimp soon after; and the death-squad cops machine-gun several beautiful young girls who jump naked into a swimming pool with some older men (such is the movie's notion of wickedness). The mixture of prurience, reactionary moralism, and mass murder might be amusing if only the film's opportunism were a little less desperate.

The same opportunism and confusions make nonsense out of *The Laughing Policeman*, in which frantic Bruce Dern and a silent, dour, cryptic Walter Matthau (in his worst performance yet) conduct a tour of San Francisco low-life in search of a homosexual killer. Again there are loads of anonymous corpses (handled by the police with a cool professionalism that becomes obscene when you realize the corpses are there only to provide a jolt and a suitable outrage), and again the filmmakers punish the wickedness and "dirty" sex they are so eagerly parading before us; as if they had just flown in from Dubuque and couldn't believe their eyes, Dern and Matthau vent their shocked disgust on everyone they meet—homosexuals, sex-show performers, black gamblers and pimps, Hell's Angels, etc. The film's point of view is that America has become a rotting sewer in which the brutal but virtuous policeman must soil himself in order to keep the rest of us out of trouble. Perhaps to retain his family-entertainment image amid all this sin, Matthau is required to slap a lovely young woman who has posed in the nude for her boyfriend—but then the script puts him down as hopelessly old-fashioned and uptight, so even his disgust is not allowed to retain any force. The attitudes in *The Laughing Policeman* keep spinning and shifting, and the movie ends up nowhere.

Philip D'Antoni, who produced *Bullitt* and *The French Connection* and is both producer and director of *The Seven-Ups*, is obviously so single-minded about the police genre he needn't pretend his commercial reactionary shlock is really something else. D'Antoni doesn't fool around. A "pure" genre film with hardly a single original or creative element, *The Seven-Ups* is nevertheless remarkably efficient and well made and thus should satisfy connoisseurs. Cops, hoods, cars, guns, chases, and shootouts have become wholly formal elements and so has a hero, a sadistic thug-cop (Roy Scheider) with no personal characteristics whatsoever. Everything is taken for granted and nothing explained, and not a single issue is raised that hasn't been settled in other movies. The pattern is set except for minor variations. In a way *The Seven-Ups* is perfect, but it has the perfection of nullity. When you see a movie like this, you hope the genre will cease—but I doubt it will.

In recent years the movies have "grown up" but not in the way some of us had hoped; the good-versus-evil simplicities of the past have given way, all too often, to a hideous new kind of simplicity in which the good has simply been omitted. What's left—a popular culture without positive heroes—is much uglier than anything we could have imagined. Once innocence is gone, however, there's no way of going back to it without hokum and self-caricature ("nostalgia"). In our new, wised-up situation we examine each film for its possible treachery and also, occasionally, for signs of genuine tough-mindedness and moral complexity. Something as vile as *Magnum Force* would have been impossible 25 years ago, but a magnificent popular entertainment like *The Godfather* would have been impossible, too. Moviegoing has become a dangerous new world in which we each must take our chances and find our way.

March 1974

SERPICO

Judith Crist

Nobody can accuse us, not to mention our moviemakers, of moderation— not when it comes to sex, violence, or cops. To protect the masses, the television censors are still blue-nosing around for S&V (so that *The Damned* was butchered beyond recognition, *The Wild Bunch* cut into further incoherence, *The Graduate* banned by a couple of stations, *The Hospital* emasculated, and even *Cotton Comes to Harlem* bleeped and shaved of its humor). But on the tube this season, cops are big, with crime shows occupying a third of the prime-time hours and the lawmen (cops, D.A.'s, private eyes, and legal eagles) are riding high.

Before television, movies were our mass entertainment, crime was a nonpaying occupation and the policeman the true-blue hero (or dead if he wasn't, as in *Rogue Cop*). But with TV's preemption of the masses, the movie-morality pendulum took a mighty swing as "realism" became the order of the precinct-house day. Cops at best were bigoted whoremasters and/or borderline psychopaths or just stupids and/or cute connivers (e.g., *Fuzz, The French Connection, The New Centurions, Badge 373, Dirty Harry,* and *Cops and Robbers,* among others). And while television's cops are still in the catbird seat, thanks to the propriety of the blue pencil, moviegoers have been clobbered with the image of the cop as pig and pretty rotten person. That is where movieland's realism presumably leads. Or is it?

Serpico reveals the cop as person—in Frank Serpico's case, in fact, as a decent person, let alone a real one. And the reality of this New York City cop is thrilling both as to fact and in the film's recounting of it. The filmmakers have simply refuted the contention of television's crime-fictioneers that reality undermines entertainment; here, the raw truth boggles the mind and outpaces the imagination. Serpico, the subject of Peter Maas's best seller, was, you may recall, the offbeat plainclothes cop—so offbeat as to be not only honest but even incensed by the dishonesty of his colleagues—whose long-frustrated attempts to turn the tide culminated in disclosures of corruption that led to the Knapp Commission and the continuing overhaul of the NYPD—and to Serpico's self-imposed exile in Switzerland to escape retaliation.

Al Pacino, that brilliant young actor whose rise has been overshadowed by his seeming similarity to Dustin Hoffman and whose excellent performance in *The Godfather* was overshadowed by the wax-filled jowls of Marlon Brando, brings Frank Serpico to remarkable reality as the intelligent young man who wanted to be a city detective, a good one, and nothing else. There's a lovely scene underlining this ambition, when an arty girlfriend takes Frank to a hip party overflowing with would-be actresses who work as secretaries, would-be writers who work as admen, would-be artists who work as clerks, and Serpico emerges as the would-be who *is*—to the amused disbelief of the others. For he is typical of a good percentage of the men who have come to police work out of a boyhood dream or a mature ambition or interest; this film seems to me the first to recognize this good core, so distracted have we been with the rottenness of the few. And it is Pacino, a compact, muscular man with a sense of high comedy and a deep passion that penetrates his every movement, who brings Serpico to life. There is an intensity to his characterization that forces us to follow and ultimately share his near-frantic righteousness, from his first awarenesses of corruption—if only in settling for a fatty sandwich on the house in return for winking at a parking violation—to his paranoid rebellion against the fat-cat group payoffs, the smooth-talking indifference and condolence of higher-ups, the political double-talk and the settle-for-half attitude of the semi-crusaders.

Pacino's performance is bolstered by a screenplay and direction that respect the city-dweller's intelligence, that tells of an eleven-year experience with sophistication and temperance and resists endless opportunities for a wallow. Seasoned writers—Waldo Salt, best remembered for *Midnight Cowboy*, and Norman Wexler, for *Joe*—show their know-how in dealing with the city and the variety of men who police it. Sidney Lumet—a director who is so very good when he's good—provides a tension rarely found in the telling of a well-known tale, and that infallible film editor, Dede Allen, shares that credit.

While Pacino provides one of the outstanding performances of the year, he is far from alone; a cast of high quality gives the authentic detail to the story. Tony Roberts, as the Ivy League plainclothes cop who shares Serpico's dedication, although politics rather than the "street" is his beat; Jack Kehoe, as the "nice" cop who takes corruption for granted; Ed Grover and John Randolph, as inspectors out for integrity rather than popularity; Biff McGuire as a solemn, religious, don't-rock-the-boat inspector; Cornelia Sharpe and Barbara Eda-Young as the girls who pass through Serpico's life, and a host of others offer splendid support.

Perhaps above all it is the setting of the city, captured in muted tones and striking images by cinematographer Arthur J. Ornitz and reflected in the score composed by Mikis Theodorakis, that gives an irrefutable honesty to the film. It's the inside of the city that we see—from the seedy clutter of the precinct house, the shadowy nighttime of school grounds, the sunlit oasis of a Bronx Park, the warehouse streets, the Village gardens, the tenement-lined, chill deserted slum street.

Where else would a character like Serpico flourish, the ultimate plainclothes cop wearing the plain clothes of the street people of the sixties and seventies, a nice first-generation Italian kid from Brooklyn settled into a Greenwich Village pad complete with arty girlfriend (later succeeded by a non-arty but bright and dedicated nurse from next door), taking Spanish at N.Y.U., reading books about ballet, being overconscientious and therefore disapproved of by his colleagues? Where else would there be so great a variety of people and their crimes? And where else—or in what other time—would we find refreshment in his distaste for the petty graft and, almost to our surprise, share his growing horror at the organized loot and the terror that emerges as the tide of corruption seems to engulf him? No doubt about it—we want to believe that there is an honest man at large in this city and Serpico is the balm in our Gilead, the physician for our post-Watergate sickness. Let others buy the Sam Ervin bromides at 33 rpm; it's the Serpicos—and the price they have paid—who might inspire us to save ourselves.

December 10, 1973

THE FRIENDS OF EDDIE COYLE

Richard Schickel

Physically he is right for the part. The slope of the belly has grown more acute with the passage of years; the face is puffy and well worn; even the complexion looks gray, with just a hint of green around the gills. But there is more than mere looks to Robert Mitchum's performance as Eddie Coyle, the aging, small-time hood with a big-time survival problem. The weariness, the hooded cynicism, the underlying toughness that seems to consist more of an ability to survive beatings rather than administer them—all have always been there, unspoken factors in a career that has consisted largely of trying to transcend roles that did not fully engage one of the most active and original intelligences in the star business. Now, at last, Mitchum achieves a kind of apotheosis in Peter Yates's strong, realistic and totally absorbing rendition of George V. Higgins's bestselling novel.

Coyle's nickname is "Fingers," because five of them were mangled as punishment for fouling up a gun-running operation early in his career. Wary, only partially daunted, in his soldier's way wise to the ways of the underworld, he is still dealing in hot guns, supplying them to a mob specializing in branch bank heists around Boston. Simultaneously, he is trying to beat a bootlegging rap by doing some minimal informing—a thief's honor warring with a middle-aged man's need to put his comfort and his family's needs first.

Coyle could easily have been played as a simple victim, a soft spot at the heart of this picture. But supplied with hard blue language by writer Paul Monash, and played by Mitchum as a man trying to walk—not run—to the nearest exit, he is an infinitely more appealing figure. Coyle is still hard enough to intimidate a reckless apprentice punk, canny enough to fight a good delaying action against the cop who keeps pressing for more and more information and strangely trusting of an old friend who is a much more clever stoolie (and who finally undoes him). In all, Coyle emerges as a complex and multifaceted character. Self-consciously, with an old pro's quiet skills, Mitchum explores all of Coyle's contradictory facets. At fifty-six, when many of his contemporaries are hiding out behind the remnants of their youthful images, he has summoned up the skill and the courage to demonstrate a remarkable range of talents.

Among Coyle's "friends," Steven Keats is a bundle of raw nerves as the kid crook trying to tough it out in a line of work he is not really mature enough to handle. Richard Jordan exudes the dank and oily atmosphere of a basement where one cannot tell the cops from the crooks they suborn; and Peter Boyle menacingly underplays the man who finally betrays Mitchum.

Peter Yates is not a director who asserts his personality in obvious ways. *Eddie Coyle* is, like his previous successes in the action genre (*Bullitt, Murphy's War*), a work which efficiently and unobtrusively establishes an ambience that helps to explicate behavior. This is not a matter of directorial "touches," but rather a case of careful overall polish that brings out the grain of his raw material. He accomplishes this with no sacrifice to the pacing of his action sequences or the suspenseful development of his story's arc.

July 2, 1973

WALKING TALL

Gary Arnold

Walking Tall, the sleeper of 1973, is a fascinating throwback, a powerhouse melodrama in the "social protest" tradition of Warner Brothers in the thirties. I don't believe this is a movie one can exactly look forward to seeing, but if you do see it, you'll never forget it.

Walking Tall recalls such pictures as *I Am a Fugitive from a Chain Gang* and *Marked Woman*, and it recalls them with an impact that is often overwhelming. Like *I Am a Fugitive* and *Marked Woman*, the new film is a fictionalized account of a rather astounding and appalling real-life story, the sort of history in which the protagonist has endured so much that he begins to seem almost mythic, a once-ordinary person transformed by circumstance into a tragic pariah. The fact that these protagonists—Paul Muni's fugitive, Bette Davis's call girl, and now Joe Don Baker's Tennessee sheriff—have more than a trace of hubris in their characters intensifies the tragic implications. To the unsympathetic, these are the kind of people who have "made trouble for themselves," and there's a measure of truth, if a lamentable want of compassion, in that assertion.

Walking Tall is based on the experiences of Buford Pusser, a crusading lawman in a wide-open county in rural Tennessee. Pusser, now thirty-five, served three terms (the statutory limit) as sheriff of McNairy County from 1964 to 1970. In the course of his six-year battle with the local vice interests, Pusser survived several attempts on his life, but his wife, Pauline, was shot and killed during one of those ambushes. Pusser's jaw was blown off in the same attack, and it has taken fourteen plastic-surgery operations over the past six years to reconstruct the lower half of his face.

In both the literal and figurative senses of the term, Buford Pusser was a marked man. The incident that led to his career as a lawman was a run-in with the operators of a McNairy County gambling casino: Pusser was rolled, beaten, carved up by a knife-wielding bouncer, and left for dead on the highway. In one of the movie's melodramatic flourishes, Joe Don Baker as Pusser rips off his shirt to reveal the knife scars on his chest when he's on trial for assault and battery, a charge brought by the gamblers after Pusser had recovered and returned to the casino to exact some rough personal justice on his original assailants. At the conclusion of the film, the hero is even more hideously marked: widowed and disfigured, his eyes glowering over a plaster cast that covers every other feature of his face, Joe Don Baker suggests a human golem, a fantastic image of suffering, perseverance, and mad courage.

Walking Tall evidently had its genesis in a 1969 CBS television documentary in which Buford Pusser was interviewed by Roger Mudd. The program was seen by Mort Briskin, a producer and screenwriter associated with Bing Crosby's production company. It was three years before Briskin got a Pusser biography into production, with Pusser himself as technical adviser and locations done in and around McNairy County, but in the meantime Briskin had manufactured a couple of hits for Bing Crosby Productions and Cinerama Releasing—*Willard* and *Ben*, the horror movies about pet rats on the rampage.

Phil Karlson, the director of *Walking Tall*, also did *Ben* for Briskin, but in this case his relevant credit is *The Phenix City Story*, made 20 years ago. *Walking Tall* is similar in style, plot, and inspiration. Indeed, the vice crowd forced out of Phenix City, Alabama, in the fifties may have relocated in McNairy County, Tennessee, among other places, in the sixties.

Karlson has had a spotty commercial career, highlighted by some vivid and interesting but not quite Grade-A melodramas like *The Phenix City Story* and *Hell to Eternity* and by some agreeable entertainments like *The Silencers*. *Ben* was perhaps the low point of his career: the production was so chintzy and the direction so inert that it looked like the end of the road.

Walking Tall appears to revive Karlson as a capable and resourceful commercial director, to reanimate his low-budget sort of effectiveness, which thrives on an atmosphere of naturalism and intense melodramatic conflict. The film could certainly be better in many respects. It's often crude and occasionally downright lurid (for example, there's one shot of a naked prostitute being whipped that might have been composed for a cheapie exploitation vehicle), and the color photography maintains a decidedly unappealing and inappropriate level of commercial "brightness." At the same time, *Walking Tall* could scarcely aspire to more power or vividness than it enjoys right now. If it's a crude picture, it's also an effectively crude picture, emotionally charged from beginning to end and emotionally shattering in climactic sequences.

To resort to the old terminology, this movie packs a wallop. Crude melodramas often do when they remain close to the surface of real life and close to the feelings of ordinary people in perilous circumstances. *Walking Tall* generates a primitive, atavistic sort of power: it awakens more apprehension and dredges up more complicated and contradictory emotions than one anticipates.

It's possible that the film was conceived as an unmitigated law-and-order morality tale. The filmmakers echo some of the self-righteous, demagogic notes struck successfully in *Dirty Harry* and *Billy Jack*, and the revamped advertising campaign asks, "When was the last time you stood up and applauded a movie?" The film received no press screenings and only negligible publicity when it was first released last spring (1973). Now that it's being revived in metropolitan markets, thanks to an unforeseen success in Memphis and several small-town localities, *Walking Tall* may be getting a rather misleading send-off. Audiences are likely to cheer at a certain point in the action—when Baker returns to the gambling house and gets even with the thugs who nearly killed him—but the film doesn't sustain a feeling of triumphant vigilante justice. The dominant emotion of the picture is dread, and its ultimate emotional effect is a combination of sorrow and exhaustion. The hero pays such a heavy price for his obstinate heroism that it seems a bit obscene to stand up and cheer. If it really affects them, *Walking Tall* is the sort of picture that should send audiences out in a subdued rather than a vociferous mood.

The film has its rabble-rousing moments (and one of the worst occurs near the fadeout), but they're mitigated by the introduction of ambivalent or contradictory material. For example, Douglas Fowley is cast as a corrupt judge, and the filmmakers use him essentially as a foil, scoring easy points by showing the honest young sheriff being frustrated time and again by the dishonest old magistrate. At their worst, these confrontations seem designed to illustrate the reactionary lament about the courts "tying the hands of the police." Still, the judge gets to score some points too, and corrupt or not, he is quite correct when he informs the hero sarcastically that there is more to the law than swinging a big stick and kicking down doors.

As a matter of fact, there must have been more to Buford Pusser's tenure as sheriff than his war with the McNairy County vice lords. One of the sociological weaknesses of the film seems to be a source of its melodramatic strength: we never see Pusser administering justice impartially, without a personal stake in the outcome. There is a single, continuing situation in the film—a state of war between the sheriff and the men whose antagonism propelled him into office in the first place—and it's not a situation that permits arbitration or compromise. Both sides are playing for keeps, and both sides play rough. In terms of melodrama the film enjoys a clear-cut conflict, and the tension keeps accumulating. At the same time this approach severely limits the conception of a lawman's duties and obligations. The lawman in this story is always a dreadfully injured and interested party.

Dirty Harry and *Billy Jack* seemed absurd from the very beginning because it was impossible to believe in the reality of their heroes. Clint Eastwood and Tom Laughlin were fairy-tale champions—lonely, ascetic, invulnerable figures with no social or family ties but with physical powers often commensurate with Superman's. There was no way they could become mythic, because they were myths to start with.

Walking Tall impresses me as a more plausible and compelling melodrama because it operates from a more realistic premise. There's no doubt about who the hero is and who the villains are, but the former is a *common* man who becomes caught up in a violent and tragic set of circumstances, partly of his own making. Susceptibilities vary in this regard, but *Walking Tall* starts with a premise I find myself susceptible to. Pusser's fate seems peculiarly involving because it happens to such an ordinary, vulnerable man, a strapping straight-arrow who has a family to protect and a living to earn and a traditional code of justice to uphold. In his pride and self-righteousness, this man can also abuse the law, and the filmmakers have been either courageous or unwary enough to show him doing precisely that.

One is never quite certain whether the film's ambivalence is intentional or inadvertent, but popular melodramas often reflect this sort of split, and it's one of the things that makes a picture like *Walking Tall* critically interesting. If it was intended as a law-and-order sermon, the movie doesn't quite come out that way. It gets deeper than that. The filmmakers are obviously persuaded of the rightness of Pusser's cause, but they're willing to show him acting foolishly and even shamefully. They're also cognizant of other people's responses and fears, like the fear of guns expressed by Elizabeth Hartman as Pauline Pusser very early in the movie. Her fear isn't characterized as unreasonable or "womanish" either. On the contrary, it's a justifiable apprehension, and every sensitive person in the audience is going to share it.

There are several scenes and images that appear to cut deeper than the filmmakers may have intended. I can't really tell if Karlson and Briskin fully appreciate the implications of a scene in which Pusser's little boy shows up at the hospital with his rifle, determined to protect his father in the wake of another murder attempt. The filmmakers seem to blunder into something complexly moving while making a simple-minded grandstand appeal. The level of writing and direction is uneven enough to keep one in doubt about how conscious and perceptive these men really are. It's impossible to give them unqualified credit as artists, but they're always such vivid melodramatists that the picture maintains an extraordinary level of intensity and human interest even when the point of view wobbles.

The images of violence are exceptionally strong, but I think Karlson uses these images in a fundamentally sound and responsible way to illustrate the authentic, awful *costs* of violence. The shots of Joe Don Baker on a rainy road at night, struggling to attract the attention of passing cars after he's been beaten and left to die, convey a sense of pain and desolation that begins to give you the chills. Karlson stays with that suffering man long enough to let the pain sink in.

I was dreading the scenes reenacting the killing of Pusser's wife before I entered the theater. Karlson's reenactment proved even more terrifying than I expected. Again, Karlson stays with his stricken characters for a long, long time. It seems an eternity while Baker cradles Miss Hartman's limp, bloody body. This violent interlude is transformed into a sustained, agonizingly intimate pantomime of pain and grief. Karlson has his faults, but playing violence false is not one of them. The emphasis is always dramatic and revelatory rather than picturesque, and when Karlson prolongs the grief-stricken scenes, the emotional scope of the movie seems to expand, encompassing a number of grievous memories from the public violence of the past decade.

Audiences should take to Joe Don Baker for many of the reasons that they take to Jeff Bridges: he's at once "real" and forceful. Physically, Baker is just a big lug, tall and beefy, built along the lines of a football guard or blocking back. In another period of moviemaking, he might have been some studio's answer to Guinn "Big Boy" Williams. He is constructed from very common clay, but he has an actor's power and range, and these attributes make him a compelling figure as Pusser, a common man with an uncommon measure of rage and grief to express. The most striking performer in a strong supporting cast is a young actress named Barbara Benet, who plays a tough, alluring bar girl who eventually becomes an informer for Pusser. She has a stunning moment when she doesn't react at all: Baker walks into the gambling den and clobbers a bouncer with his homemade shillelagh; Miss Benet, watching from a bar stool, doesn't bat an eyelash, and her composure is shocking in the extreme.

Walking Tall is a roughhewn but significant piece of work. The basic material emerges out of immediate, ongoing conflicts in this country, and almost in spite of themselves, the filmmakers appear to express a tragic vision of those conflicts. This movie might have begun as a self-congratulatory law-and-order melodrama, but it leaves one in a reflective, critical frame of mind, contemplating unhappy possibilities—the system may not be so conducive to law and order and even extraordinary heroism may not be its own reward. Perhaps the filmmakers wanted an "affirmative" picture, but they end up expressing a powerful sense of loss. It's not at all certain that the hero's sacrifices have resulted in a triumph for justice and decent, law-abiding folks. One doesn't feel that Pusser's community is now safe at last and that all the scars will heal, particularly the emotional scars left by the death of his wife. Affirmation would stick in the throat, so *Walking Tall* expresses a haunted, skeptical mood that may now be the appropriate one for both the American hero and his society.

October 4, 1973

CHARLEY VARRICK

Andrew Sarris

Once upon a time when I was a reader at Fox I learned that one of my predecessors in this line of work had been none other than the late Jack Kerouac. Rumor had it that the studio became disenchanted with Kerouac's work simply because he wrote rave reports on every piece of writing submitted to him. He seemed concerned less with finding hot properties for the studio than with making it possible for every writer in the world to make it big in Hollywood. I have no way of knowing if this story is true, but it's a lovely, warming story all the same. Still, I can understand the studio's disenchantment. The powers-that-be had cast about for a Darwinian decision-maker only to discover that they had reeled in a Franciscan fool.

I bring this up now only to demonstrate the conflict between the Darwinian and Franciscan sides of my own critical temperament. With one hand I point out the pictures I like best while with the other I wave my readers into every movie house in the land. Hence, on the Darwinian level I prefer *Charley Varrick* to *The Long Goodbye*, and *Summer Wishes, Winter Dreams* to *Late Autumn*. But on the Franciscan level, I hope my readers see all four films even though by my Darwinian calculation of viewer priorities *Charley Varrick* and *Summer Wishes, Winter Dreams* rate four Vs, and *Late Autumn* and *The Long Goodbye* only three. Certainly, all four films deserve to be seen and supported in this age of shrinking attendance and production. Why should these four films be seen? Before I try to tell you, I should warn you that it would be wise to see the films before you read the rest of this review. With *Charley Varrick* especially, half the fun in the flick is being surprised by the delicious details of the plot. Also, I don't know how long any of these movies are going to be around in this dismal period of flash exhibition.

Charley Varrick and *The Long Goodbye* fall into the general genre of film noir or bang-bang. *Varrick* fits more precisely into the sub-genre of the caper movie whereas *Goodbye* is at least nominally part of the private-eye tradition. *Summer Wishes, Winter Dreams* and *Late Autumn* deal largely with women, and therefore belong to the most despised (and most domestic) of all genres—soap opera and/or sitcom—depending on their shifting moods.

But it is only when you don't like a movie that you dump it into a category or suddenly remember that the movie medium itself is "popular" or "commercial" or "conformist" or "compromised" or "conventional." Some critics even dredge up that archaic term of academic abuse—kitsch—for movies they don't like at the very same time as they are hailing other people's kitsch (e.g., *The Way We Were*) as Fun Entertainment. By the same token, certain pundits can deliver sermons on violence for the bang-bang movies they don't like, and then turn around to pontificate on violence as a metaphor for Vietnam in bang-bang movies they do like.

Charley Varrick is my idea of Fun Entertainment, but not because of its bang-bang elements so much as because of its classical ingenuity in endowing a criminal character with moral intelligence. Director Don Siegel and his writers Howard Rodman and Dean Riesner have altered John Reese's novel considerably, and, I would say, all for the better. Walter Matthau's Charley Varrick can be said to be a romanticized and even sentimentalized variation on the mediocre meanness of the character in the novel. Hence, the movie Varrick lingers over his dying wife whereas the book Varrick thinks only of saving his own skin. Whereas the movie Varrick outwits and outlives the Mafioso hit man (Joe Don Baker), the book Varrick ends up with his head crushed by a bowling ball wielded by this same Mafioso. And whereas much of the book was focused on the sexual psyches of policemen, underworld banking procedures, and the nuances of Nevadan lawlessness, the movie zeroes in on Varrick himself as a modest, rational hoodlum with the ability to read the patterns of paranoia in the minds of his adversaries and to make his moves accordingly.

Larger than life? Of course. But then *Charley Varrick* is the closest thing I've seen to a Hawksian caper movie. In the end it isn't the money that glitters so much, but rather the mind with its grasp of anticipatory details: what dental X-rays to put in what folder so as to fool the FBI when the corpses begin to accumulate, how to set up a hysterical confederate for the hit man, how to use the confederate's corpse to bait a trap for the hit man, how to use the mob's own contacts, a flair for stunt flying, and a knack with dynamite for a magical finale of escape and retribution.

What was a minor virtue in *The Day of the Jackal* becomes a major virtue in *Charley Varrick*. The difference is in the endings. Whereas *The Day of the Jackal* ends with the triumph of bureaucratic routine over individual ingenuity, *Charley Varrick* ends with the triumph of individual ingenuity over the bureaucratic routines of both the Mafia and the police. Don Siegel is in a playful mood around the edges. An abortive police stake-out and bulletproof-vested rush provides a comic parody of the very moving Widmark-Guarino-Ihnat confrontation in *Madigan* some years ago. There is a reference in the dialogue to Clint Eastwood, and the trailer camp is named after the author of the novel. Siegel himself does a cameo bit as a ping-pong player outhustled by an Oriental advance man for the Mafia.

But where it counts, Siegel is dead serious. His classical editing of movement and milieu, characters and conveyances, results in a delicate balance between things and people not to be found in the baroque distortions of a Yates or in the squashed absurdism of an Altman. Siegel renders unto the genre what is its rightful due by never exceeding its limits as a sidelong glance at reality. More important, Siegel restores a moral equilibrium to his material by discarding the strained High-Noonism of *Dirty Harry*.

Indeed, by casting the unruly Andy Robinson as the victimized confederate, Siegel finds a more satisfying niche for this simperingly psychotic type than was devised for him in the overextended villainies of *Dirty Harry*. Siegel's women—Felicia Farr, Sheree North, Jacqueline Scott—are expressed idiosyncratically without being exploited idiotically, no mean feat for a bang-bang movie in this brutalized era. In addition, Marjorie Bennett evokes a bawdier version of May Robson as she lusts through old age for all the lurid fantasies of which the Supreme Court seems determined to deprive her. One could write a think piece about some of the sociological tidbits Siegel drops here and there. But why bother? The important thing is that Siegel doesn't inflate his caper movie with hot air. The narrative line is clean and direct, the characterizations economical and functional, and the triumph of intelligence gloriously satisfying.

November 1, 1973

Eight

COMEDY

SLEEPER

Survivor

Pauline Kael

Woody Allen appears before us as the battered adolescent, scarred forever, a little too nice and much too threatened to allow himself to be aggressive. He has the city-wise effrontery of a shrimp who began by using language to protect himself and then discovered that language has a life of its own. The running war between the tame and the surreal—between Woody Allen the frightened nice guy trying to keep the peace and Woody Allen the wiseacre whose subversive fantasies keep jumping out of his mouth—has been the source of the comedy in his films. Messy, tasteless, and crazily uneven (as the best talking comedies have often been), the last two pictures he di- rected—*Bananas* and *Everything You Always Wanted to Know About Sex*—had wild highs that suggested an erratic comic genius. The tension between his insecurity and his wit makes us empathize with him; we, too, are scared to show how smart we feel. And he has found a nonaggressive way of dealing with urban pressures. He stays nice; he's not insulting, like most New York comedians, and he delivers his zingers without turning into a cynic. We enjoy his show of defenselessness, and even the I-don't-mean- any-harm ploy, because we see the essential sanity in him. We respect that sanity—it's the base from which he takes flight. At his top, in parts of *Bananas* and *Sex*, the inexplicably funny took over; it might be grotesque, it almost always had the flippant, corny bawdiness of a frustrated sopho- more running amok, but it seemed to burst out—as the most inspired comedy does—as if we had all been repressing it. We laughed as if he had let out what we couldn't hold in any longer.

The surreal is itself tamed in Woody Allen's *Sleeper*, the most stable and most sustained of his films. (It also has the best title.) Easily the slapstick comedy of the year—there hasn't been any other—*Sleeper* holds together, as his sharpest earlier films failed to do; it doesn't sputter and blow fuses, like *Bananas* and *Sex*. It's charming—a very even work, with almost no thudding bad lines and with no low stretches. I can't think of anything much the matter with it; it's a small classic. But it doesn't have the loose,

242

manic highs of those other films. You come out smiling and perfectly happy, but not driven crazy, not really turned on, the way his messier movies and some musicals (*Singin' in the Rain, Cabaret*) and some comic movies (*M*A*S*H, The Long Goodbye*) and parts of Paul Mazursky's movies can turn one on. I had a wonderful time at *Sleeper,* and I laughed all the way through, but it wasn't exhilarating. Allen's new sense of control over the medium and over his own material seems to level out the abrasive energy. You can be with it all the way, and yet it doesn't impose itself on your imagination—it dissolves when it's finished. If it sounds like a contradiction to say that *Sleeper* is a small classic and yet not exhilarating—well, I can't completely explain that. Comedy is impossibly mysterious; this is a beautiful little piece of work—it shows a development of skills in our finest comedy-maker—and yet it's mild, and doesn't quite take off.

Woody Allen plays a Rip Van Winkle who wakes up in 2173—and that's all I'm going to say about the story, because I don't want to squeeze the freshness out of the jokes. His girl is Diane Keaton (who was practically the only good thing in *Play It Again, Sam*), and she has a plucky, almost Jean Arthur quality. She's very appealing, and in *Sleeper* you want to like her; I always felt right on the verge of responding to her (as a broad-faced, Slavic-looking poet of the future), but she isn't quite funny enough. She has good bits (like her Brando parody), but her timing is indefinite, and so is the character she plays. She's really just there to be Woody's girl, and there's nobody else—other than Allen himself—you remember from the movie. *Sleeper* could really use a *cast.* In a Preston Sturges comedy, the various characters' madnesses and obsessions bounced off each other and got all scrambled up; Chaplin and Keaton had their big fellows to contend with; the Marx Brothers had each other, plus Margaret Dumont and Walter Woolf King and Sig Rumann and those blondes wriggling in satin. But Woody Allen has no set characters to respond to. He needs a great stock company, like Carol Burnett's (Who wants to be a crazy alone? That leads to melancholy), but so far in his movies he's the only character, because his conception of himself keeps him alone.

The Woody Allen character suffers, in all his films, from sex in the head which he figures his body can't get for him. It's the comedy of sexual inadequacy; what makes it hip rather than masochistic and awful is that he thinks women want the media macho ideal, and we in the audience are cued to suspect, as he secretly does, that that's the real inadequacy (social even more than sexual). Woody Allen is a closet case of potency; he knows he's potent, but he's afraid to tell the world—and adolescents and post-adolescents can certainly identify with that. His shrimp-hero's worst fear may be that he would be attractive only to women who feel sorry for him (or want to dominate him). The latter is parenthetical because Allen hasn't explored that possibility; the thought of him with, say, Anne Bancroft suggests the sort of gambit he hasn't tried. When we see his films, all our emotions attach to him; his fear and his frailty are what everything revolves around. No one else in his pictures has a vivid presence, or any particular quality except being a threat to him, and even that quality isn't really character-ized. Maybe the reason he doesn't invest others with comic character (or even villainous character) is that he's so hung up that he has no interest in other people's hangups; that could be why his stories never really build to the big climactic finish one expects from a comedy. His plots don't tie a gigantic knot and then explode it, because the other characters aren't strong enough to carry the threads. The end of *Sleeper* is just a mild cutoff point—not bad but unexciting. The movie has a more conventional slap-stick-comedy structure than *Bananas*, and slapstick isn't something you can do with a pickup cast. The comedy isn't forced, it looks relaxed and easy, but the routines don't gather momentum—they slide off somewhere. Woody Allen loses his supporting players along the way, and one hardly notices. It's likely that he sees his function as being all of us, and since he's all of us, nobody else can be anything.

But, being all of us, he can get too evenly balanced, he can lose his edge. Nobody else could have made *Bananas* or parts of *Sex*, but others could conceivably make a movie like *Sleeper,* just as others are beginning to write in the Woody Allen manner—and one of the most gifted of them, Marshall Brickman, is co-author of the *Sleeper* script. The humor here doesn't tap the mother lode; it's strip-mining. The movie is in the Woody Allen style, but it doesn't have the disruptive inspiration that is the unbal-anced soul of Woody Allen. In interviews, Allen has often been quoted as saying that he wants to stay rough in his movie technique; I used to enjoy reading those quotes, because I thought he was right, and in *Bananas* his instinct to let the jokes run shapelessly loose instead of trimming them and making them tidy paid off. The effect was berserk, in an original way. But he tailored his play *Play It Again, Sam* in the smooth George S. Kaufman–Broadway style, and the movie version, which Herbert Ross directed even more smoothly (I hated it), turned out to be Woody Allen's biggest box-office success up to that time, and made him a mass-audience star. How could a man who really trusted the free and messy take up the clarinet, an instrument that appeals to controlled, precise people? You can't really goof around with a clarinet. (The group he plays with, the New Orleans Funeral and Ragtime Orchestra, can be heard on the *Sleeper* track, along with the Preservation Hall Jazz Band.) I think he knows that the free and messy is the right, great direction for his comedy, but he's very well organized, and, like most comedians, he really trusts success. He trusts laughs, and how can a comedian tell when they're not earned? He's a romantic comedian—he goes on believing in love and the simple, good things in life. He's also a very practical-man comedian—he's the harried, bespectacled nice guy who just wants to stay nice and be a success and get the girl. In terms of his aspirations, he's rather like Truffaut's Antoine Doinel—the unpretentious, hopeful joiner of the bourgeoisie—as a jester. In American terms, he's Harold Lloyd with Groucho's tongue.

To have found a clean visual style for a modern slapstick comedy in color is a major victory; Woody Allen learns with the speed of a wizard. *Sleeper* has a real look to it, and simple, elegant design. (The robot servants of the future, in their tuxedos, might be windup dandies by Elie Nadelman.) Physically, Woody Allen is much more graceful in *Sleeper;* he's turning into that rarity, a verbal comedian who also knows how to use his body. And his acting has developed; he can register more emotions now, and his new silly beatific look—the look of a foolish sage—goes with the wonderful infantile jokes that don't make sense. But one might say that *Sleeper* is a sober comedy; it doesn't unhinge us, we never feel that our reason is being shredded. It has a businesslike, nine-to-five look about it, and a faint nine-to-five lethargy. For a comedian, the price of stability may be the loss of inspiration. (Our most inspired comedian, Jonathan Winters, has never found his forms. But then he doesn't have that base of sanity, either.) What's missing is the wild man's indifference to everything but the joke. In Woody Allen's case, this out-of-control edge went way past Groucho's effrontery and W. C. Fields's malice into a metaphysical outrageousness, but the impulse was similar: finally, the pleasure in the joke was all that mattered. That's what put him among the great ones.

Woody Allen has become the folk hero of adolescents and post-adolescents and maybe just about all of us because we felt that if we stuck with him failure could succeed; this was, in a sense, his pact with us to get our loyalty, and it worked. We don't want to have to go through failure; we want to watch him go through it—and come out the other side. I always thought the danger for him was that he wanted to be a universal little fellow—a Chaplin—and that he might linger too long on the depressive, misfit side of his character and let the schleppy pathos take over (as he did in *Take the Money and Run*). And I thought that if he ever convinced us that he was really failing he'd lose us—who wants to watch a wispy schlep? He may not fully know it, but he doesn't need our sympathy; he's got much more than that already. What Woody Allen probably doesn't realize is that when he uses his wit he becomes our D'Artagnan. He isn't a little fellow for college students; he's a *hero*. They want to be funny, like him.

What I had underestimated was another danger. Woody Allen tips the scales toward winning in *Sleeper*, all right, but he overvalues normality; the battered adolescent still thinks that that's the secret of happiness. He hasn't come to terms with what his wit is telling him. He's dumped Chaplin (blessings) and devised a Buster Keaton–style story, but Keaton's refined physical movements were a clown's poetry, while when Allen does physical comedy—even when he's good at it—he's a very ordinary person. His gift is upstairs. It's really lucky that he cares about himself as much as he does, or he might get so balanced out that his jokes would become monotonous, like those of his imitators. If only he can begin to take control for granted, now that he's improving as a physical comedian and gaining infinitely greater skill as a director. Surreal comedy is chaos; to be really funny, you have to be willing to let your unconscious take over. That's what doesn't happen in *Sleeper*.

December 31, 1973

Fresh Frozen Woody Allen

Molly Haskell

First, the Consumer Index Rating. For moviegoers who want to know whether to hire a babysitter and stand in line for Woody Allen's *Sleeper*, and whether to eat after or before the show (for fear of stomach muscle strain), the new comedy, pitting Woody against brainwashed bullies living in the year 2173, has a fair share of laughs—four uproars, seven or eight knee-slappers, fifteen chuckles; or more than *Play It Again, Sam* and *Everything You Always Wanted to Know About Sex*, and fewer than *Take the Money and Run* and *Bananas*. In other words, enough to justify a babysitter, but not enough to keep you from feeling hungry afterward. As likable and intermittently funny as Allen is, there is little connection between gags and nothing to take up the slack when a joke fails. As with the lesser cartoons of some of the animators being featured at the Cultural Center's series, you begin to keep score of hits and misses.

There are those who think we reviewers should take our chuckles and run, but I happen to believe that we have an obligation to go beyond the first hedonistic reaction to a movie to an analysis of the aftertaste, and that we also can (and cannot help but) react to other stimuli—to books on which movies are based, to other movies in the genre (to say that a movie based on *Death in Venice* or *The Long Goodbye* should be analyzed in isolation from the original is like asking us to look at Cézanne's mountains without considering our experience of real mountains—or of other paintings of real mountains), to other critics. Reviewing, being an essentially comparative task, inevitably becomes polemical: If a book is praised as the best novel of the year it is, willy-nilly and implicitly, raised over the dead, or at least battered, bodies of other novels—books that failed to achieve the monumentality of this one, the stylistic perfection of another, the up-to-dateness of still another. The oversell is part of a campaign to get people to buy books and go to movies, but who among us can help but react to overreaction?

Woody Allen, by treating the film medium as his private sandbox—to play in, to dump on, to ignore—has become the darling of critics who jeer at other critics for taking movies too seriously and of audiences, represented by these critics, who find the attempt to develop an idea into some kind of complete and cohesive work (heaven forbid we should use the word "art") heavy going. The strained ambitiousness of so much contemporary filmmaking has induced in critics a neo-philistinism that is as intolerant of aspiration as Harry Cohn's bellwether ass.

Woody Allen plays to this, elevating sloppiness to a governing principle. This can be hysterically funny as when, at the opening of the film, he emerges from a cryonics tube, his feet wrapped in booties of Reynolds Wrap like some hastily frozen product. Or the idea of his going into St. Vincent's for a minor operation (and having found a parking place right in front, at that) and emerging two hundred years later. But as soon as it becomes necessary to establish his surroundings—the doctors who are sponsoring him and their conflict with the authorities—Allen is at a loss.

Allen the director can't turn away from Allen the performer, and Allen the performer is not always interesting enough to sustain the mutual admiration society. He mugs, nudges his audience, plays to them rather than to his fellow actors, alters the roles of his characters to suit the whim of the moment (Diane Keaton, for example, goes from screaming enemy to silent partner to active ally, all ineffectively, and is denied the consistency, even rigidity, that would give her comic plausibility), uses sight gags that would have as much, possibly more, impact in verbal form—as incidental humor pieces in *The New Yorker*, for example, where Allen and his screenwriter Marshall Brickman do time as writers; and displays a contempt for logic that is less grand than gratuitous. The initial Swiftian conceit of Woody as Miles Monroe, a proprietor of a Greenwich Village health-food store, thrust among the dehumanized Brobdingnagians of tomorrow, becomes anti-Swiftian in its indifference to scale and in its failure to define the natives with any detailed consistency. The sight gag of a garden of giant-sized fruits and vegetables, for example, has nothing to do with the physical proportions or any other characteristics that we know of the master race and hence falls flat after its momentary shock value.

Allen, with four films and considerable cultural chic to his credit, can hardly claim the figurative definition for the title of his new film, and yet he presumably means for us to do so. He has cannily promoted the idea of not taking himself too seriously into a first principle of business. He distributes his films in what appears to be a hit-or-miss fashion so that most people haven't seen all four (now five), has systematically withheld them from television, where closer scrutiny might expose his limited skills and durability as a performer, and has encouraged a "just fun" attitude toward his films while stealthily adding more elaborate sketches to his repertory in order to invite comparison with the great comedians of the past. Critics have noted the influences on him—Roger Greenspun has mentioned Chaplin, and Richard Corliss, Langdon as superior to, but recognizable in Allen's white-face, robot-servant impersonation in *Sleeper;* and Stuart Byron has suggested an affinity with Jerry Lewis.

But Allen's sense of his own identity is too strong and too obtrusive for him ever to successfully camouflage himself as a mechanical man, the way Chaplin does in *The Circus,* the way Keaton enters animistically into harmony with other organisms. Nor can he quite envision a world of "normal" people as Lewis does in *The Nutty Professor.* Allen clings tenaciously to the worm's eye view which is the source of his humor and of his success and which defines the limits of his vision. It is the humor of a stand-up comic, wit that plays off a given world, rather than inventing it. It is a verbal, parochial, ratty, ethnic, bargain-basement humor, sexist, conservative, self-centered, and the funniest lines in *Sleeper* are hangover lines, when the "morning after" happens to be two centuries later: "I haven't seen my analyst in 200 years . . . (pause) . . . I might have been cured by now." Or, to Keaton's exclamation, "You haven't had sex in 200 years!", Miles's answer: "204 if you count my marriage."

In alien territory, Allen can just about survive. He lacks the ability of a Chaplin or a Keaton to turn expediency into poetry, and his over-concrete personality—Jewish ethnic, New York—is a cross he brandishes with bravado (unlike Lewis who, in the Establishment fifties, was obliged to sublimate his). In this, Allen is very much in tune with the contemporary *Zeitgeist,* the vision of the alien as insider, the underdog as top banana. Whereas most comedians suggested, by their smallness or obesity, the plight of outsiders looking in, longing to join the beautiful people (and thus were universal), Allen, to his disadvantage and advantage, comes at a time when little of the decorum and ritual of an elitist society remains for the comedian to sabotage, and when the WASP establishment has been demoted, in movie mythology, with the ethnic occupying center-stage. Actors and actresses who normally would have played character parts or supporting roles (Al Pacino, Dustin Hoffman, Robert De Niro, Bruce Dern, Dennis Hopper, Barbra Streisand) are leading men or stars; the WASP has become a figure of ridicule. Note the paper-doll imbecility of the smart-set girls in *The Way We Were,* or the conversion of the Durk character in *Serpico* into the lightweight Lindsayite played by Tony Roberts (the actor, incidentally, who played the womanizer opposite Allen in *Play It Again, Sam*). Perhaps we could trace a parallel trajectory between the declining fortunes of Mayor Lindsay and the loss of potency of the screen WASP.

At the same time, Allen—and this is the source of the reactionary side of his wit—wants *in*. Like the traditionally upward-mobile Jewish kid, part of him wants to join the dumb goyim, the smiling blond middle-Americans whose surrogates are the lobotomized futuristic race of *Sleeper* who say "Green-witch Village" and never heard of Norman Mailer. But Allen never develops the tensions and contradictions inherent in this situation beyond showing a disinclination to become involved in a radical plot by a group called Aries to overthrow the government, and by showing a marked contentedness once he has been reconditioned as a member of the establishment. He tries to have it both ways—the vernal paradise of the revolutionaries recalls *Fahrenheit 451,* but it also plays on the negative image of carnivores in Godard's *Weekend.*

Allen is too much a product of his own biography to make the leaps of association of which the great comedians were capable, or—and this is a more serious failing—to envision an adversary as a worthwhile opponent. Allen's vision of a futuristic society, despite the elaborateness of the sets under Dale Hennesy's art direction, makes one appreciate the authority of a Stanley Kubrick. The comedian lives in a symbiotic relationship with his enemy, and this is where we appreciate the genius of Chaplin and Keaton, not just in the sublime grace (or deliberate gracelessness) of their mimetic art, but on the conceptual level, in the instinct for investing the opponent with strength—the towering mass of the bully in *Easy Street,* the numerical advantage of the cops or the army of women in Keaton's films, which give rise to feats of grace and ingenuity and intimations of the spirit's immortality that are beyond the considerable talents of Woody Allen.

January 3, 1974

PLAYTIME
Time Off

Penelope Gilliatt

"In Chicago they are actually building the décor that cost me so much to have made for my difficult film," said Jacques Tati at a showing last year of his stirringly funny and innovative movie *Playtime* (1968). It has already been seen noncommercially at festivals in San Francisco, Los Angeles, and New Orleans, as well as publicly all over Europe and in England, in its original, 70-mm. form. The delay in the national release here was caused by the reluctance of exhibitors to go to the expense of installing 70-mm. equipment. The hilarious perfectionist, onlie begetter of *Jour de Fête* (1949), *Les Vacances de M. Hulot* (1953), *Mon Oncle* (1958), and *Traffic* (1971), clung to the 70-mm. form he shot in. Now, at last, he has made for public release here a 35-mm. version that he is happy with. *Playtime* is to be cherished. It is a new step in slapstick comedy: gay, cinematically new, as if the old Mack Sennett form had been reborn as a fledgling. Its technical inventiveness, its view of modernity, and its gift to the development of a popular art, which took Tati years of his working life, are a giant stride in the career of a man who declines to repeat the beloved formula of his classic M. Hulot films (to the foreseeable fury of some of the public, which generally flies into a tantrum when men who have made it laugh change their tune). *Playtime* is to be loved for what it does for the aesthetics of comedy, not to speak of its charm and its world-irony, which is so light that its antic insult to the messianism of New Town living floats in the face of axiomatic notions of progress without doing injury, like a blow from a feather.

Tati thinks that the days when films revolved round comic heroes are over. The days of Keaton and Chaplin are gone. The school is closed. *Playtime* sees the same world of prankishness and physical catastrophe and victimization that the school's old students do; the difference is that Tati finds his film's world inhabited by everyone, not by a single comic star. The film notices in businessmen and tourists and dandy waiters the identical adherence to life and insanely funny concentration on small private projects that used to belong in vaudeville exclusively to the comic at the top of the bill. Tati's famous figure of M. Hulot is still there, his trousers hung as high as ever, his head in air, a figure loping into drastically unfamiliar situations with an umbrella carried like a military officer's stick or sometimes like a fencing foil. But his importance has receded. The director/ actor of *Playtime* has even put into the film a couple of people who, seen from the back, look just like Hulot. They wear the same short mackintosh and the same hat. They have the same bouncing walk, as if reaching up to smash a high tennis lob. Why should Hulot's role be too magnified, asks the film radically, when everybody is a little funny in life, depending on the recorder looking at them? Tati's eye is perpetually apt to catch the ridiculous in the fashionable. He can't be foxed; on the other hand, he doesn't flail in loathing of the up-to-date. He sees in modern surroundings elegance, inutility, unsuitability to the human frame; at the same time, he notices that his ungrumbling people, who seem to have no recall of the past, are appealingly spellbound by the steely present, and that they accept standardization with little cries of wonder. The charm of Venice is shown at the beginning of the film by exhibiting a photograph of a Venetian skyscraper exactly like one taken of a skyscraper in London. Beautiful! How Venetian!

The main character of the film's world is the décor. It is a heroic character, or at any rate trying to be: certainly not villainous. There are glamorous cliff faces of sheets of metal, newly laid highly polished lino in squares that come unglued and stick to people's heels, glass doors so spotless that a man gesturing through one of them to ask someone for a light mystifies the audience about the reason for the dumb show, until everything becomes clear when the door that had been invisible is opened to allow contact. For Tati, as he tells us through this subtly comic and tender film, the old style of dramatic situation is dead, and the conventional plot of exposition and dénouement is dead with it. He is not even concerned to describe the truistic condition of man pitted against a dehumanized environment. Tati shows him clasping the murderous new state of enlightened living with a bear hug, full of joy and gratitude, so that the point of its killing power is actually made with much more gravity. The inhabitants of the *Playtime* world certainly know about racism, pollution, poverty, the population explosion, drugs, melancholia, the second-rate corruption of big finance and politics, but the knowledge gets swept to the side of the mind like wood shavings in a new building. Everyone here possesses the small soul of an eremitically intent housewife. Yes, dear, I know about the refugees, but don't go leaving fingerprints on the nice new steel elevator doors.

The characters' unwitting task, which they undertake with fortitude and brave bird cries, is to make enlightened urban conditions habitable. Vestiges of shabby old hedonism linger in the uncomfortable new world that everyone in *Playtime* good-heartedly accepts as a benison. An aged elevator operator in charge of a glossy and complicated thing that seems to be operated by a computerlike signal board above his head sneaks a drag at a stinking relic of a smoke between bouts of coping with the up-to-the-minute machine. He is given arcane help by the computer, which flashes cold signs at him about the elevator's movements like a voting recorder on TV gone berserk. M. Hulot, a prospective but not overhopeful passenger, stands by patiently. He has a card that he gives to the elevator controller; the battered official, still game, who derives a certain balked dignity from his uniform but visibly doubts that he has any real control over his handsome charge, plugs on dutifully at the long job of pressing in turn the right switches for, presumably, floor, area, section, and person. This desired person lives in a head-high box in territory so hygienic that dust would be a friend. Nothing here is remotely suited to ordinary living, though complaints are never made. The withered old liftman has to stand on tiptoe to reach what must be the voice box for announcing visitors. Hulot strikes out bravely through the unknown steel Sahara, trying to adjust his naturally messy preferences to the rules of politesse. More than ever before in his films, his face expresses bewilderment without utterance. There is an element of the aghast hidden in it somewhere, but his bearing is always soldierly, even under the worst duress—obeying flashing signs about where to go in and out, crushing inner rebellion, shaking hands courteously although he is hampered by carrying his furled umbrella. The last maneuver is made successfully in spite of the umbrella; manners have been saved, even in this upside-down world.

The elegantly intelligent, modest film has Tati's peculiar quality of decorum preserved in hilarious circumstances. It may be plotless, but it has a strong narrative line. It tells the story of a day in the life of a glassy Paris that is alien to Hulot, with his affection for natural muddle. The same hours are spent by some very different people, who meet at the end of the exhausting expedition of discovery in a set piece about a pompous but jerrybuilt restaurant. Their coming together confers on the film a typical Tati mood of conviviality. At the beginning of the day, a coachload of American women tourists arrives in Paris. Most of the women wear hats all the time. Some of the artificial flowers on the hats droop, especially with evening formal wear; in the day, the flowers are neatly arranged around the crowns. They express propriety, celebration, and an excitable little-girlishness that is not particularly apt for the age of the matrons wearing them, but never mind. The sightseers also include some young American girls, one of whom later shyly makes friends with M. Hulot. We never learn his exact job: it isn't consequential. Nobody's work is, in this picture. The people in employment are middlemen or redundant or inanely decorative, like the multilingual announcer at an international trade fair, and the out-of-his-time elevator man, and customs men at airports, and baffled waiters struggling to serve inedible food in the unusable, costly restaurant, and secretaries with nothing obviously taxing to do, and mechanics causing cars in magic modern garages to go up and down in pretty patterns. Still, everyone is charmed by everything. Even the tired, carefully dressed sight-seers cry out with pleasure at the foreignness of it all, though it would save the vivacity of response that they expend if they were to admit that the experience is much like being in America. They speak in bright exclamations. "I didn't know they had a parking problem in Paris!" Men going through customs express undue excitement about duty-free liquor. Ladies get keen on cranes they could see at home, and at the sight of two cars going up and down in a garage: one red, one blue. And there's even a mechanic jumping onto a car while it is in motion. Tati/Hulot ridicules none of them. If the expensive tourist food is foul, responds Hulot in his easygoing way, the stuff in some drugstore will do fine instead. The young American girl, whom Hulot has seen through the window of the coach, passionately wants to photograph a flower stall but keeps getting thwarted by passersby and customers; in the dawn light of the next morning, she and Hulot go to the stall she likes, and Hulot persuades an old Parisian to stand next to the flower seller to be photographed. That is, until another and more coldhearted tourist with a camera shoves Hulot's gently courted girl out of the way and commandeers the puzzled old man.

Tati says something acute and physically eloquent in *Playtime* about the influence of modern architecture on human movement. The brainwashed devotees of shoebox living always walk at right angles around corners—secretaries with memos, a man wheeling a tea trolley—following the angles of contemporary architecture and T-squares. When one distraught woman upsets the pattern by running higgledy-piggledy, the effect of the unconscious precision drilling has been so powerful that it almost looks as if she is the one who is out of step. People follow signs devoutly, sometimes with chaotic results. A drunk who has been thrown out of the grand new joint at the end of the picture automatically obeys the pattern of the restaurant's neon sign, which is shaped in a curved arrow and ends in the restaurant, craftily leading hunters for fun into the jaws of the place. So the sloshed one, after a few staggers and bends made in a conscientious attempt to follow the orders of the sign, lands up again in the grandiose chaos from which he has been slung out. The polite dissident is M. Hulot, as usual. Earlier on, in a supermarket where he has bought a scarf as a present for the American girl, whom he already maybe loves, he pays, goes out through the wrong exit, and is sternly made to rearrange the handles of some serried saucepans that have broken rank with his passing. It is important to use the proper turnstile, you see, even if it is already filled with a woman shopper. Tati is much concerned with the fatuity of the rules that people are forced to accept now, though his characters do it entirely without grumpiness. No one gets impatient. Neuroticism doesn't exist in Tati's films. *Playtime* reflects reality here, as Tati's films always do (though he raises it to the poetically funny), for the truth is that many perfectly well-formed individuals in life are content to be standardized.

The film is beautifully designed, mostly in monochromes: in shades of white; in a dulled, indoor gray-green; in reflectionless steel. It includes a view of a colossal apartment building with hundreds of plate-glass windows opening without curtains onto the sight of as many happy families, all of them watching television, who seem to come from some refrigerated Norman Rockwell group portrait. Eugène Roman was the architecturally-minded designer, following Tati's vision and Tati's painstaking, technically knowledgeable drawings; the director is a beautiful quick draftsman in black ink, and tends politely to get round an expert's "No" with a more inventive "Perhaps this way?"

There are a few other happy revolutionaries, apart from Hulot himself. They include a mongrel or two, and a contented-looking woman traveler at the airport who pats a whimpering case that is presumably full of live dog. A combative other woman meanwhile objects to having her mere handbag searched. The headwaiter of the grand, fast-collapsing restaurant of the finale emerges once from the kitchen with a neat ring of black round his mouth where he has taken a gulp from a bottle of wine, the owner having put soot on it from the bottom of a chafing dish to catch secret swiggers. Another and more dolled-up waiter keeps doing his hair in the kitchen mirror before he makes his entrance with some dramatic plateful. Individualists and eccentrics survive, says *Playtime;* drab functionalism can still be sabotaged by cheek, and even by happy solemnity, as it is by Hulot's speechless, futureless, but deadly earnest feeling for the girl tourist. The trouble isn't so much that life now is standardized, suggests Tati, any more than it is altogether true to say that modern architecture is Tati's enemy. He sees that it is often foolishly unlivable-in, but he also vividly sees the dauntlessness of people coping with it. Sometimes he finds it farcically beautiful, and its inhabitants' pride in it then strikes him as intensely interesting—something comic, sincere, to be recorded.

The film is photographed mostly in Tati's favorite long-shot. He doesn't care much for close-ups. Nor does anyone else with a background in vaudeville (Keaton, Chaplin, all the rest) or in sport (Tati did early vaudeville sketches and made film shorts about rugby, boxing, wrestling, bicycling, tennis). Keaton is his hero, partly because of what Buster could do balletically. In New York last year, Tati watched a seven-year-old performing a minute of classical ballet to keep herself amused during grown-up talk in French; then he said to her in English, "You know Keaton? Yes, I thought so. They say girls can't be funny, but you are funny. You know already that it is funnier if one doesn't set out to be funny." (*Playtime* starts slowly. The grins grow. The riot comes at the end.) "For me," he said, with his usual seriousness in speaking to children, "Keaton is No. 1 on the legs."

The soundtrack is revolutionary. Tati uses the ordinary sounds of overcivilization as expressively as others use speech. We hear stiletto heels that catch in cracks, tripping toward us with a percussive tinkle on tiled floors. Businessmen, audible from afar as they go about their nonexistent activities along lengths of corridor, seem to be walking on pigs' trotters. The cushions of heavily contemporary armchairs give way when sat on with a noise like a bicycle tire being let down. A businessman's ball-point pen clicks. A tag on a briefcase makes a fluttering noise like a sail in a squall, and there is a din of squelch on the track when a drugstore attendant pumps cream around a dessert with a patented cream nozzle. The sound of an air-conditioner in the restaurant on a girl diner's naked back nearly deafens: you can practically see her skin rippling in the wind. Are the sounds vastly magnified, or does the apparent distortion come from the fact that we generally close our ears to them when they make their attack in real life? In *Playtime*, the racket of engines, machines, zips, enlightened buzzers drowns the human voice. Tati uses sparse, low-key scraps of dialogue in French and English at random, without subtitles: no need for them in the Esperanto world of international marketing and trade fairs that so fascinates him here. He even introduces a fast-talking bilingual German who is selling, of all things, a door that closes in Golden Silence.

Tati is one of the funniest men in the world. *Playtime*, which is a custard pie in the face, is also his most humane and serious observation of people's comically difficult endeavor to survive the inroads of improvements, to sustain intimacy, to save language from turning into something like a half-heard eternal cassette of officialese. Tati sees citizens who are no more than ordinarily gifted having to battle with conditions that are simply not scaled to the human figure. It typifies the film's vision that the cloud-cuckoo-land architect who designed the restaurant that so hilariously subsides into ruin is only called in to measure things too late, when they already don't work: for instance, when a dish supporting an elegant and angrily decorated fish won't go through the kitchen hatch. The irritated architect measures the width and length of the dish with due professional fuss, and the fish looks more and more uneatable. But none of the mostly identically dressed dancers and diners seem to notice the lack of food, the gradually declining timbers, and the slapstick shambles around them. It has all been a great success, they feel.

Something is over, though. M. Hulot has given the girl flowers and her scarf. What might have happened if she hadn't been only on a twenty-four-hour trip? Nice girl. The women in the tourist bus, tired but still appreciative, admire the scarf, finger it, and show each other the pictures of Paris on it. The girl goes on sitting with the box on her lap. "Someone gave me this," she says.

July 2, 1973

Lifeless Abstractionist

Richard Schickel

There is no doubt that Jacques Tati has the spirit of an artist. A short subject accompanying *Playtime* shows him to be generally observant and thoughtful, not only about his own filmmaking but also about the world around him and the people with whom he shares it. Unfortunately, he lacks the artist's talent to mold and shape his insights into truly engaging works. This film—made in 1968 but delayed in release here until a satisfactory 35-mm. print could be made from his 70-mm. original—is almost as stupefying as his more recent *Traffic* and ranks with it as one of the truly excruciating cinematic experiences of recent years.

The enthusiasm that has greeted these latest adventures of Mr. Hulot appears to be the product of critical wistfulness. Tati is the last in a once great tradition of pantomimic screen comedians. Out of a desire to keep that tradition alive, writers seize on the odd, amusing bits in his films, overpraising them while ignoring Tati-Hulot's glaring inadequacies.

Among the most obvious of these is a total lack of narrative drive, both overall and within the individual sequences of his films. *Playtime* finds him trying to keep an appointment in an automated office building, wandering through an exhibit of new industrial products, attending the opening night of a new restaurant which is trying to maintain a chic air while construction workers are still trying to finish the place.

These are promising enough settings for comedy, but Tati never develops any dramatic tension within them, partly because he seems to have no firm attitude toward them. Modernism was an actively malevolent force in Chaplin's *Modern Times;* Tati sees it as nothing more than a minor nuisance. His greatest problem, however, is that unlike Chaplin—or Buster Keaton—he hasn't the faintest idea of how to link one gag to another, building the kind of comic line that tightens, tightens, tightens around them and ensnares the audience in analogous helplessness, the kind that results from masterfully orchestrated laughter.

The air of aimlessness that hangs so heavily around *Playtime* is thickened by the fact that Hulot cannot be said to be a character in the sense that Chaplin's Tramp or Keaton's Great Stone Face was. He is passive where they were active—even revolutionary—in their relationship to the things and the people who tormented them. Chaplin was insouciantly defiant when pressed, Keaton manically inventive. Both were also incurable romantics. They were people of dimension, people with plans and aspirations and a wide range of feeling. One could identify with them, suffer, and exult with them.

Hulot, on the other hand, is just a pleasantly boring presence, a cipher who shows no feelings beyond a spaniel-like curiosity and momentary flutters of frustration that never approach the level of anxiety, let alone threaten him with breakdown. He and the people he encounters are scarcely less abstract than their settings, juiceless, and lifeless. Going to a Tati movie for laughs is about as practical as going to an exhibition of Mondrian paintings with the same goal in mind, though the painter may actually excel the actor in terms of motion and emotion.

August 6, 1973

TEN FROM "YOUR SHOW OF SHOWS"

Andrew Sarris

The funniest movie in 1973 may well turn out to be a collection of old kinescopes entitled *Ten From "Your Show of Shows."* Who would have imagined that ancient television would turn out to be so much more fun than modern cinema? Unfortunately, audiences haven't yet been cued in to the volume of laughter the show deserves. I suppose they're waiting for some prestigious critic to call the show a "breakthrough" of some sort or other. But it's already too late for a *Time* or *Newsweek* cover for Sid

Caesar, Imogene Coca, Carl Reiner, Howard Morris and their merry crew. They remain enshrined back in the supposedly humorless years of the Eisenhower and McCarthy fifties when so many humorless essays were being written about the decline of humor and satire in America.

So many of us would laugh our heads off on Saturday night through *Your Show of Shows,* but by Monday morning we would be nodding in agreement at some gloom-and-doom pronouncement in the public prints on the sad state of humor in our repressed republic. The gloom and doom were dispensed in regular dosages by James Thurber, E. B. White, Malcolm Muggeridge, Marya Mannes, John Crosby, and other eminent takers of the public pulse. Where, we were asked again and again, was America's Aristophanes, Molière, Voltaire, Beaumarchais, and Swift? On occasions, we were even asked to mourn the absence or inactivity of such supposedly trenchant satirists as Mark Twain, Will Rogers, and Fred Allen. No matter. By Saturday night we would be rolling off our collective couches in the national living room only to forget by Monday morning the art and craftsmanship we had been privileged to witness.

Of the ten skits in the current selection I would say that only three—the take-off on *This Is Your Life, Bertha the Sewing Machine Girl,* and *The Bavarian Clock*—rank anywhere near the top of the Caesar-Coca-Reiner-Morris repertory. *Big Business* and *The Music Evening* are middle-range sketches with great moments, while *From Here to Obscurity, Breaking the News, The Prussian Doorman, The Interview with the Viennese Space Expert,* and *The Movie Theatre* are closer to the bottom than to the top of the vast reservoir of revue material from *Your Show of Shows.*

Even so, there are more deserved belly-laughs in the single Caesar-Morris-Reiner demolition of *This Is Your Life* than in the total oeuvre of Woody Allen. And yet I dare say that the humor-exhumers of the future will decide on the basis of printed artifacts that Woody Allen deserves an entire chapter whereas Sid Caesar deserves at most a footnote. Hence, though 20 movies on the order of *Ten From "Your Show of Shows"* could be assembled without dropping down to the dregsier sketches from the show, there does not seem ever to have been the slightest interest in writing a book on this showbiz phenomenon.

If indeed there is such a book I stand corrected, but I've never heard of it. I've never encountered a decent essay on the subject. When I happened to mention Sid Caesar on my WBAI radio program some years ago, people congratulated me for my emotional loyalty to an obscure pleasure from the past. As I recall, the only reference I have ever made to *Your Show of Shows* in print occurs tangentially (and parenthetically) in a review of a book on the Judy Garland television show (*The Other Side of the Rainbow* by Mel Torme): "The recent history of the medium is replete with instances of sophisticated shows being swamped in Trendex terms by cornpone attractions. "It probably all began when Lawrence Welk drove the *Show of Shows* off the video screen even as Sid Caesar, Carl Reiner, Howard Morris, and an army of professionals were doing scathing satires on the folksy amateurishness of the Welk Show."

The same question therefore comes back to haunt so many of us: Why have we been so ungrateful and forgetful over the years to a group of people (and let us not forget producer Max Liebman and writers Mel Tolkin, Lucille Kallen, Mel Brooks, Tony Webster, Caesar, and many others) who have given us so much exquisite entertainment in spite of the minimal cultural encouragement provided by the medium itself and those who professed to meditate on it? But before we consider this question of our own perplexing ingratitude, we must attempt to recapture the atmosphere in which *Your Show of Shows* originally materialized.

The first big comedy star of television was Milton Berle, in many ways the stylistic antithesis of Sid Caesar. It would be startling today to rerun the old Berle shows simply to check off the innumerable times Uncle Miltie made his grand opening entrance in drag, and how often he indulged in pinky-twiddling, powder-puffing routines out of the gay grotesqueries of the Borscht Circuit. He was low-down, vulgar, dirty, boisterous, obvious, and outrageous, and the kiddies loved him even more than they loved Pinky Lee with all the latter's lisping juvenilia. Berle established the comic tradition on television of an insolent unprofessionalism by which the comedian was rewarded by the audience with bigger laughs for going up in his lines than for delivering them correctly. This tradition was later extended and perfected by Jackie Gleason, Red Skelton, and Dean Martin.

Sid Caesar was different, one might even say dialectically different. He appeared at the beginning of each show in his bathrobe to announce the various acts with dull humility. His manner and dress seemed to say: I am not a stand-up comedian with a glib line of patter, but rather a most humble artist or even artisan trying to entertain you with bits and pieces of comic legerdemain. Of course, the 'umble pie routine didn't quite come off, what with all the grandiose fanfare preceding it, and with all the abrasively pushy personality sketches which usually followed the character comedian bathrobe bit.

Truth to tell, Sid Caesar lacked the ineffable beauty and divine charm of the greatest comedians. He had first emerged from under the very large shadow of Danny Kaye, and their early airplane-movie routines were strikingly similar, but whereas Kaye started out in his Sylvia Fine period as a beguiling blend of Harpo Marx and Noel Coward, Caesar was a roughneck by comparison. He could function properly only in an atmosphere of perpetual parody. There was nothing really "straight" about him, whereas

Kaye could sing and dance with sufficient charm and dexterity to beguile even the Russian Tea Room out of its slow, surly service.

Also Kaye was the verbal dervish par excellence whereas Caesar had a voice problem in the off-putting realm between the perpetual rasp and the frequent cough. (Of course, I am speaking of the demonic Danny Kaye who kowtowed to nobody in those early days before the Queen Mother and UNICEF turned him into a dull public institution.)

Still, Caesar's voice—rasp, cough and all—was very finely tuned to the cadences (though not to the textures) of parody. In *From Here to Obscurity*, Caesar takes on a composite part that is half Montgomery Clift (the trumpet part) and half Burt Lancaster (the love scene on the surf-soaked beach), and he doesn't really evoke either actor.

Indeed, Frank Gorshin can do a better imitation of Burt Lancaster in his (Gorshin's) sleep. What Caesar successfully parodies is not any particular performer, but rather the clumsy mechanism of middle-brow allegory with low-life characters.

Actually, Caesar and Coca were far more devastating in their take-offs and put-downs of *Streetcar Named Desire* and *A Place in the Sun*, two skits not in the current series. Even so, Caesar did not so much evoke Marlon Brando as expose Stanley Kowalski, and Coca did not so much express Shelley Winters as epitomize the shrewish wife-to-be in the rowboat on the lake. Thus, *Your Show of Shows* was unique in going beyond the surface of performances to the substance of characterizations in its show-biz satires.

Nonetheless, the most precious moment in *From Here to Obscurity* is connected less with the satiric sensibility of the enterprise than with its "live" professionalism. The moment I speak of is the moment in which Imogene Coca breaks up as she watches Caesar's shrewdly sappy expression of surprise as a bucket of water splashes over his timing of the scene. But rather than exploit her breaking up for the easy laugh of amateurish audience identification, she covers the breaking up by turning her face from the audience while seeming to nuzzle Caesar's shoulder.

Every week for six or seven years, a group of talented performers would undergo the most stringent demands of both theater and cinema. That is to say that they were locked up in both the inexorable time machine of the theater and in the cold-fish-eye objectivity of the camera lens. Their opening nights were thus not only their closing nights but also their eternal incarnations. And as much as they might have been appreciated by their live audience, they knew that their ultimate fate depended on a vague, amorphous mass of viewers with whom they could communicate only through an electronic image. Performers in the theater can have an occasional bad night without jeopardizing their reputation. Performers in the cinema (and now canned television) can do as many takes as they need to become letter-perfect. But the very real charm and excitement of early live television B. T. (Before Tape) consisted of the suspenseful possibility of human error by even the most professional performers. Hence, no recapitulation of *Your Show of Shows* can fully reproduce the exquisitely wrought emotional tension of the original experience. And no revival can ever bring back the full force of that earlier laughter.

Although the current selection from *Your Show of Shows* is not ideal by absolute standards, I am not sure that I would like even the best skits to be assembled in this fashion. Ultimately, *Your Show of Shows* does not belong on the movie screen, but on the video screen, and not just the comedy sketches, but the whole show.

As it is, the laughs come too close together without the pleasing interruptions of the snazzy dancing of the Hamilton Trio, the singing of a personable tenor named Bill Hayes, and his female operatic counterpart, Marguerite Piazza, a veddy, veddy stylized twosome called Mata and Hari (a bit of a drag, I always felt, and too close to the burlesque ballets of Imogene Coca), the ever ebullient Billy Williams Quartet, and, more often than not, a guest star from the silver screen. If none of the major networks want to pick up the show, why doesn't the Educational Network pick it up in the name of early and middle fifties nostalgia and social history? Or is there an unconscious fear of demonstrating that the much-maligned fifties were infinitely more entertaining than the hyped-up seventies?

Of course, *Your Show of Shows* never sought to fulfill the tendentious rhetoric of the more solemn soothsayers of the Republic. There was none of the pseudo-significant topicality of the proto-talk-show-type comedians like Mort Sahl, Steve Allen, and even the relatively expurgated Lenny Bruce of the television medium.

Although most of the writers and performers on *Your Show of Shows* might be said to have partaken of a distinctively Jewish sensibility in their satiric orientation, they were nonetheless completely immersed in the ambience of popular culture. What makes *Bertha the Sewing Machine Girl* truly magical is not merely the lurid precision of the eye-rolling and lip-speaking "pantomime" of the silent screen, but of the emotional energy that Caesar, Coca, Reiner, and Morris expend on the enduring vitality and sincerity of that ancient form of dramatic expression. This then is the source of their stylistic conviction as satirists: a loving complicity with their mass audience on the inherent absurdity of all dramatic formulas and melodramatic mechanisms.

To return to the Jewishness of *Your Show of Shows*, it was still light years away from the more modish late fifties absurdism and alleged anti-Semitism of the unexpurgated Bruce, the Omnibus-oriented Nichols and

May, and the *Voice*'s very own Jules Feiffer. The difference between a Sid Caesar skit and a Nichols and May skit was not only a difference in period, but also in class consciousness. With Caesar, a fundamentally popular common sense was appealed to with every bellow of outrage. With Nichols and May, an elitist *frisson* of intellectual and cultural superiority was cultivated at the expense of our most sacred cows. This was the beginning of the civil war between the Jewish intellectuals and the Jewish philistines, and also the beginning of an era of cultural affluence and alienation, and of increasing fragmentation of audience sensibilities.

Thus, in a sense, *Your Show of Shows* was more a hangover from the socially united forties than an expression of the socially divided fifties. Caesar and Company steered clear of politics and any trace of sick humor. Ethnic jokes were verboten unless they had been filtered through a secondary cultural source. Hence, Italians could be caricatured only in a parody of neorealism. Germans of the Blue-Max Prussian-Yiddish School of dialects were okay. But the Black-Shirted SS Men of such later entertainments as *Stalag 17* and *Hogan's Heroes* remained alien to the circumscribed comic vision of *Your Show of Shows*.

The clinical orientation of most of the slapstick humor tended to be oral rather than anal. *Big Business*, for example, depends for most of its humor on the debunking notion that food is more important to a hungry executive than even the fate of his firm. Curiously, the basic joke in *Big Business* is redone with off-key ennui in the meeting of the media people in *The Candidate*. Then or now, it isn't that much of a comic idea on the drawing board, but who can ever forget Howard Morris's flapping his pickle with diabolically phallic force right in Caesar's drooling face.

The plastic precision with which this incredibly intricate sight gag is executed takes us into the highest reaches of humor and archetypal imagery. And to watch Howard Morris's clinging to Sid Caesar like an overly affectionate orangutan in *This Is Your Life* is to feel a primal laughter gurgling out once more from the depths of one's intestines.

Louis Kronenberger recently requested a moratorium on the use of the words "subsume," "epiphany" and "persona." I'll try to accommodate him on the first two, but I'll have to borrow "persona" one last time to try to explain why Sid Caesar has never retained a loyalty among his laughing followers comparable to that accorded to Chaplin, Keaton, Lloyd, Langdon, the Marx Brothers, W. C. Fields, and Laurel and Hardy. What they and most comedians have, and what Caesar did not, is a persona.

With the persona-performer, we can't remember after a time which gag was in which picture, and we mercifully forget all the lapses and *longueurs*. We remember only that Jack Benny was stingy, that Jackie Gleason preferred ouzo to water in the office cooler, that W. C. Fields disliked women and children, that Groucho enjoyed playing the cad, that Hardy was eternally exasperated with Laurel.

A more severely limited comedian like Jimmy Durante seemed to earn the gratitude of his admirers simply by having survived to entertain them with the same old jokes and routines. Ultimately, therefore, the strongest link between the lasting comedians and their admirers is one more of ritualistic love than of renewable laughter.

Caesar in his bathrobe of the anonymous craftsman did not ask for our love, only for our respect and admiration. What little did filter through about his "true" personality seemed to accord with the imperial cast of his name. There were rumors of his tyrannical temperament, and rumblings about his video "divorce" from Imogene Coca. And he very often played bosses and bullies, but, just as often, he played against type as the hapless schlemiel of *A Night at the Movies* and *The Bavarian Clock*, thus shrewdly indulging the audience's subconscious desire to see him dampened and virtually dismembered.

In terms of media poetics, he was anti-McLuhanist to the core, of high rather than low definition, and ultra-professional in every bone of his body. Indeed, he seemed somehow to thrive on the insane stopwatch pressure of live television where pure energy was at a premium, and where the rough edges of a performance could be blasted away with sheer gusto. He was considerably less effective on the stage and screen where a further refinement of his talents was required and never forthcoming.

Unfortunately, the current series fails to do full justice to Imogene Coca and Carl Reiner as invaluable mercenaries in Caesar's imperial army. Imogene Coca's supper-club subtlety was one of the earliest casualties of ad agency decisions to equal so-called "national" taste rather than elevate it. Whereas Lucille Ball triumphantly incarnated the West Coast nitwit housewife with more things than thoughts on her mind, Imogene Coca seemed to be powered by the cosmopolitan neon of New York as she floated through boozy mantraps, one eye beckoning and the other blotto.

As a failed femme fatale, as a hiccupping Helen Morgan with more of a whine than a catch in her voice, or as a Pavlova sinking gradually from a swan's glide to a duck's waddle, Imogene Coca represented a culture secure enough in its sensibility to laugh at some of the convulsions of art appreciation at any cost. Over the long TV haul, however, Caesar and Coca did not make a compatible couple with their strenuous idiosyncrasies. Certainly, they were no match for the witless authenticity of Lucy and Desi as a wildly Pirandellian pair of performers, or of the joyless gutter sentimentality of the Cramden couple impersonated by Jackie Gleason and Audrey Meadows.

In addition Lucille Ball was one of the most beautiful women ever to take pratfalls in any medium, and this may help explain Caesar's desperate decision to revamp his own image by taking on Nanette Fabray and Janet Blair as video wives after disposing of Imogene Coca. Despite the comeliness and talent of the newcomers, the "marriages" never really worked. Instead, Caesar seemed broader and more raucous than ever before now that Coca's slyly provocative stylization was no longer available to relieve him of some of the comic responsibility.

By contrast, Carl Reiner was always Sid Caesar's indispensable right-hand man, his genial fool, and his willing foil. In their years together, Reiner joined the select company of sterling straight men—George Burns, Bud Abbott, Dean Martin—who eventually eclipse the top banana in the eyes and ears of the connoisseurs. I remember at the time we were always nudging each other over Reiner's catatonic comedy style lurking around the edges of Caesar's hysteria.

Toward the end, I was laughing more at Reiner than at Caesar, and I am reminded particularly of Reiner send-ups of James Mason's emceeing a drama series on television, and of Mike Wallace's inquisitorial techniques on *Hot Seat*. But by then it was too late. The cost-per-thousands boys and the ratings rajahs and the sponsors' wives and the demographic samplers had taken over television, and the noble experiment with live, sophisticated entertainers was terminated. Even the survival of *Your Show of Shows* on kinescope is an accident of television history. The studio kinescopes have long since been destroyed. Only Max Liebman's personal copies have survived to remind us of a fantastic episode in the history of popular entertainment.

Summer, 1973

A KING IN NEW YORK

Roger Greenspun

The best film to open in New York last December [1973], and so to make its way into national distribution this spring, was made 16 years ago. Charlie Chaplin's *A King in New York* opened in London in 1957. It took a while to get here.

In an odd way, the delay was a good deal more famous than the movie. Everybody deplored a missing Chaplin film, and nobody seemed terribly anxious to see it. Actually, it could be seen frequently enough in Europe, and the reports were not too encouraging. Late Chaplin, from *Monsieur Verdoux* (1947) through *A Countess from Hong Kong* (1966), has presented a problem for those who had seen, say, *The Gold Rush* and thought they knew what Charlie was all about. *A King in New York* compounds the problem, having grown notorious in its absence as Chaplin's answer to the House Un-American Activities Committee. Everyone knew what Chaplin had been through in the late 1940s and early 1950s—the most ritual indignation at his mild political nonconformity, at his success, his sex life, his refusal to become a citizen, his beautiful young wife. The American Legion fought him, the Catholic War Veterans picketed him; play dates were canceled for *Monsieur Verdoux;* when he left the country after finishing *Limelight* (1953) he was barred from coming back.

He made *A King in New York* in England. All the exteriors are stock footage in obvious back projection. As it turns out, the lack of simple realism is a virtue. I don't know what I expected of the film; considering its politics, perhaps something like a harangue from the Hollywood Ten. That was all wrong. It is a gentle, surprisingly unassertive film. It opposes the Un-American Activities Committee all right—but not in the name of left-wing politics. Like all the late Chaplin movies, and as their titles begin to suggest (*Monsieur* . . . , *A King* . . . , *A Countess* . . .), its ideal is a decent, dated, somewhat displaced aristocracy. The heroes of these movies aren't the archetypal Little Tramp; but they are his fancy cousins. Whatever their pasts, they are now only pretenders to position and power. Except for the busy wife-murderer Verdoux, they have no jobs. They are all a little short of funds.

Even King Shadhov (Charlie Chaplin), fleeing revolution, feels the pinch when the national treasury, which he thought was safely awaiting him in his New York exile, is spirited off to South America by his unscrupulous prime minister. Tempted, and masterminded, by a voluptuous vision in a hotel bathtub (Dawn Addams), Shadhov turns to advertising—royal testimonials on TV, billboards above Times Square—and he almost succeeds in winning the rat race, until a little child he befriends pushes him into facing the tragedy inherent in historical process. The kid (Michael Chaplin—possibly the best performance by a Chaplin offspring in any movie, which isn't saying much) spouts a sort of new Marxist litany by fanatical rote. But he is a bright and immensely likable kid. And by a stroke of fine dramatic intuition, it is he and not the suave Shadhov who is brought low, when the Committee gets him to reveal the names of former Communists for whom his radical schoolteacher parents would go to jail— in order not to tell. The boy's betrayal is both sadder and less shattering than any adult's. He will grow out of it. Even to the perspective of 1957 the

Committee's terror must have seemed greatly diminished. Moved, but for practical purposes untouched, Shadhov returns to Europe. Not to his kingdom, but to his queen, now living in Paris on her own personal wealth, enough money to support him in the genteel extravagance to which he is happily accustomed.

There is a lot of topical cultural satire in *A King in New York*—about wide-screen movies, the way kids dance (whatever it was that preceded the "twist"), TV commercials, progressive education—none of it too startlingly on target. An extended take-off on face lifting, when Chaplin accedes to Dawn Addams's desire for a more photogenically young-looking man, simply lacks the invention to justify its time. But then Charlie will violently throw himself on Dawn Addams—after a buildup of the most inappropriate sweet talk and soft music—and the clown behind the king emerges in an explosion of vitality. It is moments like this, or the moments when Charlie laughs that simpering embarrassed, rather wicked laugh, giving away the nasty secret of a sixty-year-old monarch who really lusts after a girl in her twenties, that certify the style and the very meaning of *A King in New York*.

Essentially, it is an old man's film about the condition of being an old man—a complex, not entirely disagreeable condition. And it is at the same time a film about the power of sexual attraction, a power that for Chaplin outlasts its sublimated youthful forms—in the sweet pathos of the early features like *The Gold Rush* or *City Lights*—to become something much more serious. Also, funnier. So much of Chaplin's late humor stems from his capacity suddenly to lose, and just as suddenly to regain, composure, as if he were two utterly incompatible personalities living together under *almost* perfect control.

Sexual appetite can break that control, and its emergence means both a loss of psychic balance and an expression of physical vigor. In life, the vigor has been real enough—and prodigious. Chaplin was fifty-four when he married Eugene O'Neill's eighteen-year-old daughter, and he then began to father eight children. But on the screen it ultimately gives way to smiling regrets, to a sometimes bitter, more often bemused, nostalgia for what might have been. Dawn Addams has never been the world's greatest movie actress. But she was (and still is) an elegantly beautiful woman. And the image of Dawn Addams, radiant in feathers and furs, does as much to explain the impulses behind *A King in New York* as any care for the political rights of man.

There are other images as well: certainly, the plump, vulnerable, handsome face of young Michael Chaplin; the dignified presence of Oliver Johnston, who plays King Shadhov's loyal ambassador to the United States and who functions in the movie as Chaplin's straight man; above all, Maxine Audley as the queen, who appears for just one scene and is granted an aura of personal glamour not even allowed Dawn Addams. All these people are seen with a directness and a formal simplicity that may have seemed crude to the advanced tastes of 1957, but that seems just, perhaps even inspired, today. Some of the other crudities don't matter anymore—like the minor character actors, all British and all talking "American," as if everybody in New York City got his accent from southern Missouri. And some of the crudities—like the obvious back projection, the unreal handling of crowd scenes—merely enforce the sense that *A King in New York* is the product of an intensely personal vision. It is a marvelous vision, gracious and tough, tolerant and unillusioned. And whatever its qualities were at the the start, in the great silent comedies that Chaplin made even before 1920, I think it became better toward the end—when the view of life had grown rich with backward glances and the sight of pleasures never to be explored.

April, 1974

A TOUCH OF CLASS*

Bernard Drew

Melvin Frank's *A Touch of Class,* starring George Segal and Glenda Jackson as a married man and divorcée who meet in London, run off to Marbella for what used to be called a "rollicking" week of sex, and then return to London to set up a cozy menage, despite the fact that he loves his wife, but oh you kid, and then part for what used to be called "the bittersweet finale," is a frantic attempt to turn back the clock to those dear, dead days beyond recall.

Slick and glossy, with attractive British and Spanish interiors and exteriors, and smartly caparisoned—even Miss Jackson has been thoroughly glamorized and appears to possess a set of perfect, gleaming teeth which may be obtained at a miraculous new dentist in St. John's Wood—the movie has been directed by Frank and written by him and Jack Rose.

In those dear dead days, Frank always wrote with Norman Panama, and

* See also Molly Haskell's piece in the American Themes section.

Rose with Melville Shavelson as teams, and they were responsible for many of the scripts Bob Hope did in the forties, some of which were even good.

But they were all situation comedy, which meant an adroitly contrived rewrite of what worked last time around, and Frank has now persuaded Segal and Miss Jackson to become modern prototypes of Rosalind Russell and Cary Grant, Irene Dunne and Charles Boyer, Jean Arthur and Melvyn Douglas, and you may switch them around in any combination your memory savors.

Which is not a bad idea in itself. God knows we need comedy now. And don't Segal and Miss Jackson meet cute in Hyde Park with him playing baseball and accidentally stepping over her child?

And then don't they keep running into each other all over London until he finally gets her in a hotel room and she says that she doesn't mind going to bed with him, after all, she's a grown woman and it's been a while, but not in these sordid surroundings. Let's go away somewhere . . .

All right, Irene Dunne would have choked before she suggested that, but there are a few concessions to the fact that this is, after all, 1973, and then don't they go to Marbella after a cute moment or two in London when it looks as if his wife and children will go along, and when that is taken care of, more cute moments at the airport where he just happens to run into a fat, wise, movie writer friend who begins every sentence with "Boychick," and who is also going to Marbella and who also once had a serious affair with a woman while married, and then more cute moments at the hotel, staggering around with their luggage while they look for a room with a view of Vesuvius?

And when they finally get to bed, doesn't he wrench his back, necessitating more cutenesses with a local doctor, and once his back is back in and everything looks peaches down in Georgia, don't they have a knockdown fight right out of *Private Lives?*

And once the're back in England, in their cozy nest, doesn't he get to race all over London in ever so many cute ways, trying to please two women and be in two different places at the same time?

Still, all this might have worked had there been real ingenuity and wit, somewhere along the road, instead of dialogue like, "Two children in two years? Are you Catholic?" Segal asks. "No and I wasn't careless either," says Miss Jackson, remembering Clare Boothe Luce's most famous line from *The Women.*

Later on, in their flat, she asks a neighbor whore, "Do you have oregano?" whereupon said neighbor-whore gasps, "I hope not. I just had a checkup last week."

You see, nothing has really changed since the days when Bob Hope would say, "Cheer up, the night is young even if you aren't," and Milton Berle's "My sister married a second lieutenant. The first one got away." Except that those were funny, or so they seemed at the time.

June 22, 1973

SLITHER

Robert Hatch

The whole of Howard Zieff's *Slither* is really one slow take, which makes it perhaps the most prolonged dropped jaw in show business. I found it funny—not productive of a great many laughs, but internally warming by its appreciation of the zaniness in our modern life.

Dick Kanipsia, Barry and Mary Fenaka, Kitty Kopetzky, and other American birds of passage are transformed by only a slight application of cinematic license into a gaggle of comic-book superkids pounding down the highway in search of "wealth beyond your wildest dreams." If I were to outline the plot of *Slither*, the reader would curl his lip and turn the page. There is nothing to be said for it, except that it is the sort of thing a good many Americans can imagine themselves getting tied into; and, anyway, the plot is hardly the point. What matters is the style of these argonauts, a chuckle-headed band of amoralists endowed with the native belief that success is a good break around the next corner and protected from an inflated notion of their own cleverness by an ability to roll away from disaster. Or perhaps "slither" is the word.

Dick (James Caan), a college football star turned auto thief, has come out of jail with nothing in his pockets and little on his mind except half a clue to hidden loot. Barry Fenaka (Peter Boyle), self-proclaimed embezzler but recently fronting as a saxophonist/master of ceremonies for fraternal gatherings, knows the other half, and as soon as they manage to trade secrets (after circling each other in the manner of gang bosses they must have admired on some late show), Barry hooks up his paneled and gadgeted mobile home to his big stereo-equipped convertible and they are off for Eldorado. They are followed by a huge, impassive, black land yacht that fills them with dread.

You have to listen to the dialogue. Suddenly in the night, the parked camper begins to career as though in a hurricane. "There's someone on the roof," Dick hazards. A moment later, Mary Fenaka, who had loved Dick from the sidelines when they were in college together, says: "I want to thank you for all you've done for us," and Dick smiles modestly, aware perhaps that all he has done is try to stay alive in a situation that entirely befuddles him. And Kitty (Sally Kellerman), who pops pills and believes that she is a girl anyone would appreciate having at his side in a tough spot, is always worth attending. She speaks in a rich, husky voice and has apparently memorized a slightly out-of-date hip glossary. Occasionally, though, she coins a phrase of her own: "I'm in heat," she says, meaning to convey that she is carrying a gun.

Do I convince you? Somehow I doubt it. The quality of *Slither* is in its skewed verisimilitude, and that is hard to convey. American highway democracy, Friday night at the lodge hall, a bingo game under a Chautauqua tent, Fenaka's virtuoso control of his windshield wipers, the food and drink of the mobile millions—all these are documented with piercing accuracy. But the people passing through are not quite synchronized to the pop art super realism. They look all right—indeed they look perfect—but what they say and do is just a degree refracted. In short, they are a little nuts. And that, I think, is what Zieff wants to say about America: not vicious, not cruel, not destructive, not ugly—just a little nuts. To be sure, it is a soft indictment, but harsher judgments abound and this is a view worth considering.

March 26, 1973

Nine

THE AMERICAN FILM THEATRE

THE AMERICAN FILM THEATRE: A PROSPECTUS

Hollis Alpert

Something new and special in the way of filmed entertainment will break on the American scene in late October. It is a venture named The American Film Theatre (not to be confused with the American Film Institute), and in effect, it amounts to an amalgam, or cross-breeding, of repertory theater, subscription cinema, and the "hard ticket" two-performances-a-day method of releasing films. Offered the first season (and, it is hoped, not the last) will be a series of eight films faithfully adapted from well-known and in most cases prestigious plays. One will appear each month from October through May in selected film theaters throughout the country; each will have four performances (a matinee and an evening performance on one Monday and one Tuesday of the month during which it is scheduled to appear) after which it will be retired, temporarily at least, from circulation. What amounts to a clever marketing method for play "properties" of dubious commercial prospect, but which also has distinct cultural value, is the brainchild of Ely Landau, a self-admitted maverick in the prevailing film establishment of production, distribution, and exhibition.

The chosen plays are: John Osborne's *Luther*, Edward Albee's *A Delicate Balance*, Simon Gray's *Butley*, Chekhov's *Three Sisters*, Weill and Anderson's *Lost in the Stars*, Harold Pinter's *The Homecoming*, O'Neill's *The Iceman Cometh*, and Ionesco's *Rhinoceros*. For an independent producer these cautious days, getting even one project on the screen is a task requiring boldness, perseverance, faith, and luck; the making of eight in a body is virtually Herculean. Ely Landau, in appearance, is not exactly Herculean. He is in his early fifties, rotund, balding, with long white sideburns. He feels himself to be overrated as a businessman, but underrated when it comes to idealism.

Whether businessman or idealist, he has nevertheless managed to corral into his project such star names as Katharine Hepburn, Paul Scofield, Zero Mostel, Lee Marvin, Stacy Keach, Laurence Olivier, Karen Black, Brock Peters, and Alan Bates, among a good many other film and theatrical figures. Among his directors are Tony Richardson, John Frankenheimer,

Peter Hall, Harold Pinter, and Tom O'Horgan. Edward Albee, Simon Gray, and Harold Pinter did their own screen adaptations of their works, and where outside screenwriters were brought in, they were under orders and restraint to adhere as scrupulously as possible to the texts of the works. According to Landau, he has produced not filmed plays but motion pictures. "However," he says, "they have not been opened up for the sake of opening up. I am not inhibited by the spoken word."

It may be remembered that an earlier film produced by Landau, *Long Day's Journey into Night,* relied heavily on the spoken word and gained considerable critical acceptance, if not large commercial success. Recently, he screened advance segments of the eight new films for those members of the media who might be eager to herald his venture in advance, and it was clear from these segments that performing and interpretive standards were being emphasized over what might be called cinematic movement. Critical assessment of the filmed plays will have to await the showing of the complete versions; until that time, potential subscribers are being assured by Landau and his publicists that they have "eight enchanted evenings" ahead of them as well as, presumably, eight enchanted matinees.

Landau is not only enamored of his eight filmed plays—he even loves the story of how they happened to come about. "Am I boring you?" he will interrupt himself from time to time in the recital. With assurance to the contrary, he goes on: "I love to hear this story. I can hardly wait to hear what I will say next."

A little more than five years ago—and this is a key element in the story—after twenty largely successful years in film and television distribution and production, Landau decided to retire. Five weeks later Martin Luther King was assassinated, an event that shocked and saddened Landau and that instantly resuscitated his not long dormant idealism. He decided, with his wife, Edythe, that he would devote his retirement years to the making of a film about King that would be a visual record of the black leader's life and career. The resulting documentary was seven hours long and was donated to the Martin Luther King Foundation. Then came the problem of what to do with it. His brainstorm of an idea was to cut it down to manageable length and then hold the largest single theater party ever. The plan involved getting 1000 theaters with an average of 1000 seats each to show the film simultaneously. The ticket charge would be five dollars, and all proceeds would go to the foundation. The 1000-theater goal was not reached, but a total of 667,000 seats were filled on the night of March 24, 1970, with well over $3 million going into the foundation's fund.

Several theater owners approached Landau after that event (for which he had received only large amounts of satisfaction) and suggested that he create more such special attractions—though not necessarily philanthropic. Landau decided to go back to work. He relates:

"It occurred to me that Mondays and Tuesdays were traditionally the worst nights of the week for movie houses. What special attractions might be suitable for those nights? It's in my pattern to look for the gap or the void that no one else is filling. What was my particular niche? In looking back over my career, I decided that my niche was doing something that did not play down to the lowest common denominator in the audience. In an era of sex and violence in the movies, of racism, and of bombings of far-off populations, what might I provide? So it came to me: intellectually stimulating, thought-provoking material. In other words, good plays, and on film."

Thus was born, at least as Landau tells it, the concept of The American Film Theatre, and it has taken three years to get it on the screen. "Am I boring you?" he asks, for he has much more to tell.

Something of an intermission in the saga, here, while we go back to beginnings, back to the time when Landau, age twenty-five, was ending his army career in a southern camp. Considering business possibilities for his return to civilian life, he looked into a product called Fritos, then being distributed throughout the South. He inquired about obtaining the northern franchise and found it already allocated. Back home in New York, he found a manufacturer making a product that was much the same and convinced him to rename it Pepcorn Chips. Far afield though this story may seem, it has much to do with Landau's entering the field of television.

In the early postwar period, the seven thousand television sets in use in the New York area were mostly to be found in bars and grills, which also, in Landau's opinion, represented a prime market for Pepcorn Chips. He took to advertising the products on television, before and after the Brooklyn Dodgers ball games. Business proved brisk, but the product proved risky. Inadequate packaging resulted in Pepcorn Chips turning rancid almost overnight. Landau sadly collected the Pepcorn Chips he had sold and terminated his franchise with the company. In need of a job, he persuaded the small advertising agency that had placed the spots to employ him as what Landau terms a "gofer." What's a gofer? "Oh," he explains, "you go for this; you go for that."

At the agency he caught the television bug. "I became obsessed with the new medium," he now says. "I read everything I could about it, particularly as it affected advertising methods. I put this collected knowledge into a pamphlet I called *The Television Story* and sent it around to several ad agencies. Frankly, it was a pitch for a job. Several offers came in, and I accepted one with a small agency and became the head of its then almost nonexistent radio and TV department. Within a few years the agency was a lot bigger. In effect, I rode the early television tide."

In 1952 Landau decided to make his own films for television. These were of 15-minute length and could be sold on a syndicated basis. "I did *The Bill Corum Sports Show* and another that was an interview show featuring, among others, Eva Gabor, some prizefighters, and some minor politicians." The company he had set up was converted into one that acquired already-made half-hour filmed shows as well as a bunch of pre-1948 feature films. The company, National Telefilm Associates, prospered—so much so that it was able to acquire several television-channel franchises, among them Channel 13 in New York City.

This latter fact is what Landau is leading up to when he relates his story. For it was what happened on Channel 13 during the late fifties that determined his future course.

"When my group bought the channel," he says, "it was a shlock station oriented toward what was being shown on the other six New York channels—syndicated shows, old feature films, advertising by pitchmen."

Landau decided that Channel 13 had to be different. He introduced the *Mike Wallace Show*, which had truly in-depth interviews of 60-minute length. He made an important personality of Alex King. He had a special program of 90-minute length called *One-Night Stand*. Most important of all, he introduced a program called *Play of the Week*. "We became the maverick station of the entire country," he says. But it was the plays he produced, each running seven nights a week, that he was and still is most proud of. Among them were *Medea, The World of Sholem Aleichem, No Exit,* and *Tiger at the Gates.* He is still immodest enough to claim that his four-hour-long production of *The Iceman Cometh* (with Jason Robards and Robert Redford) is the greatest single production in the history of television.

Mrs. Carlotta Monterey O'Neill happened to agree with Landau's assessment. She asked to meet with him. She said, in effect, that no one had ever done an O'Neill play as well and as faithfully. Therefore, she was granting to him exclusive film and television rights to all of the O'Neill canon that were not already in other hands. And when those rights lapsed, they too would revert to Landau. It was agreed between them that the first O'Neill film he would make would be *Long Day's Journey into Night.* It was not much later that the clamor arose to turn Channel 13 into a public education station. Landau left his company in an attempt to buy the station for his own use. He felt that private enterprise could do a better job and serve a wider audience spectrum than what was planned for the channel. "I was defeated," he now says philosophically, "by the large foundations." Good as the job that public TV does on occasion, there are still many who re-member Landau's Channel 13 as one of television's more glorious achieve-ments.

Landau then turned to filmmaking in earnest. First came *Long Day's Journey*, made for $400,000, with a cast that included Katharine Hepburn, Ralph Richardson, Jason Robards, and Dean Stockwell. Next came *The Pawnbroker*, and once more Landau had a fight on his hands. The film, a serious and harshly moving one, was the first to show frontal nudity, in a very brief scene between Rod Steiger and a black prostitute. The Legion of Decency promptly awarded it a C for Condemned rating, and the Motion Picture Association refused to grant the picture its seal of approval. Landau fought the ruling and won a reversal. Before that happened, though, the major distribution companies had turned down the picture, and Landau was forced into distributing it himself. Now a distributor as well as a producer, he acquired several films made by others, among them *The Servant, King and Country*, and *The Umbrellas of Cherbourg*.

As can be adduced from the above, Landau has come a long way from Pepcorn Chips. Although not exactly a culture vulture, Landau apparently respects—more than that, prefers—dramatic material that has both cere-bral and social value. He puts it another way: "I respect the audience."

On the other hand, he is not so respectful of the typical week-in-and-week-out motion picture audience that supports the continuing dosage of vio-lence, sex, and horror provided by the majority of film fare. "Those fourteen million a week are not the ones I hope to attract to my subscrip-tion series," he says. "I'm not looking for a mass audience; I'm looking for a very special one. Contrary to the judgment of some of the majors, I think the audience is there and will come out to see a very worthwhile attraction in a theater that is neat and clean, that they will enter with the lights on, and that will provide a program—an appropriate atmosphere, in other words."

To this end he has signed up, at this writing, 512 theaters, in most of the fifty states, that will play the series. Subscription prices will be thirty dollars for the eight enchanted evenings and twenty-four dollars for the matinees. This works out to $3.75 per filmed play, for evenings, hardly unreasonable for a reserved seat and for shows that, in the case of *The Iceman Cometh* at least, will run four hours, with two intermissions. Landau sees as his present task the filling of 1,500,000 seats per play, and his pepped-up organization, led by him and his wife, is hard at work on it. The originally skeptical film trade is now watching the operation with keen interest.

Landau is quick to credit others for the realization of the project. There were several shoals to negotiate, important among them the initial financing of films costing an average of $750,000 each. He says:

"From the beginning, I realized I would need subsidy—not the official kind, which this country doesn't have, but subsidy from financial people, film companies, exhibitors, and, most important of all, the talent. For the major financing, I looked for a non-film-oriented company that had direct-to-consumer marketing expertise."

The third firm he went to, American Express, bought Landau's idea and enthusiasm almost at once. Landau quotes Howard Clark, chairman of the American Express board, as commenting: "We've all joined in combating pollution of the environment. Perhaps we should join in combating pollution of the spirit." At any rate, a new subsidiary called American Express Films, Inc., is joining with Landau's organization in presenting the series.

Stars of the caliber of those in the play series would have quickly used up the planned budgets and more if they demanded their usual fees. Landau had little trouble convincing them to join in, whether as playwright, director, or star, for no more than $25,000 each—a relatively low figure for a star of the popularity of Lee Marvin, appearing as Hickey in *The Iceman Cometh*, who has been known to take $750,000 for his presence in one film. Should the series turn out to be profitable, all will be further rewarded by a suitable percentage.

When American Express agreed to participate, a stipulation was made that Landau would use one of the major film companies to distribute the series. As Landau gently puts it, "They wanted the comfort of the association of a major. But so, as it turned out, did my own banks, from which I raised my own and my wife's share of the financing." Landau entered into an agreement with Columbia to co-finance and distribute, but first there was a knotty problem to be overcome. Did not the selling in advance of eight unseen films amount to a breach of the block-booking prohibition on the film industry? The divorce of production and exhibition came about in 1948 and has been rigidly interpreted by the Justice Department ever since. Back to the lists went Landau, and seventeen months later he obtained a court ruling that permitted him to book his eight films in advance. The ruling specifically allowed the repertory film concept to proceed, on the assumption that it was in the public interest. By the time the court okay came through, Columbia had cooled on the project. With all eight films in production, four in Hollywood and four in England, Landau was faced with the prospect of no theaters to play them in.

Then came what he likes to think of as one of his finest hours, metaphorically speaking. He dashed on an eight-day plane tour of the country, making grasshopperlike jumps to major national theater chains and some important minors, to sell them on his American Film Theatre. "I made impassioned speeches," he said. "I appealed to their consciences, to their half-empty houses on Mondays and Tuesdays, and I came back with a contract from each and every one of them." He also darkly hints at pressure against the plan from interests who opposed turning over one Monday and Tuesday of each month to the non-popcorn crowd.

Landau, who is on the roly-poly side, claims to have once excelled at basketball. It would be hard to envisage Landau driving past a Willis Reed or a Wilt Chamberlain for the basket, and it is almost as hard to envisage the rather gentle and jovial man bulling through a project that required the enlistment of a major corporation, of banks, of theater-chain operators, of the courts, of stars and their agents, and that now requires the mailing of ten million brochures to that "very special audience" that he hopes will want to subscribe to his series. "If we should die," he speculates a little sadly, "we will have to go the other way." By that he means the typical patterns of general release, with subsequent sale to television. Meanwhile, he sits smiling, beaming even, in his large, quiet office, where MGM used to reign, furnished with white washable plastic-covered sofas, suspended pots holding ferns, and no desk but, instead, a coffee table with only one telephone on it. Buttons on the phone light up frequently, but no buzz or ring is to be heard, merely a gentle, soothing chime. As the trade would say: Whatever happens, Landau and the series have class.

August 28, 1973

THE ICEMAN COMETH

A Pubful of Pipe Dreams

Molly Haskell

I figure we should give the American Film Theatre (and its computers) a few more productions before we jump on them with hob-nail booties, or decide what this marriage of convenience means . . . and whom it conveniences. *The Iceman Cometh*, its first offering, is a sturdy effort that manages to overcome none of the basic problems of transferring an effective stage play to another medium and of not having Jason Robards in the part of Hickey. John Frankenheimer, like Lee Marvin, does the best he can with alien material, and there are some fine performances, namely Fredric March's Harry Hope and Robert Ryan, in the shadow of death both in and out of character, as Larry Slade.

Although Slade, the disillusioned anarchist, is usually taken to be O'Neill's mouthpiece, the amount of theatrical trickery the playwright gets away with here should convince anyone that Hickey is at least as close to his playwright-huckster's heart. For contrivance and a complete disregard for sociological probability, imagine a saloon full of the disparate dregs of a melting-pot society all bandying the term "pipe dream" about like a clue on a quiz show; or the second act "awakening" when the characters, all galvanized by Hickey's spiel, dutifully trot out into the "real world" for their epiphanies and return that evening, on cue, their disillusionment complete. As if these miracles were not enough to out-Ibsen Ibsen, the third act has them all responding in unison to Hickey's fraud, wrapping themselves back up in their security blankets like flowers closing their petals at sunset. And yet O'Neill gets away with it; what's more, I think much of our enjoyment of the play is mouth-open wonder that he does.

It's not just the stylistic devices (or lack thereof) that give one pause— the uninspired locutions, the lack of an idiom tailored to each character— but the actual thrust of the play. For this is not quite the compassionate universal statement (as it was represented to me in school) that "we must all have our illusions," but rather a poetically disguised defense of alcoholism, an ode to being down and out with one's buddies, that draws on one of the most popular and seductively puritanical themes in American art.

O'Neill masks his intention by making the spokesman for moral rehabilitation a liar and a quack, and by intimating that the furies (mostly wives, also causes) from which these characters have fled are a fate significantly worse than the illusory tomorrows on which they ease their dying days. The wives had acted as a constant reproach, holding over them the promise that guilt might be alleviated in action; far better a voluptuous surrender to guilt in the conspiratorial gloom of the barroom. Jimmy speaks for them all when, confessing that it was not his wife's unfaithfulness that drove him to drink but vice versa, he says, "I had some idea of wanting a home, perhaps. But, of course, I much preferred the nearest pub."

These are not the illusions that most of us have: of being always only halfway through our lives, with as many tomorrows as yesterdays; but the impenetrable private worlds, for which "pipe dream" is too innocuous a word, of the mad, the deaf-mute, or the alcoholic.

For O'Neill's derelicts, the fog of fantasy is a group effort. The shifting alignments, the way the men reinforce each other like pawns in a chess game, are as important as the sparks of animosity. Sitting like waxworks at their individual tables and yet united by the bond of booze and a gleefully accepted failure, there is a tension between isolation and proximity that can only be expressed when integrity of space is preserved, when the entire room is at all times available to us, and our eyes are free to roam among its inhabitants, identifying with one man (never the women) after another. Close-ups become a kind of emotional quarantine, but even the two-shots, such as the constant pairing of Ryan and Jeff Bridges in the same frame, force links before they have been allowed to develop dramatically.

The fact that the father-son relationship never does emerge with any emotional force is as much the fault of casting as direction: Bridges suggests neither the tortured guilt that I imagine George Segal gave the role, nor the spoiled-darling image that Robert Redford supplied (and which Beau Bridges might have better conveyed).

Lee Marvin is an energetic, exciting actor, a man's man with a gift for bullshit palaver that no doubt suggested him (along with some imagined "star pull") to the producers as ideal for Hickey. He comes on with all the excess vitality and sanctimoniousness of the non-drinker among the drinkers, of the reformed smoker among the smokers, and is about as welcome. But he has none of the insinuating charm or the convoluted morality that Robards (whom we constantly hear in the dialogue, even occasionally in Marvin's voice) brought to the role. Once he has left his small town, we can't imagine Marvin's Hickey looking back, much less sending for the girl who will clamp into him with her forgiveness for the rest of her life. There is, beneath Marvin's strength, little sense of neuroticism or emotional depth, little indication of the layers of disillusionment that must be lifted and discarded in his dance of the seven veils, and consequently, little impact to the confession when it finally comes.

Impressive in the secondary roles are Bradford Dillman as Willie Oban the Harvard law man; Moses Gunn, particularly in the first act, giving one of his most relaxed performances in years; George Voskovec re-creating the part of the general which he played on the stage; and Martyn Green as his beloved enemy and fellow veteran of the Boer War.

But aside from Ryan, it was Fredric March's bespectacled Harry Hope that most moved me: a sweet, fumbling, myopic man perched ever so delicately on his own dream, a portrait that grows more luminous as the play catches up with it.

November 8, 1973

THE HOMECOMING AND A DELICATE BALANCE

Theater in the Camera

Paul D. Zimmerman

Artistically, the AFT is batting an impressive two-for-three. John Frankenheimer's adaptation of O'Neill's *The Iceman Cometh* is a towering, deeply affecting translation of a great play. Peter Hall's production of Harold Pinter's *The Homecoming* is even more savagely funny than his memorable production with the Royal Shakespeare Company that was seen on Broadway. Only Edward Albee's *A Delicate Balance* has been weakened by the passage of time and by Tony Richardson's humorless, ponderous direction.

A Delicate Balance, which opened in 1966, is a study of a neurotic, upper-middle-class family trying to maintain its emotional equilibrium while accommodating good friends who have abruptly decided to move in on them forever. The play, which won Albee a Pulitzer Prize, sparkled with the saber-toothed sniping that made Albee at that point our most exciting playwright. Today Albee seems diminished by time as does his rhetorically florid, hollowly bitchy world. Richardson aggravates matters with a heavy-handed approach that deprives the play of the wit and theatricality Alan Schneider used to levitate the Broadway production. Robbed of currency and comedy, Albee's nattering family—Katharine Hepburn's imperially crotchety grande dame, her ineffectual and dry-as-dust husband (Paul Scofield), her drunken maiden sister (Kate Reid), and hysterical, oft-divorced daughter (Lee Remick)—has become a household of superliterate bores.

The Homecoming, by contrast, seems more relevant and penetrating than when it first reached Broadway seven years ago. Pinter's vision of a middle-class London family locked in a furious embrace of inbred hate is given a harder, more savage tone by Peter Hall than when he first staged it. The famous Pinteresque exchanges between Max, a retired butcher, his shabby-proud chauffeur brother, Sam, and three grown sons seem even funnier and more frightening. Paul Rogers, the original Max, dominates the film, a belligerent volcano of a man brandishing his pig's nose like a weapon at his hated boys. Ian Holm is again razor-deadly as Lenny, the nihilistic son who lives by pimping and who eventually signs on his returning brother's wife (once again the marvelously mysterious Vivien Merchant) to work as the family's private whore. Cyril Cusack as the chauffeur content to be the "best in the firm" and Michael Jayston as Teddy, the returning son who has become a philosophy prof in America, stand as twin monuments to smugness and are marked improvements over their counterparts on Broadway.

The AFT productions of *Iceman* and *The Homecoming* nourish both the theater and film. Even *A Delicate Balance,* for all its failings, retails Broadway to the rest of the country at a level vastly superior to most road companies. At the same time, the AFT productions so far have provided the American screen with some of its finest writing and acting in years, redressing a balance that has veered recently toward the director as superstar. Here Frankenheimer, Hall and Richardson resist the temptation to "open up" the plays, a practice which normally lets the steam out of them, and they shy away from the cinematic razzle-dazzle that has ruined filmed theater from Richard Lester's *The Knack* to Peter Brook's *King Lear.* These films occupy a viable middle ground between stage and screen where the close-up (especially in *Iceman*) compensates for the loss of intimacy of a live performance, where the absence of "exteriors" contributes to the dramatic tension inherent in these plays about people trapped together.

What problems remain—lack of physical action and of visual material exciting in itself—are overridden by the writing of masters and screen performances exceptional in their deep focus and sustained intensity. Robert Ryan's memorable Larry in *Iceman* and Paul Rogers's Max are hard-to-beat candidates for this year's screen acting honors.

December 3, 1973

Ten

POP MYSTICISM: BETWEEN HEAVEN AND HELL

THE EXORCIST

The Making of *The Exorcist*

Hollis Alpert

The film version of *The Exorcist* is unusually blessed. In spite of what is expected to be an R (for restricted) rating, it is being made not only with full Catholic approval but has in its cast two Jesuit priests and two others who have walk-ons. For consultant and adviser on matters of demonic possession, it has no less an authority than Father John Nicola, assistant director of the National Shrine in Washington and, more importantly from the standpoint of the film, the personage who investigates for the Church manifestations of the devil among humankind. Father Nicola, to put it matter-of-factly, is a demonologist. It should also be said that he is a highly skeptical demonologist. On the job for some fifteen years, he has yet to recommend the rites of exorcism for the cases he has encountered.

The driving out of demons who have obtained control over a human has always been recognized by the Church as a function of her ministry. But despite the violence that marks our century, the rising tide of individual and mass slaughter that, if the computers are correct, will within a matter of years cause the death of one of every ten of the world's human beings, the Church has become more and more laggardly about casting out demons. This may change, however. Recently Pope Paul VI urged that more attention be paid to Satan. He characterized demonology as "a very important chapter of Catholic doctrine that ought to be studied again, although this is not being done much today."

The producers of *The Exorcist* have taken this pronouncement as a virtual endorsement of their film. "Never underestimate the power of a publicity man," said Howard Newman with a straight face. Newman is in charge of publicity for the picture, and he regards the Pope's remark as a considerable coup for his department.

What better advertisement could there be than the Pope's words? "We thus know," he was quoted as saying in the Vatican newspaper, "that this obscure and disturbing being really exists and that he still operates with treacherous cunning; he is the occult enemy who sows errors and disgrace

284

in human history." The devil, as described by Pope Paul, is the "perfidious and astute charmer who manages to insinuate himself into us by way of the senses, of fantasy, of concupiscence . . ." A cute, charming twelve-year-old girl, perhaps?

In both novel and film, it is such a girl, Regan by name, who becomes so sorely possessed, who turns evil and satanic, who apparently causes walls to emit rapping sounds, furniture to move, a bed to levitate, a bedroom to chill to zero temperature, who writhes and spits out imprecations, blasphemies, language most vile, and, to top it off, commits an obscene act with a crucifix. Since the child is crucial to the story, a rigorous search was instituted for a girl suited to the role and able to play it. She was found in Connecticut, and her name is Linda Blair. She is actually twelve years old, a paragon of normality, who loves horses and rides them well and who hopes to grow up to be either a jockey or a veterinarian. Just the sort of girl a wily demon might choose for habitation.

Linda, whose acting experience is minuscule, is a key element in a production that will use up more than six million dollars of Warner Brothers' money.* The investment, it is hoped, will result in a bonanza of near-*Godfather* proportions, and there is considerable basis for the prediction. The William Peter Blatty novel remained on the best-seller list for more than a year and was number one for a good part of the time. The "trade" edition sold 200,000 copies; a Literary Guild hardcover edition sold 350,000; the Bantam paperback has sold four million in its first six months. In England it became the number-one best-seller, and twelve foreign editions in translation have done almost equally as well. In addition, the devil is "hot" everywhere, and the fad of occultism is still thriving. The reasoning is that all this will translate into long lines at the box office.

How *The Exorcist* came into being makes for one of those peculiar success stories that has caused many an aspirant to sit down at a typewriter and try for likewise. When Blatty was a student at Georgetown University, one of his teachers, Father Thomas V. Bermingham, S.J., suggested he take demonic possession as a theme for an oratorical assignment. Current at the time (1949) was a news story of a case of possession that had occurred in St. Louis. The supranormal goings-on in the bedroom of a fourteen-year-old boy baffled doctors, psychologists, and priests summoned by the boy's fearful and bewildered family. An exorcism—the last, but one, to be sanctioned by Roman Catholic authorities—was ordered, and whatever demons were bothering the boy were at last subdued. Blatty used the case as a basis

---

* According to some tallies, the picture's actual cost was more than double this figure by the time it was released.—Editors.

for his assignment and, still fascinated by it, continued his researches into the phenomenon. In 1969, after a career with the U.S.I.A., screenwriter, and comic novelist, he sat down and wrote *The Exorcist.* The boy was changed to a girl, a couple of murders were added, and the scene was changed to Georgetown. Father Bermingham, by the way, is one of the priests who has a role in the film.

Blatty indicates in his novel possible explanations for what appears to be demonic possession of a child, but his own Jesuit educational background makes him cautious about accounting for what happened in St. Louis along rational, scientific lines.

"All attempts to explain paranormal phenomena are really a sham," he said in a New York studio, where some of the film's interiors were being shot, "because underlying them is a total lack of belief that they ever took place. As I see it, one need not assume that these forces are unnatural in any way. Matter and spirit are really two different aspects of some third thing, which I would call God. Once you make that assumption, there is nothing unnatural about the supernatural."

To this the film's director, William Friedkin, added: "Let the audience come out of the theater and decide what they want to take away from it. We're not loading the cards one way or the other. It's not a film about the occult, unless you're inclined to believe in the occult. It's not a film about demonic possession, unless you're inclined to accept such a happening."

Blatty, who up until *The Exorcist,* had regarded himself as a specialist in the comic, even the wacky, wasn't at the outset sure he could write so grimly harrowing a story. But about two-thirds of the way through, he was dead certain he was going to hit number one on the bestseller charts. "I really couldn't wait for it to come out," he said, "so I could accept the plaudits of the multitudes. Harper & Row and Bantam paid an enormous amount of money for it, then began to worry. I had to hold their hands and tell them 'eight weeks after publication, it will be number one.' I was absolutely convinced."

His uses of the devil have paid off handsomely. The deal he made with Warner Brothers for the rights to the novel, his screenplay of it, and his producership was one of the highest, if not the highest, recorded in Hollywood annals. And if receipts are as expected, his percentage of same will be enormous. Oddly enough, Hollywood was at one of its lowest ebbs when he made the deal, but this worked to Blatty's advantage, since the big studios were looking for winners, and *The Exorcist* had all the signs and portents.

Friedkin, he now says, was always his choice for director. But until he directed *The French Connection,* Friedkin's boxoffice record was on the cold side. Beginning his feature-film career in 1966, he had directed Sonny and Cher in a little musical called *Good Times,* and followed this with the so-so *The Night They Raided Minsky's,* a flop film version of Pinter's *The Birthday Party,* and a better one of *The Boys in the Band.*

When producer Phil D'Antoni tapped him for *The French Connection,* the package offered was regarded as untempting. "Every studio in town turned us down," Friedkin said. "There was little confidence in D'Antoni as a producer; I was not a hot director; and what was being offered was just another 'cop script.' Why Twentieth Century-Fox picked it up, I'll never know. It had been passed by everybody, including what appeared to be the end of the line: Cannon Films. Fox picked it off the scrap heap after eleven months of inaction."

He was still mixing *The French Connection* when he read *The Exorcist* and flipped over it. Blatty being a friend, Friedkin offered his services, Blatty took a look at the nearly finished *French Connection,* was sold, and then sold Warner Brothers on Friedkin. Upon which, *The French Connection* came out, went through the roof, and the studio had both a hot book and a hot director.

"He gives inexplicable events such a look of realism that it will almost be documentary," Blatty says. And in equally complimentary style, Friedkin says, "It's the best-written picture I've ever worked on. Everything in the book is simplified and clarified, and we've added a number of things from the original case on which the book was based. The boy of that case is now thirty-six, married, has three children, and has no recollection of what happened to him. But he's still under observation by members of the Roman Catholic Church. I've spoken to his aunt, who is seventy, and she gave me details—such as what furniture moved—that will appear in the film."

The film script follows the settings in the book: Georgetown, a mental hospital on Welfare Island, and a location trip to an archaeological dig in Iraq. But the bedroom in which the eerie events occur was built in what used to be the Fox Movietone News Studio on Manhattan's West Side. There, the entire two-floor interior of an expansive Georgetown house was designed, constructed, and expensively furnished. There are, in fact, two bedrooms that Linda Blair inhabits. The duplicate bedroom has $50,000 worth of air-conditioning equipment installed in and around it and a lot of what Friedkin calls "complicated gizmos." The air-conditioning units freeze the room to zero temperature, so that when the demon in the child manifests itself by chilling the observers near to death, the frosty breath of the actors will be visible.

"There are various kinds of beds we use," Friedkin said, "some of which are suspended in the ceiling when we're not using them. One causes levitation, another makes the girl bounce up and down. And the entire duplicate set is literally balanced on a billiard ball. At one point, the room pitches and rolls while the outside background remains stationary. Technicians just remove the supports and rock the room."

With pretty much the power they wanted, Friedkin and Blatty chose the actors they wanted: Ellen Burstyn for the child's screen-star mother (her character based, according to rumor, on Shirley MacLaine); Max Von Sydow for the archaeologist-priest; Lee J. Cobb, as a police lieutenant; and Jason Miller (actor and author of *That Championship Season*) for Father Karras, a skeptical priest-psychiatrist.

But it was the child, Regan, who required the most careful casting, due to the very horrendous nature of the role and its physical difficulties. "There were well over a thousand girls the studio looked at before I ever saw any," Friedkin said. "And, after I began looking, I stopped counting after five hundred. Finally, Blatty and I narrowed the list down to twelve, and of those, we tested only one—Linda Blair.

"First of all, I felt she *had* to be no more than twelve years old. She also had to be pulled together, in the sense that I could feel she would not be psychologically damaged in any way by playing the girl. I didn't want her so beautiful that she would seem like Elizabeth Taylor in *National Velvet*, or so bright that she would appear to be some kind of *Wunderkind*. The girl had to meet certain balances both mentally and physically. For the twelve girls I was interested in, I had their mothers, or whoever came with them, read the novel *with* the child—parental guidance, so to speak, to ensure that the child could talk about the content of the book without embarrassment.

"Some of the girls, or their parents, then dropped out on their own. I discussed the book with those that remained, and frankly, I was amazed at the relative level of their sophistication. Little girls have changed since I was little. But Linda Blair was the least embarrassed, the least upset, and had the most comprehensive view of the material. We were convinced that she would not be damaged by the experience."

Even so, Blatty insisted that Linda undergo a thorough physical examination, and psychiatric experts were consulted, before she signed her contract. "She's turned out to be quite a fantastic actress," Friedkin said.

The advance publicity stills for the film will not show Linda in her more awful moments. For many of her scenes, she has had to undergo two hours of make-up application for her four-hour workday; and the make-up becomes hideous, as her diabolical possession becomes stronger. For those scenes, Friedkin keeps the set as private as possible.

Both Friedkin and Blatty are convinced they will have a knockout of a film, and confidence seems to ooze from each of them. And why not, if even the Pope is on their side?

February 13, 1973

Ultimate Power Struggle

Charles Champlin

What the industry calls the want-to-see, the anticipation for a film which precedes the reviews or the word of mouth, has probably been higher for *The Exorcist* than for any other film of 1973.

William Peter Blatty's scarifying bestseller about a movie star's daughter possessed by the devil was not the first about demonic possession, but deriving its details from a contemporary case history as it did, his book had a rare credibility. And Jesuit-educated Blatty saw it all not only as an incomparable horror story but as a true contest of good vs. evil, God vs. Satan.

The movie, which Blatty produced and wrote and which William Friedkin (*The French Connection*) directed, is now here. It is a genuinely shocking movie, which in its ferocious strength and bloodcurdling events denies any possibility that what we are witnessing is anything but a titanic struggle between God and the Devil localized in the deranged and cruelly abused form of an innocent twelve-year-old girl.

In its uncompromised treatment of its theme, *The Exorcist* becomes quite as much a movie landmark as, say, *Who's Afraid of Virginia Woolf?* did in its year for its own reasons. It is strong and frequently revolting stuff.

Readers of the book are advised that it has been delivered with only the most minor trims. Those who never read the book are seriously forewarned that it is a long shriek from the parlor game devilishness of *Rosemary's Baby*.

Ellen Burstyn, from *The Last Picture Show*, is the movie star, finishing a film on location in Washington and living divorced in Georgetown with her daughter (played with endearing innocence and then with frightening unrecognizability by Linda Blair, a Connecticut schoolgirl).

There are inexplicable rustlings in the attic, laughed-off complaints that the girl's bed is shaking, then a crude prank during a dinner party. A spinal tap (shown in needlessly clinical detail) reveals nothing physiologically wrong.

The possession tightens—strange voices and vile language from a terrified and then withdrawn and surly child. Psychiatrists have nothing to offer

but many-syllabled evasions. The mother's campy director (Jack Mac-
Gowran in his last role) dies mysteriously and ghoulishly during a visit to
the girl.

The mother, understandably hysterical, at last seeks out Father Karras
(Jason Miller), a priest-psychiatrist at nearby Georgetown U.

In the movie, as in Blatty's expertly paced book, the race to exorcise
whatever demons are in possession of daughter Regan runs a nerve-tearing
accelerating parallel with Regan's maniacal and destroying furies. The
exorcist himself is an old, frail archaeologist-priest (Max von Sydow),
obviously modeled on the Catholic philosopher-theologian Teilhard de
Chardin, who was himself said to have performed an exorcism in Africa.

Von Sydow is just back from a dig at Nineveh, where we see him in the
film's prologue, Blatty's effective device to suggest the timelessness of the
struggle about to begin.

At the technical level, Friedkin's movie is startlingly clever. (The special
effects are credited to Marcel Vercoutere.)

The girl's bed shakes jarringly and rises; the girl levitates; her skin
erupts in open wounds; "Help me" appears in welts across her abdomen;
her room is suddenly wind-whipped and icy cold, breaths steaming. Her
face is the most ghastly and distorted since Dorian Gray's, thanks to make-
up man Dick Smith.

The swift and unexpected resolution is, of course, the book's and the
movie's secret, and its meaning, even more in the movie than it was in the
book, is for the viewer to speculate on.

The most disappointing change from book to movie is, in fact, the loss of
Blatty's always-brief considerations of what it all means: Why an innocent
girl? Was what we have seen murder or martyrdom? Who won, and what
kind of read-out is there, if any, for all of us, skeptics and believers alike?

The movie plays, spectacularly, as a jolting drama which can be enjoyed
(in the most flexible sense of the word) as an adult suspense shocker with
overtones. But the reading of the overtones is left to the audience, even
though the existence of those overtones is by no means confined to those
who can believe that the battle has been indeed between the forces of God
and those of the devil. By strong inference, the events also can be taken as
good vs. evil, and as aimed at a kind of self-loathing which modern man
frequently finds in himself.

Jason Miller gives a darkly forceful performance as the priest who has
deep doubts about his own faith and heavy guilts about his abandonment
of his Greek immigrant mother (Vasiliki Maliaros).

As the distraught mother, Ellen Burstyn is clearly the up-to-date star
actress rather than a movie queen, and her portrayal of a woman driven to
the edge by events beyond reckoning is stark and strong. Her own language

is strong even before things go wrong, which is probably in character but which seems a dramatic miscalculation because it makes the daughter's sudden obscenities slightly less jolting (though they still jolt).

The surprise of the cast is William O'Malley, a Jesuit priest from Rochester, N.Y., high school teacher and drama coach, here playing a Jesuit priest, Karras's confidant. No promotional cameo, his is an important supporting role and O'Malley brings it off with an easy and likable professionalism.

Lee J. Cobb's part as the homicide detective who is more perceiving than he lets himself appear is brief but effective. Von Sydow is also effective as the dying priest trying with his last strength to save a life. In less dignified hands than his and Miller's, the crucial moments of the exorcism would come off less successfully than they do.

Kitty Winn (from *Panic in Needle Park*) plays Miss Burstyn's secretary, and very well.

Dissonant, eerie excerpts from the work of Penderecki, Webern, and other modern composers make up the striking and enhancing musical background.

December 26, 1973

Back to the Ouija Board

Pauline Kael

Shallowness that asks to be taken seriously—shallowness like William Peter Blatty's—is an embarrassment. When you hear him on TV talking about communicating with his dead mother, your heart doesn't bleed for him, your stomach turns for him. Some people have impenetrable defense systems. You can't kid around with a man who says that he wrote *The Exorcist* because "as I went along writing my funny books and screenplays, I felt I wasn't making a contribution to the welfare of the world." He says that he looks upon it "quite frankly as an apostolic work." That the work has made him a millionaire doesn't make him a liar. Blatty is apostle to the *National Enquirer,* and to *Cosmopolitan,* in which the novel was condensed—so those Cosmopolitan Girls could make conversation without looking tired around the eyes. The crushing blunt-wittedness of the movie version, which he produced, tends to bear out Blatty's apostolic claims.

Directed by William Friedkin, who won the Academy Award as Best Director of 1971 for *The French Connection,* the film is a faithful adaptation of the Blatty book—and that's not a compliment. Blatty did the intractable screenplay, so Friedkin may have been faithful in spite of himself. The picture isn't a gothic horror comedy, like *Psycho* or *Rosemary's Baby;* it has been made as a heavy, expensive *family* picture. It's faithful not to the way many people read the book—as a fast turn-on entertainment—but to Blatty's claims about what the book was intended to be. It's an obtuse movie, without a trace of playfulness in it. A viewer can become glumly anesthetized by the brackish color and the senseless ugliness of the conception.

Following on the success of *Rosemary's Baby* (Rosemary gave birth to a cloven-hoofed infant, her actor-husband having mated her with Satan in exchange for a Broadway hit), Blatty, a veteran screenwriter, developed an outline for a novel about the demonic possession of a child, and Marc Jaffe, of Bantam Books, subsidized the effort. Harper & Row picked up the hardcover rights, and the movie deal (stipulating that Blatty was to produce) was made even before publication. Blatty, who once hoaxed people by impersonating a Saudi Arabian prince, and whose screen credits include a hand in *Darling Lili, The Great Bank Robbery, What Did You Do in the War, Daddy?, Promise Her Anything, John Goldfarb, Please Come Home,* etc., is not an austere writer. The key personnel in *The Exorcist* are (a) Chris MacNeil (Ellen Burstyn), a beautiful movie-star mother, divorced, agnostic; (b) her twelve-year-old daughter, Regan (Linda Blair), who becomes a foul-mouthed, sex-obsessed, blaspheming, church-desecrating murderess; (c) Father Damien Karras (Jason Miller), a tormented Jesuit psychiatrist who is losing his faith; (d) a joky, warmhearted Jewish police lieutenant (Lee J. Cobb); (e) a distinguished, ascetic priest, Father Merrin (Max von Sydow), whose archaeological work has somehow—it's not made clear how, in either the book or the movie—released the demon that takes over Regan.

The book features a murder victim—a British movie director—whose "head was turned completely around, facing backward"; little Regan rotating her head; little Regan masturbating with a crucifix and grabbing her mother and forcing her mother's face against her bloody vagina; vomit propelled from Regan's mouth into people's faces. And what Blatty didn't manage to have his characters do he had them talk about, so there were fresh atrocities every few hundred words. Like the pulp authors who provide flip-page sex, he provided flip-page torture, infanticide, cannibalism, sexual hysteria, werewolves. The book is a manual of lurid crimes, written in an easy-to-read tough-guy style yet with a grating heightening word here and there, supposedly to tone it up. ("When the Mass was over, he polished the chalice and carefully placed it in his bag. He rushed for the seven-ten train back to Washington, carrying pain in a black valise.") The book turns up on highschool reading lists now, and the Bantam edition carries such quotes as "Deeply religious . . . a parable for our times" and *"The Exorcist* should be read twice; the first time for the passion and horrifying intensity of the story, with a second reading to savor the subtleties of language and phrasing overlooked in the mounting excitement of the first perusal."

For the movie, Blatty had to dispense with a subplot about the butler's daughter, and, of course, he couldn't retain all the gory anecdotes, but the basic story is told, and the movie—religiously literal-minded—shows you a heaping amount of blood and horror. This explicitness must be what William Friedkin has in mind when he talks publicly about the picture's "documentary quality." The movie also has the most ferocious language yet heard in a picture that is rated R, and is thus open to children (to those whose parents are insane enough to take them, or are merely uninformed). *The Exorcist* was budgeted at four million dollars, but, what with swiveling heads, and levitations, and vomit being spewed on target, the cost kept rising, and the picture came in somewhere around ten million. If *The Exorcist* had cost under a million, or had been made abroad, it would almost certainly be an X film, but when a movie is as expensive as this one, the M.P.A.A. rating board doesn't dare to give it an X. Will people complain? I doubt it; the possible complainers have become accessories. Two Jesuits appear in the cast and served, with a third, as "technical advisers," along with a batch of doctors. Besides, the Catholic Church is hardly likely to be upset by the language or actions in a film that says that the Catholic Church is the true faith, feared by the Devil, and that its rituals can exorcise demons. The two heroes of the film are von Sydow and Jason Miller, both playing Jesuits; Georgetown University cooperated with the production, which was shot partly in Georgetown; and one of the Jesuit actor-advisers enriched us, even before the film was finished, with information about its high moral character ("It shows that obscenity is ugly . . . vicious ugly, like the Vietnamese news"). The movie may be in the worst imaginable taste—that is, an utterly unfeeling movie about miracles—but it's also the biggest recruiting poster the Catholic Church has had since the sunnier days of *Going My Way* and *The Bells of St. Mary's.*

Whatever Blatty's claims, if *The Exorcist* scares people that's probably all it has to do, in box-office terms, and basically that's all the whole unpleasant movie is designed to do. "People only go to movies for three reasons, to laugh, cry, or be frightened," Friedkin has said. And "There are only three reasons to make a movie, to make people laugh, to make them cry, or to frighten them." The scaring here is a matter of special effects and sound and editing—the roaring-animal noises from the attic coming at the right instant, Regan's bed shaking just enough, the objects in her room flying about without looking silly, and so on. If the audience ever started giggling at the sounds and tricks, the picture might collapse, because it's entirely mechanical and impersonal. Von Sydow brings some elegance to his role, and the make-up that ages him is one of the most convincing aging jobs I've ever seen, but once you perceive that his Father Merrin is saintly and infirm, that's it. As Father Karras, the most active character, Jason Miller does the gloomy, tormented John Garfield bit—and it's a wheeze by now. All the performances are; there's nothing the actors can do with the juiceless stock roles.

The book's success may relate to its utter shallowness; the reader can go at a fast clip, following the plot and not paying any attention to the characters. But in the movie version the psychology, which is tiresomely moralistic (as in a fifties TV drama), is dead center. There we are with the free-thinking mother feeling guilty about her divorce and its effects on Regan; we may not know why the demon picked on Regan, but we're tipped that that broken home—the first step to Hell—gave the Devil his chance. And there we are with the creaking goodness of the Jewish cop, and the jocular bonhomie of the Jesuits. It's all so tired that we can keep going only on fresh atrocities. Apart from the demonic special effects, which are done in staccato quick cuts, the picture is in a slugging, coercive style. It piles up points, like a demonstration. Friedkin, beloved of studio heads for such statements as "I'm not a thinker. . . . If it's a film *by* somebody instead of *for* somebody, I smell art," is not a director given to depth or mystery. Nor is he a man with a light touch—a failing that appears to have been exacerbated by the influence of *El Topo*. He has himself said that Blatty's book took hold of him and made him physically ill. That's the problem with moviemakers who aren't thinkers: they're mentally unprotected. A book like Blatty's makes them sick, and they think this means they should make everybody sick. Probably Friedkin really believes he is communicating an important idea to us. And the only way he knows how to do it is by surface punch; he's a true commercial director— he confuses blatancy with power.

As a movie, *The Exorcist* is too ugly a phenomenon to take lightly. Its gothic seriousness belongs to the class of those old Hearst Sunday-supplement stories about archaeologists defiling tombs and the curses that befall them, and it soaks into people's lives. A critic can't fight it, because it functions below the conscious level. How does one exorcise the effects of a movie like this? There is no way. The movie industry is such that men of no taste and no imagination can have an incalculable influence. Blatty and Friedkin can't muster up any feeling, even when Father Karras sacrifices himself—a modern Christ who dies to save mankind. We in the audience don't feel bad when the saintly Father Merrin dies; we don't even feel a pang of sympathy when the words "Help Me" appear on Regan's body. From the mechanical-scare way that the movie works on an audience, there is no indication that Blatty or Friedkin has any feeling for the little girl's helplessness and suffering, or her mother's, any feeling for God or terror of Satan. Surely it is the religious people who should be most offended by this movie. Others can laugh it off as garbage, but are American Catholics willing to see their faith turned into a horror show? Are they willing to accept *anything* just as long as their Church comes out in a good light? Aren't those who accept this picture getting their heads screwed on backward?

Somewhere in the publicity for the film there was an item about William Friedkin's having looked at five hundred little girls before he chose his Regan, and, indeed, Linda Blair is a sparkling, snub-nosed, happy-looking little girl, who matches up perfectly with Ellen Burstyn. I wonder about those four hundred and ninety-nine mothers of the rejected little girls—or about the hundred and ninety-nine, if that's a more reasonable figure. They must have read the novel; they must have known what they were having their beautiful little daughters tested for. When they see *The Exorcist* and watch Linda Blair urinating on the fancy carpet and screaming and jabbing at herself with the crucifix, are they envious? Do they feel, "That might have been my little Susie—famous forever"?

January 7, 1974

GODSPELL

Bruce Williamson

A band of raggle-taggle Jesus freaks singing their hearts out all over New York's parks, skyscrapers, and neon signs makes *Godspell* a giddy delight, at least during the first hour of the movie version of John-Michael Tebelak's hit musical. Co-scenarist and director David Greene uses members of the original cast to fine advantage at the outset, showing them as ordinary bustling New Yorkers who chuck away their wigs, neckties, taxicabs, ballet lessons and platform heels to spread the word of the Lord. Composer Stephen Schwartz's score has plenty of youth and exuberance—

and the same might be said of the company as a whole. They zip through their illustrated Bible stories—everything from the good Samaritan to the Crucifixion—with incredible energy. And the cityscapes are pretty, the choreography charmingly inventive in a clap-hands-and-shout sort of way. But even the blithest spirits tend to flag after a while, and *Godspell* wears down its audience while the cast is still going strong. Nearly two hours is too long for an enterprise so frail and essentially formless. This show-biz improvisation occupies a patch of terra incognita somewhere between *Sesame Street* and the Gospel According to *Laugh-In.*

July 1973

JESUS CHRIST SUPERSTAR

Hollis Alpert

It's a terrible story, really. There's this droopy little fellow with sad eyes and long hair, dressed in what looks like white sackcloth, wandering through the deserts and hills and fields of present-day Israel. He's followed around by a bunch of nondescript young people, who appear to adore him for no apparent reason; nor do they seem to have any particular place to go or any particular mission to accomplish, except now and then they mention going to Jerusalem. Now, for some reason, there are a few priests (you can tell they're priests by the strange headpieces they wear) who worry about the little fellow. So they get hold of one of his followers, who is black and very mixed-up, and give him some money to point out this man who leads these young people around—even though he's in *plain sight* all the time, and they know exactly who he is. Meanwhile a fat king called Herod, who wears yellow-tinted glasses, mocks the little fellow and chortles with glee when some soldiers carrying spears and submachine guns bring him before a Roman called Pontius, who has the fellow whipped for no apparent reason and then has him nailed to a cross. Oh, the black, mixed-up man tosses his money away and finds a lonely tree and hangs himself, after complaining that he didn't really want to betray his friend anyway.

What story is this? *Jesus Christ Superstar*, of course. It's now a movie, after a vastly successful career as a stage musical; and though I already knew the story by heart, having read it in several versions and seen it in various film versions, I found it astonishingly fascinating to watch.

Rock operas are hardly new by now, neither on stage nor on film, and the recent film version of *Godspell*, which tells precisely the same story, is already on view and doing well. Yet, *Jesus Christ Superstar* suffers not in the least by comparison or by familiarity. Both musicals have made the transition to film successfully, although poles apart in style. *Godspell* posits a clown Jesus, whose followers skylark with him through a cinematically vivid Manhattan; it's all joy and freshness and high spirits until the inevitable mystical passion of the conclusion. *Jesus Christ Superstar*, on the other hand, goes to the original place of the happening or the myth (depending on one's degree of devoutness) and deposits its bus load of participants amid some desert ruins supported by modern-day scaffolding, whereupon they burst into song and continue unflaggingly in, for the most part, musical rhymed couplets until the stark ending on the cross. They then board the bus and head elsewhere, perhaps to enact the same story all over again.

What makes *Jesus Christ Superstar* pertinent (at least for me) is that the filmmakers and those who created the stage version take the Passion of Christ less as gospel than as theatrical religious ritual, there being considerable theory to this effect. Therefore, once more young people have come to Israel to repeat the ritual in their own, somewhat unsophisticated terms, while infusing it with modern, indeed campy, touches. "Everything is fixed, and you can't change it," the sorely beset little leader grates from tortured lips to Pontius, who wonders why he must scourge and kill this inoffensive man. And when Judas wonders why he must betray the man he follows and loves, he is given much the same reason. Taken as story, motivations are entirely missing, but as ritual, events must take their course—they are preordained.

As a feat of filmmaking, Norman Jewison's handsome production is particularly admirable. There were problems to be solved: for one, the very transfer from the stage conventions to what would work in the film medium; for another, achieving pictorial fluidity, while never for a moment deserting the opera's musical structure; and, perhaps most important, making the whole affecting. He does all these. When Mary Magdalene, sung and acted superbly by Yvonne Elliman, wonders in her long and lovely plaint why and how she loves that man, and holds the screen for a full four or five minutes (a very long time by cinematic reckoning), one might expect the film to become static. But no. With rare and careful grace, and no tricks, Jewison achieves movement—not action, but the kind of filmic movement that is achieved in the editing room.

Using almost no one from the Broadway cast, Jewison has found marvelous faces, lithe bodies. Ted Neeley, for all the blandness of the operatic Jesus, has a touching quality in his physical appearance and meets the voice demands of the role. Carl Anderson is an electrifying Judas; Joshua Mostel makes for a gorgeously funny Herod; Barry Dennen is perfect as the puzzled Pilate. The dance episodes are stunningly performed. Not a familiar face in the interracial lot, yet there is no one who is inappropriate. And should the music leave one unmoved, and the story contain nothing remotely resembling suspense, there are still backgrounds to enthrall: mysterious ruins, rocky configurations, shimmering desert expanses. At one point, Judas is found on his knees in the desert. A strange rumbling is heard, and over a rise in the barren landscape five monstrous, snouted tanks appear. One doesn't even bother to seek the meaning of the anachronism, for it is a visual tour de force, a surreal apparition that, at the same time, reminds us in no uncertain terms of the actual world we live in—or at least the world where the film was made.

July 17, 1973

Passion in the Desert

Paul D. Zimmerman

Hopefully, *Jesus Christ Superstar* will staunch the flow of recent tribal rock musicals that transport the Passion of Christ into a contemporary, counter-cultural context. There are pitfalls aplenty in a Jesus who sings the blues, and director Norman Jewison, in his screen translation of the ballyhooed Broadway rock opera, manages to parlay them all into one of the true fiascos of modern cinema.

To give his story a specious kind of authenticity, Jewison shows his hippie Jesus and his commune of hyperthyroidal acolytes pouring out of a tourist bus amid the monumental escarpments of the Middle East. This realistic backdrop provides Jewison with majestic sunsets and the big look of a major musical, but the price is parody. Broadway go-go choreography looks just plain silly in the middle of the desert, despite Jewison's efforts to rev it up with slow-motion and freeze-frame gimmickry. Seeking an effect of timelessness, the director mixes ancient amphitheaters, modern tanks, Biblical costuming, a tourist bazaar, and a traditional Crucifixion in a mélange that isn't so much timeless as mindless.

The mixed setting, for all its strain on our credulity, leads to fatal foolishness everywhere. The Sinai setting undercuts *Superstar's* original theme—Jesus as rock idol. There just isn't very much of a credible rock audience at the Fillmore Middle East. But beyond this, the anachronisms lead to fatuous fakeries like Judas betraying Jesus after escaping pursuit by a flock of tanks, Jesus being pelted with bagels, the Apostles assuming the attitude of Leonardo da Vinci's famous fresco at a Last Picnic.

Jewison's Jesus often recalls Charles Manson, camping out a lot and surrounded by beautiful women who anoint him in their spare time. He is described as having "that look you rarely find" but, in fact, Ted Neeley, as Jesus, seems a dead ringer for all those sentimentalized figures one sees in second-rate religious art. He is a peevish figure, constantly berating his Apostles for not loving him enough and worrying about whether people will talk about him when he's gone. Like Carl Anderson as Judas, Neeley is pushed by Andrew Lloyd Webber's eclectic score into the screaming falsetto blues made popular by Janis Joplin, until the shrieking style grows shrewish. Yvonne Elliman sings Mary Magdalene with a sweet and touching clarity, but the role turns Magdalene into a valet, constantly changing Christ's tunic and trying to get his mind off his work. God himself is played, as is customary, by sunlight streaming through clouds.

There are a few bright moments—especially a bit of twenties musical parody when Herod (Joshua Mostel), a kind of drag king, taunts Jesus to "walk across my swimming pool." And an aria by Jesus asking to know the meaning of his death gathers some power until Jewison cuts away pretentiously to a gallery of Crucifixion oils by Western masters. At the end, the cast piles back into the tourist bus, all of them except Jesus. How did the tour leader write up that afternoon's outing? "We danced and sang and Jesus was crucified and a good time was had by all." Lord, forgive them. They knew not what they were doing.

July 9, 1973

JONATHAN LIVINGSTON SEAGULL

Michael Korda

> . . . o the laughter of holy white birds flying after.
> —JOHN MASEFIELD

I confess to a certain bias against the anthropomorphic view of animal nature, and a guarded faith in the behavioral theory of such scholars as Konrad Lorenz. It seems to me a mistake to suppose that animals share our feelings, fears, and triumphs, or our moods. An acquaintance of mine summed up the matter, after twenty years of raising eagles, by saying, "They're bloody savage bastards, and I don't trust them a moment." Birds *are* somewhat special, with their habit of staring fixedly into space and their glazed looked of hostility. Theirs may be—who knows?—a full, rich life, but if so, it is closed to us. Yet, they exert a certain fascination, for they are free in ways we are not, physically able to soar, fly, to enter into a third dimension of time and space that we can know only by means of the most cumbersome and expensive machinery. It is hardly surprising therefore that we tend to identify with them: not for nothing did Don Juan appear to Carlos Castañeda in the guise of a raven, or fate in the form of a white falcon. Birds have a dramatic quality, combined with a certain reptilian remoteness.

Given this, I was hardly surprised at the success of *Jonathan Livingston Seagull,* and even less so to find that I liked the movie of this spectacular bestseller. Children (at least those I know), being pragmatic rationalists, are likely to dismiss the movie as merely being a documentary about talking seagulls, and I would be the first to admit that there is something disturbing, at least at the beginning, about hearing real seagulls in lively conversation with one another, especially when it becomes quickly evident that they are in fact lecturing to us about the failures and weaknesses of the human race. There is an instinctive human reaction against this kind of thing, a feeling that however low man may have fallen, we surely do not yet need to be preached to by a flock of seagulls.

Let me just say that within ten minutes Hall Bartlett's magic, like author Richard Bach's, takes hold of the viewer. I let myself go and was soon flying high above the California coast with J. L. Seagull, suffering with him as he tries to fly higher and faster than any seagull has ever done and to make seagulls understand that their strength is in their wings, not in their beaks and their frenzied struggle to steal food from one another. If suspension of disbelief is the criterion of art, then *Jonathan Livingston Seagull* is great art.

Few movies make me cry; this one did, perhaps because I'm fond of animals, even birds, more likely because the seagull's dreams are so common to all of us—to be free, to soar, to do good, to understand the meaning of life. There is something pathetic and touching about Jonathan's confrontation with his vicious, garbage-stealing flock, in his epic flight across snow-covered mountains where no seagull has ever flown, about his arrival in what I take to be seagull heaven (the film is obscure on this point), and his return to the flock as a kind of seagull Christ. I don't think that I've ever seen a more *beautiful* movie, and it is possible to enjoy it simply as a nature film, which in a way it is, what with the spectacular surf, the clouds, the rocks, and the endlessly wheeling birds against the changing sky. On this level, you'd have to be blind not to like *Jonathan Livingston Seagull*. But its real fascination lies deeper. However ludicrous the arguments of Jonathan with his girlfriend or his parents, however odd it is to hear longings and fumbled dreams of adolescents expressed from the beak (I was about to say lips) of a seagull, Jonathan's courageous leap into the unknown, his desire to fly like an eagle instead of a gull, his passion to liberate himself from the sordid scavenging of the flock, his apotheosis in the snow of an unfamiliar forest, and his return as a mythic feathered prophet of flight, all are wonderfully moving. For Bach has hit on a perfect working metaphor: flight is freedom, Jonathan's desire to perfect his flying abilities is our desire to perfect our soul, his flock is our daily life, his ambition to soar is our ambition to live beyond everyday life, to transcend ourselves. If the beginning of the film is halting and disturbing, even lachrymose, the rest of it is superb, a parable couched in the form of a nature film of overpowering beauty and strength in which, perhaps to our horror, we are forced to recognize ourselves in a seagull obsessed with the heights. There are ludicrous moments, to be sure, the worst being the appearance of an elderly seagull *guru*, a kind of web-footed Buddha, who instructs the soul of Jonathan Seagull in the arts of patience and meditation, but despite these jarring notes, *Jonathan Livingston Seagull* is an emotional experience.

November 1973

THE DAY OF THE DOLPHIN
The Porpoise of Life

Paul D. Zimmerman

He rises majestically from the sea, a joyful child of nature, innocent, playful and free. His name is Alpha, the star of *The Day of the Dolphin*. And, for director Mike Nichols, this beautiful aquatic mammal embodies the qualities of trust, loyalty and childlike innocence that have all but vanished from the human community. When Alpha and his tank-mate, Beta, are kidnapped by malevolent men who play cruelly on their trusting natures and program them as weapons of warfare, we realize that the same profound misanthropy that pushed Swift to abjure mankind in favor of horses drives Nichols to prize the virtues of dolphins above those of men. Looking at Alpha, George C. Scott, as a marine biologist, remarks: "We should have become like what they are—all instinct and energy." But Scott introduces the dolphins to the human world instead—by teaching them to speak English.

Nichols does everything to arouse our admiration for his sea heroes. Scott lectures on the dolphins' extraordinary powers—they can carry on simultaneous conversations with a neighbor and with another dolphin miles away, their language transmits complex and subtle information, they are intensely alive and receptive in all of their senses. The lyrical ballet of the blonde skater in *Carnal Knowledge* finds its parallel here in Nichols's rhapsodic *pas de deux* for dolphins, plunging and soaring through the sea to the strains of baroque water music.

But it is the job of the story, written by Buck Henry from Robert Merle's novel, to convince us that dolphins are better than people. To this end, Nichols applies coat after coat of mythic lacquer: the myth of growing up—with Alpha and Beta adored, punished, ruled and finally renounced by their foster parents, "Pa" and "Ma"—Scott and Trish Van Devere; the myth of man's rape of nature, which moves Nichols to depict even Scott's seemingly benign education of his charges as an inevitable corruption; the myth of the destruction of the private paradise, in which an all-powerful, all-malevolent government turns into a combination of Captain Hook and the CIA and despoils Scott's island kingdom.

But these layers of myth rest upon a bedrock of pop melodrama. Nichols's cherishing of childlike innocence turns Alpha into an idealized Disney figure, laden with marzipan sentimentality as he nuzzles Scott, crooning "Pha loves Pa" in a voice half pussycat, half babykins. When the unnamed villains (identified only as the directors of a philanthropical "foundation") outfit Beta with a mine to blow up the Presidential yacht, Alpha is sent to stop her just like Rin-Tin-Tin with fins. So cynical has Nichols become that he feels no obligation to identify the men manipulating Beta or their purpose—they are simply the sinister forces of the anti-life conspiracy, located chiefly now in "government" itself. Paul Sorvino, as a seedy spy for hire who helps Scott recover his kidnapped *Kinder*, symbolizes the idea that man's morality is perennially at auction. In the same way, Nichols refuses to identify the President on the yacht, using the office imprecisely because it has become an empty symbol suitable for melodramatic manipulation.

But the film's final and most grievous failing lies in Nichols's manipulation of the audience. He arouses our sure-fire anger by having bad men lie to innocent lovable porpoises. He arouses our sure-fire anguish when

Scott—who is nothing more than an expensive embodiment of the conventional idealistic scientist—sends his beloved Alpha back into the sea to save him from the iniquity of man. We are heartbroken as Alpha croons "Pha loves Pa" even as we realize these are feelings drawn from us by a director who knows how to exploit them without sharing them. And manufactured feeling rather than the communication of real feeling distinguishes artifice from art.

December 31, 1973

Eleven

FAVORITES

THE MERCHANT OF FOUR SEASONS

Lost Love, Found Despair

Andrew Sarris

Rainer Werner Fassbinder's *The Merchant of Four Seasons* may be the most exquisite achievement in cinema to reach these shores from Germany since the Golden Age of Murnau, Lang, Pabst, *et al* in the years Before Hitler. Unfortunately, New York audiences seem to have become studiously indifferent to German movies. It's not anything one can put one's finger on and label as bias, prejudice, or backlash bigotry. It is simply a matter of massive non-interest. Even ultra-German projects like *The Damned* and *Ludwig* sneak into the art-house market only on the Italian passport of Luchino Visconti. Indeed, if it were not for the New York Film Festival and for Richard Roud's predilection for Fassbinder, Straub, and Herzog the contemporary Germany cinema would be completely unknown in these precincts. As it is, even critics who should know better tend to lump together Fassbinder, Straub, and Herzog into one esoteric stew of excruciating stylization.

The basic problem with German cinema is that there is no middle ground between the mandarins and the masses, between the festival palaces and the grind houses, between lonely artists and lowly artisans. Straub with his uncompromising formalism and Herzog with his grotesque humanism exemplify this problem of program-note cinema. I can't say that I've ever really enjoyed Straub and Herzog. I've always respected them, yes. I've even admired them on occasion. But I would never send my friends to see their films. I think they should be shown at the New York Film Festival for the benefit of that ever-growing contingent of film scholars concerned with the new boundaries of the medium. Fassbinder, I think, can provide pleasure even for the ordinary moviegoer dwelling within the older boundaries of life. In a sense, Fassbinder deftly balances style (Straub) with humanity (Herzog) in such a way that *The Merchant of Four Seasons* manages to break the heart without betraying the mind. Fassbinder's achievement is aided in no small measure by the extraordinary presences and performances of Hans Hirschmuller as the hapless victim, Hanna

Schygulla as his beautiful and dilettantishly compassionate sister, and Irm Hermann as his sensually ungainly wife.

We are not too far into *The Merchant of Four Seasons* before we feel the reverberations of *Wozzeck* and *Mother Courage*, but Fassbinder strikes a very distinctive tone of his own on the tin drum of despair. From a certain angle, the produce-peddling protagonist can be viewed as an especially mediocre specimen of Everyman. He has been rejected by the Great Love of His Life, and settles for second-best with a sullen woman who is embarrassingly taller than he is. His previous service with the Foreign Legion had been a disillusioning debacle, and his family has virtually disowned him as a social disgrace. He is a growlingly inarticulate clod of a creature with a constant buzzing in his brain from which he can never escape. He has been discharged from the police force for consorting with a prostitute in the station, and he has transformed this transgression into a tavern anecdote in a futile attempt to understand its significance in his life. But everything in his life is out of sync and out of proportion. He lives by a different clock and on a different scale from everyone else. He earns and he yearns, but only drink can ease his suffering.

For once, the distancing devices of rack focus and artificial color schemes serve to express the chasm between what a character feels and what he is able to communicate to others. Fassbinder does not stop with Rosebud as a psychological spring; he presents the full flowering of the rose in all its tawdry triviality as an objective fact and in all its sublime stature as a subjective fantasy. The death and funeral of Hans is one of the great passages in modern cinema, and the intimation of his great and lost love one of the modern cinema's most lyrical ironies. Earlier, Hans approaches a state of spiritual communion with his sister, but a lapse of concentration on her part sends him scurrying back to the chilling sanctuary of his own introverted psyche, and he is thus doomed forever to emotional isolation. The spine-tingling irrevocability of this sequence constitutes a dramatic spectacle of the highest order and establishes Fassbinder as one of the most forceful filmmakers of the seventies, a man for both the coterie and the crowd. And if one needed any additional motivation to see *Merchant of Four Seasons*, there is Hanna Schygulla with the eyes and lips and womanly wiles to lead one to hell itself.

November 22, 1973

DAYS AND NIGHTS IN THE FOREST

David Denby

It's clearly much harder these days than it was a decade or so ago for a foreign film without obvious mass appeal to get a commercial booking in New York. Even if it is lauded when it plays at the New York Film Festival or the Museum of Modern Art, all too often there is no substantial commercial follow-up. Distributors don't want to take a chance and exhibitors, with notable exceptions, would rather schedule Bogart, Garbo, and Groucho festivals into their houses during those periods when they don't have a hit on their hands. What's more, the mass audiences are largely indifferent to foreign films, except for French and Italian farces and an occasional stunner like *Last Tango in Paris*. The theaters on the East Side, a number of them originally built as art houses ten or twenty years ago, now play the most conventional American stuff; theater owners have apparently come to feel that East Side people won't go to Times Square anymore, and a lot more money can be made showing crime caper and young romance pictures than something slightly different from overseas. All of this at least partially explains why it is only now that Satyajit Ray's marvelous *Days and Nights in the Forest*, after languishing for more than two years, is to receive regular commercial bookings. It is the best picture around right now, and there's no reason why, properly promoted, it shouldn't be a hit.

The great Indian director, of course, was hardly obscure or a beginner when *Days and Nights in the Forest* was shown at the Film Festival in 1970. His *Apu* trilogy was already world-famous, and *Devi, The Music Room*, and *Two Daughters* had been much praised and written about. None of these previous films, though, was so easily accessible to the Western viewer or offered deeper pleasures. While *Days and Nights in the Forest* is completely absorbing as narrative, the picture may also be enjoyed as a meditation on vanity and moral blindness, and as a study of the relationship of civilization to violence.

In Ray's script, an adaptation of a novel by Sunil Ganguly, four thirtyish Calcuttans—educated, Anglicized and very bourgeois—travel to the countryside for relaxation, the pleasures of friendship, and social/

erotic adventure. However, it quickly becomes clear that each of these men is self-dissatisfied and unresolved in some way that makes him slightly dangerous to others and to himself. The two intellectuals, Ashim and Sanjoy, have settled into business life after giving up their little magazine, and their self-contempt finds a release in weary condescension; the shallow, sensual athlete, Hari, recently jilted by a dazzling girl, has become aggressive and vengeful; and the fourth man, Sekhar, is tolerated by the others but he's the least attractive of the lot—a chattering, hysterical little conformist, terrified of women and incapable of experience.

We know from what Ray has written about his own explorations of the Bengali countryside (the setting for *Pather Panchali,* his first great film) that such voyages into a culture very different from that of the city provide a splendid opportunity to look, listen, and learn. But these young men, likable in so many ways, are too narcissistic to *see* anything. In part, their blindness is induced by the double caste system that operates on their behalf—granted a high social status by birth and education, they also in their relations with women assume an attitude of superiority and inherent male "dignity" that would put an ordinary Western male chauvinist to shame. Casually, they appropriate the impoverished villagers for labor or sex, never recognizing them as human beings until the villagers' suffering and violence begin to threaten them as well. At the same time, Ashim and Sanjoy begin flirtations with women of their own class, and each suffers the most wrenching embarrassment (leading to self-knowledge in one case, mortification in the other) before admitting that the woman has felt and suffered more than he. Somewhat chastened, the four men go back to the city.

Ray's method is gentle; he exposes his heroes' folly but avoids the vindictive oneupsmanship of a film like *Carnal Knowledge.* Slowly, firmly, the director makes his point, and we may be amazed, finally, at the intensity he builds up out of nothing. A silly, flirtatious little game, with the four men and two women sitting in a circle trying to remember famous names, serves to crystallize the whole dramatic situation for us: we see each one's character, his social, sexual and cultural ambitions, and his relation to the others with almost unbearable clarity. When the sequence is over we sigh in relief, grateful for the mastery that can produce such a response without slugging us over the head. See *Days and Nights in the Forest.* If it becomes a hit, the whole foreign film scene could loosen up a bit.

May 3, 1973

THE ADVERSARY

Gary Arnold

Satyajit Ray's *The Adversary* is a beautiful film, an exceptionally perceptive and moving account of what it feels like to be young, serious, intelligent, and undecided about the future in a modern urban civilization. To the
best of my knowledge, no other contemporary movie has communicated the
attitudes typical of bright young men and women of the educated, liberal
middle classes as honestly or comprehensively as *The Adversary.* Ray
seems to understand their self-consciousness, their tastes and aspirations
and frustrations, as thoroughly as Hollywood misunderstood them back in
1970 with projects like *Getting Straight, The Strawberry Statement,* and
Zabriskie Point.

It's wonderfully ironic that it should turn out to be an Indian director
who makes the first authentic and indisputably relevant "youth movie" of
the seventies. It's not so surprising that Ray is the director to do it, since
Ray and François Truffaut are probably the greatest humanists of their
filmmaking generation.

The Adversary takes place in Calcutta, and this setting may endow Ray's
vision of a young man at a turning point in life with a special measure of
poignancy. The protagonist lives in a modern city and expresses a modern
consciousness. One recognizes him in many young people here, and it's
likely that many older people will recognize themselves at an earlier stage of
life. But seeing this familiar, representative figure against the vast, teeming
backdrop of Calcutta gives the story an awesome resonance. If the hero
should fail to find himself, to assert his individuality, to discover a useful
and satisfying way of life, he threatens to vanish without a trace. In this
setting individuality looks like the most precious and precarious of qualities to be asserting.

The Adversary is having its American premier at the Inner Circle
Theater, which also launched Ray's *Days and Nights in the Forest.* Both
films are based on novels by the Bengali writer Sunil Ganguly, and according to an interview with Ray in the Winter 1972/73 issue of *Sight and
Sound,* a new film called *Company Limited* completes an informal trilogy
dealing with contemporary Indian problems.

Whether this new trilogy becomes as famous as Ray's *Apu* trilogy remains to be seen, but I would love to see a resurgence of interest in Ray's work among American art-house patrons. A Ray vogue among aspiring young filmmakers wouldn't be such a bad development either; his characteristic simplicity and lucidity of expression might prove a more useful model and inspiration than the examples set by flashy grandstanding directors. For the purposes of either social or psychological realism, Ray is our most illuminating and exemplary film artist.

Days and Nights in the Forest appealed to enough Washingtonians to keep it going for three weeks, and I think it's conceivable that *The Adversary* can improve upon that showing. Since the material reflects significant aspects of their experience so closely, students may feel more attraction for *The Adversary* than *Days and Nights,* which dealt with a slightly older group, out of school or job-hunting and into professions. *The Adversary* is also a better-looking movie. The black-and-white photography (by Soumendu Ray and Purnendu Bose) is strong and expressive but also modulated. For some reason much of *Days and Nights* looked overexposed, uncharacteristically "primitive," with lighting contrasts so harsh that the Indian countryside resembled a lunar landscape.

The hero of *The Adversary* is named Siddhartha, a detail which should not be misconstrued by the many admirers and disparagers of Herman Hesse. The Siddhartha of Sunil Ganguly and Satyajit Ray may be trying to find himself, but he has a good idea of where to look. There's nothing mystic in his style of thought or behavior.

Siddhartha's outlook is essentially rational and secular. He's reserved and introspective, a young man with a contemplative, "literary" sort of temperament, which includes a keen sense of nostalgia for childhood settings and memories. While he shows no inclination toward mysticism, he is tempted to associate himself with extremist political activity, an alternative already chosen by his unnostalgic, ruthless younger brother, a terrorist belonging to one of the militant left-wing parties in Calcutta.

The deceptively simple narrative deals with Siddhartha's attempts to find a job. When we first see him, he is on his way to be interviewed by a state selection board for a position as a botanist. He ruins whatever chances he may have had by answering questions far more sincerely and candidly than a person looking out for his self-interest is obliged to. The climactic scene of the film occurs during a second job interview for a civil-service position. Siddhartha again kills his chances for immediate "success," but he demonstrates a moral courage and independence that are admirable and inspiring in themselves, and we can at least hope that they'll sustain him and help shape his character and work in the future.

As both written and played, Siddhartha is the most convincing embodiment of a thoughtful, intellectual young person I've ever seen in a movie. His personality comes out naturally in that opening job interview, and we see that a dominant element is the pride he takes in his intelligence. You hear it in his reply to the question, "Do you like flowers?" "Not without exception . . ." he begins, qualifying the response in a way that is bound to lose him a few points with the interviewers but seems unavoidable (or compulsive) in a bright, articulate, unwary young man.

Dhritiman Chatterjee, the young actor who plays Siddhartha, has a dark, gentle, expressive face and a quiet, intent, watchful manner. He projects a credible and sympathetic image, at once physically and psychically appealing. The actor doesn't contradict the sensibility attributed to the character; thought processes and conflicts of feeling seem to be accurately reflected in Chatterjee's face.

Through a series of encounters that seem casual, almost inadvertent, we see the alternatives open to someone like Siddhartha at the age of twenty-five. A former medical student, he has left school some time before the story begins, following the death of his father, a hard-working and prosperous businessman. The death has resulted in a lower standard of living for the family and a less privileged position for Siddhartha, the eldest of three grown children, who can no longer afford a prolonged scholarly career.

It appears that Siddhartha commences his search for a straight, permanent job after a considerable period of idleness and aimlessness. It's a matter of both necessity and self-respect. Although the ostensible head of the family, Siddhartha has not been contributing to its income, and he can exert no influence or control over his younger sister and brother, diverging in worrisome directions of their own, one toward materialism and dreams of celebrity, the other toward radicalism and dreams of revolution.

Siddhartha feels at once protective toward and estranged from his sister and brother. Their preoccupations worry him, but he can't honestly disapprove of them. His sister ignores him when he advises her to be cautious about a romantic involvement with her boss. Siddhartha looks even more foolish and priggish when he approaches the boss and suggests that his sister not be kept overtime quite so often. Sexually inexperienced and jobless himself, how can he hope to carry any conviction or authority along with his sense of concern?

His brother reminds him, somewhat contemptuously, that Siddhartha was the one who first exposed him to the works of Che Guevara. Committed himself, the younger brother has no respect for the uncommitted, the indecisive, the ambivalent. He dismisses Siddhartha as a bourgeois coward. Earlier the job interviewers had suspected he was a Communist, misunderstanding his explanation of why the Vietnam war was the most significant event of the period. (Their idea of the right answer is the moon landing.)

Siddhartha's ambivalence and conscience clearly disqualify him for certain things, like the materialism of his sister, the fanaticism of his brother, the hedonism and cynicism of a college chum, and the certitude of the civil-service bureaucrats. Since he can't continue to remain immobile and unemployed, the question is, can he find a reasonable way out?

The question is not answered, but for once the dilemma itself is honestly and adequately dramatized. We know exactly what's at stake, how much the character stands to lose if he's compelled to give up his self-respect in order to make a living. There are hopeful indications as well as bleak ones. Siddhartha's "revolt" at the second job interview could prove personally liberating, if practically ineffective, and he meets a girl, a college student named Keya (Joyshree Roy), who seems to share many of his own sentiments and aspirations.

We don't know what will become of Siddhartha, but we're inspired to care about him intensely. Perhaps he's submerging himself as the film ends, but it's equally possible that he'll emerge with renewed strength and confidence in the future. We can't be certain if we're watching the turning point in a purposeful life or a wasted life, and this uncertainty contributes to the film's emotional impact. Our hopes and apprehensions about Siddhartha and Keya begin to merge with those we feel for other young people, for our children, for the race.

Posed atop a Calcutta skyscraper, watching masses assembling for a rally in the streets below, Siddhartha and Keya become epic images of pathos. They project the beauty and vulnerability of yet another generation of the young. Abstracted from this sea of humanity, the young have never looked more beautiful, or more vulnerable.

May 24, 1973

DAVID HOLZMAN'S DIARY

Vincent Canby

The fever began in Paris with Henri Langlois and his Cinémathèque Française, where, in the fifties, a generation of cineastes discovered that it was actually possible to survive 12 to 18 hours a day sitting in the dark watching old movies. No bends. No laughing or crying fits. No hallucinations uninvited. One might be a bit dizzy and inarticulate when one emerged, but the traumas were seldom fatal. In the 1960s the fever, not unlike a kind of medieval ecstasy, spread to America, where the effects were initially apparent on the postwar young. They were the most easily susceptible, but the older generations were also touched.

We learned to look at movies, especially commercial American movies, with a new respect, to recognize the art within Hollywood's assembly line product, as well as the contributions of the individual artists involved. This was all to the good. Then the fever turned into a kind of madness.

It was healthy to recognize the extraordinary heritage of films. It was one thing to appreciate this history, but it was quite another to start relating only to films, and to relate one film only to other films quite cut off from everything else in the world. It took just one more small step to recognize the camera as a holy instrument, as incapable of falsehood as The Redeemer.

"Cinema," said Jean-Luc Godard, "is truth twenty-four frames a second."

If you can swallow that without choking (and I'm not sure that Godard ever did), you can swallow anything, and you can make a good case for saying to hell with the formal study of literature, music, painting, philosophy, history, politics, and maybe even ceramics. If truth is there to be discovered by any Eclair camera, why fool around with all that other junk? Get a nice portable 16-mm. camera, a tape recorder, and go to work. Which is, I'm afraid, one of the reasons why film courses are blooming on college campuses everywhere. Movies, given a certain basic technical skill, are not difficult to make, and if you study any series of moving pictures long enough, you can come up with some quite impressive truths to justify them.

The last word on this latter-day movie madness is Jim McBride's rambunctiously funny and wise first feature, *David Holzman's Diary*, which was made in 1967 but is only now having its debut engagement in New York at the Whitney Museum of American Art. McBride made the movie in five days, for a cash outlay of $2,500, shortly after graduating from the New York University film school. It looks like a fact-film, heavily influenced by the cinéma vérité work of Ricky Leacock, D. A. Pennebaker, the Maysles brothers, Andrew Noren, and Andy Warhol, but it is fiction of extremely witty order, largely improvised but most carefully composed.

As the title says, it has the form of a diary photographed by a completely self-absorbed movie nut named David Holzman (L. M. Kit Carson), who you have every reason to suspect has probably just graduated from the NYU film school, owns a camera and a tape recorder, and wants desperately to make a movie though he hasn't much in mind except himself.

One of the things that makes this movie remarkable is that McBride and his collaborators Carson (who, I assume, made up most of his own dialogue) and Michael Wadleigh (the cameraman, who was later to direct *Woodstock*) had the perspective to see what was going on in the comparatively new cinéma vérité form at that time. Two years later Milton Moses Ginzberg was still looking upon the camera as a magic instrument in *Coming Apart*, a pretentious first feature about a mad psychiatrist (Rip Torn) who tries to fix truth by photographing his own life. *Diary* even predates Norman Mailer's haymaker of a pseudo-cinéma vérité film, *Maidstone*. There is nothing of interest in either of those two films that isn't done better by McBride, Carson, and Wadleigh.

Diary covers eight days in the mixed-up life of David Holzman, who early on tells us that "objects, people, and events" seem to speak to him, that he's just lost his job, that he's been reclassified 1-A by the draft, and that he is attempting to get some grasp of his life by photographing it. He quotes Godard on truth and proceeds to examine himself as well as his friends, including Penny (Eileen Dietz), his girl, a pretty, rather grumpy model whom David introduces to us first with a still picture and the comment that she's a bit of a slob and has a dirty neck.

There's a lot of Antoine Doinel in David's preoccupation with self, with his inability to understand the feelings of others. When Penny gets fed up with David's stalking her around his upper West Side apartment with camera and tape recorder, when she slams out of his pad forever, all David can say is "I don't quite get her sense of privacy."

Another friend of David's, an artist named Pepe (Lorenzo Mans), warns David that "some people's lives are good movies and some people's lives are bad movies." Pepe is especially upset by David's footage of Penny. "She's ridiculous," he says. "She's trite. She behaves melodramatically. She's just not credible."

Pepe becomes what I take to be a kind of devil's advocate on behalf of cinéma vérité. He suggests that David's efforts to understand himself and his life through film are doomed to failure. David, he says, is too busy wondering about how he should frame himself, where he should put his hands. "Your decisions stop being moral decisions and they become esthetic decisions," says Pepe. "Your whole life stops being your life and becomes a work of art—and a very bad work of art this time."

In a quote that is not included in *David Holzman's Diary*, Godard once said that the best critique of one film is another film. In addition to being a very appealing portrait of a young man with an obsession, who trails girls in and out of subways with his camera, who interviews a woman in a Thunderbird who wants to take him to bed, who explores the architecture and faces of the upper West Side—*David Holzman's Diary* says more than any written review I've read about some cinéma vérité movies I've liked (*Salesman, Showman, Primary*) and some I haven't liked (*Gimme Shelter*).

The films aren't mentioned by name (some weren't even made then), but the arguments that Pepe raises, as well as the actions of David himself, highlight questions we all have about the quality of truth that can be captured by the cinéma vérité camera.

These questions have not only to do with whether the presence of a camera distorts life, and with the awful possibilities for distortion through the process of selection that goes into editing a film, but with the way David's camera allows him to stand outside his own life, to be a disengaged spectator. Carried to an extreme, it becomes an escape from any commitment whatsoever. At the end of *David Holzman's Diary*, David is totally bereft.

There is much that cinéma vérité, which is also called direct cinema, can do, but it's a complete fiction to suppose that it can necessarily teach us to see and hear any more efficiently than a fiction film as intelligent as, say, *Mean Streets*, or *American Graffiti*, or *David Holzman's Diary*.

Historical note: McBride's second film, *My Girlfriend's Wedding*, which played the Whitney last week and was made in 1969, is a fairly tedious cinéma vérité portrait of a young English woman named Clarissa. His third film, *Glen and Randa*, was released commercially in 1971. It's a post-Bomb story about two unlikely nature children wandering through the forests and the debris of cities on the Pacific coast, which, after the Bomb, has been altered to touch Boise, Idaho.

December 9, 1973

PULP

William S. Pechter

Outside of Peckinpah's films, in which, at least before *The Getaway*, the violence has always been used with a serious intention to disturb, the movie which seemed to me the most disturbingly violent of those of the past few years was an icily skillful British film, *Get Carter*. A gangster film, with

Michael Caine as a vicious thug avenging the death of his brother by a series of murders as he works his way toward the man he's after, *Get Carter* was made so disturbing not by the violence itself, ugly as that was, but by the utter affectlessness with which it was presented; it was perhaps the most affectlessly violent film since *Kiss Me Deadly*, but without an equivalent of the allegorical framework by which the violence in *Kiss Me Deadly* is given meaning. No sympathy is asked for the avenger or his victims, nor are we allowed to take any vicarious pleasure in his successful completion of his task; minutes after he completes it, he, too, is killed, by a disinterested hireling. Nor is there even a suggestion that this final twist is intended as a slap in the audience's face, in the way that such thwarting of an audience's expectations in Hitchcock's films is a deliberate assault on the spectators' sensibilities, but, in being this, is at least an acknowledgment of them.

The writer and director of *Get Carter*, Mike Hodges, has now made another film with Michael Caine, and, if short of the work of the best directors, there has been a more impressively versatile one-two punch in films, I can't recall it. *Pulp*, too, is a thriller, but a thriller in a very special vein: something like *Beat the Devil*, if not as good, and something like *Gumshoe*, but better. Indeed, unless I'm mistaken, it even features in a small role (the only other in which I've seen him) the actor who played the Arab chieftain in *Beat the Devil*, and who, when told that Humphrey Bogart, Robert Morley, and company have landed clandestinely on his country's shores to sell vacuum cleaners, utters the memorable line: "Ah, hut to hut, I suppose." In *Pulp*, as the head of a typing pool who has been stimulated by a pornographic novel his staff is preparing, he speaks, to the book's author, a few other memorable lines: "You have my card. Don't hesitate to touch me."

Mickey King, the film's narrator-protagonist, played by a pokerfaced Michael Caine in a performance scarcely less good than that of Albert Finney in *Gumshoe*, is the author of that novel, a successful writer of pulp fiction (*The Organ Grinder*, *My Gun Is Long*, etc.) under such pseudonyms as Guy Strange, Les Behan, Paul R. Cumming, and as the promising new literary discoveries from Egypt and Algeria, O. R. Gann and S. Odomy. Summoned to ghost-write the memoirs of an ex-star of Hollywood gangster movies now living in retirement in the same Mediterranean country as the writer, he suddenly finds his employer assassinated and himself the target of an assassin's bullets as the presumed recipient of the star's secrets of a covered-up scandal. Though in fact the deceased star hadn't confided in his biographer, the latter now launches an investigation into the matter on his own to discover the identity of his intended killer before it's too late; but he uncovers the facts of the case only to find himself at the end immobilized by a leg wound, the unwilling house guest, presumably for his lifetime, of the guilty party, the country's "New Front" political leader, at whose estate the writer spends his days composing and reciting a pulp fantasy of revenge on his "host" to which nobody listens.

All this is recounted in a style half pulp itself, and half witty parody of it. "The old man's headed for the big sleep," the movie star's bodyguard tells the ghost writer, as though the former had read too many detective novels; "then I knew he'd get his picture in the paper," the writer remarks of a character he has just found murdered, and later he describes the series of events in which he finds himself embroiled as being "like a pornographic photograph: difficult to figure out who was doing what, and to whom." At the movie star's Art Deco villa, a wizened old woman in black dress and shawl sits and stares into the swimming pool ("Has mama eaten this week?" her son inquires); and when the star is killed (by a man disguised as a priest, which occasions a police line-up of priests), and his sculpted sarcophagus installed in a mausoleum with stained-glass windows depicting him in his most famous film roles, there is a juke box featuring excerpts from his films' soundtracks outside, and the mother is forever provided with coins with which to play it. A clue from a clairvoyant ("He was wearing a dirty mackintosh. Clairvoyants usually do.") leads to an Antonioniesque ghost town of the old and maimed, and eventually to a second narrow escape from assassination ("Remember that thou art pulp, and unto pulp thou shalt return," the writer eulogizes over the mangled corpse of his hired would-be killer). But his escape from being silenced is short-lived. As we last see him, his leg in a cast, reading aloud while his captor shoots boar in a pit ("Where *do* you get your ideas from, Mickey?" his one remaining listener asks as she leaves him), he is wishfully exclaiming, "I'll get the bastards yet!" and then, with more conviction, "Ooh, I wish my leg didn't itch."

This column hasn't gone in much for consumer guidance; here is some: see *Pulp*. You may have a hard time doing this, since the film, after opening in San Francisco, unreviewed, on the bottom half of a double bill with a Charles Bronson movie (this despite a cast including, along with Caine, Lizabeth Scott, Lionel Stander, and Mickey Rooney in a flamboyantly amusing performance) is thus far having its only New York performance as part of a limited engagement of a series of movies (works by Arrabal, etc.) reputed to be without commercial possibilities. I think the fact that the very real commercial possibilities of *Pulp* can't be seen constitutes probably the biggest gaffe in film distribution since the mishandling of the Marlon Brando–Gillo Pontecorvo film, *Burn!;* the idea that film distributors have a grasp of at least the commercial side of movies is one of the great undying myths, like that of *Time* magazine's at least getting its facts straight. But then, when you withhold a "risky" movie from distribution, or simply dump it unadvertised into release, you are, of course, always right, since you're dealing in self-fulfilling prophecy.

Try to see *Pulp* without my having to tell you that it's great or a masterpiece when it isn't, or even that it's unfailingly good. (Most of the less good jokes are clustered near the beginning.) But though it would be well worth seeing merely because of its being a hugely funny entertainment, it isn't simply that either. I don't know anything about Mike Hodges, its writer-director; to judge from the hard clarity of his style, my guess is that he's had considerable experience in filmmaking before, perhaps for television, although *Get Carter* is his first credited feature. Impressive, however, as is the diversity between that film and this, no less impressive is how much similarity that diversity masks. In a curious way, though I probably wouldn't have said this about either without having seen both, the two films now strike me as peculiarly if unspecifically political in character, involving, as they do, corruption in high places and the sexual exploitation of a lower-class girl by those in power. And both films portray the insurmountable frustration of trying to call the powerful to account. Don't get me wrong; *Get Carter* resolutely eschews "significance," and, like the rest of the film, the ending of *Pulp* is lightly done and very funny. And yet somehow the two films, taken together, seem to me to take on an added resonance, and finally to issue in a single distinctive cry of impotent rage.

March, 1973

KID BLUE

Jay Cocks

Robbing trains and stirring up trouble, he is known as Kid Blue. But when he gets fed up with a bandit's life, he uses his proper name, Bickford Waner. Bickford (Dennis Hopper) leaves his outlaw ways behind him and heads down the trail to Dime Box, Texas, where he puts up at the boardinghouse and lands a job sweeping out the barbershop. Polishing shoes or eating supper with the other boarders, though, Bickford just seems to stir people up. "You got no respect, boy," a shoe salesman (Ralph Waite) informs him one evening. "What am I supposed to have respect for?" is all Bickford wants to know.

There are obvious and deliberate echoes here of Brando's classic challenge in *The Wild One*. "What are you rebelling against?" one harried adult asked him, and Brando just shrugged and said, "Whatya got?" What is different in *Kid Blue* is the tone. Brando's cyclist was a threat, an aggressor; Hopper's outlaw is a puzzled, slightly paranoid victim. Trying to go straight and live right, he only makes the citizens more suspicious. They are resentful in some vague way, and the sheriff, Mean John ("But only my friends can call me that") Simpson, is disbelieving. "I seen boys like you before," he tells Bickford, "and there's no good in ya."

Proud custodian of all the vested moral interests of the community, Mean John makes sure that Bickford receives regular doses of harassment. After some puzzling personal encounters and some unprofitable employment, Bickford decides to be the lawless kid everyone suspects he is. He concludes that the only way to save his pride and salvage his honor is to rob the fattest safe in town.

Kid Blue is a quirkish, laid-back, jolly film, rich in resonance, full of scrupulously affectionate detail for a West that changed too fast and too often ever to be called "Old." It is a wry paean to a life of crime, and displays a robust contempt for law, order, and the encroachments of civilization. Bickford, as dexterously played by Hopper, shows signs occasionally of becoming a kind of surrogate James Dean, a prairie rebel without a cause. Hopper started working in films about the same time as Dean (they appeared together in *Rebel Without a Cause*), and in rather the same style. But Hopper is an actor of quick cunning, and he manages to get the movie back on course whenever it tends to become a little sentimental about the lot of the misunderstood loner. He has the uncanny ability to transform himself instantly from a ravaged outcast into a kid in a cowboy outfit on his way to First Communion.

Scenarist Edwin Shrake has provided some good, funky dialogue, and James Frawley is a director who gives his actors time and room to move around in their parts. Warren Oates is exemplary as a factory worker enamored of the ancient Greeks ("They went around barefooted, wearing sheets and other comfortable things, and men could love each other and not be ashamed"), and Lee Purcell is fetching as his wife. Peter Boyle as a preacher with an interest in aeronautics and narcotics, and Ben Johnson as Mean John make a fine couple of Texas crazies.

There is also an absolutely smashing, irresistibly sexy performance by Janice Rule as an "actress" called Janet Conforto, who shows up in Dime Box one day "to do a single." The photography (by Billy Williams, who shot *Women in Love*) is elegant without ever being too fussy or ostentatious.

Mellow and good-humored and not entirely serious about itself, *Kid Blue* shows it is still possible to bring a newer, fresher, more contemporary tone to the Western while still honoring what is best and strongest in the traditional form.

May 14, 1973

IF I HAD A GUN

Pauline Kael

Why does one film reach an audience when another film—like the first one, only better—fails to? Is it a tide in the affairs of men, or clever promotion, or both? There is no tide and no promotion for the Czechoslovakian film *If I Had a Gun*, which strikes me as considerably more skillful than such successes in this country as *Loves of a Blonde* and *Closely Watched Trains*. It's true that the subject—the Nazi Occupation as seen through the eyes of a Slovakian boy of perhaps thirteen—is not exactly calculated to create panic at the box office, but it's also true that the small fashion for Czechoslovakian films has passed and that there were no public-relations people working for this one. There's some minor irony involved, because the man who directed *If I Had a Gun*, Stefan Uher, though he is only forty-two now, was the first New Wave director in Czechoslovakia and the man who—with the *The Sun in the Net*, in 1962—broke new ground. When that film was banned in the director's native Slovakia, it was taken up by the young film enthusiasts in Prague, and it influenced the Prague directors whose work we saw—the group that since the fall of Dubček has been demoralized and disbanded. Uher, however, who went on working in Slovakia, experimented with cinéma vérité and with poetic dream styles, and revived the prewar Slovakian Surrealism, and, in 1971, made *If I Had a Gun*, from Milan Ferko's volume of wartime reminiscences. Ferko, too, is Slovakian—a culture that movie audiences here have had practically no acquaintance with. Because of a shift in internal politics which I can't pretend to understand, filmmakers seem able to do in Slovakia what can't be done now in Prague.

The major surprise of *If I Had a Gun* is the contrast between the sophistication of Uher's style and the mixture of folk witchcraft and Christianity in his peasant characters. The villagers suggest the mad Polish peasants that Jerzy Kosinski described in *The Painted Bird,* but Kosinski was writing from the perspective of a terrified child, an outsider wandering alone from one nightmare encounter to the next; the boy of *If I Had a Gun* lives with his family in relative security, despite the Nazi Occupation, and though the village life is semi-surrealist, the petty cruelty and the superstition bounce off him and are mixed with discoveries and pranks. An old woman's refusal to give up the money she has hidden for her funeral, though it might save the life of her granddaughter, touches that macabre peasant spirit of Kosinski's account, but *The Painted Bird* is out of Hieronymus Bosch, and this is closer to Brueghel. There's a pagan, healthy quick-wittedness about this boy's perspective—life as seen by a resourceful young human animal. The behavior and events in the village have the lunacy of a put-on, yet it's all part of his growing up: seeing where a black-marketeering uncle's loot is stashed, and watching a Jewish woman being hauled off; serving as an altar boy, and watching his grandmother prepare a witch's brew; peeking at girls bathing, and eavesdropping on the Nazis. The principal effect of the war is on his fantasy life; he lives in a maze of self-glorifying revenge dreams in which he destroys the Nazis and becomes the village hero. Few movies have dealt so effectively with the way historical events affect our fantasy lives; at the climax of the film, when the boy actually does get a crack at the Nazis, we see how his dreams change.

The movie is episodic, but it doesn't feel that way; there are so many jokes and incidents that they run together, and they trip by so fast that they're always just a little ahead of the viewer. The abrupt, sprinting film rhythms make the life of the villagers seem spontaneous. Nothing is loitered over (with the possibly unavoidable exception of a too ingratiating Russian soldier hiding in the town), and nothing looks programmed (except, at the end, after the Nazis leave, a celebration that includes the arrival of the Russians). The film, which is in black-and-white, has a large cast, expertly deployed, especially in the fantasies. Uher is a superb technician; this is probably the most precise and stylized of the Czechoslovakian films to open here. Probably there is no way for *If I Had a Gun* to reach much of an audience in this country (it has already closed at the theater in which I saw it), but it's a small classic. It shares with the Czechoslovakian films that succeeded here the sense of recording a modest chapter of the human comedy, yet it has a knobbiness—an eccentric spring and speed—all its own. And it's "dry"—it doesn't make us feel how alike we all are, but how different. Maybe Slovaks are a little crazier than Czechs, and craziness is what those other films lacked.

February 17, 1973

WEDDING IN WHITE

Roger Ebert

Jeannie is the kind of girl you can never remember from high school: sort of pretty in a faded way, not very bright, and weighted down with a vast lack of confidence. She's sixteen years old and very much in awe of her friend, Dollie, who uses lipstick and has lots of nice clothes and an extensive collection of cheap costume jewelry. The admiration she feels for Dollie, in fact, is about the only sharp emotion in her life; for the rest, she's listless and indifferent.

She lives with her family in Canada, in about 1943. Her father is a beer-guzzling good old boy in the Home Guard, and her brother is in the army. One weekend he comes home with a friend, and what with one thing leading to another the friend sort of rapes her, and she confesses to her mom: "I think I'm in trouble." Her father, enraged, beats her and plans to send her away, but one drunken night he conceives a plan to marry her off to his best buddy, Sandy. Now Sandy is a drunken and worthless character of about sixty, but so what? "No other man would touch her," her father says.

Out of this commonplace story about ordinary people, the Canadian writer and director William Fruet has fashioned *Wedding in White,* a poignant, bitter, sometimes surprisingly funny slice-of-life. It really does re-create its wartime society; everything about it is right: the clothes, the dialogue and particularly the prejudices and ignorance. We don't feel we're being told a story; it's more like we're glimpsing the small joys and tragedies of unfortunate relatives.

The movie, which won the Canadian Film Festival, works so well, I think, because the performances are good; this material could never stand being fancied up by overacting. Donald Pleasence, that superb actor who is unsurpassed in his ability to project banal evil, provides the force behind the plot as the father. Carol Kane, as Jeannie, seems almost transparently vulnerable. Doris Petrie, who plays the mother, has a wonderful scene toward the end—she pleads with her husband to understand their child— that seems just right in revealing that she has been defeated by life in everything except a stubborn, lingering hope.

The movie examines its small Canadian town with something of the same attention Peter Bogdanovich revealed in *The Last Picture Show*. The girls go to a dance, for example, and the band is made up of three elderly women on accordion, drums, and piano: Their two-step dance rhythms sound memorized to death. The dimestores, the soda fountains, the slang, all work toward the final effect.

And the effect is simply that of a small domestic tragedy. The girl's life has been ruined, not by her pregnancy but by her father's ignorance. Yet she's too dim to even quite understand that; it's impossible for her to rebel, unthinkable to question her father. The movie ends without a message, without a statement, without any indication that the characters understand their own motivations.

In most movies, that would be a weakness, but here it's a strength, because Fruet wants only to show us these people as they are. The result is one of the most merciless, strangely touching portraits of character I've ever seen in a movie; only Mike Leigh's *Bleak Moments*, from last year's Chicago Film Festival, comes to mind in comparison.

April 1, 1973

Twelve

REFLECTIONS

IMAGINARY MOVIES

Paul D. Zimmerman

After months in the screening rooms, dutifully sitting through all the current movie trends and fads, Paul D. Zimmerman decided it would be simpler to review these films before they're made.

Leon Phipps is an eighteen-year-old passing sensation striving to become the first starting black quarterback in the history of pro football. Sam Dowd, the fifty-one-year-old veteran signal caller, is the only man who stands between rookie Phipps and a first-string berth. The two meet at the New York Gothams' training camp and fall in love. The story of their courtship, marriage, honeymoon, and heartbreak, conducted under the pressure of the team's struggle toward the Super Bowl, forms the basis of *Hold the Signal Caller Snugly*, the latest in a series of films that use life as a metaphor for sports.

Director Tommy Trend beautifully balances comedy and pathos, as in the locker-room scene after the final exhibition game when Phipps and Dowd announce their betrothal to their startled teammates. Predictably, there are some harsh words from a few old veterans, some objecting to the match because of the age difference, others on religious grounds (Phipps is a Druid, Dowd a founder of the First Pentecostal Church of the National Football League). But most of the Gothams are content to shrug their shoulders and return to their petit point.

Undaunted by the jeers of the rival clubs, Phipps and Dowd carry on, yelling endearments to each other from the sidelines, exchanging small gifts at halftime, caressing on extra points (Phipps holding). But their brazen disregard of football's unwritten rules breeds a tension in the club, until it is discovered that Dowd is dying of Dutch elm disease.

At this point, the team rallies around Sweet Sam, picking up patches of his yellowed uniform as they fall about the field during the climactic Super Bowl. When he starts losing his cleats, Phipps takes over, delivers a touching eulogy to his fallen friend (for which he is assessed a delay-of-game penalty) and then scampers in ever-decreasing circles 300 yards for the winning score.

This is that rare film that will move not only the fans of life and death but also those interested in the larger question of what to call in third-down, long-yardage situations.

We've had *Shaft, Superfly,* and *Slaughter,* but none of these break-through films has so fully embraced the black experience as *Mocha Jiver.*

Jimmy Jiver (Pigmeat Markham) represents a totally new kind of black hero—diffident, nonviolent, pudgy, pocked and, at fifty-eight, slowed by arteriosclerosis. He and his blood brother, Stump, a paralyzed Vietnam veteran, run numbers in Harlem for the Mafia. While pimps, hustlers, and drug kings drive Cadillacs and dress in furs, Jiver rides to work in a customized Sherman tank and Stump is pulled about by a team of blondes.

But Stump wants to get out of the numbers game. One night, he stuffs his suitcase with sevens, nines, and sport shirts and skips town. The Mafia tracks him to a dance hall in Atlantic City. While Stump is watching a tango contest, a dark, terribly attractive young hit man administers the most prolonged and lascivious kiss of death ever filmed. The next morning, Jiver wakes to discover Stump dead in his toaster.

With Senator Ed Brooke's hard-rock score belting out "Some Break-fast," Jiver vows revenge. His chance comes at a Mafia wedding two days later. Disguised as a plate of black olives, Jiver lies quietly in the middle of the banquet table and artfully anticipates the punchlines to the Godfather's best jokes. I won't give away what happens next, but, if you like a story that ends with one wheezing black facing a fully armed phalanx of Mafiosi, then *Mocha Jiver* is your cup of Joe.

The Western has proved to be a durable genre. But its true limits had gone untested until *They All Wore Hoods.* Adapted by a twenty-two-year-old Armenian director, Armen Miranda, from the Pierre Franzblau novel, it tells the story of three nuns who hold up a train filled with candy and then survive a 600-mile trek through Blackfoot country to deliver their booty to a beleaguered Boys Town.

From the early planning stages in a Carmelite convent, through the brilliantly choreographed candy caper, Miranda makes us appreciate what it is to be a nun in the Wild West: habits tangled in Western saddles, tongue-lashings from saloon tarts, knapsacks filled with sourballs cutting painful strapmarks into alabaster shoulders.

The trek across the barren Badlands of North Dakota to the lodestar of Father Flanders' Boys Town is more than a mission of mercy. For Sister

Sarah, who devoured her bastard baby, it represents an act of contrition. Sister Serena still half believes the Mexican legend that she is the Sun Queen. And Sister Jethroe, the leader of the group, sees the trip as the road to salvation through physical fitness. In the end, their faith pays big dividends. The dread Blackfoot surround them and are about to ravish them when, as though by a miracle, the savages settle for three pounds of rock candy.

Three unknowns perform perfectly as the three sisters—Jenny Stripe is a touching Sister Sarah, outwardly gay but wearing a blonde hair shirt beneath her robes; Marsha Brite, as Sister Serena, talks to the sun with a conviction that persuades us that someone indeed inhabits that fiery orb, and Mark Rosenthal as Sister Jethroe executes the most perfectly choreographed set of calisthenics ever filmed. Miranda understands the existential nature of the story, gradually registering the dismay of the sisters as they learn that Boys Town has a firm rule against sweets. We leave them turning back toward the sun, readying themselves for the 600-mile march back to the convent, saddened but in no way P.O.'d.

In recent films we've seen the emergence of a new breed of cop. Sometimes he hates blacks, sometimes Puerto Ricans, sometimes hippies. *Filthy Lieutenant Katz* hates everyone—Portuguese, Tahitians, members of the Hanseatic League, lefthanders, insurance salesmen, esthetic realists, jaywalkers and the victims of violent crime. But, most of all, Filthy Lieutenant Katz hates himself, a point driven home in a brilliant opening sequence when he beats himself to a pulp in a deserted alley.

A veteran of the force, Katz has seen everything—murder, rape, robbery, gluttony, sloth—even a rare print of Hedy Lamarr in *Ecstasy*. Now, eleven months away from retiring to Constabulary Village, Katz is suddenly saddled with a new sidekick, Percy Chelli, fresh out of Harvard Police University and filled with fuzzy-headed liberal notions—for example, that every man should be apprised of his rights before he is shot.

On their first patrol, Katz disabuses Chelli of his illusions by firing twelve shots at random into a crowd waiting for a bus. "They were innocent bystanders!" screams Chelli. "Nobody's innocent," snaps Katz. Nonetheless, Katz is suspended by the Homicide Division on the ground that his victims had no chance to make a phone call before they died.

Frustrated by this miscarriage of justice, Katz declares war on the surviving members of the Warren Court in the salty language characteristic of these new tough-cop movies (Justice Douglas is "that banana," Marshall "an old prune" and White "that dumb kumquat"). Director Bull Ryan, on leave from New York's Tactical Patrol Force, has a good feel for action, whether it's Katz strangling former Justice Arthur Goldberg in a crowded elevator or pursuing Earl Warren across forty miles of busy California beaches, both men in dune buggies. In the end, Katz gets Warren with a warning shot between the shoulder blades and is restored to the force. Standing triumphantly over the slain former Chief Justice, a cruel smile on his lips, Filthy Lieutenant Katz tells him: "You might have gotten away, Earl. You might have lived if you'd only reversed yourself."

September 24, 1973

ABEL GREEN (1900–1973)

Vincent Canby

"But the writing of American newspaper columnists, at its most advanced, is as the writing of Walter Pater compared to that of the two weeklies, *Variety* and *Time.* . . . *Variety* bangs away at the language in an innocent, hearty and insatiable manner. . . ."
—H. L. MENCKEN, *The American Language, First Supplement*

It will be interesting to see how long that manner, more hearty and insatiable than innocent, survives the death last week of Abel Green, seventy-two, the editor of *Variety* since 1933, the man whose style was his total content, the only person who, in 1973, might say when he was going out to lunch at "21" that he was grabbing some groceries. A.G., as he signed his cryptic, often illegible staff memos jotted on small sheets of green note paper, was responsible more than anyone else for the marvelously mixed-up, manic tone of what Bill Greeley, a *Variety* television reporter, once called "the last of the home town weeklies," the home town being as easily Jean Seberg's Marshalltown, Iowa, as Hollywood, New York, Paris, Rome, London, Las Vegas, Miami, Hong Kong, or wherever else some film was being shot, some hoofer was hoofing, or some friend of Abel's had found time to write a postcard. It was largely because of Abel that *Variety* became the panoramic, gossipy, often scoopfilled (and sometimes dead-wrong) showbiz chronicle that might run a carefully prepared, highly technical breakdown on a film company's financial affairs, cheek-by-jowl with an A.G. story beginning:

"Darryl F. Zanuck is still nursing a fractured jaw, now pretty well healed, as a result of an accident in his Hotel Plaza (N.Y.) suite this past summer when, expecting an important overseas phone call, he slipped getting out of the shower. Coincidentally he also fractured the same right ankle, a skiing accident heritage, but that has since healed and he continues his two-mile walks in Central Park.

"However, when his face hit the bathroom wall, he also broke five teeth which cannot be replaced until his mouth is fully mended. . . ."

Under Abel's editorship, reading *Variety* was always like browsing through an elegant flea market of information. You were as likely to learn the name of the next president of CBS as you were to learn that Walter Winchell, then in New York for a testimonial dinner, was having a dreadful time with his teeth, or, as Abel called them, his choppers.

Turning to the back of the paper on a Wednesday morning, the day *Variety* comes out, you might read under the New York Chatter column, a space usually reserved for social notes, a rather terse sentence to the effect that "The attorneys for Mrs. Jonathan Bell Small announce that she did not give birth to a baby last week in Doctor's Hospital."

I recall these things with respect and admiration for the man who gave me a job in 1959 and several weeks later was threatened with a lawsuit over something that I'd written about an actor in a play review.

He brushed the matter aside without smiling. "I don't worry when they threaten to sue," he said. "Only when they reprint you in your entirety."

A.G. was a small, button-eyed man, given to wearing bow ties (a disgruntled former reporter is said to have written a novel about him titled *God Wears a Bow Tie*, though I've never been able to find it), whose hair remained a constant, quite startling raisin color as long as I knew him. The basis of his success was an unsentimental enthusiasm for all aspects of show biz, and he had no patience with reporters whose enthusiasm flagged, or who might rebel at the idea of working less than the seven-day week he worked. On what was supposed to be the reporter's day off, he might ring him at home at 7 A.M. and ask "Did I wake you?" and, without waiting for an answer, suggest three or four story leads to be checked out before lunch.

The enthusiasm was dumbfoundingly indiscriminate to outsiders, having to do with getting the best tables at supper clubs (boites or nighteries, he called them), the best seats at the theater, the best rooms in hotels when he was traveling (he was furious when he once was given a suite at the Carlton Hotel in Cannes "overlooking the broom closet"), as well as the best stories. All life was reviewed as if it were *Variety* material, to such an extent that when he wrote about the funeral of his close friend, Harry

Edward Gould, Sr., two years ago, he noted the "S.R.O. attendance of over 1,000 at Temple Emanu-El."

The death of Mr. Gould obviously shook A.G. as few events had shaken him until then. He became aware of his own mortality and was prompted the next week to write a follow story, or thinkpiece, of the sort that only he could have thought up. Under the headline, "Gould's Death Cues N.Y. Ease-Up Talk/Among Other Show Biz Gadabouts," the story started:

"Since the sudden passing of Harry Edward Gould, Sr., at 72, a common attitude of his contemporaries has run 'you can bet your life I'm gonna pass up many of these benevolent balls, charity fund pitches, and political rallies and just mail in the money—maybe that's one way all of us will last a little longer. And that goes for first nights and all the doings so many of us feel like we don't want to miss.'

"Overall feeling is that the current economic stress, necessitating back-to-hard-work, the social whirl is not only taxing, but needlessly woos basic physical exhaustion, even fatalities."

Abel himself had had a heart condition that was corrected by surgery several years ago, and he did cut down on his first nights and benevolent balls, but his prose and punctuation remained exuberantly uninhibited by textbook precedent or by anything resembling consistency. When Toots Shor's Restaurant closed, Abel's lead sentence read: "The raison d'etre for el foldo . . ."

When A.G. began covering the show-biz scene, he was still in his teens and show biz was mostly Broadway, but as it expanded so did he, into films and television as well as theater, vaudeville, nightclubs, radio, records. He really did know everybody. He was a gadabout, worldwide, and no trip he ever took was ever a true vacation. It always resulted in stories that read like what-I-did-on-my-summer-vacation as written by three or four different people, all trying to communicate as much as possible, as quickly as possible, without much differentiation between important news and trivia. He didn't drop names, he made a literary style of them.

On his return from a Las Vegas trip in February, 1961, he did a wrap-up piece that contained the following sentence:

". . . Spot Frank Sinatra, Victor Borge, Bobby Darin, Dinah Shore, Andy Williams, the Folies Bergère, the Lido de Paris, the Harold Minsky revue with Johnnie Ray, 'La Plume de Ma Tante,' Davis and Reece, Billy Gray, Prof. Backwards (Jimmy Edmondson), not to mention lounge acts like Duke Ellington, Sarah Vaughan, Arthur Lyman, Billy Daniels, Jerry Colonna, Monseigneur Strings, Dick Contino into the plush hotels that dot the fabulous milelong Strip and it's little wonder that they make 'paying their dues' in the casinos a pleasure."

It wasn't that Abel didn't know how to write short sentences, but when he got started, he couldn't stop.

The same story also contains the sort of information that only Abel would have been able to get away with:

"The Sands steamroom is 'the 10 Downing Street' of the town, especially when Sinatra is on the scene. The 6 P.M. thaw-out incidentally sees a strange galaxy of specially made robes which were presented to 'the clan.' Sinatra's billing is 'The Pope.' . . . 'J.F.' is the billing for Sands boniface Jack Entratter's 'Feet' because of those special shoes he wears. . . ."

As an editor, A.G. was not as interested in the style of a reporter as he was in whether or not he was on top of a story, which, to A.G., meant having it, if possible, before it happened. This sometimes prompted stories of pure speculation, the sort that quote unnamed "industry observers." It also prompted most reporters to turn out reams of copy, which is not always such a great idea, and to dig for stories, which is.

Because *Variety* has never been dependent on any one branch of show biz for advertising, it has always been more free to be critical of all branches, and, for the most part, its film and television reviews have been highly independent, so independent that some years ago Warner Brothers pulled all advertising from the paper because of an only-fair review of *Gypsy*. As it turned out, the *Variety* review was the best the film received.

In battles that *Variety* reporters had with their sources, Abel maintained a kind of pious aloofness, acting like the nice cop who steps in to soothe a suspect (source) after the bad cop (the reporter) has roughed him up. It usually worked. And since, at least during the years I knew him, he seldom expressed any strong critical opinions of films or plays, which he did not review, he could always sympathize with a producer or director or star whose work had been ridiculed by the reviewer. It was my impression that this sympathy was genuine, for, in recent years, the general direction of many movies and plays baffled and bored him.

A.G. was truly offended by Lenny Bruce's material, and said so in print, only to be called "that aging hipster" by Bruce, which offended him even more. Above all, Abel wanted to be hip, but it became increasingly difficult for a man who was at heart a puritan. A.G. the editor eventually won out over A.G. the moralist and *Variety* now reviews pornographic films as a branch of show business but, I suspect, he must have justified this to himself by recalling that journalists, after all, do not make news but only report it.

The quintessential Abel Green is to be found in his annual wrap-up pieces in which, in the first issue every January, he would look back over the year before and summarize the events of major importance. Riots, cataclysms, revolutions, wars and natural disasters got thoroughly and breathlessly homogenized with references to fads, box-office data, and general show-biz news. He had a gift for covering absolutely everything in a way that only a non-pro would find anti-climactic. Thus, in January, 1960, he wrote:

"Finis to the Frantic Fifties, fraught with frenetic foibles. Kiss the decade goodbye in the names of Khrushchev, Castro and Charles Van Doren. . . ."

After several feet of this kind of prose, Doris Arneel, the wife of an old-time *Variety* reporter, once put down the paper and said simply: "Abel writes faster than I can read."

May 20, 1973

JOHN FORD (1895–1973)

Roger Greenspun

John Ford lived for seventy-eight years. He directed movies during six decades of American filmmaking. And he died a few days ago, full of honor and official admiration. For younger audiences, he may almost have to be saved from his admirers: how do you praise the favorite filmmaker of the Nixon administration? For such audiences, coming to Ford at this stage may be a shock to their expectations. It is like discovering that the Poet Laureate actually wrote great poetry.

By any standards, Ford is very great. In this country, only Hawks and Hitchcock come close to him. I don't quite mean the John Ford of official imagination, an imposing figure of exceptional simplicity, like a mesa in Monument Valley. I don't mean to exclude that figure either; it is not false, it is only much too incomplete. Like a great poet, Ford imbues his work with subtlety, richness, complexity, and a sense of irony that is very close to the tragic. But like a great poet, Ford pushes none of those qualities upon us.

I know from experience what happens when a class of contemporary college kids has to deal with the image of John Wayne leading the cavalry out on a dangerous mission. The response is mainly negative and wholly superficial. The film is *The Horse Soldiers* (1959), one of Ford's late masterpieces. To despise it, you must not only miss the authority of Wayne's performance, the beauty of the visual compositions, the poignancy that attends a social structure—even a military structure—soon to be destroyed. You must also fail to appreciate where the cavalry is headed and why, and what strange and ambiguous pacifistic conclusions lie deep in enemy territory at the end of the mission.

Andrew Sarris has suggested that "too many of his characters wear uniforms without any torturous reasoning why" for Ford to be popular with ideological critics of the Left. The uniform in Ford is above all a way of codifying conduct, signifying community. If a filmmaker begins by questioning the propriety of his characters' situation, then his film is likely to remain at the level of its beginnings. To the best of my recollection, this never happens in Ford, though I think it sometimes happens in the movies most praised by ideological critics of the Left.

Like some major directors of his era, but especially like Renoir, born in 1894 and thus one year his senior, Ford's career peaked twice—once in the middle-to-late thirties and once again in the middle fifties to the early sixties. Also like Renoir, Ford won his important recognition (and most of his Oscars) with films made in the thirties. By serious critics, if not by audiences, the work of the fifties went largely ignored. In 1956, the year of *The Searchers*, arguably the greatest American movie, both the New York Film Critics' and the Academy awards went to *Around the World in 80 Days*. And I remember seeing my own favorite, *The Man Who Shot Liberty Valance* (1962), in the bottom half of a double bill in the second-best theater (out of two) in New London, Connecticut.

The famous earlier movies, from *The Informer* (1935) to *How Green Was My Valley* (1941), parallel a rising social consciousness in Depression America and a growing general awareness of film as art well suited to the work Ford was giving his audiences. World War II brought a temporary end to all that (and a temporary interruption to Ford's commercial career), and when it was over, the old consensus, which could embrace both a John Ford and a Franklin Roosevelt, had given way to new divisions and new ideas of what was serious. Ford followed a conservative tack, keeping his characters in the armed services and mostly making Westerns.

The prewar movies for many of us these days range from the almost unwatchable to the magnificent. They tend to be very artful, even arty (this, rather than oversimplicity, was always Ford's weakness), and the current crop of highly astute, scholarly critics probably underrate them. They happen to include several of the movies that Ford most wanted to make and that he remained proudest of. For movies like *How Green Was My Valley*, *The Grapes of Wrath* (1940), or *Young Mr. Lincoln* (1939), he had every reason.

It's worth recalling the characteristics of a John Ford movie. They are characteristics that you might find badly imitated—especially in the "quality" Westerns a few years back—but never properly repeated. They include the breathtaking sense of location, the leading actors—Wayne, Fonda, Jimmy Stewart—and the strong stock company—Ward Bond, Victor McLaglen, Ben Johnson, Woody Strode, many others. Some of them grew up with Ford; some grew old with him.

There was the gift of being Irish, not just for the movies set in Ireland, but all the way west in America and to the South Pacific beyond. There was a lot of sentiment and some sentimentality. And of course there was the marvelous presence of Maureen O'Hara and the singing of songs like "I'll Take You Home Again, Kathleen." These belong to everybody's experience of Ford, and you can't ignore them unless you ignore the way his movies look and feel. I can't imagine that Ford believed the world quite existed in the image of his films. But within those films he was always able to provide a world in which moral choice is meaningful, though not easy, and in which it was possible to say that people had a function.

Off and on toward the end, though at least as early as *The Searchers*, I think that world became a country of the mind. One reason why Ford's last films are so special to me, even the relative failure of *Cheyenne Autumn* (1964), is that they seem like an old man's personal and very privileged meditation. To most critics at the time I believe they appeared trivial. But the places of those films—the desert town of Shinbone that may become a garden (*The Man Who Shot Liberty Valance*), the Pacific island paradise of Haleakaloa that is well-ruled by children (*Donovan's Reef*, 1963), even the beleaguered mainland China mission where everyone learns the meaning of sacrifice (*Seven Women*, 1966, Ford's last movie)—those places exist not on a map but in the thoughts of an artist for whom vision and memory had become the general landscape.

Probably the notion of "John Ford—American" will stick. In any case, it surely eclipses the literary Ford, the adapter of O'Flaherty, Maxwell Anderson, O'Neill, or O'Casey. But "American" raises as many questions as it settles, and there is less to say for Ford the chronicler of American history (he has been treated this way) than for Ford, a witness to the contradictions in being an American. Ford was no specialist in happy endings. Of course he made some comedies. But his Westerns, which could have gone either way, generally went down in mood, or went into an elegiac contemplation of irreconcilable values.

He may have felt that his world had come to an end before he did. That may be why the work of his late survival is so extraordinarily moving. But his earlier work is also moving, and he was one of the few whose public acceptance and whose achievement, for a while at least, went hand in hand. His audiences perhaps really did understand him, and for how many major twentieth-century artists can you say that? Only for a few of the film-makers, those who flourished as John Ford flourished, when movies were very popular and when they openly celebrated, or at least hoped for, a shared community of feeling.

September 9, 1973

JOHN FORD:
THE GRAPES OF WRATH

Andrew Sarris

Who is the actual (or even predominant) author of a film? This question had perplexed film scholars long before auteurism added a new dimension to the debate. (*Vide* the voluminous briefs filed in the expressionistic-camera case of Murnau vs. Mayer.) Even when we stipulate multiple authorship in a collaborative art form, we find that the problem has not been solved. Certainly *The Grapes of Wrath* (recently revived at the Whitney Museum) could not have become a motion picture if Darryl F. Zanuck or some other producer had not willed it into being by purchasing the rights to John Steinbeck's novel. The next-in-command after Zanuck was associate producer-scenarist Nunnally Johnson, who adapted the novel into a screenplay for John Ford to direct. Ford, in turn, worked very closely with Gregg Toland on the camera set-ups, but there was a great deal of second-unit work as well, and the final editing was very much a studio operation. But even if we could imagine a single ego which encompassed all the creative and productive functions represented by the names Steinbeck, Zanuck, Johnson, Ford, Toland, *et al.*, we would still be confronted with the autonomous assertions of the players on the screen, not only on the stellar level of Henry Fonda's Tom Joad nor on the archetypal level of Jane Darwell's Ma Joad, nor on the grizzled grandeur level of Charles Grape-win's Grampa Joad, nor on the messianic level of John Carradine's Casey, but down also to such cameo gems as Paul Guilfoyle's wry-mouthed born-troublemaker and Grant Mitchell's benignly tut-tutting New Deal bu-reaucrat.

We would be confronted also with the vast area of affecting accident recorded by the camera for display on a canvas which extends in both space and time. Even the constituent viewer elements of the editorial "we" would provide a bewildering diversity of viewpoints and associations, and the passage of time would actually alter the "look," "sound," and "feel" of the film. When *The Grapes of Wrath* was screened for students at a Yale seminar I gave in 1970, the hostile reaction baffled me at first, but then I realized that what had seemed unusually courageous in 1940 seemed unduly contrived in 1970. And what had once seemed the last word in "realism" now seemed strangely stylized. Besides, the New Dealish optimism which had initially inspired the project had evaporated over the years with the swings to the Right of McCarthyism, Eisenhowerism, and Nixonism, and with the growing realization that the original Okies of *The Grapes of Wrath* were destined to become the staunchest supporters of Ronald Reagan in California.

Rebecca Pulliam provides a thoughtfully radical critique of *The Grapes of Wrath* in the *Velvet Light Trap No. 2* (August 1971), and concludes: "As with the Protestant ethic and New Dealism, John Ford à la 1940 stays within certain safe limits of expression and does not assault the confines of its preconceptions any more than he penetrates the political organization. Certainly, a man cannot be blamed for the shortness of vision of his times. But the makers of this movie were unfortunately caught without a new vision—between decades and between myths."

Of course, one can argue that few movies of any decade or any country can be said to be genuinely radical in opposition to the social substance upon which they feed. Eisenstein dutifully excluded Trotsky from the October Revolution in *October,* and one would search in vain for any signs of Hollywood pacifism between Pearl Harbor and Hiroshima. Even so, Ford's conservative evolution in the fifties and sixties has misled modern film historians into theorizing about a conservative conspiracy back in 1940 to subvert Steinbeck's scathing critique of American society by substituting New Dealish homilies. It all depends upon one's frame of reference. Compared with other Hollywood movies of 1940, *The Grapes of Wrath* doesn't seem conservative at all. But compared with the writings of Che Guevara, Pablo Neruda, and Eldridge Cleaver, *The Grapes of Wrath* seems more like a hymn to honky capitalism and rugged individualism. Even so, it would be a mistake to view the alleged betrayal of a sacred literary source in purely ideological terms. Steinbeck's "choric interludes" which Ms. Pulliam considers crucial to the novelist's cosmic conception of suffering humanity would have loaded down the screen with a kind of rhetorical bombast reminiscent of D. W. Griffith's universal-brotherhood superimpositions in *Birth of a Nation,* and his recurring refrain of Lillian Gish's (and Walt Whitman's) "Cradle Endlessly Rocking" in *Intolerance.* Indeed, Steinbeck's "choric interludes" seem today only to increase the novelist's biological distance from his protagonists, who, by absorption into the mass of abstract mankind, became a small detachment of lowly marchers in a veritable army of avenging ants on the picnic blankets of the bourgeoisie. A very pitying expression of liberal guilt, to be sure, but hardly the heady stuff of which revolutions are made. It is perhaps more than a coincidence that both Steinbeck and John Dos Passos, from whose "newsreel" and "camera eye" in *U.S.A.* Steinbeck had borrowed his "choric interludes," turned conservative in their later years, thus reflecting the ultimate rupture between the New Deal–Old Left of one generation and the New Left of another.

Back in 1940, however, the problem of adapting Steinbeck's novel to the screen must have been one more of poetics than of politics. We are a long way from Theodore Dreiser's ideological commitment to Eisenstein over Sternberg for the film version of *An American Tragedy*. Still, even Eisenstein with all his clickety-clackety montage never demonstrated how a long novel could be faithfully adapted into a short movie. As it is, *The Grapes of Wrath* runs for 129 minutes, not too long by the one-shot standard of *Gone With the Wind,* but appreciably longer than the slightly under ninety-one-minute average running time of Ford's twenty-six features in the thirties. Ford, especially, had become a legend on the set for replacing precious literary lines with eloquent silences. The trick was to find the visual equivalents for wordy plots. Don't tell 'em, show 'em. Indeed, most critics had been brainwashed by high-brow aestheticians into believing that talk was the mortal enemy of cinema as an art form. Hence, the process of reducing and simplifying a novel for the screen enjoyed the highest aesthetic sanction.

Modernistic film aestheticians like Jean-Luc Godard and Roland Barthes can debate the contrasting ideologies of words and images, but in the forties there was very little critical precedent for examining the tensions between word and image, screenwriter and director, content and form, substance and style. There could be a disparity of effectiveness, but not a disparity of meaning. Thus critics could applaud John Ford's stylistic contribution to *The Grapes of Wrath* without suggesting in any way that he was undermining the thematic thrust of John Steinbeck's novel and Nunnally Johnson's screenplay. That there could be an ideological contradiction between the beautiful pictures of Ford and Toland and the angry words of Steinbeck and Johnson would have seemed as strange a notion in 1940 as any similar critique of the stylistic beauties of the neorealistic films would have seemed a decade later. At the very least, Ford and Toland could be charged by a retroactively revolutionary tribunal with diminishing the urgency of this enterprise with their eye-catching compositions of light and shadow on windswept fields and weather-beaten faces. There is even a ceiling (of a diner) photographed a full year before *Citizen Kane*, and a novelistic flashback shortly before *Rebecca* and a year before *How Green Was My Valley*. Thus, another film classic turns out to be more expressionistic than its realistic reputation would indicate. The term used to circumvent this stylistic contradiction is "poetic realism."

Only long after the event has it become possible to conclude that Ford's personal concerns were particularly inimical to Steinbeck's biological conception of his characters. Whereas Steinbeck depicted oppression by dehumanizing his characters into creatures of abject necessity, Ford evoked nostalgia by humanizing Steinbeck's economic insects into heroic champions of an agrarian order of family and community. But both Steinbeck and Ford share a kind of half-baked faith in the verities of outhouse existence and a sentimental mistrust of machinery. Neither Steinbeck nor Ford would have fitted very comfortably in the Soviet scheme of things with its worship of industrialization. However, the early forties were years of Popular Front sentimentality once the temporary embarrassment of the Nazi-Soviet pact had been forgotten and forgiven, and in this ecumenical era it did not seem too farfetched to link the rural evangelism in *The Grapes of Wrath* with world revolution. After all, more seemed to be at stake than a crass studio's desire to make money from a downbeat project. The minds and hearts of the moviegoing masses were thought to be hanging in the balance. Why depress and alienate these masses needlessly by reproducing Steinbeck's vision of existence as a dung-hill of despair? In hindsight, we might note that only a Luis Buñuel at his most outrageous would be capable of rendering all the gruesome horror of Steinbeck's saga on the relatively squeamish screen. But what would Buñuel have evoked with his lurid fidelity to Steinbeck, tacticians of the time might have asked, beyond the nervous laughter of the sophisticates and the revulsion of the general public? By contrast, the strategy tacitly agreed upon by Zanuck, Johnson, and Ford enabled the audience to identify itself with the sufferings of the characters, partly by making these characters active rather than passive, partly by stressing their coherence as a family though not as a class, and partly by offering hope in the future through Jane Darwell's concluding we-the-people speech, in its own way almost as controversial as Charles Chaplin's world-peace speech in *The Great Dictator*. Still, it is worth remembering that Odetsian audiences in Manhattan balconies cheered wildly in the forties when Ma Joad dispensed her populist manifesto: "Rich fellas come up an' they die, an' their kids ain't no good, an' they die out. But we keep a-comin'. We're the people that live. Can't nobody wipe us out. Can't nobody lick us. We'll go on forever."

Resounding rhetoric aside, *The Grapes of Wrath* is graced with subtler virtues than its dated "message" would indicate. After being overrated in its time as a social testament, it is now underrated both as a Hollywood movie (not glossily mythic enough) and as a Ford memento (not purely personal enough). What *does* stand up to every test of time, however, is Henry Fonda's gritty incarnation of Tom Joad, a volatile mixture of the prairie sincerity of *Young Mr. Lincoln* with the snarling paranoia of Fritz Lang's *You Only Live Once*. Once more, Fonda was passed over for top acting honors by both the Academy and the New York Film Critics. Possibly, his was too unsettling a performance for facile audience identification. Fonda-Joad's physical and spiritual stature is not that of the little man as victim, but of the tall man as troublemaker. His explosive anger has a short fuse, and we have only his word for it that he is tough without being mean. Indeed, it is mainly his awkwardness in motion that suggests his vulnerability whereas there is a tendency in the devious blankness of his expression to make him seem more sullen than he has any right or motivation to be. Consequently, his putatively proletarian hero becomes ominously menacing in that shadowy crossroads where social justice intersects with personal vengeance. Fonda's Joad is no Job, and as much as his mouth spouts slogans of equality, his hands are always reaching for a club or a rock or a wrench as an equalizer against the social forces massed against him. His is ultimately the one-man revolution of the ex-con with whom society can never be reconciled. By contrast, Jane Darwell's Ma Joad is the pacifier and unifier and high priestess of liberal reform at the altar of the sacred family.

Even within the Joad family, however, the significantly generational conflict between Charley Grapewin's Grampa Joad and Jane Darwell's Ma Joad is generally misunderstood and misinterpreted as the affectionate squabbling of rural types. But what is actually transpiring is nothing less than the transformation of the Joad family from a patriarchy rooted in the earth to a matriarchy uprooted on the road. It is no accident that, even in the casting, Charley Grapewin's Grampa dominates Zeffie Tilbury's Grandma Joad as completely as Jane Darwell's Ma Joad dominates Russell Simpson's Pa Joad. Once on the road, the men have a tendency to wander and finally run away altogether either via drink or via distance. The women of the family must then hold the fort and save the children as poverty and unemployment destroy the authority of the paterfamilias.

Ford's own feelings are so powerfully patriarchal that when Grampa dies, something in the movie seems to die with him. Hence, the complaint of many critics that the first third of *The Grapes of Wrath* is superior to the final two-thirds. Parker Tyler noted astutely that even the surface of the screen seemed to change from lyrical dustiness to an antiseptic enamel finish. Ford's concern with the sacraments of the soil is expressed in the poetically sifting hands of John Qualen's maddened Muley and Grampa himself, and it is in this primal property gesture through which we sense the conservative commitment of Ford's feelings to the dirt shriveled by the wind into dust, but still drenched in all its dryness with the blood, sweat, and tears of generations. Later, in *They Were Expendable*, Ford even redeems Russell Simpson (who is so diminished in *The Grapes of Wrath*) by casting him as Dad, chief of the shipyard, and a haunting hold-out who sits on his porch with his rifle perched on his lap, and his dog poised by his side, waiting, waiting, waiting for the invading Japanese. As doggedly loyal-to-the-land Dad, Russell Simpson revives the patriarchy which disappeared in *The Grapes of Wrath* somewhere on the road between Oklahoma and California.

October 18, 1973

ABOUT THE CONTRIBUTORS

HOLLIS ALPERT is film critic and an editor for *Saturday Review/World* magazine. His most recent novel, his sixth, is *Smash;* he is also the author of a collection of essays on film, *The Dreams and the Dreamer*, and a biography, *The Barrymores*. He has taught at New York University, the Pratt Institute, and Yale.

GARY ARNOLD is film critic of *The Washington Post*.

VINCENT CANBY is film critic of *The New York Times;* he was a critic and reporter for *Variety* from 1960 until 1965, and is an associate fellow of Pierson College, Yale. His first novel, *Living Quarters*, will be published in the spring of 1975.

CHARLES CHAMPLIN is film critic of *The Los Angeles Times;* he was host of the *Film Odyssey* series for NET.

JAY COCKS reviews for *Time*.

JUDITH CRIST is film critic of *New York* magazine and *TV Guide*. She has been film critic of *The New York Herald Tribune, The World Journal Tribune*, and NBC-TV's *Today* show. Her reviews were collected in *The Private Eye, the Cowboy, and the Very Naked Girl*. She is an adjunct professor at the Columbia University Graduate School of Journalism and in *Judith Crist's TV Guide to the Movies*.

DAVID DENBY writes on film for *Harper's* and was formerly critic of *The Atlantic*. His pieces have appeared in *Film Quarterly, New York* magazine, and *The New York Times*, and he has taught at Stanford and University of California at Santa Cruz. He was editor of the three previous volumes in this series. He conducts a regular program on film for WBAI-FM.

BERNARD DREW is film critic and feature writer for the Gannett News Service. He has written original material for movies and television.

ROGER EBERT is film critic of *The Chicago Sun-Times*. His pieces have also appeared in *Esquire, The New York Times, Film Comment*, and *The Critic*. He is lecturer in film at the University of Chicago and he wrote the original screenplay of *Beyond the Valley of the Dolls*.

JOSEPH GELMIS is film critic of *Newsday* and the author of a collection of interviews, *The Film Director as Superstar*. He is an adjunct assistant professor at State University of New York at Stony Brook.

PENELOPE GILLIATT is a film critic for *The New Yorker* and was formerly film critic of the London *Observer*. Her latest books are *Nobody's Business*, a collection of short fiction and a short play, and *Unholy Fools*, a collection of writing on film and theater. She has also written two novels, *One by One* and *A State of Change*, and two collections of stories, *Come Back If It Doesn't Get Better* and *Penguin Modern Stories No. 5*. Her original screenplay for *Sunday Bloody Sunday* is available in hardcover and paper.

ROGER GREENSPUN, formerly a film critic for *The New York Times*, now writes for *Penthouse* and *Changes*. He also teaches film at Rutgers, where he is associate professor of English. His pieces on film have appeared in *Moviegoer, The New York Free Press, Second Coming, On Film, Cahiers du Cinéma in English, Film Comment, Sight and Sound*, and *The Village Voice*.

MOLLY HASKELL is a film critic for *The Village Voice* and *Viva*, and a freelance writer on film and theater. Her pieces have appeared in *Vogue, Saturday Review, Intellectual Digest, Show, USA, Film Comment, Film Heritage, Inter/VIEW, Cahiers du Cinéma in English*, and *Ms*. She is the author of *From Reverence to Rape: The Treatment of Women in the Movies*.

ROBERT HATCH is film critic and executive editor of *The Nation*.

PAULINE KAEL is a movie critic for *The New Yorker* and was formerly the movie critic of *McCall's* and *The New Republic*. She has written for *Partisan Review, Sight and Sound, Film Quarterly, The Atlantic* and *Harper's*. Her criticism has been collected in *I Lost It at the Movies, Kiss Kiss Bang Bang, Going Steady*, and *Deeper Into Movies*. Her long essay "Raising Kane" appears in *The Citizen Kane Book*.

MICHAEL KORDA is film critic of *Glamour* magazine and editor-in-chief of Simon and Schuster. He is the author of *Male Chauvinism: How It Works*.

WILLIAM S. PECHTER is film critic of *Commentary*. His pieces have also appeared in *Commonweal, The Kenyon Review, Moviegoer, Sight and Sound, The London Magazine, Contact, Tulane Drama Review, Kulchur, Film Quarterly*, and *Film Comment*, and have been collected in *Twenty-four Times a Second*.

ANDREW SARRIS is film critic of *The Village Voice*, associate professor of cinema at Columbia University, and a member of the program committee of the New York Film Festival. His books are: *The Films of Josef von Sternberg* (1966), *Interviews with Film Directors* (1967), *The Film* (1968), *The American Cinema: Directors and Directions 1929–1968* (1968), *Film 68/69*, co-edited with Hollis Alpert (1969), *Confessions of a Cultist: On the Cinema 1955–1969* (1970), and *The Primal Screen* (1973).

RICHARD SCHICKEL was film critic of *Life* from 1965 until its demise in 1972. He now reviews films for *Time*. He was producer-writer-director of the PBS series, *The Men Who Made the Movies*. His books include *The Disney Version*,

The Stars, The World of Goya, His Picture in the Papers, The Platinum Era, Harold Lloyd: The Shape of Laughter, and a collection of film criticism, *Second Sight.* He co-edited *Film 67/68* with John Simon.

BRUCE WILLIAMSON is film critic and contributing editor of *Playboy* magazine and has taught at St. John's University, Long Island; he was a film critic at *Time* magazine from 1963 to 1967 and has written satirical songs and sketches for revues in New York and London.

PAUL D. ZIMMERMAN is film critic of *Newsweek* and the author, with graphic designer Burt Goldblatt, of *The Marx Brothers at the Movies.* He has taught at the Columbia University School of Journalism.

INDICES

TITLE INDEX

348

NAME INDEX